BLOOMSBURY

Time Out
NUS

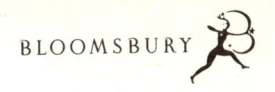

Student Guide

The first *Time Out & NUS Student Guide* is a comprehensive guide to student life, covering all the major aspects of higher education, from application to graduation and beyond. It will prove invaluable – whether you're a prospective student, wondering where and how to apply; or if you're already a student, worrying about accommodation, money, part-time work or what do in the summer holidays.

Time Out has been London's best-selling weekly listings magazine for over twenty years, and for the past fourteen years has produced a free Student Guide, which is distributed to 100,000 new students in London.

For over seventy years, the National Union of Students (NUS) has been providing support for student unions and a national voice for students.

After a decade of co-operation on the *London Student Guide*, we decided to pool our expertise and resources to produce a book that would be the complete reference work for every student. All students have doubts and worries about what college life will be like. But don't worry: armed with the *Time Out & NUS Student Guide*, you will never be a fish out of water....

First published 1991

by Bloomsbury Publishing Limited, 2 Soho Square, London W1V 5DE

Copyright (©) Time Out Group Ltd/National Union of Students 1991

British Library Cataloguing in Publication Data. A CIP record for this book is available from the British Library.

ISBN 0 7475 0 9166

Printed in Great Britain by Clays Limited, St. Ives plc.

Publisher's note

The information in this book was correct to the best of the Editor's and Publisher's belief at the time of going to press. While no responsibility can be accepted for errors or omissions, the Editor and Publisher would welcome corrections and suggestions for items to include in future editions of the book.

All rights reserved; no part of this publication may be reproduced, stored in a retrieval system, or transmitted by any means, electronic, mechanical, photocopying or otherwise, without the prior written permission of the Publisher.

Produced by
Time Out Magazine Limited, Fifth floor, Tower House, Southampton Street, London WC2E 7HD (071 836 4411).

Editor Julie Emery
Senior Managing Editor Peter Fiennes
Managing Editor Marion Moisy
Art Director Kirk Teasdale
Design Iain Murray, Warren Beeby
Publisher Tony Elliott
Financial Director Kevin Ellis
Project Co-ordinator Adele Carmichael
Advertisement Director Lesley Gill
Advertisement Sales Director Mark Phillips
Cover designed by Kirk Teasdale and Warren Beeby
Cover Photography Paul Rider

© 1991 Time Out Group Limited and National Union of Students

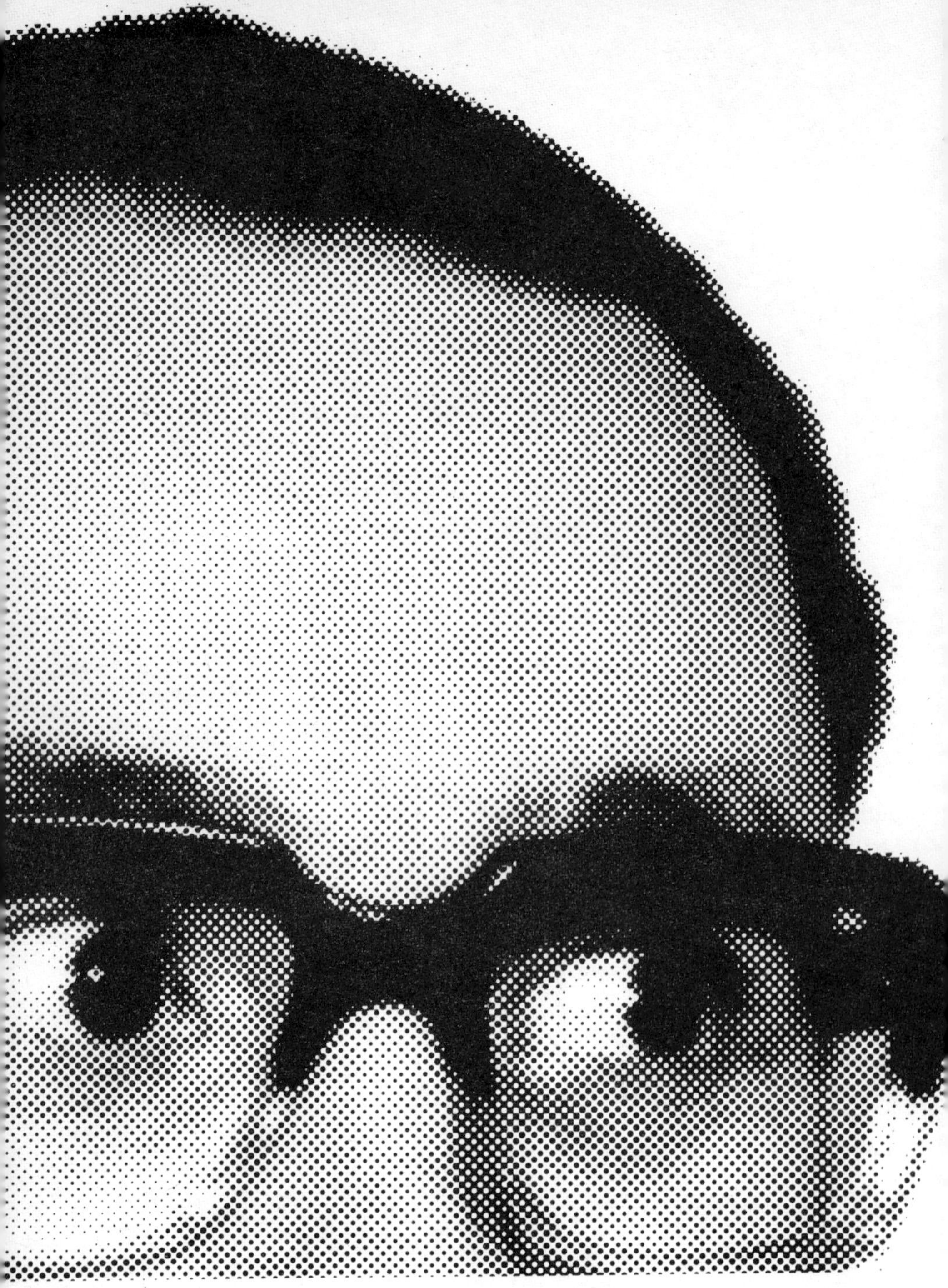

2	How to Apply	172	Health and Stress
28	Overseas Students	200	Study Techniques
44	Mature Students	210	Studying Abroad
50	Students with Disabilities	220	Lesbian and Gay Students
60	Arrival at College	228	Women Students
72	Money	236	Black Students
94	Accommodation	244	Rights
116	Basic Living	254	Employment
146	Student Unions	278	Travel
160	Sex and Relationships	306	Index and biographies

contents

This page could determine just how far you'll get as a student

Are you a young person aged 16 to 23 or a mature student in full time education?

If so you can get around 30% off nearly all National Express or Caledonian Express fares to anywhere in mainland Britain.

With one of these it could be a very long way

All you need is a Discount Coach Card. It costs only £5 and is valid for a whole twelve months.

You can use it any time on any of our coaches to any of our hundreds of destinations time and time again. Most people save the cost of the card the first time they use it.

DISCOUNT COACH CARD »

To apply or get more details, see any National Express or Caledonian Express agent or most Student Travel offices.

introduction

The *Time Out & NUS Student Guide* is a guide for all students in higher education. Whether you're considering applying to a university, polytechnic, teacher training college or the Open University, the guide will help you decide when, and how, to go about it. You'll find advice on what to do if your application is unsuccessful and whether you should take a year out between school and college.

The guide is for current as well as prospective students. There are comprehensive chapters on money, accommodation, student unions, health, travel and legal rights. We suggest ways to make the most of your academic career; but also explore the wider opportunities that college offers.

We hope we've made the book an interesting read, but we've also tried to make it as useful as possible. At the end of each chapter, you'll find lists of useful addresses and suggestions for further reading. And throughout the book, we've included quotes from the famous and the not-so-famous on their student days.

All the information was checked and correct when we went to press, but please remember that phone numbers change, self-help groups close down and companies can go out of business.

Practical & Financial
From helping you decide where to go and what to study, to finding a place to live, and surviving the first few traumatic weeks, we've outlined the administrative steps you have to take, and highlighted all the pitfalls along the way.

Money may be too tight to mention for most students, but we give advice on how to get every penny you're entitled to and how to make it last. And if you need to build both your bank balance and your c.v., we suggest ways to make extra money and enhance your job prospects.

Academic & Social
Many new students find that college is their first opportunity to establish their individuality and to live independently from family and social pressures. There are chapters which deal with the unique circumstances faced by women, black, overseas, mature and lesbian and gay students. But we haven't forgotten that studying will also play an important part in your college career, so we've included advice on how to study effectively, to maximise your exam potential and what to do if you fail.

Let us know what you think
We hope you enjoy the *Time Out & NUS Student Guide* and that it helps you get the most out of your time at college. But if you disagree with anything that's written in this book, please let us know; your comments are always welcome.

Time Out would like to thank Durex, the sponsor of the Guide. However, we would like to stress that the sponsor has no control over editorial content. The same applies to advertisers. No organization or business has been listed because they have advertised.

Abbreviations
ACFHE – Association of Colleges of Further and Higher Education; **ACU** – Association of Commonwealth Universities; **ADAR** – Art and Design Admissions Registry; **BA** – Bachelor of Arts; **BEd** – Bachelor of Education; **BSc** – Bachelor of Science; **BTEC** – Business and Technician Education Council; **CDP** – Committee of Directors of Polytechnics; **CNAA** – Council for National Academic Awards; **CRAC** – Careers Research and Advisory Centre; **CRCH** – Central Register and Clearing House for Teacher Education; **CVCP** – Committee of Vice-Chancellors and College Principals; **DES** – Department of Education and Science; **Dip Ed** – Diploma of Education; **FE** – Further Education; **HE** – Higher Education; **HNC** – Higher National Certificate; **HND** – Higher National Diploma; **LEA** – Local Education Authority; **MA** – Master of Arts; **MSc** – Master of Science; **NUS** – National Union of Students; **OU** – Open University; **PCFC** – Polytechnics and Colleges Funding Council; **PCAS** – Polytechnic Central Admissions System; **SCOTVEC** – Scottish Vocational Education Council; **SCE** – Scottish Certificate of Education; **UCCA** – University Central Council on Admissions; **UCMC** – NUS Wales; **UFC** – Universities Funding Council;

how to apply

Application Procedures **4**

Filling in Forms **11**

Applicant's Diary **14**

Choosing a Course **16**

Choosing where to Study **19**

Taking a Year Off **24**

Further Reading **25**

Useful Addresses **25**

Choosing a course and a college is a complex business. **Laura Matthews** from NUS emerges unscathed from the UCCA and PCAS Clearing systems, with the perfect plan for applying.

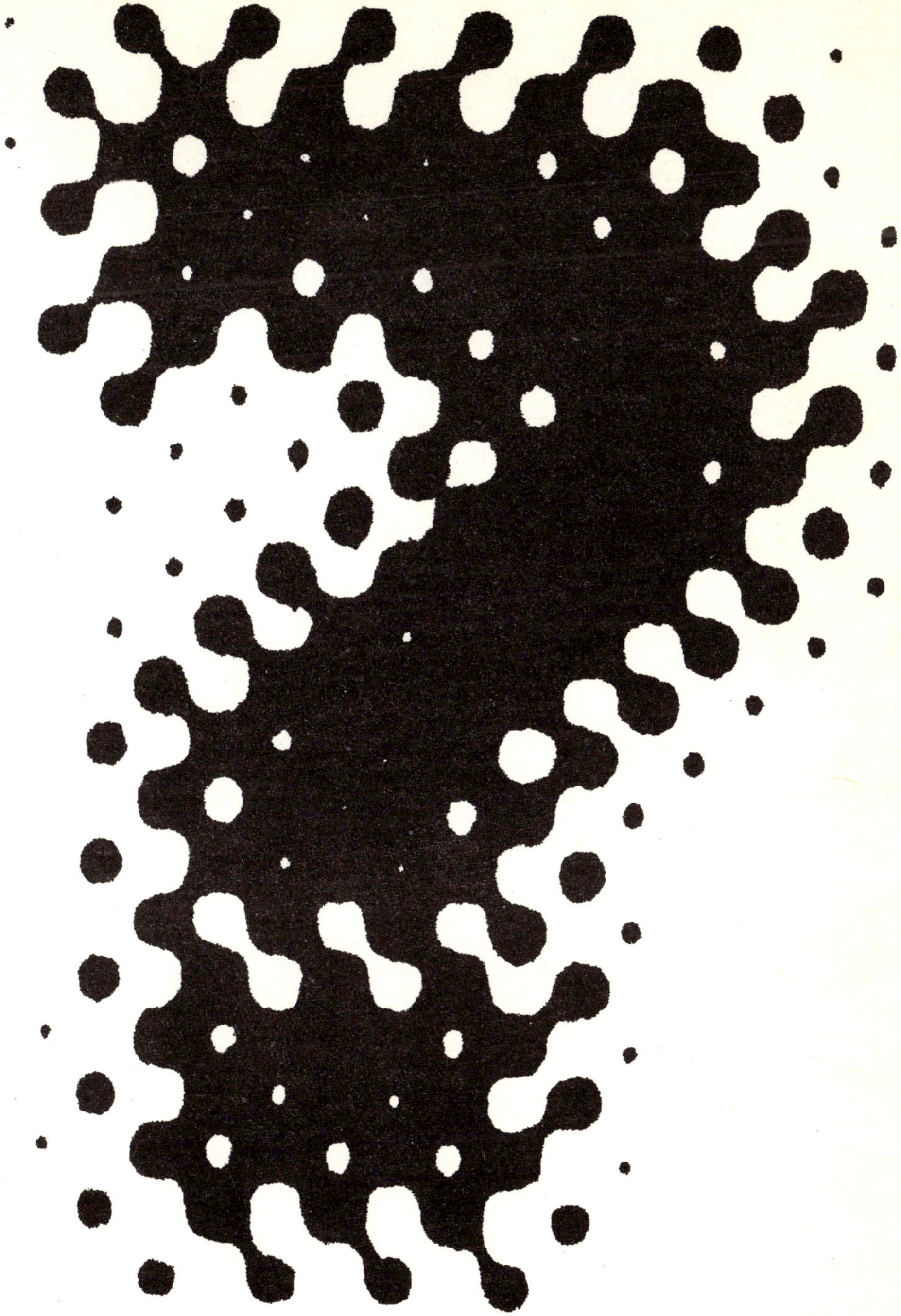

The decision to enter higher education entails many other choices. No two colleges are the same; indeed, no two courses are the same. Studying at Keele University, a campus university in the middle of a field a good thirty minutes' bus ride from the centre of Stoke-on-Trent, will be very different from studying at Manchester Polytechnic, in Manchester city centre. Also, while the core components of courses might not differ from college to college, the specialist course options will vary significantly in content and in the way they are taught, according to the character, pet subjects and political views of the lecturers giving the courses.

So, in addition to mastering the application procedure, you will need to be able to recognize the differences between courses at different colleges which appear, on initial inspection, to be offering exactly the same subjects for study. You will have to find out about the things – social life, accommodation, the student union – which the college prospectus won't tell you about in any great detail. In this chapter, we advise on how to deal with the complex and often bewildering application procedure and suggest some criteria for deciding on the right course and college.

Application Procedures

The majority of courses are applied for through the Universities Central Council on Admissions (UCCA) and the Polytechnics Central Admissions System (PCAS), which process applications for courses at UK universities, polytechnics and colleges. What they do not do is advise on choice of course, qualification or institution; entrance requirements; scholarships and grants; or admission prospects. What they do is register, distribute and co-ordinate applications centrally, relay offers and rejections, and provide safety-net procedures in case initial applications are unsuccessful. Each body produces a handbook, detailing all the courses and institutions which it covers, and a single, common form on which you apply to colleges included in either or both schemes.

There is nothing to stop you applying through PCAS as well as UCCA, or holding conditional offers from both. However, once you have firmly accepted an offer through one, you should withdraw immediately from the other. PCAS and UCCA are located in the same building and use the same computer. This means that applications through the systems are processed to a similar timetable, so you can make informed choices. But if you apply through both PCAS and UCCA, your applications will be considered quite separately, and will not affect each other.

The entry fee is £7 per scheme (£14 for both) and payment must be attached to the form. The systems and procedures of each are similar, but there are some differences between them, and each application procedure is outlined separately below.

UCCA

UCCA co-ordinates applications and admissions to full-time undergraduate courses at UK universities and university colleges. A small number of university colleges are not included in the scheme, which also doesn't cover applications to the Open University, nor to postgraduate courses, part-time or evening courses, nor to diploma or certificate courses which last less than, and up to, one year.

The UCCA handbook details the university courses available, and the application procedures. You won't be able to fill in your application form without it, because it shows the

How to Apply

course codes which must be included. You can obtain the free handbook, *How to Apply for Admission to a University*, from your school or college, or direct from UCCA (*see below* **Useful Addresses**).

The form allows five choices of courses and universities. You can apply for more than one course at the same university, although you may not name Oxford or Cambridge more than once, nor may you apply to both in the same year, unless you are applying for choral and/or organ awards on a music scholarship.

You must enter the universities in course code order. You may not indicate a preference. A full explanation of other details required is provided at the front of the handbook (*see below* **Filling in Forms**).

Once you have completed the form and passed it to your referee, he or she will forward it, along with a confidential statement, to UCCA before the closing date, usually around mid December. Within a month to six weeks you will receive an acknowledgement letter from UCCA. This will give you: your UCCA serial number, which must be quoted in any correspondence; details of the courses; and universities to which your form has been forwarded. Check these carefully. Mistakes can be rectified, but you cannot change your mind or apply again until next year. By mid May, you should have received details of offers, as well as rejections, from all your choices, have made a firm acceptance of one offer and be holding another for insurance.

If you have not been made any offers at this stage you will automatically become eligible for Clearing, the last-minute process by which students without places are matched with unfilled course places (*see below* **Clearing**).

PCAS

PCAS co-ordinates applications and admissions for all full-time and sandwich first degree, Diploma of Higher Education (DipHE) and Higher National Diploma (HND) courses at 72 polytechnics and colleges, with the exceptions of initial teacher training (Bachelor of Education, or BEd) and degrees and HNDs in art and design. You can obtain a copy of the free handbook, *Guide for Applicants*, either from your school or college, or direct from PCAS (*see below* **Useful Addresses**).

You can apply to only four polytechnics or colleges, naming the same institution more than once if you want to be considered for different courses at the same place. You must enter the courses in alphabetical order, by polytechnic or college name, and not indicate any preference. All your choices will be treated as equal. The PCAS handbook provides a thorough explanation of everything you need to include on the form, along with course codes (*see below* **Filling in Forms**).

When you have completed the form, you should fill out the acknowledgement card (you've got to stamp it yourself) and hand both to your referee. He or she will complete the reference section (page 2, which you should neither write on nor detach at any stage), and then forward the form to PCAS. Your acknowledgement card will arrive back from PCAS within a few days of your form being submitted. It will notify you of your PCAS registration number. About a month later, you will be sent a letter which will confirm your registration number and the institutions and courses you have applied for. Check the details carefully, as mistakes must be put right as soon as possible. You can alter your application in only three circumstances:

Pass your exams – FIRST TIME

With GCSE, A-levels, or a Professional exam behind you, you can achieve your ambitions at college or at work.

An RRC home study course enables you to fit in your exams with your commitments and your lifestyle.

You have all the materials you need immediately to hand; there's nothing extra to buy. You work at your own pace and at a time that's convenient for you, while your highly qualified personal tutor is always there to provide unrivalled back-up by phone or post to help you through the course – and particularly that final revision. With 60 years' experience and over 400,000 exam successes you can rely on RRC's home study methods.

Many GCE A-level and GCSE courses, including:

- Accounting • Biology
- Business Studies • Chemistry
- Computer Studies • Economics
- English • French • Geography
- Gov't & politics • History • Law
- Mathematics • Physics
- Religious Studies • Sociology

Over 40 Professional courses including:

- Accounting • Banking • Chartered Secretaries • Estate Agency • Health Service • Law Degree • Management (MBA) • Marketing • Micro-Computing • Photography • Purchasing and Supply • Radio Amateurs.

SEND OR PHONE FOR FREE PROSPECTUS

Call **081-947 7272** quoting Dept No. below.

Or please tick your choice and return the coupon. ☐ Professional courses ☐ GCE A-level and GCSE courses

Mr/Mrs/Miss/Ms _____

Address _____ Postcode _____

Course(s) of interest _____

RRC The Rapid Results College

Dept DZ100, Tuition House, 27/37 St George's Road, London SW19 4DS.
Tel: 081-946 1102 (24-hr) or fax 081-946 7584 quoting Dept No above. CACC Accredited

How to Apply

- If you have a disability and the polytechnic or college can't make appropriate arrangements for you, you will be allowed to make another choice through PCAS;
- If the course you have applied for is marked 'subject to approval' in the PCAS handbook, or if it does not appear there at all but is listed in the institution's prospectus, and approval for the course has not been obtained for the year in which you wish to enter, you will be offered a chance to apply for another course at the same college, or allowed another choice through PCAS if this is not possible;
- If the course you have applied for is unavoidably withdrawn, you are entitled to a new choice, as above.

Final offers are made between mid-August and late September, and you will only have a limited period in which to reply – so it is important that you are at your correspondence address during this time. If you cannot avoid being away, make sure somebody else will act on your behalf. If you don't reply to your offer in time, you could lose your polytechnic or college place. If you do not receive offers from any of your initial choices you will be eligible for Clearing in September, and you will automatically be sent details.

Clearing

When you become eligible for Clearing (*see above*), you will automatically be sent a Clearing entry form and instructions.

Clearing can help you in the following situations:

- You have received no offers from your initial application;
- Your examination grades fall below those required in your conditional offers (*see below* **Offers**);
- You have not applied previously that year and wish to make a late application.

Clearing, although co-ordinated by UCCA/PCAS, gives you the chance to shop around, contact institutions direct and secure verbal offers (which UCCA will confirm). Because there is less time at Clearing stage than during previous stages in applying, you will have to work hard at it, and to be prepared to make decisions quickly, if you are going to maximize your chances of getting on a course which will suit you.

It's not a good idea to plan a holiday around the time that results are published (September). In an emergency, you should make sure that somebody else will deal with your correspondence.

Applying to institutions outside UCCA and PCAS

Initial teacher training (BEd): Apply to the Central Register and Clearing House (CRCH) for initial teacher training outside the universities in England and Wales. Your school or college should be able to provide you with a CRCH booklet and application form. If not, you can obtain a form from CRCH direct (*see below* **Useful Addresses**). Your application, with its £6 fee and confidential report, must reach CRCH by mid December. You can apply for up to three courses. If you receive no offers from your initial choices, you can select three more under the Continuing Application Procedure (CAP). Offers will have been made by the end of July; if, in September, you either hold no offer, or have not achieved the entrance requirements, you will automatically enter the Clearing system, which is also open to late applicants.

CULTIVATE YOUR INDEPENDENCE

WITH

THE CHAIN WITH NO NAME

THE NETWORK OF INDEPENDENT RECORD STORES
FROM ABERDEEN TO PENZANCE

OFFERING A **FIRST CLASS DEGREE** OF KNOWLEDGE +
EXCLUSIVE RELEASES FROM **ROUGH TRADE** DISTRIBUTION

ABERDEEN ONE UP • **BARNSTABLE** UPFRONT • **BATH** RIVAL • **BEESTON** OASIS • **BLACKBURN** ASTONISHING • **BIRMINGHAM** PLASTIC FACTORY • **BOLTON** X RECORDS • **BRIGHTON** ROUNDER • **BRISTOL** REPLAY • REVOLVER • **BURNLEY** ASTONISHING • **BURTON** OASIS • **CAMBRIDGE** RHYTHM (mail order) • **CANTERBURY** RICHARDS • **CARDIFF** SPILLERS • **CHELTENHAM** BADLANDS • **CONGLETON** BEAT ROUTE • **COVENTRY** SOUNDHOUSE • SPINADISC • **CROYDON** H&R CLOAKE • **DERBY** BPM • OASIS • **DUMFRIES** BARNSTORM • **DURHAM** VOLUME • **EASTBOURNE** POWERPLAY • **EDINBURGH** AVALANCHE • FOPP • **GLASGOW** FOPP • MUSIC MANIA • **HUDDERSFIELD** BIG TREE • **HULL** OFF BEAT • **IPSWICH** SPIN DIZZY • **KINGSTON** BEGGARS BANQUET • **LANCASTER** ERE EAR • **LEAMINGTON SPA** SOUND HOUSE • **LEEDS** JUMBO • **LEICESTER** ROCK A BOOM • **LINCOLN** RADIO CITY • **LIVERPOOL** PROBE • **LONDON** MOONFLEET • RHYTHM • ROUGH TRADE • RUTHLESS • SISTER RAY • SOUNDSTORE • TERRAPIN TRUCKING • VINYL EXPERIENCE • **LOUGHBOROUGH** LEFT LEGGED PINEAPPLE • **LONGEATON** OASIS • **MANCHESTER** EASTERN BLOC • PICCADILLY RECORDS • **MAIDSTONE** LONGPLAYER • **NEWCASTLE** VOLUME • **NEWPORT** ROCKWAY • **NORTHAMPTON** SPINADISC • **NOTTINGHAM** SELECTADISC • **OXFORD** MANIC HEDGEHOG • **PENZANCE** SOUNDCHECK • **PERTH** GOLDRUSH • **PLYMOUTH** RIVAL • **PRESTON** ACTION • **ROMFORD** EXIT/FOREST • **SHEFFIELD** RECORD COLLECTOR • WARP • **SUNDERLAND** VOLUME • **SWANSEA** MUSIQUARIUM • **WAKEFIELD** JAT • **WALSALL** BRIDGE • **WIGAN** ALANS • **WORCESTER** MAGPIE • **WINDSOR** REVOLUTION • **YORK** RED RHINO

How to Apply

Colleges and institutes of higher education outside PCAS: For courses not covered by PCAS, other than teacher training courses, you must apply direct to the institution.

Art and Design Degree and HND courses outside UCCA and PCAS (England and Wales): Apply to the Art and Design Admissions Registry (ADAR) (*see below* **Useful Addresses**). The ADAR handbook costs £5. Art and design courses often have more flexible entrance requirements than many others: A levels, BTEC, foundation courses, or even your portfolio alone could all be acceptable. For foundation courses, you should apply direct to your chosen institution, as early as possible, since competition is fierce.

The Open University: You can obtain a copy of the Open University Guide to the BA programme from the Open University Undergraduate Admissions Office (*see below* **Useful Addresses**). Together with information on courses, study methods and so on, you will also receive an application form. The OU year is based on the calendar year rather than the academic year, and the deadline for applications to BA Undergraduate courses is the end of September. The Open University advises that applications be made as early as possible, since courses are often oversubscribed by 100 per cent. There are no formal entrance requirements for OU courses, but you must be 18 or over at the start of the year the course starts, and you must be resident in the UK when courses start, in February. For information on course fees, *see below* **Choosing where to Study**.

Offers

Once your application form is received by an institution, either via a Clearing house or direct, it will be evaluated. You will receive one of three responses to each application:

- Rejection. The institution will not consider you for a place;
- Unconditional offer. The institution is offering you a place on the course you have chosen that does not depend on the results of examinations or interviews;
- Conditional offer. Most offers made by institutions are of this nature. You have been offered a place on your chosen course, dependent upon your obtaining satisfactory grades in examinations not yet taken or for which you are awaiting results, or upon your performance at an interview. The required grades will be specified, so you know what you are aiming for. Some offers will also specify which subjects you must get particular grades in.

If you firmly accept an unconditional offer, you have in effect accepted a place on a course and should cancel all your other applications and withdraw from Clearing schemes immediately. Time-scales for accepting or declining offers might vary, and will be clearly specified when the offer is made. Don't delay – if you miss the deadline you could miss out on your place. If you are holding conditional offers from the UCCA/PCAS schemes you will have to accept or reject them through UCCA/PCAS within the given time-scale. Be prompt, but give yourself enough time to think carefully and compare any offers that have been made to you.

By mid May you might hold one offer which you have accepted firmly, and one provisionally from each of UCCA and PCAS. If you had applied through CRCH, this date is mid July. You can hold as many offers as you like from individual colleges outside Clearing House schemes. If you had a conditional offer depen-

ICA

• Exhibitions • Film & Video • Music & Live Arts •
• Talks & Conferences • Bar & Cafe • Bookshop •

Open Daily 12noon-11pm

"Seriously weird".
The Observer

A Student ArtPass Membership costs only £10, lasts a year, and gives you:

- Free entry for yourself and a friend
- All tickets half-price (eg Cinema tickets for £2)
- Monthly programme mailings
- Invitations to private views

Institute of Contemporary Arts
The Mall, London SW1
Box office 071 930 3647

nearest tube Piccadilly Circus, Charing Cross

How to Apply

dent on grades, and your results fulfil the conditions, you will be asked to make a firm acceptance before a deadline, and to withdraw any other applications. If you don't get the grades required in any conditional offers, there could still be a chance that you will be considered by the institutions from which you hold offers, especially if your grades were close to the conditions. Phone the colleges as soon as possible to find out if they will still accept you. If you haven't got on to a course you originally applied for, you will be sent Clearing forms by UCCA, PCAS or CRCH.

Filling in Forms

Applying to universities, polytechnics and colleges means filling in forms. Your applications are meant to impress, so you will need to fill them in clearly and accurately (especially the UCCA/PCAS form, as it will be photocopied and reduced). Most forms will be accompanied by clear and detailed explanations, but if you do need help, ask tutors, teachers or careers advisers. It's better to ask than to get it wrong – after all, your application form is an advertisement for you. Incomplete application forms will not win you hotly-contested places. You need to demonstrate both that you are capable of pursuing, and able to benefit from, a course, and that you are serious about getting on it.

If you are a mature applicant, you might feel put off by application forms that are clearly oriented towards people applying straight from school or college with orthodox qualifications. But don't let that stop you from selling yourself in the way which suits you. PCAS and UCCA encourage mature students to use the form as flexibly as possible – particularly the sections on education, further information and examinations – to give details of their employment history and other relevant information. If you are a mature applicant, the 'further information' section on the form is crucial, especially if you do not possess traditional entry requirements. Take extra care to explain your reasons for wanting to go into higher education, and the experience which will go towards supporting your application. It's a good idea to send a copy of your c.v. to the institutions you are applying to (not to a Clearing House), explaining why you want to return to education and giving a broader picture of your qualifications and experience. Quote your UCCA/PCAS registration number when you send your c.v. (*see also page 44* **Mature Students**).

Key points

Get off to a good start. This could be your only chance to advertise yourself to your chosen institutions. Remember the following points:

Clarity: If the instructions say 'black ballpoint', use one. Write in capitals, or type if that is required, but don't type unless specifically permitted.

Accuracy: Check your spelling and get the course codes right. Make rough drafts of any long passages.

Relevance: You're selling yourself – so emphasize your academic achievements, but don't be too limited in your approach. Mention any other relevant interests or experience.

You will generally be asked to provide the following information:

Personal details: Name, address, nationality and so on. This is straightforward, but less so for overseas applicants (*see page 28* **Overseas Students**).

RICHMOND COLLEGE LONDON

Richmond College is a residential US liberal arts university college offering the Bachelor of Arts and Master of Business Administration degrees. With campuses in both Richmond, Surrey and central London (Kensington), the College has an international student body of over 1100 representing 83 nations. *Courses offered include:*

- Business Administration
- International Business
- Economics
- History
- Studio Art
- History of Art
- English Literature
- Psychology
- British Studies
- Political Science
- Mathematical Sciences
- Computer Science
- Combined Social Science
- Pre-Engineering
- Pre-Chiropractic

For further details and a copy of our brochure, contact:
Director of Admissions (Dept TO), Richmond College, Queens Road, Richmond, Surrey TW10 6JP.
Tel: 081-940 4487   Fax: 081-332 1297
ACCREDITED BY THE MIDDLE STATES ASSOCIATION OF COLLEGES & SCHOOLS

It's time to change the course of your life

Phone now for your **FREE** Prospectus of the exciting range of degree-level courses at this lively, multi-cultural Polytechnic.

Tel: **071-753 5066/7** (direct lines)

The Polytechnic of North London
166-220 Holloway Road, London N7 8DB

PNL

There's never been a better time to join Labour

Form:
- I wish to join The Labour Party.
- Surname
- Forename ___ Title ___ ☐ M ☐ F
- Address
- Postcode
- Date of Birth
- Trade union (if eligible)
- Annual membership subscription.
  - ☐ £10 if employed
  - ☐ £3 if a student / unwaged / part-time worker / retired / on a government training scheme.
  - ☐ £5 trade union (if union is affiliated to the Labour Party).
- I enclose an extra donation of £
- ☐ I enclose cheque/PO made payable to *The Labour Party*
- ☐ I wish to pay by Access/Visa/American Express/ Diners Club
- ☐ I wish to pay by Direct Debit. Please send details.
- I agree to abide by the rules.
- Signature ___ Date ___
- To: Membership Processing, The Labour Party, FREEPOST, London SE17 1BR
- Phone: London 071-701 1234

KM

The Conservative government is in a real mess.

They know the poll tax would lose them the next election. So they've bribed us with a £140 discount - hoping we don't notice the higher VAT bills that will pay for it.

And they have come up with a half-baked scheme to combine a property tax with the poll tax - a twin tax torture.

But it's not just the poll tax.

Our inflation is the highest of our industrial competitors. Mortgage and interest rates have hit record levels.

The NHS no longer guarantees high-quality treatment. Schoolchildren share textbooks in crumbling schools.

Labour will scrap the poll tax and replace it with fair rates. We'll build a first-class economy able to compete abroad. And we'll invest in health, education and jobs.

Join us today - all you have to do is fill in the attached form.

How to Apply

Address: Remember that correspondence will continue until September – make sure that you will be at your correspondence address until then, or that you can get hold of your mail quickly.

Choice of college and course: Get the course codes right, and list courses in the order specified in the instructions. *See below* **Choosing a Course** and **Choosing where to Study**.

Education from age 11: Make it complete, but keep it simple.

Examinations – results known: You must include everything, even failures or low grades. Some Clearing Houses require this and, in any case, you won't be penalized for failing and trying again – it shows determination, motivation and honesty. The UCCA/PCAS form will have space for BTEC/SCOTVEC qualifications. If an application form does not have designated space for your qualifications, make sure that you include them anyway, perhaps on a separate sheet.

Examinations – results not known: Include everything. Don't miss things out just because the application form does.

Further information: This is the most difficult section of all, and the space (and, it is safe to assume, the importance) given to it on the UCCA/PCAS form has been increased. Jot your ideas down first and make rough drafts before you write on the form. You must be concise, and avoid being bland. 'Sport' says nothing about you but, for example, being a member of your local hockey team shows qualities of team spirit and enthusiasm. Guard against being too wordy – not only can you run out of room on the form, but you could find yourself with nothing left to talk about at an interview.

You should include any positions of responsibility you have held at school; relevant employment experience; and any skills you have. Don't be afraid of including off-beat activities – if you've got interesting and unusual hobbies, then so much the better (but don't embellish or make things up; the pretence could be hard to sustain at an interview). Remember: selectors aren't looking for superheroes, they're looking for students likely to contribute to, and benefit from, the course.

Ethnic monitoring: This usually applies only to UK residents, and is used for statistical purposes; for example, to monitor application and admission rates. The information will not be passed on to your chosen institutions if you are applying through UCCA/PCAS, and will always be treated confidentially.

Referees: After you have completed your application form, you should pass it to your referee who will write a confidential statement. Give your referee enough time to do this properly, as the confidential statement is important. If you are at school (or college) your headteacher (or principal) should be your referee. If this is not possible, or not applicable, you should find someone who can write you a suitable academic reference. An academic reference is far better than a personal one, since it is, after all, your academic aptitude that institutions want to be sure of. Although some individual teachers and tutors might let you look at and discuss the statement, this is probably the last time you will see your form.

applicant's diary

Year a

June/July
Obtain Clearing House handbooks, college prospectuses and alternative prospectuses. Take day trips to places and institutions you are considering.

August
Research and choose your course and institution (see **Choosing a Course** and **Choosing where to Study**). Make sure that you have all the application forms you need if you will not be getting them from school or college.

Early September
UCCA/PCAS/CRCH begin to accept application forms. Get hold of application forms and handbooks when you return to school or college.

Mid October
Closing date for Oxbridge applications through UCCA. Offers begin to be made.

Year b

January
Investigate halls of residence/private accommodation availability. Beware – deadlines for hall applications vary, and can be very early. Write to your local education authority for your maintenance grant application form (you might be able to obtain this from your school/college). *See page 72* **Money**.

February-April
Interviews and open days.

Early December
Get your form to your referee in good time.

Mid December
Closing date for UCCA/PCAS/CRCH. Late applicants will be considered at institutions' discretion only.

Mid May
You could have received one firm and one insurance offer from UCCA and/or PCAS.

June
A level examinations.

August
A level results published. Places confirmed. You should now hold on to no more than one firm offer.

September
Clearing. Late applications (June Year B onwards) also considered.

October
Courses start.

December
The deadline for applying for LEA grants is the end of the first term. If you do not apply now you won't be eligible for a grant for the rest of the course.

Choosing a Course

Choosing a specific course is a major decision. It is vital that you choose the right one, since you will probably have to stick at it for several years. To give yourself the best chance of academic and personal satisfaction, you should research carefully what is involved in studying a specific subject at a particular institution, and make sure that it will fit any career plans you have. No matter what subject you are going to study, you should consider the following points:

Entrance requirements: Don't waste your limited number of applications on courses for which your qualifications aren't applicable. Check in prospectuses, handbooks and *University Entrance – The Official Guide* (*see below* **Further Reading**). At this stage it is a good idea to identify your 'insurance' application – a course and institution where the entrance requirement is lower than the other options you are considering. You should also check for any other general requirements: GCSE (or equivalent) as prerequisites, for example.

Alternative qualifications: A levels are not the only acceptable qualification for entry to higher education. Indeed, over half the entrants to polytechnic courses have qualifications other than A levels.

Probably the best-known alternatives are Business and Technical Education Council (BTEC) National Certificates and Diplomas. Generally, a minimum of 3 units, with merit at level 3 will be required. You can offer BTEC in combination with A level.

Similarly, the International and the European Baccalaureates are acceptable entry qualifications. Scottish students will normally hold the Scottish Certificate of Education (SCE), which is acceptable to all UK higher education institutions.

Overall, higher education institutions are becoming more flexible with respect to entry requirements. The range of acceptable qualifications and, possibly, credits for work experience will usually be detailed in an institution's prospectus. If you need further clarification, write to the academic registrar of your chosen institution.

Access courses: Begun in 1977, there are now over 640 access to higher education courses designed for mature students who 'missed' the traditional routes into higher education. The Education Counselling and Credit Transfer Information Scheme (ECCTIS, *see below* **Useful Addresses**) publishes an annual *Access to HE Courses Directory*, detailing the courses, where you can take them and what degree programmes they lead to. Access courses are taken in further education colleges, which often have franchising agreements with the local higher education institution enabling access students to transfer immediately to higher education courses on completion of their pre-degree access year. *See also page 44* **Mature Students**.

Course structure: You'll have to decide whether you want to go on a course which features a placement year in industry or a year abroad, and if so, whether you want the placement to be compulsory or simply an option. Think about whether it will count towards your assessment and, if so, by how much. Some courses give the chance to follow options outside the main subject choice department, and if you are applying for one of these, you'll have to decide what proportion of 'outside options' you want and find out how free a hand you will have in choosing them. You'll have to decide whether you want a course which concentrates on one discipline, or whether you want to study two or more subjects together. Many institutions

How to Apply

offer joint honours (with a main discipline), and combined studies are becoming increasingly popular. The length of the course might be a deciding factor. Degree courses in England last three years, although some institutions offer the opportunity to do a foundation year first. In Scotland, honours degrees take four years, the first of which is a foundation year.

Course content: In weighing up courses which are more practical or more theoretical in content, think about whether you want to do field trips and laboratory work, and what proportion of the course assessment will this take.

Teaching methods and academic environment: Ask yourself whether you want a course which is taught by largely traditional methods – lectures, seminars and tutorials – or one which is more unorthodox. Some courses involve a high number of compulsory teaching hours, and the range of the available teaching hours could influence your choice. Consider the size of the department: a large department could be a bit depersonalized, but will probably have many subjects on offer; there could be more personal supervision in a small department, but the range of available specialities is likely to be more limited.

Assessment methods: Courses vary between those assessed mainly by examination and those with a large continuous assessment content.

Career relevance: You'll have to decide between courses that are directly vocational and those that are more esoteric. Some courses could exempt you from parts of professional examinations you might want to take later.

New subjects: If you are applying for a course in a subject area you have not studied before, you need to ask yourself whether you fulfil all the prerequisites. Look for hidden requirements, such as numeracy and languages (you'd be surprised where they crop up, in archaeology, for instance). There are courses that start with a foundation year or otherwise enable students to sample a range of options before committing themselves to one discipline (especially in the social sciences). Think about the opportunities you would be offered for a change of plan after you had started the course.

If you are applying for a language course, you should ask yourself whether you want to learn a new language, what facilities you would prefer to have, and whether these are available. You'll also have to decide whether you want a language or a literature-based course, and find out whether courses involve some time abroad.

Getting information

Asking yourself the above questions will help you develop a well directed strategy. You could be either delighted or dismayed when you begin to assess the actual courses available by looking at the institutions' prospectuses (available from your school or college careers library, or from individual institutions themselves). What is more likely is that you will want to know more than the prospectus tells you. You should discuss your expectations from a course, and your preliminary choices, with teachers, tutors or careers advisers.

Do you know anybody who has studied your chosen subject at the institution which interests you? Talk it over with them. If you have the chance to go to an open day, or to an interview, ask students and academics any questions you have (*see below* **Open Days and Interviews**). Every year, the *Guardian* holds 'Higher Education Fairs' in Birmingham, Bristol, London and Manchester, while *The Times* organizes one fair, 'Directions', in London.

"I had important course decisions to make. Was it to be Greek Drama or the Medieval Variety? I chose Medieval because the Greek tutor had a beard and was called Graham. Medieval Drama, on the other hand, was to be taught by a magnificent woman with silver hair and a purple shawl. No contest. I've always made all major career decisions in this remarkably whimsical manner. For example, I work for Channel Four because the Commissioning Editor has a nice Irish accent and wears groovy socks. LWT's opposite number wears a lot of grey and has a flat in Balham."

Julian Clary, comedian and presenter of *Sticky Moments* (English and Drama, Goldsmith's College, London, 1977-80).

These Fairs are advertised in the newspapers holding them.

Alternative prospectuses: Usually produced by the student union, alternative prospectuses (APs) are a useful, sometimes humorous, and more student-centred source of information about courses and institutions. The AP gives you the insider's view. It is intended to provide prospective students with an impression of what it's really like to study at an institution, based on the experience of current students. As well as offering subject-centred evaluations of what's available academically, they also give information about the environment of the institution, campus, town or city, and on the role of the student union, together with study facilities like libraries, laboratories and equipment.

APs are available from the student union of the institution, although not all student unions produce them. You could encourage your school or college to obtain them on your behalf, as they are extremely useful to all potential students.

A strategy for course choice

Assess your priorities among course structure, content, academic environment, examination methods and career relevance, then make preliminary selections of about a dozen courses for closer investigation. Read prospectuses and APs, talk to careers advisers, teachers and tutors, and take advantage of open days to talk to students on your proposed course (unfortunately, most open days and all interviews take place in spring and summer, too late to inform your choice when first applying). Gradually narrow your options. You will be able to dismiss some courses immediately. Naturally, the type and location of the institution will play a large part in influencing your choice of course (*see below* **Choosing where to Study**).

How to Apply

Look at the entrance requirements of your shortlisted courses, making sure that you will have the main qualifications and meet any general requirements such as minimum GCSE (or equivalent) standards in subjects other than your main discipline. Identify, if you can, the grades or levels you need to obtain to satisfy offer conditions for your preferred courses. It is prudent to select one course for which the entrance requirements are lower than for others. This is your insurance application.

Don't include more than one insurance application on multiple application forms for Clearing Houses, since they offer few enough choices already. If you are applying through UCCA/PCAS, finalize your shortlists of five and four courses respectively. Unless you are particularly single-minded and won't consider any alternatives, it's a good idea to use all the choices available.

Choosing where to Study

Your course and institution cannot be separated: you can't have one without the other. Obviously, the choice of where to study is subjective, but there are a number of differences between institutions which make useful points of comparison and contrast.

Courses: Make sure that the course you want to do is available, and that the teaching and assessment methods suit you (*see above* **Choosing a course**). You should also decide whether you want to go to an institution which has a single subject-area focus (ie education, social sciences); or one which is multi-faculty, with everything from accountancy to zoology catered for.

Atmosphere: Some higher education institutions, particularly universities which are structured on collegiate lines, have formal traditions, such as the wearing of academic dress on occasion and regular dining in college. Others are far more relaxed. You will have to decide whether collegiate camaraderie or free-range style suits you best. The profile of the student body will also affect the atmosphere of an institution. Would you prefer to study in a place where there is a high proportion of traditional school-leaver entrants or a high percentage of undergraduates, or one which has a more mixed student population, with a higher number of postgraduates and researchers? Would you prefer to study as one of thousands, hundreds or tens of students?

Student union and other facilities: You should ensure that any passionate interests you have will be catered for. What are local cinemas, theatres and nightlife like? Are there adequate sports facilities on and off campus? Do student union clubs and societies cover your interests? Are the facilities you require for religious worship close at hand? On site, you should check library and laboratory facilities. Study conditions will affect your work. Make sure also that any special needs you have, from childcare to wheelchair access, are catered for – check with institutions before you apply, as well as attending open days.

City vs campus: Campus institutions have classrooms, laboratories and libraries, housing and a range of other facilities all on one self-contained site. They have the advantage of creating a feeling of community, and providing easy access to everything you might need as a student. However, campuses are often some distance from town centres and their amenities, and the isolation from the real world which this can entail is a drawback and a deterrent to many. Conversely, living out in the town can lead to feelings of isolation, and not being part of the student body. Travelling to college can

19

also be both inconvenient and expensive. Other drawbacks include high rents in the private sector (especially in London and the South-east of England; *see page 94* **Accommodation**). But there are advantages for those who prefer to live in a varied community, not surrounded by other students, and with a range of social and leisure opportunities readily available. By using college and student union social facilities you should be able to meet your fellow students easily.

Location: The cost of living is lower away from metropolitan areas, especially in the South. You should also consider how close you wish to be to your family home, especially if this is the first time you will be living on your own. You might find that you are commuting back and forth regularly. How convenient, and how expensive, will this be? Are you moving to a student town? Some towns have a number of higher education institutions, and therefore a relatively large student population. Do you want to be in a student town, or would you prefer anonymity and a broader social mix?

Studying in London: If you study at a college in London, you will probably not be based in central London (Buckingham Palace, Oxford Street and the West End). You're more likely to be studying in south-east London (if, for example, you're a student at Goldsmiths' College or Thames Polytechnic), north-west London (Middlesex Polytechnic), east London (Polytechnic of East London or Queen Mary and Westfield College) or even Surrey (Royal Holloway and Bedford New College or Kingston Polytechnic). If you do attend a college based in central London (such as University College), you probably won't be able to afford to live in the centre of town. Most students living and studying in London spend at least an hour every day travelling to and from college, which can be expensive, tiresome and frustrating.

Although the student grant has an additional London weighting, most students find it insufficient to pay for the excessively high rents charged by private landlords (£55 a week is the norm) and higher cost of living in the South-east of England, and in London in particular. Despite this, London is a great place in which to study. The cosmopolitan and eclectic mix of people, places and pastimes mean that whatever you want to do in London, there's bound to be somewhere to do it and someone to do it with. Although you might never have any money, you'll never be bored.

The Open University: You might decide that you do not wish to study away from home, or you might not be able to afford being a full-time student for several years, in which case the Open University could suit you very well. This unique institution prides itself on being 'genuinely open', having no entrance requirements or interviews, and being flexible. It offers not only undergraduate degree courses, but also postgraduate courses, business courses, leisure courses and a range of other continuing education courses. Open University study is mainly at home in your own time, from texts and other materials provided, and radio and television broadcasts. However, you will have a local tutor-counsellor, and go to a residential summer school in your first year. The minimum time it takes to do an Open University degree course is three years, but most students spread their workload over five or six years, to fit in with their other commitments. For those who have not studied for a long time, the Open University runs foundation courses from February to October each year.

How to Apply

The cost of an Open University degree is about £390 for the first year (including summer school fee), and £120-£240 for subsequent years, depending on the course taken. Your local education authority might contribute towards fees, employers might assist on work-related courses, and if you are on a low income the Open University itself might make an award to pay most of your fees. Information is available from the Open University's Central Enquiry Service (*see below* **Useful Addresses**).

Open days and interviews

Open days: Colleges invite prospective students to open days, usually through tutors and careers advisers, but sometimes by placing advertisements. If you are invited to an open day, take the opportunity to go along, have a look at the institution, campus and town, and meet the students in your department and in the student union. Open days are invaluable for finding out facts about the courses and institutions that prospectuses and college representatives won't tell you. They are most useful if you are still thinking about where and what to apply for, but even if they take place after the closing dates for applications, you should still go along to get to know where you might be studying.

By the end of an open day, you should have had the chance to talk to a whole range of people, and to see what facilities are on offer for study, leisure, welfare, sport and childcare, from your student union, department and institution. If you are disabled you should also have had the chance to examine any special facilities you require, such as access routes (*see page 50* **Students with Disabilities**).

Talk to academics and students in your department and find out how the course is taught and supervised, how the workload develops over the duration of the course, and what facilities are available. Ask to see teaching rooms, the department or faculty library, laboratories and language labs (if appropriate). Ask students already on your course about the atmosphere of the department. Is it impersonal, or close and sociable? Are there departmental weekends away or other social events? How flexible are teaching and assessment methods in practice? How much teaching is compulsory, or simply available? How interesting, useful or complementary are certain courses? Is it worth following extra course units in order to support your main course units? Which outside options are preferred by students in the department? On your tour of the department you should ask how accessible the study facilities are, both in terms of the number of people competing for them and opening hours.

You should also ask for a tour of the main library you will be using. Is it updated regularly? Does it get the periodicals you will need? Does it get overcrowded? Ask to see the information technology services, if you think you might be using them. Find out whether training on computers is provided for beginners, if you need it.

Other facilities you might be interested in finding out about include the student health service and (although it might seem rather a long way off) the careers service.

Talking to students currently at the institution will give you a chance to ask not only about courses and so on, but also about the town you will be living in. What is the cost of accommodation, and which areas are cheapest? How easy is it to travel around? What facilities exist off campus, and will your particular interests and hobbies be catered for?

"I had an interview at Kent and was unimpressed with that; Hull made me an offer without even seeing me, so I was unimpressed by that too. Warwick was the least bad option. It's not the sort of place you fall in love with immediately, but I grew to like it eventually.
Campus universities are very useful in one sense, because everything you need is there, but it's such an artificial world: you never see any old people, kids or dogs. And the accommodation was not particularly splendid: sharing one flat with eleven...

At many open days there will be time set aside for you to be shown around and introduced to the student union. If there isn't any allotted time, it's still worth going along to the student union to talk to staff and students.

The student union will be able to provide you with information on its role in the college, and on what facilities are on offer. Find out about welfare, housing, counselling and financial advice services. Also see what societies and clubs there are. Is there a women's group, a lesbian and gay society, a sports club? What social events does the student union organize; and, probably most important of all, where is the bar?

Talking to people in the student union, as well as reading the alternative prospectus, will give you an insider's view, minus the glossy photographs and slick literature, which it is otherwise hard to obtain from official sources. For fuller information on student unions, *see page 146* **Student Unions**.

Interviews: You might be asked to attend an interview at one or more of the institutions you have applied to, either prior or supplementary to a conditional offer being made, or as the sole condition of your offer. Not every institution uses interviews as a selection procedure, and you are more likely to be asked to go to an interview if you are applying with unorthodox entrance qualifications. Make sure you know why you are being interviewed before you go.

When you attend an interview you should be smartly dressed, punctual, polite and well prepared. Remember, you are selling yourself in what is becoming an increasingly competitive market, and you need to project yourself as someone who will contribute to, and benefit from, a course of study. Everybody else will dress for the occasion, so don't put yourself at a disadvantage, and avoid scruffiness.

How to Apply

Being well prepared doesn't mean that you have to prove you know everything about the course you are applying for. What it does mean is that you should be able to talk competently about your academic and personal interests and to ask relevant questions about the institution, the department and the course you're trying to get on to.

If you have never had an interview before, or feel out of practice, talk to teachers or tutors, and careers advisers; indeed, anybody with interviewing experience. Ask somebody to run through a mock interview with you, so you can practice your replies to likely questions, as well as general interview technique. This kind of preparation will enable you to feel far more relaxed and familiar with the real thing, and consequently to perform more effectively.

As far as specific preparation goes, you should have assessed the demands of the course (*see above* **Choosing a course**) and carefully read prospectuses. It is helpful to prepare a list of questions in advance on a variety of subject areas. This will show the interviewer that you have considered your choice of course seriously, and will avoid embarrassing pauses while you try to think of something to say. Interviewers like to be asked questions, since interviews should, after all, be a two-way process of information exchange. When an institution has shown sufficient interest to invite you for an interview, return the compliment by showing interest in what they have to offer you. Taking brief notes (both with you and while you are there) is fine.

Certain questions will invariably arise in various forms. Be prepared for: Why are you considering doing this subject? Why do you think you are suited for it? (Especially if you have not studied the subject before). What have

**...other men was as hygienic as living in a zoo. I hear there's a plaque where I used to live, which is a bit disturbing.
It was a real effort to get off campus, but it was worth it when I did: it was great to go to a real pub instead of spending all my time talking to other students in the union bar, where the carpets were permanently soggy and fag-stained, and ridiculous student politics were all over the place."**

Simon Mayo Radio 1 DJ (History and Politics, University of Warwick, 1977-1980).

you done previously that is relevant to the subject? What are you looking for from your studies, both personally and in terms of a future career? How will you cope with a less structured workload? How will you manage to recommence study (if you are a mature student or have taken time off)?

You might be able to play it by ear, but a few stock examples and standard answers which you can fit in and tailor to meet the requirements of the interview panel will add to your confidence; and if you are confident, you will express and present yourself in a positive way.

When you answer questions about yourself, don't be apologetic or hesitant; after all, that's one subject you'll know more about than anyone else. Show confidence in your ability, and enthusiasm for your non-academic activities. Use examples of projects and jobs you have undertaken, enjoyed and succeeded at, to prove your ability and interest. Don't rush into answering any question. Taking the time to think about what you are going to say, especially if you are asked anything unexpected, will keep you calm and probably improve your answer. Although an interview will primarily concern your academic field of study, you can only gain by demonstrating a broad range of academic and non-academic interests.

At the end of an interview you should thank the interviewers, no matter how you are feeling, and find out when you will be informed of the outcome. Afterwards, you should identify any areas which you think need polishing up for any further interviews, and prepare answers to any questions you hadn't expected. If you have a series of interviews, you might well be asked similar questions again and again, and learning from your mistakes can only be to your advantage.

Taking a Year Off
Deferred entry

If you wish to delay your entry to a course, you must indicate this on the application form by changing the date at the top of the front page. There will be space on the form for you to explain why you propose taking a year out between school or college and higher education, and what you intend doing in that year. If you are applying for a course outside UCCA/PCAS, make sure that deferred applications are acceptable.

If you do decide to take a year off, you might be considering one of the following:

Travel: If you decide to travel abroad, you will need money. You might also want to show that you have done more than taken a glorious holiday for an extended period. There is a range of opportunities for working abroad, although these are often unpaid or provide only pocket money. If you are interested in working abroad you should contact your school or college careers advisory service (*see also page 254* **Employment**).

Voluntary work: If you are interested in voluntary work – bearing in mind that you will probably not be entitled to receive Income Support or other welfare benefits – you must make sure that you can support yourself. You should speak to careers officers (*see also page 254* **Employment**).

Employment: Getting a job during your year off will allow you to build up some useful skills (such as typing and office administration) as well as giving you experience in money management. If you are especially careful, you might also manage to save some money for the under-financed student years ahead. At any rate, you will increase your chances of better-paid vacation work, and maybe gain some useful extra experience for your future. However, after

How to Apply

working for a year, you might find it hard to readjust to studying, and to surviving on a student grant or loan.

Pros and cons of taking a year off study

Self-confidence, social skills and overall awareness develop in ways not always possible in the school environment. You could also gain useful experience, and learn about self-sufficiency. Deferring entry will not put you at a disadvantage when applying, and will provide you with the opportunity to prepare fully for the year ahead. But you could get out of the habit of studying and lose some enthusiasm for continuing your education. Some people feel they have wasted their free time by not planning it adequately.

If your applications are unsuccessful

If, after Clearing and contacting institutions to check if they have places, you still do not have a place, either because you have received no offers or because your examination results were not sufficient to satisfy the requirements of conditional offers, it's still not the end of the road, either academically or for your career.

After speaking to teachers or tutors and careers advisers, you should be able to develop a strategy for your future. You will need to define your priorities. It's a good idea to make a list of your aims and objectives. The decision whether to persevere with applications, or to give up the whole idea of education, will have to be made by you; but you should obtain information and advice from as wide a range of sources as possible. Deciding not to re-enter education immediately is now not as final as it used to be, since most institutions are becoming more flexible about admissions, and many employers offer the opportunity to follow courses.

You will need to decide whether you are prepared to try again in a year's time to go on with your education, and to evaluate the likelihood of applications being successful the next time round. You could stay on at the same school or college, or you could enrol at your local further education college. Will you study the same subjects, or go for a complete change? When reapplying, you will need to ask yourself where you went wrong last time, and to be more flexible about the type of course and institution you choose. Look carefully at the entrance requirements of different courses and different establishments. You might consider enrolling on a course which requires an alternative entrance qualification instead (*see above* **Choosing a Course: Alternative qualifications**), with a view to moving back to your initial strategy later.

If you decide that you don't want to continue with formal education, but find employment instead, you should talk to your school or college careers advisory service about your options and chances. You might be able to pursue qualifications while you are at work, whether at evening classes, on day release or by Open University study. Employment certainly does not have to mean the end of formal study. Increasing numbers of mature students are applying for, and entering, higher education courses. In some cases 'mature' can mean as young as 21. There is often greater flexibility in entrance requirements for a mature applicant – your aptitude and ability to benefit from a course will be judged on criteria broader than the achievement of particular grades in examinations. The increasing availability of access courses gives yet another avenue into higher education (*see above* **Choosing a Course: Access courses** and *page 44* **Mature Students**).

Further Reading

The UCCA handbook, *How to Apply for Admission to University*, and the PCAS handbook, *Guide for Applicants*, are vital. If they are not stocked at your school or college, they are available free from UCCA and PCAS (*see below* **Useful Addresses**).

All of the following publications should be available in colleges and schools, libraries and careers offices:

University Entrance – The Official Guide (£11.95).
Published annually by the Committee of Vice Chancellors and Principals (CVCP) and the Association of Commonwealth Universities, this provides an outline of each institution UCCA covers. Course tables are divided into subject groups, listing entrance requirements (subjects and grades), non A level qualifications, statistics on how many people applied/were accepted (very useful for deciding on 'insurance' options). For each subject group, a brief guide to differentiating between different courses within it is given. The book also covers what is involved in following various disciplines at university level.
Colleges and Institutes of Higher Education – Guide.
Published annually by the Standing Conference of Principals (SCoP), the free Guide gives a profile of all colleges and institutions of higher education in England and Wales, including courses offered and general information.
Polytechnic Courses Handbook.
Published annually by the Committee of Directors of Polytechnics (CDP), the free book includes: profiles of polytechnics; a section on first degree courses broken down into areas of study; sections on HNDs, advanced non-degree courses and second stage advanced courses.
Higher Education in the UK – a handbook for students and their advisers (Longmans, £12.95).
Produced by the Association of Commonwealth Universities, the guide contains a directory of what is available at universities, polytechnics and colleges throughout the UK.
A-Z of first degrees, diplomas and certificates (Kogan Page, £6.95).
An annual guide to qualifications awarded by universities and polytechnics in the UK. Lists by subject name.
Which Degree? (Newpoint, £7.95 per volume); Vol 1 Arts, humanities, languages; Vol 2 Engineering, technology, the environment; Vol 3 Mathematics, medicine, sciences; Vol 4 Business, education, social sciences; Vol 5 Universities, polytechnics, colleges.
The Kogan Page Mature Students Handbook by Margaret Korving (Kogan Page, £8.95). Outlines a variety of courses including access courses, open and distance learning courses, degree and advanced courses, by regional availability.

Useful Addresses

Association of Colleges for Further and Higher Education (ACFHE) c/o Swindon College, Regent Circus, Swindon, Wiltshire SNl IPT (0793 513193).
Association of Commonwealth Universities (ACU) John Foster House, 36 Gordon Square, London WCIH OPF (071 387 8572).
Art and Design Admissions Registry (ADAR) Penn House, 9 Broad Street, Hereford HR4 9AP (0432 266653).

How to Apply

British Technical Education Council (BTEC) Central House, Upper Woburn Place, London WCIH OHH (071 388 3288).

Careers Research and Advisory Centre (CRAC) 2nd Floor, Sheraton House, Castle Park, Cambridge CB3 OAX (0223 460 2777).

Central Register and Clearing House for Teacher Education (CRCH) 3 Crawford Place, London WI 2BN (ex-directory).

Council for National Academic Awards (CNAA) 344/354 Grays Inn Road, London WCIX 8BP (071 278 4411).

Educational Counselling and Credit Transfer Information Service (ECCTIS) PO Box 88, Walton Hall, Milton Keynes, MK7 6DB (0242 518724).

National Union of Students (NUS) Nelson Mandela House, 461 Holloway Road, London N7 6LJ (071 272 8900).

NUS Scotland 12 Dublin Street, Edinburgh EHI 3PP (031 556 6598).

NUS/USI Northern Ireland 34 Botanic Avenue, Belfast BT7 IJQ (0232 244641).

Open University Walton Hall, Walton, Milton Keynes MK7 6AA (0908 274066).

Polytechnic Central Admissions System (PCAS) PO Box 67, Cheltenham, Gloucestershire GL50 3SF (0242 227788).

Scottish Vocational Education Council (SCOTVEC) Hanover House, 24 Douglas Street, Glasgow G2 7NQ (041 248 7900).

UCMC/NUS Wales 107 Walter Road, Swansea SAI 5QQ (0792 643323).

Universities Central Council on Admissions (UCCA) PO Box 28, Cheltenham, Gloucestershire GL50 1HY (0242 222444).

30 Entering and Leaving the UK

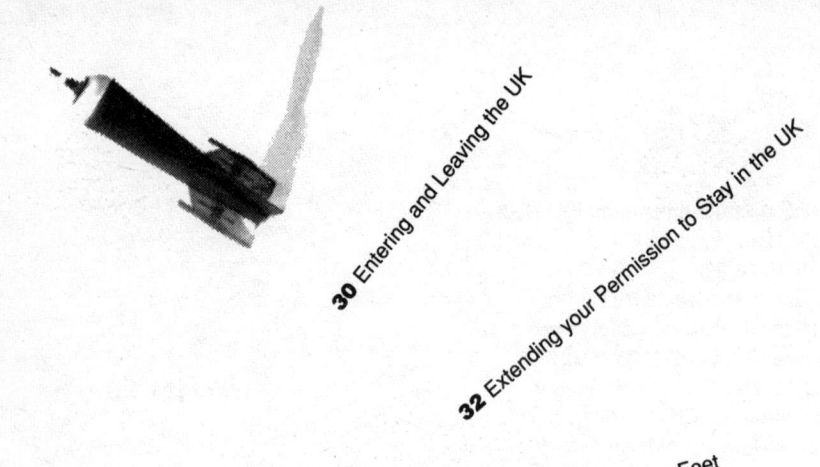

32 Extending your Permission to Stay in the UK

35 Finding your Feet

36 Money Matters

38 Working in the UK

41 Useful Addresses

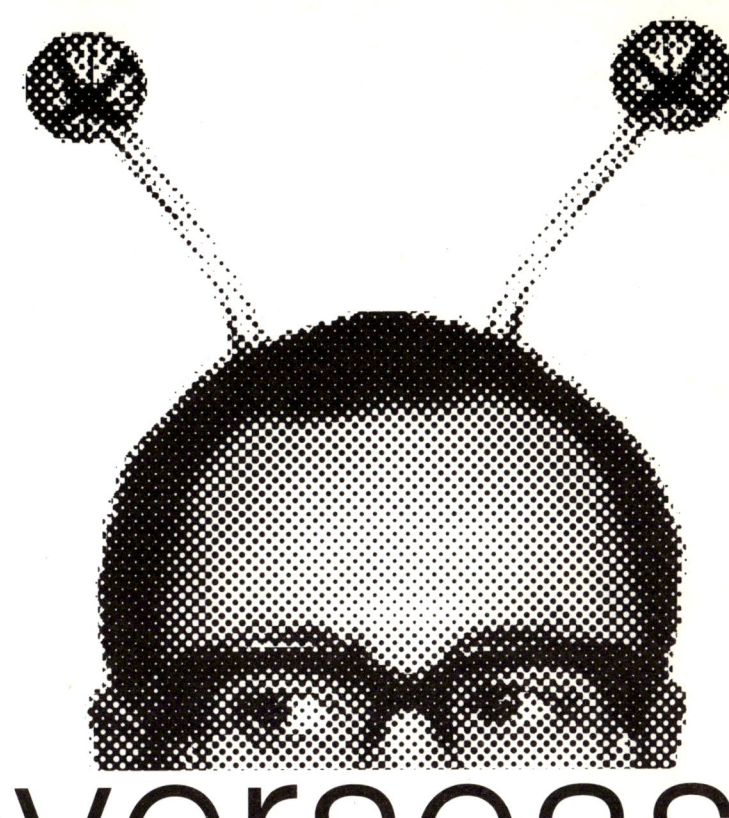

overseas students

Overseas students in the UK can find it difficult adapting to an alien and often confusing culture. **Linet Arthur** and **Maeve Sherlock** from the UK Council on Overseas Student Affairs steer a path through the maze of rules and regulations and recommend ways to make studying in the UK a trouble-free and satisfying experience.

It's never easy becoming a student. You're surrounded by new people, you can spend hours struggling with unfamiliar lecture halls, tutors and books and you're having to cope with an exhilarating but usually baffling new way of life. This process can be particularly daunting for overseas students. After all, you'll also have to adapt to a new country and culture.

There will also be numerous rules and regulations influencing your life which are different to those faced by British students: rules about whether you are allowed into the country; how long you can stay; whether you can work while you are here; and whether you can be accompanied by your family. An understanding of these rules and regulations will make it easier to cope with the pressures you may face while studying in the UK.

Entering and Leaving the UK

There are very strict immigration laws governing who is allowed to enter the UK, for how long and for what purpose. It is important to understand the ways in which they affect you. This section explains the different conditions imposed by the Home Office and gives advice on what to do if you are thinking of travelling abroad.

European Community students

European Community (EC) students are allowed to enter the UK freely and their passports are not stamped on entry. The countries of the EC are: Belgium; Denmark; France; Germany; Greece; Italy; Ireland; Luxembourg; The Netherlands; Spain; Portugal. Spain and Portugal, although members of the EC, do not become full members until 1 January 1993. Students from these two countries will face restrictions on their working rights until 1993 (*see below* **Working in the UK**).

Other students

When you enter the UK, your passport is stamped by an immigration officer. This stamp determines your conditions of stay in the UK.

Most overseas students are given a **Code 2 stamp**, sometimes called a 'restriction on employment':

A Code 2 stamp allows you to stay in the UK until the specified date. You will only be allowed to work during college holidays or part-time during the college term (up to 15 hours per week) if you first get permission from the local Job Centre. (Look in your local telephone directory under Employment Service to find the nearest Job Centre.)

If you are a male overseas student with a restriction on employment and you are accompanied by your wife, then she will be given a **Code 1 stamp**:

This stamp allows your wife to stay in the UK until the specified date; she is free to take up employment without having to obtain permission first. If you are a female overseas student, your husband may not enter the UK as a dependant.

Some overseas students are given a **Code 3 stamp**, sometimes called a 'prohibition on employment'. This means that you are allowed to stay in the UK until the specified date, but are not allowed to work.

If you are a male overseas student who is prohibited from working, and you are accompanied by your wife, then she won't be able to work either.

Leave to enter the United Kingdom, on condition that the holder does not enter or change employment paid or unpaid without the consent of the Secretary of State for Employment and does not engage in any business or profession without the consent of the Secretary of State for the Home Department is hereby given for/until

**Code 2 stamps
(employment restriction)**

Leave to remain in the United Kingdom, on condition that the holder does not enter or change employment paid or unpaid without the consent of the Secretary of State for Employment and does not engage in any business or profession without the consent of the Secretary of State for the Home Department is hereby given

until _____

_____
on behalf of the Secretary of State
Home Office

Date _____

Leave to enter the United Kingdom, is hereby given for/until

**Code 1 stamps
(no employment conditions)**

Leave to remain in the United Kingdom, is hereby given

until _____

_____
on behalf of the Secretary of State
Home Office

Date _____

Leave to enter the United Kingdom, on condition that the holder does not enter employment paid or unpaid and does not engage in any business or profession, is hereby given for/until

**Code 3 stamps
(employment prohibition)**

Leave to remain in the United Kingdom, on condition that the holder does not engage in employment paid or unpaid and does not engage in any business or profession, is hereby given

until _____

_____
on behalf of the Secretary of State
Home Office

Date _____

**Code 5N stamps
(visitors–employment prohibition)**

Some overseas students are given the **Code 5N stamp**:

This stamp is usually given to visitors, students on courses lasting less than six months, and prospective students (who have not yet registered on a course). It means that you can stay in the UK for six months from the specified date, but are not allowed to work.

Extending your Permission to Stay in the UK
Changing from visitor to student

If you entered the UK as a visitor and have been given a 5N stamp (*see above*), it can be hard to extend your stay in the UK or to become a student. Indeed, it is impossible if you are a 'visa national'. A visa national is a citizen of a country whose subjects need a visa in order to be admitted into the UK (*see below* **Re-entry visas** for a list of visa national countries).

If you are a citizen of one of these countries and have entered the UK as a visitor, but now want to study, you will have to leave the UK and obtain a visa to come back as a student. You do not necessarily have to return to your home country in order to make the application – it can be made from anywhere outside the UK. It is likely that if you needed a visa to enter the UK, you will also need one to enter most other European countries.

While you are still in the UK, if you have at least two months' leave-to-stay remaining, you can apply for a visa to go to another country by making an application to that country's embassy in the UK. Once you arrive in that country, you can then apply to the British Embassy for a visa to re-enter the UK as a student – although there is obviously no guarantee that you will be successful. If you are a visa national and entered the UK as a prospective student, you can apply for an extension of your permission to stay, like any other student (*see below* **Continuing your stay as a student**).

If you are not a visa national and entered the UK as a visitor, you can apply to change to student status. If you do this, you must be careful to show that you have genuinely changed your mind since you arrived in the UK. If you always intended to study but did not say so when you entered the country, this could be seen as an intention to deceive the immigration officer and used as a reason to refuse your application, even though you satisfy all the student requirements. If you want to apply to change your status, you should write to the Home Office (*see below* **Useful Addresses**), sending the following:

• A reasonable explanation of why you changed your mind after entering the UK and decided you would like to study here;
• Your passport;
• A letter of enrolment from your college showing that you will be studying full-time;
• Proof of financial support.

Continuing your stay as a student

If you wish to stay in the UK for longer than the date stamped in your passport, you must apply to the Home Office before your leave to remain expires. If you apply for an extension of stay after your current leave to remain has expired, and the Home Office refuses your application,

Overseas Students

then you will not be able to appeal against the decision.

In order to extend your leave to remain, you should send the following documents to the Home Office (*see below* **Useful Addresses**) by Recorded Delivery Post (ask at any Post Office):
- A letter requesting that your leave to remain be extended, listing the items that you have enclosed;
- Your passport;
- Your police registration certificate (if you have one);
- A letter from your college stating that you are enrolled on a full-time course (at least 15 hours per week) and that you have been attending your course regularly;
- A bank statement showing that you have enough money to pay your fees and maintain yourself, or evidence that you are receiving a scholarship.

Take photocopies of the letter and documents and keep them in a safe place.

If, for any reason, you do not have all these documents available, you must still write to the Home Office before your leave to remain expires. Explain that you need to extend your stay, enclose as many of the documents as you can, and state that you will send the remaining ones as soon as possible.

Some colleges have a special arrangement with the Home Office to consider applications to extend stay for students on campus. Check whether your college has such an arrangement. If you make a written application for an extension of stay, the Home Office will take about four months to process it. You can usually get an extension on the same day if you apply in person to the Home Office at Lunar House in London (*see below* **Useful Addresses**), but you must take all your documents with you.

Late applications: If you apply for an extension to your leave to remain after the date which is stamped in your passport, you should ask your college for a letter of support, explaining why your application was late and confirming that you are enrolled at the college. If possible, the letter should state that you have a good academic record.

In the case of late applications, it is important to send all the required documents with your application. This is because you have no right of appeal if the Home Office refuses your application and you applied late.

Early applications: The Home Office will only consider applications if there are two months or less before your current leave to remain expires. As it will take about four months for staff to process your application if you apply by post, you will be left without a passport and, for a period, with no official leave of entry. However, as long as your application for extension is made before the date stamped in your passport, leave of entry is extended until the application has been processed. If your application is refused for any reason, you will be given some additional time (usually 28 days) to arrange your departure.

Registering with the police

The stamp in your passport will state whether or not you are required to register with the police. If you are a citizen of the European Community or the Commonwealth, or if you intend to stay in the UK for less than six months, you probably won't have to register with the police. If you are required to register with the police, you must do so within seven days of arrival in the UK. It is also necessary to inform the police every time you change your address while you are in the UK.

JOIN INTERNATIONAL STUDENTS HOUSE CLUB

London's friendliest meeting place for students from around the world

restaurant
coffee shop
bar
study room
mini shop
television rooms
laundry
general services office
welfare & advisory service
debates
dances
musical evenings
films
art & drama
dinners
excursions & outings
special events
football
cricket
hockey
tennis
squash
table tennis
badminton
snooker
pool
multi gym

SPECIAL OFFER
ONE MONTH'S FREE
MEMBERSHIP

International Students House Club is the friendly meeting place for all overseas and UK students. The Club offers many facilities, but perhaps more important is the chance to make friends with students from all parts of the world ¶ The Club is open to all full time students, student nurses, au pairs and professional trainees ¶ Take up this offer of one month's free membership and discover the warm welcome that is waiting for you at the International Students House Club.

Phone or write for free membership details to:
International Students House
229 Great Portland Street
London W1N 5HD
Telephone 071-631 3223

Nearest Underground Stations:
Great Portland Street
Regents Park

Overseas Students

There is a charge of £36 for registration. You will need to present your passport and two passport-sized photographs of yourself. If you're living in London you should go to 10 Lambs Conduit Street, London WCl between 9am and 4.45pm, Monday to Friday. In other parts of the country you should visit the nearest police station for advice on where to register.

Travelling abroad

If you are leaving the UK (on holiday, for example) but are planning to return, you will again have to satisfy the immigration officer, on your return, that you meet the necessary requirements for entry into the UK as a student.
So, before you travel abroad, you should:
* Check whether you need a re-entry visa (*see below*);
* Check that your passport is not going to expire while you are away (if it is, you should apply for a new one in plenty of time before your trip);
* Check that your current leave to remain will not expire before you return.

If your leave to remain does expire while you are away, you must take the following documents with you:
* Evidence that you are a student enrolled on a full-time course in the UK;
* Evidence that you have enough money to support yourself (bank statements; a letter from your sponsor).

Before you leave, you should also check whether any of the countries you want to visit have a visa requirement and, if they do, obtain the necessary visas from the relevant Embassy or High Commission. You'll need a visa for a country even if you are only travelling through it.

Whether or not your current leave to remain has expired, it is sensible to carry these documents with you every time you leave the country.

Re-entry visas

If you are a citizen of one of the following countries you are a 'visa national' and must obtain a re-entry visa before you travel abroad:
Afghanistan, Albania, Algeria*, Angola, Bangladesh*, Benin, Bhutan, Bulgaria, Burkina, Burma, Burundi, Cambodia, Cameroon, Cape Verde, Central African Republic, Chad, China, Comoros, Congo, Cuba, Djibouti, Egypt, Equatorial Guinea, Ethiopia, Gabon, Ghana*, Guinea, Guinea-Bissau, Haiti, Indonesia, India*, Iran, Iraq, Jordan, Korea (North), Laos, Lebanon, Liberia, Libya, Madagascar, Mali, Mauritania, Mongolia, Morocco*, Mozambique, Nepal, Nigeria*, Oman, Pakistan*, Philippines, Poland, Romania, Rwanda, Soa Tome e Principe, Saudi Arabia, Senegal, Somalia, Soviet Union, Sri Lanka*, Sudan, Syria, Taiwan, Thailand, Togo, Tunisia*, Turkey*, US Pacific Trust Territories, Vietnam, Yemen, Zaire.
(Students from countries marked * may not always need a re-entry visa. Contact your student adviser for more information.)

A re-entry visa can be obtained from the local passport office. You will not be given a re-entry visa if your current leave to remain is about to expire. If you cannot obtain a re-entry visa before you travel, you can obtain an entry visa at a British Embassy or High Commission abroad, but you must have with you all the documents you would normally need to extend your stay.

Finding your Feet

It's not unusual to feel lost and confused when you first arrive in the UK. Most colleges hold a special introductory event for all students to help them settle in, which may be called an 'orientation event', an 'intro evening' or an 'intro fair'. It is worth attending this, or any events for overseas students, as it will give you the chance to meet other students, to find out about the way the college works and to ask questions about college life.

Clubs and societies

Try not to spend all your time on academic work. Joining a club or society is a good way to meet other students with similar interests. Many of these societies can also give valuable experience which might be useful when you are looking for a job after you finish your course. You may find that there is a society for students from your country, or one for all overseas students.

Every college in the UK has a student union which represents the students at that college. Most unions contribute money towards social activities, sports and societies. If you find that there isn't a society for students from your part of the world, or one that covers an activity that interests you, then tell the student union: you might be given help in starting one.

You may also want to get involved in politics at your student union and stand for office as a committee member. Overseas students are usually encouraged to play a full role in student unions.

Cultural attitudes

When you arrive in the UK, you may find it difficult getting to know other students. Don't give up. Everyone finds it hard, and it is especially hard for overseas students who are trying to adapt to life in a new country. Try to involve yourself in activities that help you to meet other students, such as clubs and societies. Don't be put off if other students seem reserved or unfriendly when you first meet them – they're probably just as nervous as you are.

You should be aware, however, that racism does exist in the UK and you may encounter it in some form during your time here. If you believe that someone is behaving towards you in a racist way, you should discuss the matter with your student adviser or someone in your student union. Almost all colleges in the UK have anti-racist policies, and there are also national laws to counter racial discrimination and racial harassment. You do not have to put up with racism and there are people to help if you are confronted by it (*see page 236* **Black Students**).

You may find that some attitudes in the UK are very different to those you are used to at home. Attitudes to alcohol or to sex, for example, may seem alien at first. It's important not to feel that you have to change your behaviour in order to conform. It doesn't matter if you want to drink orange juice rather than alcohol at the pub, or if you prefer to go to bed early, or feel that you need to spend more time studying. Conversely, some British attitudes and laws are less liberal than those you may be used to: it is, for example, illegal to smoke, buy or sell cannabis here.

Money Matters

As an overseas student it is particularly important that you manage your money wisely and do not run short of funds unexpectedly. You need to work out a realistic weekly or monthly budget planned across the year which includes allowances for food, accommodation, social activities, fuel bills, books, laundry and, if you need it, child care. For ideas on how to draw up a budget, *see page 116* **Basic Living**.

You will also need to plan for costs you will face when you finish your course, such as travel

Overseas Students

and shipping costs. When you are making travel arrangements, be sure to take advantage of any special student deals or student reductions available. You will probably find it useful to buy an International Student Identity Card (ISIC), which allows you cheaper travel, as well as discounts on many cultural and social activities around the world. The ISIC may be bought at your local student union travel shop, or by mail from NUS Services Ltd (*see below* **Useful Addresses**). *See also page 278* **Travel**.

Don't forget that your expenditure will vary considerably from month to month. For most overseas students, the greatest costs are incurred in September or October, at the beginning of the academic year. It is normal to pay rent in advance; if you are in a college hall of residence you will usually be expected to pay a whole term's rent in advance. During the winter months you will also face higher fuel bills, which are normally paid on a quarterly basis (three months at a time) after you have used the fuel.

Transferring money from abroad

There are three main ways to transfer currency into the UK:

Bankers draft: Money is transferred from a bank overseas to its sister bank in the UK. A cheque is then issued for the money and sent by post. You can cash the cheque at the bank in the UK. This method can take a long time and depends on the efficiency of the postal service. If the cheque is lost in the post, it can be re-issued, but again this is a lengthy process because the bank will have to check that the money has not already been withdrawn before cancelling the first cheque and issuing another. The cost is about 30p% (ie £3 for every £1,000) and the minimum amount is £10.

International money transfer: This is for non-urgent transfers between banks. A system called 'swift' is used, which is faster than sending a bankers draft by post, but your transfer will not take precedence ove. other, more urgent, bank business. The cost is 25p% (ie £2.50 per £1,000) and the minimum amount is £10.

Express international money transfer: This is for urgent transfers between banks. The money is transferred by telex. The cost is 30p% (ie £3 for every £1,000) and the minimum amount is £17.

Further details about how to transfer money and the length of time it is likely to take are available from any large high street bank.

Before currency transactions can take place, the appropriate amount must be placed with the sending bank in your home country, or placed directly in the appropriate central bank.

Welfare benefits

Welfare benefits are paid by the UK government to people on low incomes. Sometimes they are given as cash payments (such as child benefit), and sometimes they are made by reducing the level of charges which people have to pay (as with community charge benefit).

All overseas students in the UK must be able to support themselves without recourse to public funds. Public funds are:
- Family Credit (given to families on a low income);
- Income Support (given to people who are unemployed);
- Housing Benefit (help towards the rent of people on a low income);
- Housing as a homeless person (emergency council housing for people without a home).

Overseas students are not allowed to claim any of these.

Benefits that overseas students can claim include:
- Free medical treatment on the National Health Service, if you are on a course lasting six months or more (this also applies to your spouse and children);
- Help towards free prescriptions, dental and optical treatment, if you are on a low income;
- Community charge benefit, if you are on a low income;
- Child benefit, as soon as you or your child has been in the UK for six months;
- Free state education for your children.

Community charge

In common with all British students, overseas students will have to pay 20 per cent of the full rate of the personal community charge (the poll tax). If you are staying in the UK for less than six months you are unlikely to have to pay anything at all. Spouses of overseas students will normally have to pay the full rate, but may be able to apply to the local council for a reduction, if they are on a low income.

Working in the UK

While studying in the UK, you may also want to work part-time or during the holidays. Alternatively, your course may include a work placement, or you may want to gain some work experience after finishing college. If you want to work, you must first get permission from the Department of Employment, by following the procedure below, unless you are a national of a European Community country. Until 1 January 1993, nationals of Spain and Portugal also have to seek permission if they want to work.

Check your passport stamp to see if you are allowed to work. Only students with a restriction on employment will be given permission to work in the UK. Students with a prohibition on employment are not allowed to work. You can apply to the Home Office for your stamp to be changed from a prohibition to a restriction, but before doing this you should seek advice from your college welfare officer, student adviser or student union.

Part-time and holiday work

If you have been given a restriction on employment, you can still be given permission to work for up to 15 hours a week during term-time and full-time during the holidays. The procedure for obtaining permission to work is as follows:

1) Find an employer who is willing to offer you a job (*see page 254* **Employment**);

2) Obtain form OW1 (application for permission to employ an overseas worker) plus the explanatory leaflet OW5, from any Job Centre or local Department of Employment office (listed in the telephone directory);

3) Ask your employer to complete the form;

4) Return the form to the Job Centre, along with the following documents:
- Your passport;
- Your police registration certificate (if you have one);
- A letter from your college, giving your name, address, date of birth, nationality, the title and duration of your course, and stating that the employment will not, in their opinion, interfere with your studies.

The Job Centre can give permission for you to take a job, so long as there is no suitable local person available and willing to fill the vacancy, and so long as the terms and conditions of employment offered to you are no less favourable than those on offer for similar work in your area. Permission to work must be obtained each time you change jobs.

Practical training while on a course
Some courses (usually called sandwich courses) involve a work placement, or practical training, as part of the course. Permission for this sort of work has to be obtained by your college department. If the Department of Employment approves the request, the permission will cover any work taken as part of the course.

Postgraduate students
If you are a postgraduate student you can undertake teaching and demonstration work (ie laboratory demonstrations) without permission, provided that the work does not exceed six hours a week and provided that you do not have a prohibition on employment. If you do have a prohibition, you must apply to the Home Office to have it lifted before undertaking teaching and demonstration work.

Postgraduate research assistants
Permission to be employed as a research assistant by a college, even if the purpose of the research is to gain a PhD, is only given in very special circumstances. Your college should apply to the Home Office on your behalf. For information on making an application, your college should contact UKCOSA (*see below* **Useful Addresses**).

Practical training and work experience after study
If you want to train or gain work experience in the UK after completing your course, your employer must complete form OW22 (available from the Job Centre) and send it to the Home Office with your passport and police registration certificate (if you have one). You may be granted an extension of stay as a trainee if the offer of training is considered to be satisfactory, and if there is no reason to believe that you do not intend to leave the UK after training. Further information about this scheme is available in leaflet OW21 at your local Job Centre.

Students on nursing courses
Information about applying for permission to take employment as a nurse is available from CHAT, Royal College of Nursing, 20 Cavendish Square, London WlM 6AB (071 629 3870).

Doctors and dentists
As a doctor or dentist, you may be given an extension of stay for postgraduate training in a hospital if you can produce evidence that you have limited or full registration with the General Medical Council (GMC). Write to the GMC Overseas Registration Division, 153 Cleveland Street, London W1P 6DE (071 387 2556). These extensions are given for 12 months at a time, and the maximum length of time you can stay for this purpose is four years.

Working holidays
If you are a Commonwealth citizen, aged between 17 and 27, you may apply to the Home Office for an extension of stay as a working holidaymaker. You must satisfy the Home Office that you want to stay in the UK for an extended holiday before returning to your own country, and that you only intend to take employment connected with your holiday (ie any temporary job). An extension of stay may be given for up to two years, on condition that you do not have recourse to public funds (*see above* **Money Matters: Welfare benefits**) and that you can pay for your journey home.

LOW FEES

Study English at the LONDON STUDY CENTRE
Munster House
676 Fulham Rd.
London SW6
071-731 3549

Arels Felco

Open all year except Easter and Christmas.
Fees: £98 for 4 wks., £228 for 12 wks.
15 hours per week.
We help you look for accommodation.
Enrol direct. No intermediaries.
Recognised by the British Council.
Cambridge University & ARELS Oral Examinations.
Library, Language Laboratory & Satellite T.V.
All levels from Beginners to Advanced.

Run by Young People for Young People

A Superior Hostel!

Near Albert Hall and Hyde Park.
As recommended by the Observer
Large lounge, colour TV, pool table
etc, showers in most rooms.

Beds from £7 per night,
including continental Breakfast.

**The Albert Hotel
191 Queens Gate
London, SW7 5EU
Telephone 071 584 3019**

EXPLORE
England and Wales with yha

☆ 240 Youth Hostels in spectacular locations
☆ Budget accommodation
☆ Flexible and relaxed - 'go as you please'
☆ *Great Escapes* low-cost adventure holidays

For a **Great Escapes** brochure and **The Place to Stay** leaflet
(with details of how to join YHA) write to:
YHA, Trevelyan House, 8 St Stephen's Hill, St Albans, Herts, AL1 2DY
or telephone (0727) 55215.

Overseas Students

Taxation

Overseas students and their spouses who take up employment will automatically be subject to UK taxation laws. Everyone who works is allowed to earn up to a certain amount per year (called the personal allowance) before they start paying income tax. In 1990 the personal allowance was £3,005. Provided that you and your spouse do not earn in excess of the basic personal allowance, you do not have to pay tax on any interest you earn on money brought into the UK for maintenance costs during your studies. Ask for details about this when you open a bank or building society account. For details on when and how to open a bank account, *see page 72* **Money**.

National Insurance

Overseas students who are working in the UK must pay National Insurance contributions. To do this, you should get a National Insurance number from the National Insurance Contributions Department at your local Social Security Office. You should be prepared to give written details of your job and you will be issued with a National Insurance number within the next few weeks. You can start work as soon as you have applied for a number, even if it has not yet been issued.

Work permits

Once you have finished your studies, you will not be allowed to stay in the UK in order to work. If you want a work permit, you should leave the UK while your employer makes an application to the Department of Employment on your behalf. It is not possible for you to apply for a work permit yourself; only your employer can do this. Work permits are only granted in areas of skill shortage or for jobs in specified categories. You will find more information about who can get a work permit from leaflet OW5, at your local Job Centre.

If you apply for a work permit to take a permanent job, and you are refused, this could threaten any application you make in the future for leave to remain as a student in the UK.

Useful Addresses

The following organizations will be able to offer further advice with any problems you may face as an overseas student in the UK. You should always write or telephone for an appointment first.

The Africa Educational Trust Africa Centre, 38 King Street, London WC2 8JT (071 836 5075). The Trust awards some small grants to African students without sufficient funds, who are reaching the end of their course.

British Council 10 Spring Gardens, London SW1A 2BN (071 930 8466). The British Council will give advice about educational opportunities for overseas students in the UK. It also offers direct help and support to students funded by the Council.

British Council Accommodation Unit The British Council, 11 Portland Place, London WIN 4EJ (071 389 3003). The Accommodation Unit helps with finding long-term accommodation for overseas students and has lists of hostels. This office deals with accommodation in Greater London only, phone for details of regional offices.

British Travel Centre 4-12 Lower Regent Street, London SW1 (071 730 3400). A comprehensive tourist information and booking service where you can get free leaflets and advice on all aspects of travel in the UK.

Citizens' Advice Bureaux: There's a Citizens' Advice Bureau (CAB) in most towns in the UK,

which will offer free advice on a wide range of issues, from fees and awards to problems with landlords. You can find the address of your nearest CAB in the telephone directory.
Educational Grants Advisory Service c/o Family Welfare Association, 501/503 Kingsland Road, London E8 4AU. This service aims to put students in touch with sources of funds, such as trusts and charities. Applications should be made in writing, giving details of your educational and financial position. If it is considered that a student has a reasonable chance of securing some assistance, a form will be sent. Overseas students are not advised to write unless they are entering their final year of study. The Service's staff is very small and there may be some delay in the handling of enquiries.
The Experiment in International Living 'Otesaga', West Malvern Road, Malvern, Worcestershire WR14 4EN (0684 562577). An association aiming to help overseas students immerse themselves in British culture, by arranging short stays (from three to ten days) with British families in their homes. This is not an accommodation service, rather it's a chance to join the family; and although no work is involved, students will be expected to help with tidying, washing up and the like. Fees range from £65 for three days to £110 for a week.
Home Office Immigration and Nationality Department, Lunar House, Wellesley Road, Croydon CR9 2BY (081 686 0688). You can apply for an extension of stay to the above address. If you want advice on immigration matters, it is best first to visit one of the independent advice agencies or your student adviser.
Joint Council for the Welfare of Immigrants (JCWI) 115 Old Street, London EC1 9JR (071 251 8706). JCWI offers information and advice on immigration.
Law Centres: Some towns have a Law Centre where people can obtain free legal advice from a qualified solicitor. You can check whether there is a Law Centre in your area by phoning, or writing to: Law Centres Federation, Duchess House, 18-19 Warren Street, London WIP SDB (071 387 8570).
National Union of Overseas Students c/o NUS, 461 Holloway Road, London N7 6LJ (071 272 8900). The NUOS is an organization of overseas students which aims to raise issues of concern to overseas students.
NUS Services Ltd Bleaklow House, Howard Town Mills, Mill Street, Glossop, SK13 8PT (0457 868003). NUS Services Ltd sells International Student Identity Cards (ISIC) by mail order.
The Refugee Council Bondway House, 3-9 Bondway, London SW8 1SJ (071 582 6922). The Council gives advice to refugees on welfare and financial matters, as well as maintaining links with refugee community groups.
Student advisers: Most colleges have a student adviser, sometimes called a student counsellor, welfare officer or accommodation and welfare officer. This person is likely to have good contacts, both within the college and outside, and will be able to offer advice and assistance.
Student unions: If you are studying at a university, polytechnic or further education college, you will be able to find help and advice at your student union. Some student unions employ full-time student welfare advisers; some have elected overseas student officers; others are very small and rely on volunteers only.

Overseas Students

Tourist Information Centre Victoria Station Forecourt, London SWl (071 730 3488). A service run by the London Tourist Board to help visitors find accommodation when they arrive in the UK. A comprehensive range of guide books and maps is sold at the centre which is open daily; there is a telephone enquiry service Monday to Friday.

UK Council for Overseas Student Affairs (UKCOSA) 60 Westbourne Grove, London W2 5SH (071 229 9268). UKCOSA offers help and advice to colleges and overseas students. The telephone casework service is open from 1 to 4pm, Mondays to Fridays, but overseas students should first ask a college adviser for help, before contacting UKCOSA.

United Kingdom Immigration Advisory Service (UKIAS) 2nd Floor, 190 Great Dover Street, London SE1 4YB (071 357 6917). UKIAS gives free advice on immigration and employs qualified solicitors to represent people at immigration appeals. There is also a refugee unit which represents asylum seekers at appeals against refusal of asylum/refugee status.

The World University Service 20-21 Compton Terrace, London Nl 2UN (071 226 6747). WUS makes small grants to final-year students from developing countries taking degree, higher professional, diploma or postgraduate courses. The average award to any one student is £350. Refugee students are given preference. WUS also provides an advisory service to refugees and gives information about other sources of help, particularly entitlement to local education authority awards.

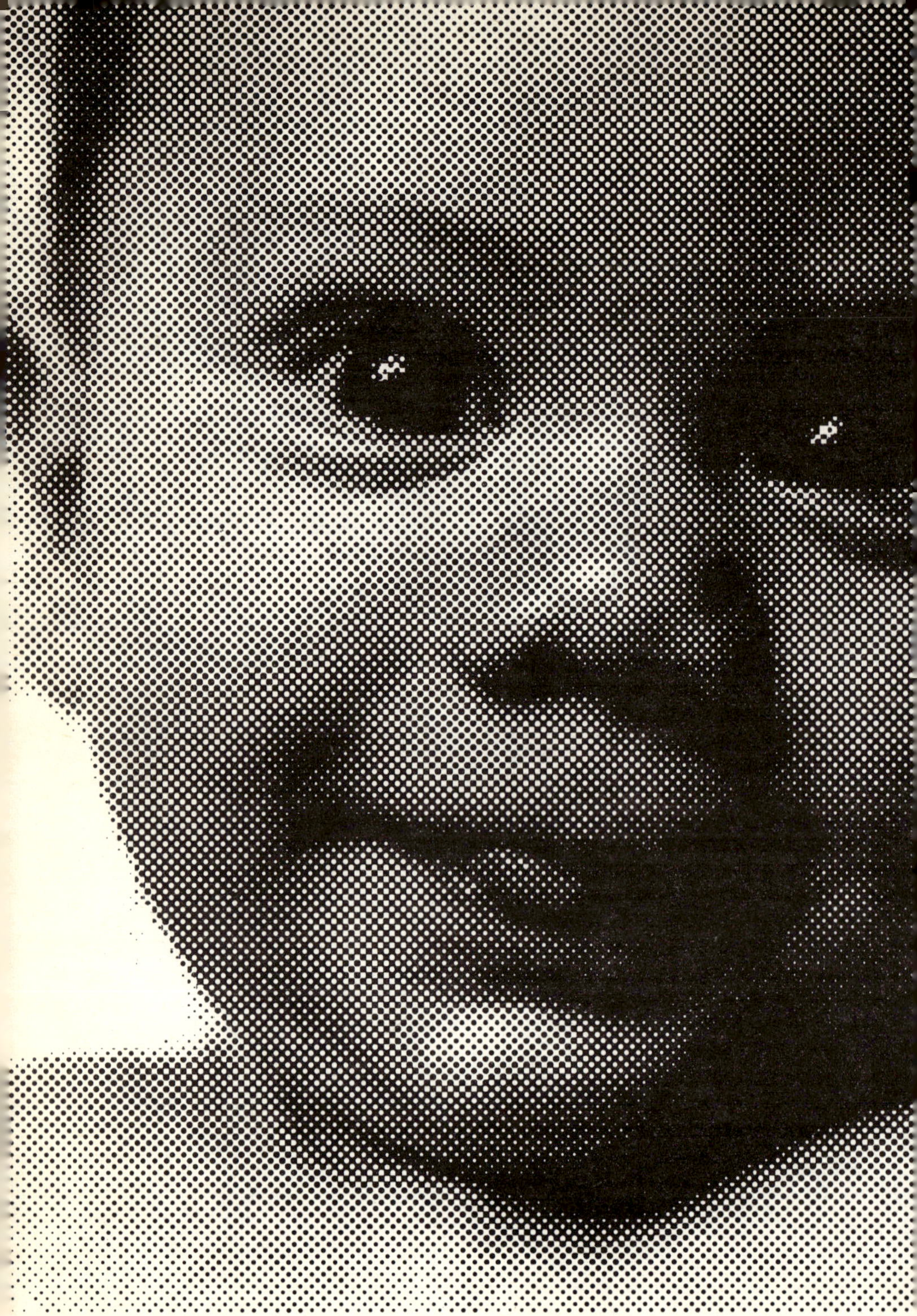

Taking the Plunge **46**

Access Courses **47**

Applying **47**

Living with a Difference **48**

The Open University **49**

Further Reading **49**

Useful Addresses **49**

mature students

The decision to return to education is often a difficult one. **Margaret Davine** from the Mature Students Union writes about balancing family and study commitments, and urges you to take the plunge.

The Government's stated policy of increasing the number of students in higher education is being implemented in spite of a drop in the birth rate which has led to a declining number of eighteen year-olds entering higher education. This means that more 'non-traditional' entrants are being encouraged to apply for degree courses, most notably mature students. One in seven university students is now a mature student; at polytechnics and colleges, the proportion of older students is even higher.

Despite this, and despite the increasing flexibility of application procedures designed to recruit students without traditional qualifications, older students still face many difficulties at college. Most, however, find that learning to cope with these problems only adds to the satisfaction they get from completing a degree course. In this chapter, we discuss some of the hurdles mature students are likely to face and offer advice on how to approach and overcome them to get the most from college life.

Who are mature students?

It's not possible to pigeonhole mature students precisely – they are as varied a bunch as school leavers are. Anyone over 21, and who has taken a break from education for a few years after school, is a 'non-traditional' student; some people who already have degrees will be seeking a change of direction, others will have found a new vocation for which a college qualification is essential; while yet others might feel that high-level education is the only way they'll do themselves intellectual justice.

It's the specific issues facing mature students that best define them as a group. Because they are older than most undergraduates, they are more likely to have families, and the attendant financial responsibilities. They might also find integration into the mainstream of college life difficult because they have different attitudes and priorities to younger students.

Taking the Plunge

Even though most colleges try to attract mature students, the fact remains that the education system is in the main geared to people arriving straight from school. When making your initial enquiries, there are a number of questions to ask that will indicate how serious the college is about catering for mature students.

For those who already have a family, it's a good idea to ask about any childcare provision run by the student union or the college; alternatively, babysitting circles are sometimes set up by mature students themselves. And ask whether the timetable allow for flexible teaching arrangements, so that lectures and seminars can be fitted around family commitments. Also, find out whether you can attend study skills courses. Other enquiries you might make are: does the college or its student union organize any relevant self-help discussion groups; are the college's student counsellors used to dealing with mature students' problems; and are the careers guidance staff equipped to advise older students?

If you have a family, it generally makes sense to go to a local college. However, where an access course (*see below*) guarantees places in an adjacent area, you might feel that the advantages of attending a course for which you are specifically prepared outweigh the disadvantages of moving away. In theory, where you study is up to you, but family pressures are sure to have some bearing on your decision. You will need plenty of information on the course, the college and the town (*see page 2* **How to Apply**).

Access Courses

Access courses are an alternative way for adults without formal qualifications to go to college. Some access courses are specifically designed for women, disabled people or students from ethnic minorities; the majority last one year and are full-time. There are about 400 access courses on offer, run by local education authorities, borough councils, universities, polytechnics and by the Open University. Whether they are called Foundation, New Direction, Preparatory, Bridging, Fresh Start or Springboard courses, they are all likely to have a study skills element.

The linked access courses are especially worthwhile as they guarantee an interview, and often a place, on an associated degree or diploma course. They also give you the chance to bypass competitive entry requirements, and often provide exactly the skills you need to make a confident return to education. Access courses are generally recognized by universities and polytechnics, because they test a your ability to complete a course and to persevere with study.

Educational Counselling and Credit Transfer Information Service (ECCTIS, *see below* **Useful Addresses**) publishes the annual *Access to Higher Education Courses Directory*, which has details of access courses throughout the UK.

Applying

These days, most colleges are keen to raise their student numbers and, specifically with older students in mind, are increasing the variety of courses on offer and making application procedures more flexible. To secure a place, you'll need to persuade the admissions tutor that you've prepared for the course and are capable of completing it. However, you might not be expected to satisfy the same entry requirements as younger students. Many colleges either have

"George Bernard Shaw said that youth is wasted on the young, but it was not really so in my Oxford days. I went late, via the adult Ruskin College (I never really tried to go the usual route, because I thought you had to do every subject you did at school, only worse). I worked hard, but still learned to write fast to get the essays done on time."

Norman Willis TUC General Secretary (Economics & Political Science, Ruskin College, Oxford, 1955-57).

special mature entry schemes, or are willing to take students with no formal qualifications if they attend an access course (*see above*).

Colleges are increasingly offering more part-time courses, intended specifically for older students with financial and family commitments. Birkbeck College, University of London, specializes in part-time degree courses; much of the teaching takes place in the evenings.

If you already have experience of higher education or have relevant work experience, this might count towards your qualification and so shorten the length of time you have to study. Contact ECCTIS for more information.

There are several ways to obtain advice on college application. Educational Guidance Services for Adults (EGSAs) are independent organizations catering specifically for mature students (*see below* **Useful Addresses**). Local authority careers services can also be of help, as can universities, polytechnics and further education colleges themselves. Check at your nearest central library; these are normally well stocked with education reference books and prospectuses.

Application procedures are covered comprehensively in **How to Apply** (*page 2*) and are the same for mature students as for school-leavers.

Living with a Difference

Mature students have needs and requirements quite different from most school-leavers. For example, some mature students are very conscious of being set apart from others by their age – a feeling which is often reinforced by having a different lifestyle from the majority; many mature students also differ in already having family or relationship commitments; and they all share the common problem of trying to adapt to full-time study after a break, in some cases a long one.

At the present time, the most significant difficulty will probably be financial pressure and, in some cases, considerable hardship. If you have never received a local education authority grant before, you'll be entitled to one, whatever your age; but if you've ever received a grant before, the Authorities can be very tight-fisted. For details of mature students' entitlements to grants and welfare benefits, *see page 72* **Money**.

Coping with the course

You might be worried that you will not be able to cope with the pressures of studying and preparing for examinations after spending time away from the education system. However, if you've completed an access course, you will be just as well prepared for the rigours of academic study as students who have recently left school, if not more so, as degree study requires an altogether different approach than A level study.

Moreover, during the years between leaving school and going to college, you will have had experience in organizing your time, budgeting, meeting deadlines and dealing with authority figures. These are all things which school-leavers are having to learn as they go along – hopefully some of the skills, at least, will be second nature to you already.

It is often difficult for mature students to separate academic from family problems, since study-related stress is frequently caused by welfare difficulties. You might find that you are trying to cope with family commitments in inadequate living conditions and with insufficient funds. However, most tutors and lecturers will be sympathetic (many will have children of their own) and will be flexible – they might extend essay deadlines, for example.

Mature Students

Sources of help
Absence from the education system also means that you might be unsure of your entitlements. Information concerning student financial support and welfare benefits will therefore be essential, and student union welfare officers can ensure that nothing is overlooked. College welfare and counselling services will also be able to help with any difficulties you have.

Support can also be had from mature students' societies, which meet regularly for social events, to organize campaigns on issues such as childcare, or just to have a good moan about the problems of being a mature student; many groups also run babysitting circles. If there is no such society at a college, union officers will be able to help you set one up; *see page 146* **Student Unions**.

Making the most of it
Clearly, returning to study after a gap can be a daunting prospect but, by taking the opportunity to get involved in the social life of the college, you minimize the differences between yourself and the mass of undergraduates. The students who get the most out of college life, irrespective of their age, are the ones who make the greatest effort to get involved in as many aspects of college life as possible.

Age and experience can be great advantages when it comes to planning, prioritizing study schedules or having a level-headed attitude to deadlines. There will be hurdles to overcome, but most mature students find that returning to education is the best decision they ever made. Most people who take the challenge find it stimulating, fulfilling and great fun, and wouldn't have missed it for the world.

The Open University
Open University (OU) study is based on tutorials and assignments marked by correspondence, plus periods at summer school. As work is done from home, there won't be any relocation, but it can take between five and eight years to gain an honours degree, and there will be very little sense of student life. The OU can, however, be a sensible option for those who have very little time to spare, or who want to carry on their jobs. *See also page 2* **How to Apply**.

Further Reading
The Mature Students' Handbook by Iris Rosier and Lynn Earnshaw (Trotman, £9.95).
The Kogan Page Mature Students' Handbook by Margaret Korving (Kogan Page, £8.95).
Returning to Study by Christopher Beddows (Heinemann, £3.95).
Study for Survival and Success by Sander Meredeen (Paul Chapman Publishing, £5.95).

Useful Addresses
Credit Accumulation and Transfer Scheme CNAA, 344-354 Gray's Inn Road, London WC1X 8BP.
Educational Counselling and Credit Transfer Information Service (ECCTIS) PO Box 88, Walton Hall, Milton Keynes, MK7 6DB (0242 518724).
Educational Guidance for Adults Centre (EGSA) PO Box 109, Hatfield, Herts (07072 79499).
Mature Students Union 6 Salisbury Road, Harrow, Middlesex HA1 1NY (081 863 3675).
Open University PO Box 88, Walton Hall, Milton Keynes, MK7 6AA (0908 274066).

Applying to College **52**

Money Matters **53**

Support in College **56**

Further Reading **58**

Useful Addresses **58**

students with disabilities

Emma Delap from Skill investigates the ways in which colleges try to meet the needs of students with disabilities, and explains what you can do to get the aid and benefits to which you are entitled.

No one likes to be labelled, and that includes people with disabilities. Although you might not consider yourself disabled, you should still find some useful information in this chapter. The term 'students with disabilities' is used here to refer to students with physical disabilities such as spina bifida or cerebral palsy; sensory disabilities such as hearing or visual impairments; or learning difficulties such as dyslexia. It also refers to students with medical conditions such as diabetes or epilepsy, and to those with mental health problems.

This chapter is not meant to exclude you from the other sections in this book, aimed at all members of the student population, but to provide extra information and advice that you might find helpful.

Applying to College

Your initial approach to applying to college is the same as anyone else's: decide which course you want to follow, find out which colleges offer it and then consider where you want to live. The specialist careers officer at your local careers office should be able to help you with this. *See also page 2* **How to Apply**.

Once you have drawn up a list of possible colleges, contact them to check that they can help with any special arrangements you need. People often ask questions like 'I have a hearing impairment – which colleges can I go to?' It is understandable that people should want to go to the college with the best support facilities, but it wouldn't be feasible, or desirable, for all students with a certain disability to go to only one or two particular colleges. The more students with disabilities contact colleges asking for particular arrangements, the more aware colleges will become that they need to make provision for these members of the student population.

Should I tell the college (and UCCA/PCAS) about my disability or medical condition?

If you need any special arrangements or support facilities for your course or for daily living, then the answer is yes. Most colleges now have a tutor or adviser for students with special needs. If you are applying for higher education at degree or similar level, contact the tutor or adviser for students with disabilities at the colleges which interest you to discuss your needs before you fill in your UCCA or PCAS form. In some cases, it's a good idea to try to arrange an informal visit before applying. For example, if you have mobility difficulties, only you can judge whether you would find the layout of the campus manageable. The sooner you acquaint the college staff with the nature of your disability, the sooner they can fully understand your needs and begin to help you as much as possible.

Be sure to start making your enquiries early. Even if the colleges are willing to help, there might be practical difficulties to overcome, so it's best to discover these in advance. Be reassured that even if you are turned down by a particular college because of your disability, UCCA and PCAS will let you make a substitute choice.

If you are applying to do a course of further education, for example, GCSEs, A levels, BTEC, City and Guilds or a preparation for other courses, there are two options open to you: local mainstream further education colleges or specialist residential colleges. Local colleges provide a wide range of courses, some designed for those with special educational needs. The majority of specialist colleges are independently run. As well as providing social and independence training, such colleges offer courses in practical and vocational skills, often leading to external qualifications such as GCSEs, BTEC and City and Guilds.

Students with Disabilities

Checklist for Applying for College:
- Start thinking about courses and colleges at least 18 months before courses begin;
- Choose your course subject;
- Find out where it's available;
- Prepare a list of questions you need to ask;
- Make initial contact with the college. Speak to the tutor or adviser for students with disabilities, your proposed department's admissions tutor and, where relevant, the accommodation officer;
- Make an informal visit to the college if necessary;
- Make a final decision before filling out your application forms.

Only you can decide which college suits you best, but it will be helpful to discuss the options with the specialist careers adviser, who should also have a copy of the COPE Directory, which lists all the residential specialist colleges (*see below* **Further Reading**). Skill, the National Bureau for Students with Disabilities (*see below* **Useful Addresses**), publishes a series of guides to higher education for people with disabilities which are a helpful source of information about access and facilities in colleges (*see below* **Further Reading**). Many colleges and student unions now produce their own booklets or leaflets for students with disabilities, which are useful as initial sources of reference.

Moving away from home?
If you have special accommodation needs, let the college housing officer know what they are – if there's suitable accommodation they can usually guarantee it to you for the duration of your course. Some colleges have adapted accommodation for people with physical disabilities. Others are becoming increasingly aware that this is something they need to provide. Don't hesitate to ask to inspect the accommodation and to enquire whether any modifications can be made.

Who do I ask about help and equipment at home?
If you need specialist equipment, such as a bed hoist or a shower chair, or personal care help, contact your home social services. They, together with the social services in your college town, should be able to make the necessary arrangements. Students in higher education with personal care needs often use the Community Service Volunteers' (CSV, *see below* **Useful Addresses**). The CSV's Independent Living Scheme provides a volunteer helper to enable you to live independently. The college can normally arrange for necessary accommodation for them as well.

What about transport?
If you have mobility difficulties, you might have to arrange help to and from college at the beginning and end of term. If travelling on public transport on a daily basis is impossible or difficult, see if the college can provide local accommodation. You will usually find the college staff understanding, and you should be given any available on-campus accommodation. Check with the local council about special travel arrangements for people with disabilities, and find out about schemes for getting a taxi on a daily basis.

Money Matters
You are entitled to a mandatory (automatic) grant only if you're doing a degree or similar level course. For any other courses, you'll have to apply for a discretionary grant, making you dependent on the generosity, or otherwise, of your local education authority. *See also page 72* **Money**.

Will I get any more money because of my disability?
If you are getting a mandatory grant, you can also apply for Disabled Students' Allowances, three separate allowances intended to meet the extra costs of a disability when attending your course.

1) Up to a maximum of £1,000 per year for general expenses.
2) Up to a maximum of £3,000 per course for major items of specialist equipment.
3) Up to a maximum of £4,000 per year for non-medical personal help.

All three allowances are means tested, and are awarded according to need.

What can I claim from each allowance?
The following are merely suggestions of what you could use the allowance for. Further guidelines on applying for allowances are available from Skill.

General allowance: If you are unable to study in the library, you might need to buy more books or to do extra photocopying, and your heating bills at home might be higher. You might need a special chair or table to study; and if, for example, you have a visual impairment, you need to pay for transcription services. You can also claim for extra clothing or dietary expenses.

Specialist equipment allowance: This can be used to buy computer or word processing equipment if, for example, you have dyslexia or writing difficulties. If you have a visual or hearing impairment, there is a wide range of equipment which could be essential to your studies, such as a braille printer, a radio microphone or an induction loop system.

Non-medical personal helper allowance: This is intended to pay for someone to facilitate your full participation in academic work: for example, a sign language interpreter, a notetaker, a reader or, perhaps, someone to help you with mobility around campus.

Where do I get my allowances?
You apply for the allowances from the awards section of the local education authority which pays your grant. All LEAs have their own policy for assessing how they award the money. Usually, they ask you to write them a letter detailing your needs and expenses. They might also require a supporting letter from your tutor or doctor; or, maybe, assessment details, for example, in the case of dyslexia. Sometimes LEAs require detailed quotations of prices of equipment.

Can I get help with travel costs?
If you receive a mandatory grant, you can also claim reimbursement of travel costs that you necessarily incur as a result of your disability, for example, if you need to use taxis instead of public transport. The amount you receive is usually the difference between what you have to pay and the costs a non-disabled person faces for the same journey. Make sure you keep an accurate record of your travel expenses during term-time, as claims to LEAs are normally submitted at the end of each term.

Can I get any special arrangements for top-up loans?
Students with disabilities doing relevant courses are entitled to apply for loans along with everyone else (*see page 72* **Money** for details). The only special arrangements regard the calculation of the borrower's income for repayment, as follows:

Students with Disabilities

- If you receive any disability-related benefits, they will be ignored as income;
- The loans administrator has the authority to delay the start of repayment of the loan, and/or can allow a longer period of time to repay it for students receiving disability-related benefits;
- If you are concerned about your ability to repay a loan, contact the Loans Administration Director at the Student Loans Company.

What are the new Access Funds?
The Education (Student Loans) Act 1990 introduced three Access Funds – for undergraduates, postgraduates and students in further education – to be administered by individual colleges. These funds are intended to help students who otherwise would suffer serious financial hardship. There is no specific fund for students with disabilities, although they can apply for the Access Funds like everyone else. See page 72 **Money** for details.

What about benefits?
It is almost impossible to talk about money without lifting the lid off that Pandora's box – social security benefits. People with disabilities are entitled to two main types of benefit:
- Income-related and income maintenance benefits intended to meet the ordinary costs of living (Income Support and Housing Benefit);
- Extra costs benefits to cover the expenses specifically incurred as a result of having a disability (Mobility Allowance and Attendance Allowance, for instance).

Income Support (IS) is a 'safety net' benefit intended to provide a basic income for those with insufficient income to meet their needs. Housing Benefit (HB) is intended to help with rent.

When your needs are assessed, you could be eligible for one of the premiums used as part of the Income Support assessment, such as the Disability Premium or the Severe Disability Premium.

As a student with a disability, you can claim IS and HB only if:
- You would qualify for the Disability Premium; or
- You would qualify for the Severe Disability Premium; or
- You are receiving the Disabled Students Allowance, along with your grant, by reason of deafness; or
- You previously got IS under the old regulation's definition: you were a disabled student unlikely to obtain a job within a reasonable period, given your disability, if you were not in further education; or
- You got IS as a disabled person at school.

The last two categories no longer apply where you have ceased to be in receipt of IS for a continuous period of 18 months or more. For information on how to qualify for the Disability Premium or Severe Disability Premium, contact Skill or your local social security office.

Can I still get incapacity benefits while at college?
Severe Disablement Allowance, Sickness Benefit (SB) and Invalidity Benefit (IB) are income benefits for people who are unable to work (SB and IB are only paid if you have made sufficient National Insurance contributions). In theory, you are allowed to follow a full-time course and still receive these benefits. However, the DSS may sometimes decide that following a full-time course calls into question your incapacity for work, and the benefit will then be stopped. In such a case, you have the right to appeal.

What if I'm doing my course part-time?
Some students with disabilities or medical conditions find that, for physical reasons, a part-time course is better suited to them. A mature student with a hearing impairment, on a social sciences course, tells of her experience:

'I am part-time, not merely because of the children – my parents are very helpful there – but because of the strain. I find that I have to use a lot of readers to make up for things I miss in class, and therefore need the time. Also, I find that trying to listen or lip-read is very tiring, so part-time is enough.'

If you are planning to study part-time, you will not be eligible for any grant or Disabled Students' Allowance. However, if you do not have to sign on as available for work to receive Income Support because of your disability, you will be able to retain it for the duration of your course. Otherwise you will be bound by the 21-hour ruling (*see page 72* **Money**).

What do I do if I'm still short of money after trying all these things?
It must be said that students with disabilities can find it hard meeting the extra expenses they incur, and often have to seek other sources of money if they are not eligible for statutory funds or find them insufficient. Some colleges have their own funds. There are also trusts, charities and local groups which specifically try to help students with disabilities. Contact Skill for a list of relevant trusts.

Support in College
Some students require certain support services or special arrangements to enable them to participate fully in a course; for example, a student with a hearing impairment might need a sign-language interpreter or a notetaker, and one with a physical disability might need special parking arrangements on campus or to use the services of a typist. Some of these arrangements or services cost money; others, such as relocation of lectures to ensure accessibility and special library loan arrangements, might require only the co-operation of college staff.

Before you start your course, it can be difficult to know exactly what support you will need. Skill produces an information sheet, *Identifying the Needs of Students with Disabilities in Further and Higher Education* (free), which can be used as basic guidelines.

If you think you will benefit from certain services, speak to your tutor and to the adviser for students with disabilities. In the experience of one second-year law student, 'the college staff are the one group of people who won't let you down. There's always someone who can advise you... A good rapport with your personal tutor is very important'.

Exams
Many students require special arrangements to be made for exams, to enable them to fully exercise their knowledge and abilities. Helpful arrangements might include extra time, enlarged-type papers, rest periods, the use of specialist equipment and, perhaps, a scribe (amanuensis). If you have particular requirements, discuss them with your department in good time so that they can be implemented. Skill produces some guidelines on examination arrangements (*see below* **Further Reading**).

A student describes how his college was supportive when he required special help to sit his exams: 'In July I had some kidney trouble and had to go into hospital. This meant I missed the exams... [the tutor for students with special needs] arranged for my exams to be postponed to the first two weeks of September. I took the

Students with Disabilities

"Be as flexible as you can [and] give yourself plenty of time to look at as many alternatives as possible. Go and see the college for yourself before you start. Don't depend on what other people say – what some people say is good might not be good for you. I don't recall seeing any other disabled students at Liverpool. I had to switch courses from history to politics because the history building wasn't accessible, so I learnt the hard way."

Chris Davies Presenter on BBC2's *One in Four* (Politics, Liverpool University, 1972-75).

exams in my own room, typing them on a word-processor. [The tutor for special needs] made sure that I received the extra time I was entitled to. On the whole, my exams went exceptionally smoothly. This was due to the willing co-operation of the college and the efforts made by [the tutor for special needs]. I cannot thank them enough.'

Social life

When you are applying to a college, check whether the student union building and the bars and cafés are accessible to you. If you're concerned about issues affecting people with disabilities, you could get involved in a disabled students committee, or set one up if none already exists. Alternatively, you could join a local group of people with disabilities – your local CAB (Citizens' Advice Bureau) or library should be able to tell you where it's based. If you're interested in sport, investigate the college and local authority facilities. If you need any specific advice, the British Sports Association for the Disabled should be able to help (*see below* **Useful Addresses**).

If you experience any personal problems, or need someone understanding to talk to, make use of student counselling services or other organizations specifically for people with disabilities. It might be more helpful talking to someone with similar experiences – there are a number of groups which you can contact (*see below* **Useful Addresses**).

Few students find their time at college a completely easy, trouble-free time, and it is fair to say that students with disabilities can encounter more difficulties and obstacles than their non-disabled peers. However, do not be disheartened by this. At the end of his first term, one student with MS (multiple sclerosis) on a social work course felt that although he had had to 'battle for everything', it was still 'really worth it; everyone should go for it'. Another student, who was half-way into her second year of law studies and still embroiled in allowance negotiations with her education authority, said: 'the setbacks and hassles are balanced by the fact that it's been well worth doing. I'm pleased I'm doing the course.'

A young overseas student, speaking after she graduated from an Urban Policy & Race Relations course, summed up how she felt about her disability at college: 'The college didn't really know what to expect when I arrived. They were all very sympathetic and everything, but they didn't understand I'd been looking after myself for years. Learning English when I arrived in this country and getting my A levels – these were issues that I had to deal with. Being blind is what I've always been.'

Further Reading

Skill Information Sheets: Skill produces a wide range of information sheets, available free. Contact the information officer for more details (*see below* Useful Addresses).
Skill Publications: (a full publications list is available from Skill on request) *A Guide to Higher Education for People with Disabilities: Part One – Making your application* (£3); *A Guide to Higher Education for People with Disabilities: Part Two – Universities* (£3.50); *A Guide to Higher Education for People with Disabilities: Part Three – Polytechnics, institutes & central institutions* (£3.50); *Examination Arrangements for Students with a Disability* (£3); *Meeting the Personal Care Needs of Physically Disabled Students at College* (£2.50); *Provision for Students with Disabilities in Higher Education* (£3).
Other Publications: RNIB runs a student support service, an employment service and a benefit rights office, which all produce useful information. RNID runs a Higher Education Communication Support Service, with information on how to obtain the support you need. See below **Useful Addresses** for details.

COPE Directory (£10.45 incl postage and packing): a compendium of post-16 education and training in residential establishments for handicapped young people (available from Wiltshire Guidance Services, County Careers Centre, County Hall Annexe, Bythesea Road, Trowbridge BA14 8EZ).
Careers Information for Students with Disabilities (£5 from Open University Office for Students with Disabilities, Walton Hall, Milton Keynes, MK7 6AA).

Useful Addresses
Organisations for specific disabilities
The following organizations can help with general or specific enquiries:
Association for Spina Bifida and Hydrocephalus (ASBAH) ASBAH House, 42 Park Road, Peterborough PE1 2UQ (0733 555988).
British Dyslexia Association 98 London Road, Reading, Berkshire RG1 5AU (0734 668271). **Helpline** 1-5pm Mon-Fri.
British Epilepsy Association Anstey House, 40 Hanover Square, Leeds LS3 1BE (0532 439393). **Helpline** (0345 089599) 9am-4.30pm Mon-Thur; 9am-4pm Fri.
Dyslexia Institute 133 Gresham Road, Staines TW18 2AJ (0784 459498).
MIND (National Association for Mental Health) 22 Harley Street, London W1N 2ED (071 637 0741).
Multiple Sclerosis (MS) Society 25 Effie Road, London SW6 1EE (071 736 6267).
Muscular Dystrophy Group of Great Britain Nattras House, 35 Macaulay Road, London SW4 OQP (071 720 8055).
National Schizophrenia Fellowship 28 Castle Street, Kingston-upon-Thames, Surrey KT1 1SS (081 547 3937).

Students with Disabilities

Royal National Institute for the Blind (RNIB) 224 Great Portland Street, London W1N 6AA (071 388 1266).
Royal National Institute for the Deaf (RNID) 105 Gower Street, London WC1E 6AH (071 387 8033).
Spastics Society 12 Park Crescent, London W1N 4EQ (071 636 5020).

General
Association of Disabled Professionals c/o Ms SJ Maynard, 170 Benton Hill, Horbury, Wakefield, West Yorks WF4 5HW (0924 270335).
British Sports Association for the Disabled The Mary Glenhaig Suite, 34 Osnaburgh Street, London NW1 3ND (071 383 7277).
Community Service Volunteers 237 Pentonville Road, London N1 9NJ (071 278 6601).
DGCIS (Disabled Graduates Careers Information Service) The University of Reading, Bulmershe Court, Woodlands Avenue, Earley, Reading RG6 1HY (0734 318659).
DIAL UK (National Association of Disablement Information and Advice Lines) Park Lodge, St Catherine's Hospital, Tickhill Road, Balby, Doncaster, South Yorkshire DN4 88N (0302 310123).
DIG (Disablement Income Group) Millmead Business Centre, Millmead Road, London N17 9QU (081 801 8013).
Disability Alliance 25 Denmark Street, London WC2H 8NJ (071 240 0806).
RADAR (Royal Association for Disability and Rehabilitation) 25 Mortimer Street, London W1N 8AB (071 637 5400).
Skill: National Bureau for Students with Disabilities 336 Brixton Road, London SW9 7AA (071 274 0565). Runs an information and advice service on all aspects of post-16 education for young people and adults with disabilities and learning difficulties.
SPOD (Association to aid the sexual and personal relationships of people with a disability) 286 Camden Road, London N7 0BJ (071 607 8851/2).
TRIPSCOPE (Information and advice on transport systems at home and abroad for people with disabilities) 63 Esmond Road, London W4 1JE (081 994 9294).

Before you Go **64**

Being Prepared **65**

Survival Kit **66**

The First Few Days **67**

Intro Fairs and Events **68**

Making Friends and Influencing People **71**

Finding your Feet **71**

arrival at college

The first week at college is a bewildering experience which most people never forget, although many would like to. **Gavin Hamilton** guides you through the minefield of registration, intro fairs and having to make conversation with complete strangers.

During the first few weeks at college, chaos and confusion rule. The amount of information you are asked to take in, the variety of people you are expected to meet and the number of different things you are required to do in such a short space of time can make it a frustrating experience.

The worries and anxiety that new students often feel usually result from a fear of the unknown. This chapter is intended to dispel any anxiety you might feel about starting college, and to equip you with the knowledge you need to survive the first few weeks.

Before You Go

Assuming you get the required A level grades in August, the college sends you a letter confirming the place on your chosen course, followed a few weeks later by half an Amazonian rain forest stuffed into a brown envelope. This is the start of a bombardment of literature from college sources (official and unofficial) over the coming weeks.

The college literature comprises information about college facilities (such as the sports ground and medical centre); where, when and how to register; how to pick up your grant cheque; and possibly the procedure for applying to the college's Access Funds, along with details about the government's top-up loan system (*see page 72* **Money**). Your department might send you a brief reading list to spur you into academic action before the start of term. It could be worth borrowing one of the books from a local library and looking at it briefly to get an idea of what you're letting yourself in for, but don't, whatever you do, go out and buy every single book on the list and proceed to take copious notes – you probably won't be expected to read every book on the list, and you'll find out what the priorities are when you get to college.

The student union might send details of events planned for intro week (often called freshers' week); a list of the various clubs and societies operating within the union; and possibly a guide to union and local facilities. If your application for a place in college accommodation has been successful, you should receive the relevant information on getting there and moving in. If you haven't been allocated a place, you might be given some advice on how to find private rented accommodation (*see also page 94* **Accommodation**).

It's tempting to study all this correspondence meticulously, perhaps too meticulously, searching for clues about life at college. There's no need to spend hours reading all the leaflets and booklets if you've got better things to do, because they don't tell you very much. Instead, jot down in your diary where and when you're supposed to register and what you have to take with you. If you're feeling keen, make a few notes on the student union clubs and societies that interest you.

Finding out more

The official literature tells only half the story. With a little detective work, the other half can be uncovered.

The glossy brochure from the accommodation office doesn't reveal much more about a hall of residence than how many people live there and how much the fees are. Ring the hall office and ask what items of furniture each room is allocated, whether rooms have washbasins and what the communal kitchen and bathroom facilities are like. Also, find out about other hall facilities, such as the bar, shop and launderette.

Arrival at College

If you're fortunate enough to know someone who has done your course, or who has studied your subject, ask if you can borrow their notes and coursebooks, or whether there's a good introductory textbook – *Philosophy Made Simple* (Heinemann), for example, is the bible for first-year philosophy students and enables them to sail through the first year.

Many student unions produce an 'alternative prospectus', usually written by the students, whose frank comments about college facilities, course subjects and student types are in stark contrast to the gloss of the official prospectus. Ring the student union and ask them to send you a copy.

You might know someone who is (or has been) a student at your college, or someone who has lived in the town where you will be studying. Have a chat with them about the best pubs, clubs, cinemas and cafés, or whatever else you're interested in. Even if their recommendations turn out to be misguided, at least you will know a bit about the place before you get there.

If you're feeling adventurous, you could go down to your college a day or two before term starts. Have a look around the area, and investigate some of the places recommended by the alternative prospectus.

Being Prepared

The more you prepare for college before you're let loose on campus, the easier it is to cope with the excesses of the first few weeks. Many things you find out about only after you arrive, but there are some preparations, such as putting together a survival kit, that you can make before you leave.

From the information sent to you through the post, work out what you have to register for, and where and when you must do it. The first few days as a new student are hectic, to say the least, but planning your time carefully cuts down on the hassle. You might find it useful to draw up a timetable of the things you have to do, then you would know how much time remains for other activities.

Essential purchases: There are some things worth acquiring before you go because your grant or parental contribution probably won't cover them during term-time. Do your best to secure the following: radio-cassette player or stereo; kettle; toaster; iron and ironing board; bicycle; reading lamp; everything in the survival kit

Food

If you're living in private rented or self-catering college accommodation, you might not be provided with any kitchen equipment, crockery or cutlery, so be prepared to bring your own. It's also worth bringing some food, certainly enough for the first few days. You could even cook something at home before you leave, and reheat it when you need to. If you've never had to cook for yourself before, you could practise a recipe or two at home to show off your culinary skills when you get to college: most good bookshops have simple cookbooks for students who've never cooked before. Avoid takeaway meals if possible, they're far too expensive. *See also page 116* **Basic Living**.

Opening a bank account

If you haven't got a bank account by the start of term, you should open one pretty sharpish. Students have to pay out several large sums of money during the first weeks of term, and if you're wandering round with a big wadge of notes and nowhere to deposit it, you could find that it starts diminishing fast. The advantage of

63

survival kit

Essential items for the first few days: Food and kitchen equipment (if in self-catering accommodation); tea, coffee, milk and sugar, mugs and teaspoons, alarm clock, condoms, coins (for phone calls and coffee machines) and phone cards, bottle opener or corkscrew, Alka Seltzer and aspirins, first aid kit, posters and pictures, Blu Tack and drawing pins, a dozen passport-sized photos, stationery and a book of stamps, toilet roll, hairdryer and toiletries.

Arrival at College

opening an account during intro week is that all the major banks and building societies have stalls at college intro fairs. You can compare the different packages on offer, meet the respective student advisers and open an account with the bank that most impresses you. Be aware that all the banks are out to persuade you to sign on the dotted line and that they use all manner of hard-sell tactics to tempt you. *See page 72* **Money** for more advice on opening an account.

The First Few Days
Travelling to college
Some people manage to cadge a lift from their parents to get their gear down to college. Going by car is blissful because your luggage allowance can be greater than if you take public transport. You can take your stereo, your cheese plant and whatever else you can cram into the family car. Travelling down by train or coach has its advantages: you don't have to put up with concerned parents, or introduce them to anyone at the other end; but you do have the hassle of carting your luggage around station platforms, and coping with unreasonably small luggage racks. If you're lucky, your college or student union will lay on some form of transport from the station. If you're not so lucky, it might be best to gratefully accept the offer of a lift from your parents or to try and persuade a friend to drive you to college.

The first night
If you're living in hall, introduce yourself to the person living next door to you at the first opportunity – it's better than bumping into them unexpectedly when you've just come out of the shower. Even if you are as different as chalk and cheese, at least you'll have someone to go to dinner with that evening and walk to college with the next morning. What you do in between is another matter.

The first night is what you make it. The best advice we can give is: at least do something and, if in doubt, follow the crowd. If everyone is going down to the hall or union bar, go down there as well. There's nothing worse than being stuck in your room, afraid to go out for fear of making a fool of yourself. This will happen only if you do something along the lines of running stark naked through the bar shouting 'Elvis is alive and well and living in Peckham'. Just behave normally and no-one will bat an eyelid. Rest assured that everyone is just as nervous and unsure of what to say as you are. Just talk about what you feel happy talking about. No-one is going to bite your head off for saying the 'wrong' things.

Registration
Registration means standing in a series of different queues. Queues during intro week are boring only if you don't talk to people. They are, in fact, a great place to widen your acquaintance.

You have to register for the following things:

Course, department and faculty: You usually have to register with your faculty first (which might not be in your department), then with your department (where you might be invited to stop for a cosy chat with your personal tutor), and then sign up for your course options (which might again be in different department buildings). And that's before you get any lecture timetables and reading lists.

NUS and college student union: You will get an NUS card if your union is affiliated to NUS (the vast majority are). All students are automatically members of the student union and for all full-time (and most part-time) students, the card is free. You need at least two passport-sized photos. Colleges that aren't affiliated to the NUS are generally part of some sort of union or guild, so new students receive a membership card for this. *See also page 146* **Student Unions**.

Grant cheque: Grant cheques are sent to your college by your local education authority. To pick up the pennies, you show the award letter from your local authority and proof that you have registered with your faculty. Grant cheques are notorious for arriving late. Be patient and don't take it out on the college administrative staff – it's not their fault.

Loan: To apply for a government-sponsored top-up loan, which you might not want to do at the start of term, you have to get a number of different forms from your college confirming your student status. For more details on grants and student loans, *see page 72* **Money**.

Library: Again, registering at the library is a simple exercise, but one which needs to be fitted into a busy schedule. You might need a couple of passport-sized photos and proof that you have registered with your department and faculty. *See also page 200* **Study Techniques**.

Health centre: An essential, but often forgotten part of the registration process, signing on at the doctor's should help set you up when your body lets you down. *See also page 172* **Health and Stress**.

You must keep a careful eye on your finances, particularly during the first week of term. Many people have been known to blow their grant cheques in the first flush of newly found financial freedom, only to spend the rest of term in abject poverty. Try to set aside a sum of money for the additional costs you're likely to face at the start of term, such as joining clubs and societies, and socializing. Do your best to work out a budget based on planned weekly expenditure. *See also page 116* **Basic living**.

Intro Fairs and Events
College events

During the first week, students are bombarded with invitations to all manner of parties, meetings and events arranged by the college to 'meet the principal', 'meet the lecturers' and 'meet your hall tutor'. Don't attend these beanos just because you think that crying off means certain ostracism for the rest of your time at college. Most lecturers arrange these events out of a sense of duty to make first-year students feel at home. Meeting college staff in a social context isn't a very good way of getting to know them – they're more likely to notice your face if you sit, wide awake, in the front row of their lectures – but events like this are a good way of meeting other students. Even if you just talk to people afterwards about how false and embarrassing the whole exercise was, it's often better than trying to introduce yourself to people across a crowded bar.

Student union intro fairs

Nearly all student unions arrange some sort of event (normally called the 'intro fair' or 'freshers' fair') for clubs and societies funded by the union, as well as external bodies such as the high street banks, to come along to sell their wares to first years, or sign them up for membership. The atmosphere is chaotic, confusing and can be intimidating.

Intro fairs are a great chance to get involved in all kinds of extra-curricular pursuits. Societies include everything from champagne tasters, weird one-offs (the Cilla Black Appreciation Society, underwater tiddlywinks and so on) to sporting, religious, political, cultural and course-related societies. Your student union might publish a handbook or intro fair guide with details of all the clubs and societies operat-

Arrival at College

"The main problem for new students is that you come up to college seeking wisdom, but find only cleverness. In the first year, you wonder whether you are wrong about everything; in the second, whether it's the university that's wrong; and in the third, when you're just beginning to sort it all out, you have to leave."

Rabbi Lionel Blue (History, Balliol College, Oxford, 1950-53; Hebrew and Aramaic, University College London 1953-56).

ing in the union, and external organizations taking stalls at the fair. Try to decide which ones you're going to join before you spend any money. Be selective: find out what's on offer and then decide which ones you can realistically get involved in. It's easy to wander around in a daze signing up with groups and societies all over the shop. Before you part with any cash, ask where your money is going and what you will get in return. If you join a society, find out when their first meeting is and try to attend. That's when they plan their activities for the term and it's your best chance to get involved. If you miss the first meeting, and turn up at the next meeting instead, you might find it a lot more difficult to get involved. *See also page 146* **Student Unions**.

Some organizations (usually external) give away a number of freebies. National newspapers, such as the *Guardian*, furnish new students with free copies of that day's paper. Other organizations give away magazines, pens, wall planners, balloons, even condoms. Fortunately, plastic bags are usually given away too, so you should have no trouble finding one in which to put all your gifts.

Freshers' balls

Most student unions put on some form of entertainment for the new students. The quality of these events varies enormously and can depend upon the finances and facilities of the union, as well as the imagination and ability of the union's social secretary and entertainments committee. Some have just one event; others put on events over a week or even a fortnight. Most have a 'freshers' ball'. Despite the grand billing, the event is rarely a black tie and ballgown affair (although some hapless punters have been known to turn up in their fanciest glad rags, only to spend the entire evening cringing with embarrassment in the corner of the bar). Don't be put off if you don't like the look (or the sound) of the band, as live music isn't the only attraction – the disco, or the cabaret, or the spectacle of drunken second and third years making fools of themselves might be far more entertaining.

Try to avoid any intro events not organized by the union, such as parties in local nightclubs. These are normally promoted by enterprising young things with the sole intention of lining their own pockets. The DJ often turns out to be a local Gary Davies, without the eyebrows. And if the beer is watered down, the bar prices won't be.

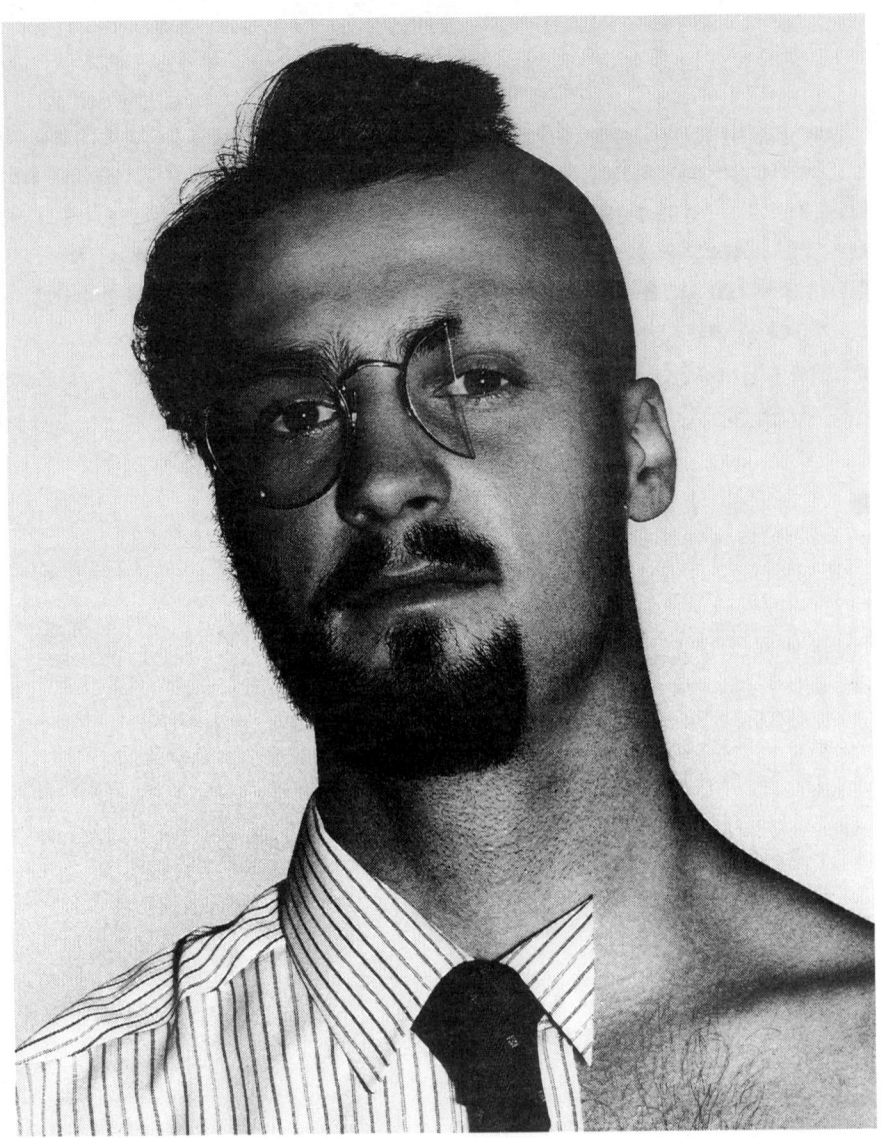

Don't forget, a Young Persons Railcard trims a third off.

If you are aged 16-23 it's worth remembering that a Young Persons Railcard cuts a third off most rail fares for a year. It's just the job for getting to interviews or for visiting friends. Pick up a leaflet for conditions of use at main BR Stations or Rail Appointed Travel Agents. It's a snip.

YOUNG PERSONS RAILCARD

Making Friends and Influencing People

It has been said that you spend your second year at college trying to lose the friends you made in the first year. However, that's a much better situation to be in than not having any friends at all.

Some new students have been known to wear T-shirts stating essential information, such as 'Name: Joe/Joanna Student. Home town: Birmingham. Course: Biology. A levels: Biology, Chemistry and English. Year off: office work then Australia for three months'. That answers all the boring questions people ask. Then you can get down to the real stuff like 'Where's the bar?', 'Isn't the food in the hall canteen disgusting?' or 'Don't you think that lecturer is barking mad?'.

The only way to meet other students is to talk to as many people as possible. That's not to say that you have to begin conversations with predictable questions. But everyone is in the same boat, and sooner or later someone has to break the ice. If you do it sooner rather than later, embarrassing moments can be avoided. And if you take an instant dislike to someone, you have more time to look elsewhere for more congenial types.

Falling in love with someone in intro week, with whom you consequently spend all your spare time, might well be romantic and an instant tonic to feelings of homesickness and loneliness. However, you will be losing out on the fun of the first few weeks. After the initial excitement of intro week and your *grande passion* have died down, you suddenly realize you don't know a soul on your course or in your hall. *See also page 160* **Sex and Relationships**.

Alcohol will probably play a large role in social events during the first few weeks; cheap promotions in the bar and wine and cheese parties abound. You might feel that a drink or two helps your confidence and relaxation, but watch your alcohol intake. Drinking too much too often will cost you both friends and money in the short term, and affect your health in the longer term. If you do drink, moderation is the key word.

You don't have to drink to have a good time and meet people: don't be pressurized into drinking if you would rather not. Many people do not drink at all, whether for religious or cultural reasons, or for the good of their health, so you won't be the only one. Most bars now offer low- and no-alcohol drinks – so not drinking doesn't mean not socializing. *See also page 172* **Health and Stress**.

Solitary confinement

It might seem an easy option to lock yourself away in your room, contemplate your navel and kid yourself that getting out and meeting people really isn't that important, that it will all happen in the fullness of time, and that you just need to wait and be patient. The people who enjoy their first few weeks at college are usually the ones who go out of their way to be friendly. After all, there are hundreds of other first years trying to do exactly the same thing, so it's hardly difficult. Shutting yourself up and copping out solves nothing in the long term, and it will seem a long term indeed if you don't make any friends.

Finding your Feet

After the upheaval of travelling to college, fighting your way through intro week and making friends and influencing people, the idea of sitting down and getting on with your course might seem positively therapeutic.

Lectures usually start the Monday after intro week; tutorials get going about a week later. The delay gives you time to explore all the nooks and crannies of your department building. It's important to locate the lavatories. If you're caught short when your lecture is about to start, and the only loo you know of is the one in the student union building on the other side of the college, you might lament your lack of interest in the departmental toilet.

Seek out the notice-boards for your course and your year – you don't want to walk into a relocated third-year economics lecture on the contribution of structuralist theory to the study of development economics when you're a drama student looking for the lecture on Samuel Beckett. Test the coffee machine in the common room. The chances are that it spews out a liquid with the texture and taste of ground charcoal. The department next door might have a better machine. Find out where your pigeon-hole is – if you don't know, you might miss memos from your tutor and important notices from the head of department. If you get lost, it's always better to ask someone than to spend hours fuming over a badly-designed college map.

Coping with coursework

During the first couple of weeks your work schedule will begin to fall into place. Don't be tempted to leave essays to the last minute, or you could find yourself in a mad panic just before the end of term when everybody else is beginning to wind down, and you won't do yourself justice.

Initial workloads vary between courses and institutions. Some new students will find themselves dropped in at the deep end with all-day lectures and assignments starting straight away; others will find that their contact hours (the time actually spent in lectures and tutorials) at college are few, and that they are not set assignments until as late as mid-term. Having said that, in

"**The year 1991 is going to bring hard times for students economically. However, Leo is very prominent this year and if you are creative there is no limit to what you can achieve. Regarding loans, students can't expect something for nothing: struggle maketh man. Because we live in such a materialistic society, people with money have more chance, perhaps, of going on to higher education than other people. But you have to battle against authority. I made my way through the world having been given absolutely nothing. If you want to make it, you can.**"

Russell Grant Astrologer.

general you can expect your workload to increase over the term, and if your contact hours are few you will be expected to do a large amount of work independently. It's a good idea to plan your work at this stage of the term, but it's equally important to give yourself time to enjoy yourself and go on meeting people.

Tutors will be on hand to advise and direct your work. Some colleges offer study skills training – which is a good idea, not just for people who are returning to study after a break, but for everybody new to higher education. Take advantage of any advice you can get in the early days, it will be invaluable throughout your college career. *See also page 200* **Study Techniques**.

After the first few lectures and tutorials, some people find that their course isn't what they expected. It might be that some of the course options on offer in the prospectus aren't actually available, because the lecturer responsible for the option is taking a sabbatical or has left. Or you might find a subject taken as a subsidiary more interesting and challenging than your main one and, as a result, you want to switch. Don't despair. Most colleges are used to such eventualities and have procedures to let students change courses. You normally have to rely upon someone else leaving, or switching from, the course you want to switch to. But don't think you can change to a course you wanted to do originally but for which you didn't make the grades. College authorities got wise to this move a long time ago. *See also page 200* **Study Techniques**.

Putting it in perspective

After the first few weeks at college, you should feel more settled and at home. If you still find the college environment confusing and disorientating, it might be that you haven't made the effort to fit in. Many people who drop out of college or fail their finals, do so not because they fail to cope with the academic demands, but because they are unable to come to terms with their college environment and to adjust to student life.

You might want to go home at the earliest opportunity. Stay at college for at least the first three weekends. Going home the weekend after you arrive is a bad move if you want to enjoy college. If you've got a boyfriend or girlfriend at home whom you can't bear to be away from, persuade them to come and see you. If the relationship is going to last, your partner won't mind.

There's no sense in deciding you hate every minute at college and that you want to jack it all in just because you haven't met the right people or frequented the right places. Very few people are lucky enough to meet students with whom they hit it off straight away, and stay friends with for the rest of their time at college. You might encounter a great many people during the first week, but you're sure to keep making new contacts throughout your time as a student, even up until the last week of the final term.

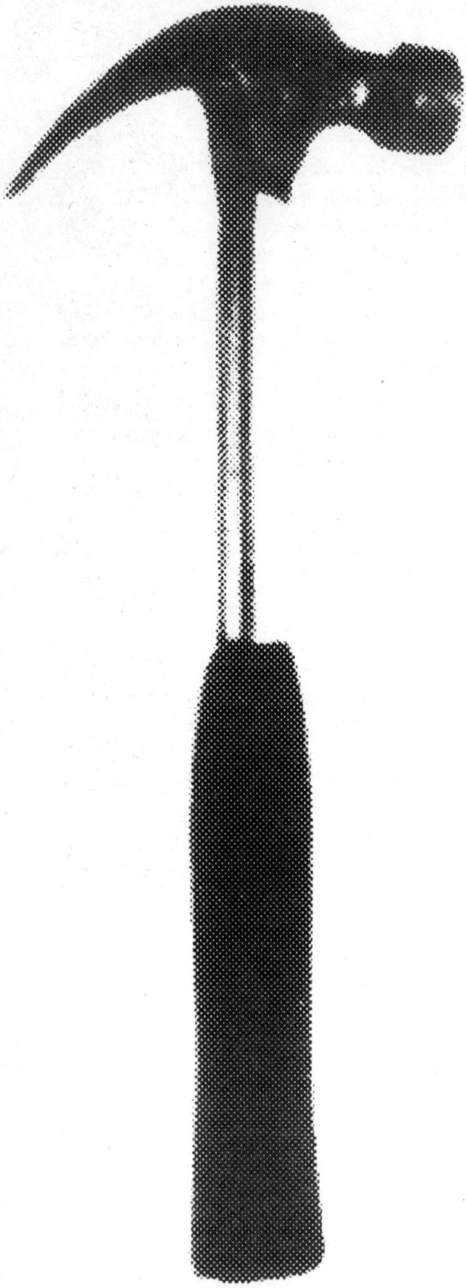

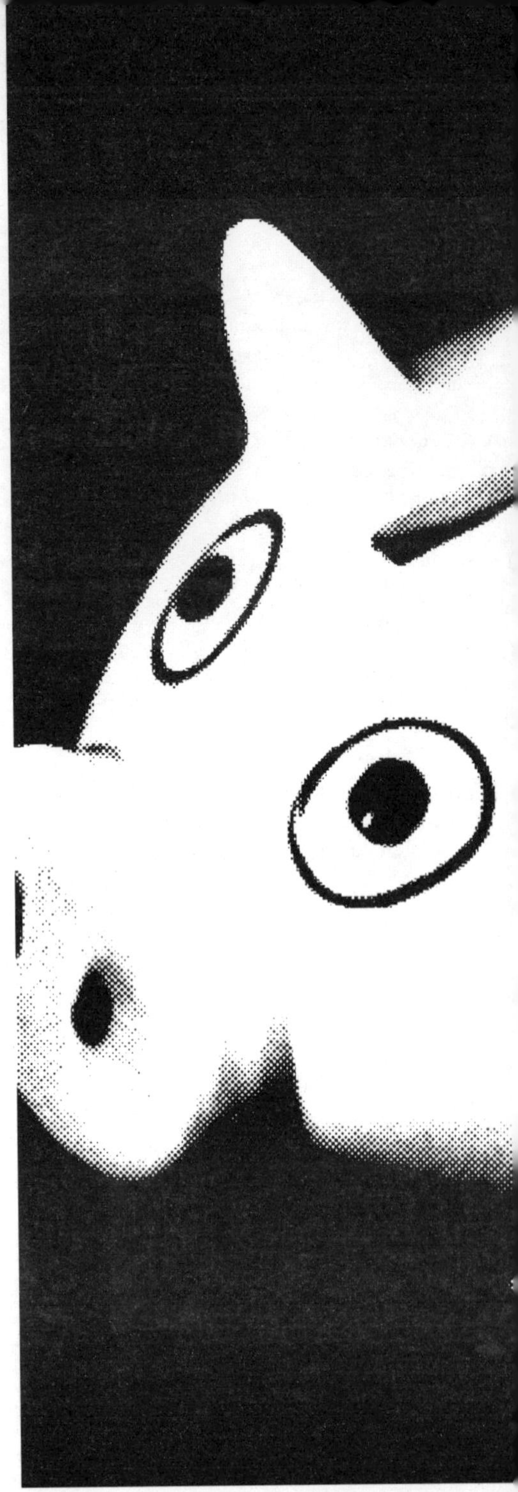

money

Student Grants **74**

Government-funded

Student Loans **83**

Social Security Benefits **84**

Access Funds **87**

Alternative Financial

Assistance **89**

Banks, Building Societies

and Credit Cards **90**

Further Reading **92**

Useful Addresses **92**

Many of the horror stories about poverty-stricken students are true. **Paul Allender** and **Julie Harvey** from NUS outline sources of student income and tell you where to pick up the pennies; while **Gavin Hamilton** takes a look at the banks and building societies.

Research done by NUS, based on the Retail Price Index (RPI) over a 12-year period, shows that since 1978/79 the purchasing power of the maintenance grant has fallen by 24 per cent. As a result, over that period many students have had to rely increasingly on state benefits – housing benefit and income support – in order to keep their income above the official poverty level. However, since 1990 most full-time students have not been allowed to claim these benefits, even over the long summer vacation. And the government now expects students to take out loans to help towards their living costs.

The year 1990 proved to be a watershed in the history of student financial support. Following a year-long passage through Parliament, the Education (Student Loans) Act was passed, and so introduced 'top-up' loans on 1 September 1990 for students in higher education. The maintenance grant will now remain frozen at the 1990/91 levels, and the loan facility will be increased each year until its value is equal to that of the grant. A conservative estimate by NUS suggests that the loan element could equal the grant by as early as 1999.

This new system of financial support is likely to result in unprecedented levels of debt. There is much evidence, ranging from NUS surveys to research done by Bristol Polytechnic's Department of Economics and Social Science, to suggest that loans will deter many people from entering higher education, in particular people from low income backgrounds.

The other elements of government-funded support available are Access Funds and, for a minority of students, welfare benefits. In this chapter we outline the main features of the new system.

Student Grants
Mandatory awards

Mandatory awards are the main type of grant available for students studying higher education courses. In England and Wales they are administered by the local education authorities; in Scotland by the Scottish Education Department; and in Northern Ireland by the Library and Education Boards.

The award consists of tuition fees, a basic rate of maintenance and, in some cases, additional allowances – for instance, for extra weeks of study or for dependants. If you qualify for an award, your tuition fees will always be paid. However, the maintenance grant is subject to one or more of three means tests – against your own income, your parents' income, or your spouse's income – so you might not receive the full amount. Indeed, some students will find that they are not entitled to any maintenance from their authority.

In order to qualify for a mandatory award there are several conditions that you must fulfil:

1) Are you intending to study on a designated course?
2) Do you meet the ordinary residence criteria?
3) Have you done any previous study which affects your entitlement?
4) Are you an 'assisted' student?
5) Has your conduct shown you to be 'unfit' to hold an award?
6) Have you applied on time?

Designated courses: To be eligible for a mandatory award you must be studying or intending to study on a designated, full-time course. These include:
- First degree courses;
- Diploma of Higher Education courses;

Money

- Higher National Diploma;
- Courses of initial teacher training, including part-time courses and the Postgraduate Certificate of Education;
- Courses provided by a university leading to certificates, diplomas, or other qualifications comparable to a first degree, which last for at least three years.

A more comprehensive list of designated courses is available from the Department of Education and Science (*see below* **Useful Addresses**).

Ordinary residence: The second condition is that you must have been 'ordinarily resident' in the UK for the three years prior to the start of your course. This means that you have been in the UK legally for a settled purpose (usually, any purpose other than tourism). You should not have been resident for any part of the three years wholly or mainly for the purpose of receiving full-time education.

Some students who do not fulfil this test can still be eligible. These are: some EC nationals, who can establish 'migrant worker' status, and keep their children with them; official UK refugees or asylees and their spouse or children; and students who fail the residence test only because they, their partner or parents were temporarily employed outside the UK. The residence test is obviously quite complex in some cases, and you should contact NUS if you need further advice (*see below* **Useful Addresses**).

Previous study: Only previous study for which you received support from public funds will affect your entitlement to a grant. If you have already attended one or more courses of full-time higher education (above A level or Scottish Higher Standard), where the courses were over two years in length, then you are not entitled to a mandatory award. This ruling applies if you attended more than one term and seven weeks of the second term, but failed to complete the course.

Comparable part-time or correspondence courses only disqualify you if you completed them. Bursaries for courses at long-term residential colleges, such as Hillcroft College, Surbiton or Ruskin College, Oxford do not affect your entitlement. For further details of these bursaries, contact Adult Education Bursaries (*see below* **Useful Addresses**). Previous study does not disqualify you if you are intending to complete a Postgraduate Certificate in Education.

Previous attendance on courses lasting two years or less does not disqualify you for a subsequent award, but your entitlement will be reduced, unless the new course is a BEd in a 'shortage subject' such as physics, chemistry or maths, where entitlement is preserved in full. The same may also apply to other subjects such as craft, design and technology or business studies, should the LEA use its discretion to classify them as a shortage subject.

In general, though, the award will be reduced, and the crucial factor determining subsequent funding is the length of the new proposed course:

- If the normal duration is two years or less, the grant will only be paid for the final year;
- If the normal duration of the course is more than two years, then two years are deducted from the duration of the award, which will then only cover the remaining final years.

Assisted student status: If you have been given paid leave by your employer to study, and the sponsorship is at least equivalent to the course fees and the maintenance grant, then you will not be entitled to a mandatory

75

award. Sponsorship of less than £2,995 (in 1990/91) will not affect your entitlement to a grant.

Unfit conduct: The Education Authority may decide not to pay a grant to someone they feel has shown him- or herself 'unfit' to hold an award. NUS has not heard of a single example of a student denied an award on this basis.

Deadline for application: Finally, to be eligible for a mandatory award, you must send your application before the deadline; otherwise, the authority is under no obligation to give you a grant. Even if you are unclear about your eligibility, you should still submit an application within the time limit. The later you leave your application, the greater the risk of your first grant cheque being late. Preferably, the application should be made as soon as a provisional place of study has been secured on a course.

In any event, in England, Wales and Northern Ireland, applications must be made by the end of the first term of your course. The Scottish Education Department operates a strict closing date of 31 December for all applications.

Should you find that for some reason you have not applied on time, it is worth asking the college to hold your place over until the following year, and then making sure that you apply on time.

Where to apply

England, Wales and Northern Ireland: You should apply to the local education authority (or Education and Library Board, if in Northern Ireland) in whose area you were ordinarily resident on 30 June, 31 October or 28/29 February, according to whether the academic year of the course begins in the autumn, spring or summer respectively.

If you're not sure which authority to apply to, write to the one you think will be responsible, before the closing date. Notice of this application should then immediately be given to all the other education authorities concerned: your position is protected if it subsequently turns out that a different authority is administering the award.

Scotland: Scottish students should apply to the Scottish Education Department Awards Branch (*see below* **Useful Addresses**).

You should keep a photocopy of all the forms you send. Also, where the length of the course you wish to take is variable (for instance, where there is an option to study abroad for a year), you should apply for the longer period, even if you do not plan to take the longer option. This will ensure that you receive funding for the entire course.

When applying, you will have to sign a clause which binds you to repaying any overpayments, even where you could not have realized a mistake had been made.

How much is the grant?

All students who qualify for a mandatory award will have their fees paid by the education authority. How much maintenance you receive depends on the outcome of a means test (*see below* **How much grant will you receive?**). However, in 1990/91 the full maintenance grant for students living in London was £2,845; it was £2,265 for students living elsewhere; and £1,795 for students living in their parental home. Students from Scotland receive less – £2,780, £2,200 and £1,660 respectively – but some help is available for travel costs (*see below* **Travel**). Students who study abroad as a necessary part of their course will receive a different rate of grant. It is these basic rates of

Money

grant which will remain frozen until the loan is of equal value.

There are also supplementary allowances available, depending on your circumstances (all allowances and entitlements mentioned below are based on 1990/91 levels):

Extra weeks of study: If you are required to attend your course for more than 30 weeks and 3 days per academic year (or more than 25 weeks and 3 days if you're studying at Oxford or Cambridge University), you are entitled to additional payments. The allowance is £63.15 per week if you're studying in London, £47.30 if you're studying elsewhere, and £33.15 if you are living with your parents. For Scottish students, it is £58.85, £43.10 and £26.40 respectively.

If you have to attend your course for 45 weeks or more in an academic year, then you'll receive a grant for 52 weeks.

Older students: If you are aged 26 or over before the start of your course, and have received at least £12,000 in taxable income (whether earnings or income support) over the three years prior to being a student, then you are entitled to the Older Students Allowance. The allowance is £250 for students aged 26 at the start of the course; £455 for those aged 27; £675 for those aged 28; and £880 for those aged 29 and over.

Disabled students allowance: If you have a disability, and as a consequence of attending a course are obliged to incur additional expenditure, you could qualify for extra maintenance of up to £1,000 per year. There is also a special equipment allowance of £3,000 per course, plus an allowance of up to £4,000 per year to pay for non-medical helpers who might be needed, such as interpreters, readers, typists and so on. *See page 50* **Students with Disabilities**.

Travel: The basic rates of grant include £195 travel allowance for students living in the parental home, and £125 for those living elsewhere.

If you have a disability, or are a medical, dental or nursing student attending clinical training away from college, you can claim for extra travel expenses. Always try to keep an accurate record of costs. Extra help is also given for overseas travel as a necessary part of the course.

The Scottish maintenance grants include £60 allowance for travel. Within limits, all students receiving a Scottish grant can claim for travel expenses in excess of this amount. Claims should be made on the form AB4, issued to colleges in December each year.

Medical insurance: If you study abroad as a necessary part of your course, and have to take out medical insurance, you should apply to your education authority for reimbursement.

Dependants allowances: Dependants allowances can be claimed for a spouse, children and other adult dependants. You will not receive any help for an unmarried partner, another award holder, or for someone not resident in the UK. Dependants allowances are means tested against the income of the dependants. The maximum that the education authority will pay is:

• Spouse or other adult dependant; or, if no adult dependant, first child: £1,525;
• Child of less than 11 years at the start of the academic year: £320;
• Child aged 11 to 15 at the start of the academic year: £640;
• Child aged 16 to 17 at the start of the academic year: £845;
• Child aged 18 or over at the start of the academic year: £1,215.

STUDENTS' UNION

durex THE SAFER SEX SYMBOL

DUREX SAFE-PLAY IS A TRADE MARK OF LRC PRODUCTS LIMITED.

Money

Two homes grant: An allowance of £540 can be claimed if you have to maintain a home for yourself and a dependant, in addition to your term-time residence.

Single parents: If you are a single parent you are entitled to whichever of the following is most favourable to you:
- A higher income 'disregard' (a proportion of income that is ignored) under the student's 'own income' means test;
- The Older Students' Allowance (if eligible, *see above*);
- or an additional dependants' allowance of £755.

Students with one or more dependants under 19 may also choose a higher income disregard for dependants instead of the dependants' allowances.

Vacations: Authorities can make weekly payments of up to £53.50 during the vacations to students who would otherwise suffer hardship. As the majority of full-time students can now no longer claim housing benefit and income support, NUS is urging authorities to make greater use of this discretionary allowance.

Special teacher training bursaries: If you are on a teacher training course lasting up to two years, and specializing in maths, chemistry, craft, design, technology or modern foreign languages, you are eligible for an extra £1,500 per year. If you are training to teach physics you are entitled to an extra £2,000 per year. Unlike the other supplementary allowances, these allowances are not means tested.

Further details about these bursaries can be obtained from the Teacher Supply and Training Branch (*see below* **Useful Addresses**).

How much grant will you receive?

The maintenance grant is means tested (*see above* **How much is the grant?**), so you might find that you do not actually receive the full amount from your education authority. Any shortfall is meant to be met by you, your parents or your spouse, as appropriate. Should meeting the shortfall prove difficult, some suggestions which may be of use are made under **Alternative Financial Assistance** (*see below*).

Students' own income means test: Your own income during the academic year will reduce the award pound for pound if it exceeds certain limits. Some sources of income are wholly disregarded; check with your education authority or student union, but exceptions include: earnings, child benefit, income support and housing benefit. There is also a general income disregard of £615 and and a scholarship income disregard of £2,995.

Parental means test or 'contribution': This applies to all students who do not have 'independent status'. Orphans always have independent status. Otherwise, to be treated as independent you must have:
- Reached the age of 25 before the beginning of the academic year for which the award is being assessed; or
- Been married for two years prior to the beginning of the academic year for which the award is being assessed (your spouse's income is then means tested); or
- Been self-supporting for periods totalling three years prior to the start of the course. Self-support includes periods of employment, registered unemployment, YT training, and times when you supported a dependant aged under 18.

There are few other situations in which a parental contribution is not assessed – check with your education authority for details.

Parental Contribution Scales 1990/91

Residual income	Scale 1	Scale 2	Residual income	Scale 1	Scale 2
£11,500	£60	£45	£28,000	£3,497	£2,623
£12,000	£131	£98	£29,000	£3,747	£2,810
£13,000	£274	£206	£30,000	£3,997	£2,998
£14,000	£417	£313	£31,000	£4,247	£3,185
£14,700	£517	£388	£32,000	£4,497	£3,373
£15,000	£577	£433	£33,000	£4,747	£3,560
£16,000	£777	£583	£34,000	£4,997	£3,748
£17,000	£977	£733	£35,000	£5,247	£3,935
£18,000	£1,177	£833	£36,000	£5,497	£4,123
£19,000	£1,377	£1,033	£37,000	£5,747	£4,310
£20,000	£1,577	£1,183	£37,210	£5,800 •	£4,350
£21,000	£1,777	£1,333	£38,000		£4,498
£21,600	£1,897	£1,423	£39,000		£4,685
£22,000	£1,997	£1,498	£40,000		£4,873
£23,000	£2,247	£1,685	£41,000		£5,060
£24,000	£2,497	£1,873	£42,000		£5,248
£25,000	£2,747	£2,060	£43,000		£5,435
£26,000	£2,997	£2,248	£44,000		£5,623
£27,000	£3,247	£2,435	£44,944	• (max)	£5,800

Money

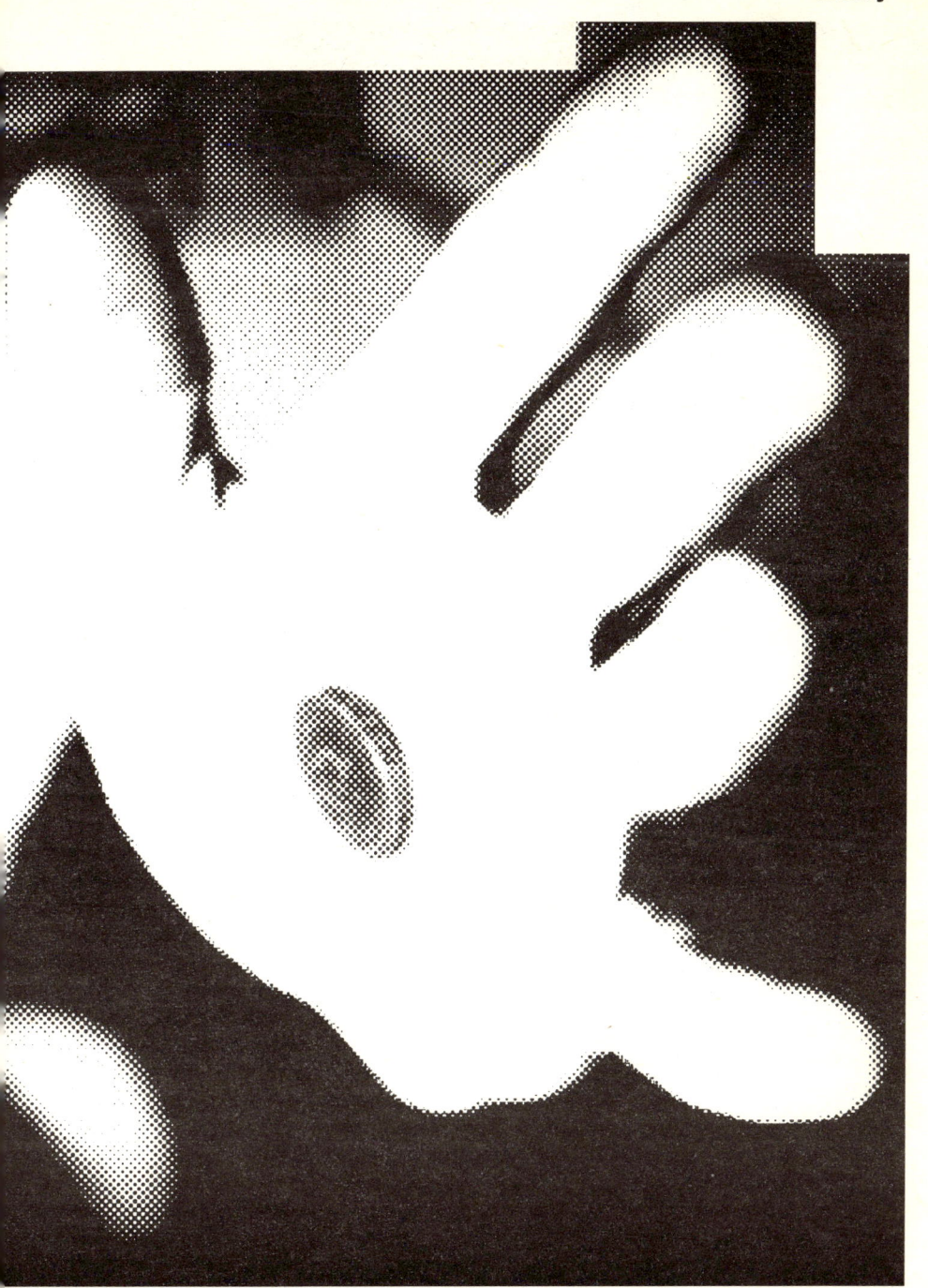

81

The parental contribution is based upon your parents' 'residual' income. Residual income is the total income of your parent(s) for tax purposes. The income which is taken into account is usually that of the last tax year before the academic year for which the grant is being assessed. Certain deductions are made from the income. The main deductions are: £1,505 for adult dependants (other than a spouse and yourself); and the gross amount of tax-allowable loan interest (principally mortgages). Deductions are also allowed, within limits, for life insurance and pensions. Check with your education authority or student union for more detailed information.

Once you have calculated the residual income using the table **Parental Contribution Scales**, you can approximate the expected parental contribution. A further £100 is deducted from this contribution for every other child dependent upon your parent(s). Your authority pays the remainder of the grant.

Notes on Scales: From 1 September 1988, two scales of parental contribution have operated. Scale 2, the reduced scale, was introduced by the government to compensate for loss of tax relief on non-charitable covenants. It came into effect on Budget Day 1988, affecting all students whose parents intended to covenant their contribution to the grant. The contribution expected by Scale 2 is 25 per cent lower than Scale 1. Students who started their course from 1 September 1988 will have their parents' income assessed according to Scale 2.

Late arrival of grants

One of the best ways to ensure that your grant does not arrive late is to apply early, and to fill in all the forms carefully. Do not leave any questions unanswered. Make sure you enclose all the required documents, such as evidence of income.

Grant cheques are usually sent to your college for collection. If your grant is late, first check with your authority whether this is due to missing information. If so, send in the information required as soon as possible. Perhaps your college has failed to send off the acceptance form to the authority.

Increasingly, grants are arriving late, sometimes very late, because the authority is experiencing difficulty administering the number of applications received. Unfortunately, there is very little that can be done about this as there is no statutory time limit within which the authority must complete the administration. Should this happen to you, it might be worth checking the overdraft facilities offered at your local bank. Also, see if your college or student union is able to offer any help.

Warning

Seek the advice of your student union before abandoning or transferring a course, as strict regulations apply regarding future entitlement to a grant. Again, it's best not to take a year out without first receiving, in writing, permission from your education authority to do this. *See also page 200* **Study Techniques.**

Discretionary awards

There is a huge array of courses that do not qualify for a mandatory award. If your chosen course is one of these, you can apply to the education authority for a discretionary award. However, the authority is almost entirely free to decide whether or not to make an award and, if it does, how much it will be.

Authorities might set age limits on eligibility for discretionary awards. Some do not support courses outside their borough or county, particularly if a similar course is available at a local college. Many authorities insist upon a minimum period of residence within their area. Your examination results could also affect your application.

The authority will probably issue a booklet on their policy regarding discretionary awards. Many authorities set an early deadline for applications, so it's best to apply as early as possible.

If you are attending a course designated for a mandatory award, but fail to qualify because, for example, you have previously studied, you can apply for a discretionary award. If your application is successful, you will receive a grant on the same basis as a mandatory award, subject to the appropriate means testing.

Government-funded Student Loans

The aim of the scheme is to provide a non-means tested loans facility to students in higher education, which must be repaid after completing the course.

Eligibility for a loan

You must satisfy a number of conditions to be eligible for a student loan. Firstly, you must be attending an 'appropriate' full-time higher education course and meet the ordinary residency criteria (*see above* **Student Grants: Mandatory awards**). In addition, you must meet the age requirements for borrowing under this scheme. Previous study does not disqualify you for a loan.

Eligible Higher Education courses: The course must be full-time, except where the course is a part-time course of initial teacher training. It must be higher than A level standard (or BTEC National Certificate or Scottish Higher Level), but below postgraduate level. The only eligible postgraduate course is the Postgraduate Certificate of Education (PGCE). The course must also last at least one academic/calendar year. Courses at private colleges are only eligible if specifically designated. Contact the Department of Education and Science for details.

Age requirements: To be eligible, you must be under the age of 50 at the start of the course.

How to apply

In the first instance, application for a student loan is via your college – ask your student union where you should go. The college loans administrator will issue you with an eligibility questionnaire, which will be used to check whether you meet the conditions outlined above. To aid this process, you will need to take several items with you:

• Birth/adoption certificate (if you do not have a UK certificate, you will need to take your passport and an official letter detailing your name at birth, and date, place and country of birth);

• Mandatory award letter, if you have one;

• Evidence of bank/building society account number, as the loan will be paid directly into your account.

If you are eligible, the college will send an eligibility certificate in your name to the Student Loans Company (SLC), a government-run company which had to be set up because banks refused to administer the scheme. You will also be given an application form. From this point on, you deal with the SLC (*see below* **Useful Addresses**).

On the application form, you are asked to give names and addresses of two 'contacts'.

These are not guarantors, but will be used by the SLC to help trace you should you later default on repayments.

You can only submit one application per academic year. You should therefore think carefully about how much of the maximum loan facility you will require before submitting your application. You can apply to the SLC for a loan at any point in the academic year, but the deadline for applying is around the end of July (check with your college for the final date). Upon receipt of your application, the SLC will send you an agreement form, which you must sign and send back to the SLC. The loan will then be paid into your bank account.

Terms and conditions

Interest: The loan will accrue interest immediately on a daily basis. The rate of interest changes each September and is based on fluctuations in the Retail Price Index (RPI) over the twelve months ending with the previous July. The RPI in July 1990 was 9.8 per cent; thus, from the following September, the interest of the loan is 9.8 per cent. In September 1991 the interest rate will change to reflect the July 1991 RPI figure. As the interest charged is variable, and reflects inflation, sometimes the interest is less than that charged by banks, and sometimes more. Interest will continue to accrue during periods of study, deferment of repayments, or default.

Repayments: Repayments start in the April after completing or leaving a course. The SLC has the discretion to allow some graduates with disabilities to start repayment at a later date, or to allow them a longer repayment period (*see page 50* **Students with Disabilities**).

Repayment is by direct debit from your bank account. Other methods of repayment (cheque, standing order) must be negotiated with the SLC.

There is a fixed repayment period of five years for courses lasting less than five years, and a seven-year repayment period for courses lasting five years and longer. Repayment will be in monthly instalments of approximately equal amounts, subject to adjustments in subsequent annual interest rates.

For examples of monthly repayments, consult the booklet 'Loans for Students, a brief guide 1990/91', available from the Department of Education and Science, Publications Despatch Centre. Scottish students should contact the Scottish Education Department. *See below* **Useful Addresses** for both.

Deferment: You can defer repayments for a year if your income is below 85 per cent of the national average wage. In 1990/91, if your gross income fell below £965 per month, you could apply to the SLC for deferment. If your income is still below the deferment threshold a year later, you can re-apply for further deferment immediately. Only your own income is taken into account. Income received from state disability benefits will be disregarded.

Cancellation of loan: Any loan still outstanding will be cancelled after 25 years, or when you become 50 (or 60, if you started the course at the age of 40 or over), whichever is sooner. This automatic cancellation is not available should you default on repayments without the SLC's agreement.

Social Security Benefits

Along with all the other changes made in September 1990 to the student financial support system, the vast majority of full-time students were taken out of entitlement to Housing Benefit, as well as Income Support during the

Money

Maximum Student Loan Available (1990/91)

Students living	final year	full year
in London	£460	£340
elsewhere	£420	£310
at home	£330	£240

PGCE students will receive a full-year's loan. Students who study abroad as part of their course are eligible at the 'elsewhere' rate.

summer vacation. Until then, Housing Benefit formed an important part of a student's overall income, especially during term time and in areas of high private-sector rent, such as London and the South-East. Loss of Income Support during the summer will be a serious blow to those students who do not find work and are unable to return to their parents' home during the holiday.

The government's position is that the student loan will compensate for loss of benefit for the vast majority of students, and that the Access Funds will provide for the minority who still find themselves in hardship (*see below* **Access Funds**). NUS has disagreed vehemently with this scenario, stating that the majority of students will be worse off as a result of being taken out of benefit entitlement. Some of them (for instance, students living in private sector accommodation in London) will lose substantial amounts of income. A student with an average weekly rent of £50 in London will lose nearly £725 during term-time alone.

Some groups of students can still claim Housing Benefit and Income Support. They are:

- Students who are single parents, including those with a foster child;

- Students with a disability. The definition of 'disability' covers those who meet the conditions for award of the Income Support Disability Premium or Severe Disability Premium. It also includes those who received Income Support as a 'disabled student' for the 18 months prior to 1 September 1990, plus those who make a claim after that date who have received either Income Support or Housing Benefit (or both) in the preceding 18 months, either as a 'disabled student', or as a 'severely mentally or physically handicapped' student. A further definition of disability in this context is those deaf students who are eligible for the disabled students allowance as part of their mandatory award;

- Student (heterosexual) couples with a dependant child or children. Both partners are required to be students;

- Students aged under 19 years of age following a course of further education;

- Students who are pensioners, ie those who meet the conditions for award of the Income Support Pensioner Premium or Higher Pensioner Premium;

- Persons in receipt of a training allowance;

- 'Certain persons from abroad' whose funds from abroad have been disrupted temporarily;
- Refugees who are attending a course for the purpose of learning English will be able to claim Income Support (and therefore Housing Benefit) while studying.

The last three groups will not be entitled to Housing Benefit alone; they will only receive Housing Benefit if they are in receipt of Income Support.

- Additionally, a (heterosexual) partner of a student, who is living with them, can claim Income Support and Housing Benefit. This is an important point to remember; students can 'transfer' a claim to their partner.

For these groups of students, who are able to continue to claim benefits (it is estimated that they number between 40,000 and 50,000), the student loan affects the way in which their income is treated. The loan is treated as 'notional income' – it is assumed that the maximum amount is being received regardless of whether or not the student is receiving anything. This is then divided by 52, as the loan is intended to be for the whole year and not just the period of study. For most students, a £10 weekly disregard is applied to the income from the loan. In 1990/91, this disregarded the entire loan, as it amounted to less than £9 per week.

The grant income will continue to be treated as it was before the social security changes: a fixed amount for books, equipment, travel and the student rent allowance are disregarded, and the remainder is divided by the number of weeks in the three terms, plus the two short vacations.

Full-time students were also taken out of entitlement to Unemployment Benefit, with no exempt groups. But as very few students were entitled to Unemployment Benefit anyway, the practical effect is not that great. However, by taking full-time students out of Unemployment Benefit entitlement, the government is depriving some people, who have paid their National Insurance contributions, of payments that they would have received were they not students.

Other benefits: There are a number of other benefits to which students or their partners could be entitled.

Child Benefit is available to anyone who satisfies the required residence conditions – either a child lives with them, or they contribute to the maintenance of a child by at least the weekly rate of Child Benefit. Child Benefit has been frozen since 1987 at £7.25 per week. In April 1991 it was increased to £8.25 for the first child only.

Family Credit is a means tested benefit for those with children and on low wages. In addition to satisfying the residence requirements, the claimant, or their partner, must work at least 24 hours per week, and must be responsible for a child who is a member of their household. Applicants must have less than £8,000 savings, and their income must be below a certain level, depending on the size of the family and the ages of the children. Once awarded, Family Credit is paid for 26 weeks, regardless of changes in circumstance.

One Parent Benefit is available to anyone who is receiving Child Benefit for a child living with them, where they are not living with their spouse or anyone else 'as husband or wife'. In the academic year 1991/92 One Parent Benefit is £5.60 per week.

There are a number of disability benefits that some students are entitled to. Invalidity Benefit and Severe Disablement Allowance can be paid during the period of study, but the student's ability to pursue a full-time course can bring into question their incapacity for work. Attendance Allowance is also payable during term-time, as is Mobility Allowance, provided the student satisfies the eligibility conditions.

The other benefits students might be entitled to are the range of health benefits: free or reduced-rate prescriptions, glasses and dental treatment. This is based on the fact that students have low incomes. However, since the introduction of the Student Loan System in September 1990, students might not receive much or any help towards these costs. The student loan is treated as 'notional income': students are considered to be receiving the maximum loan, regardless of whether they are receiving a loan or not. The only exceptions to this are those students who meet the conditions for receipt of Income Support: a £10 weekly disregard is applied to their income from the loan.

Students wishing to apply for reduced rate prescriptions, dental treatment or glasses should obtain form AG1 from the DSS or a post office. In addition, those students who are actually receiving Income Support will qualify for free prescriptions, dental treatment and glasses. See also page 172 **Health and Stress**.

Access Funds

The government introduced Access Funds supposedly to compensate for students being taken out of entitlement to Housing Benefit and Income Support. The funds are administered by colleges, and it is wholly at the discretion of the college authorities as to how they make payments from the funds. However, it is clear that the amounts provided do not compensate for the loss of benefits. Nationally, £25 million has been provided for the funds, while government savings from taking students out of benefit entitlement amount to at least £68 million, and probably nearer £100 million. A total of £5 million has been provided for further education students, £14 million for undergraduates, and £6 million for postgraduates. If every undergraduate in the country received a payment from the Access Funds, each would receive about £27.

Given that a student with an average weekly rent of £50 in the private sector in London will lose out by around £725 per year, it is obvious that the Access Funds are grossly inadequate. Nevertheless, students are left with no option but to resort to the Access Funds. The student grant has now been frozen, while, at time of writing, the loan is a maximum of £420 (£460 in London) per academic year, and social security benefits are no longer available to the vast majority of students. So, students are put in a position where they either sink further into debt or apply for a payment from the Access Funds.

Students wishing to make an application for a payment should approach their college (check with the Registrar's office or the student union as to which department within the college is dealing with Access Funds) and request an application form. Each college's form will be different, depending on the criteria they have adopted for payment. It is probably worth checking with the student union to find out whether they have a list of criteria which the college administration is using to decide how to make payments.

NUS has advocated that the funds should be used to partially compensate for loss of housing benefit: that a student who has lost out by having housing benefit taken away, should receive some compensation for this, provided the loss is

GRANT & CUTLER

London's largest foreign language bookshop

FRENCH, GERMAN, SPANISH, ITALIAN
PORTUGUESE, SCANDINAVIAN and more...

Over 100,000 books in stock

LITERATURE, LANGUAGE-TEACHING, DICTIONARIES, CINEMA
HISTORY, CASSETTES, VIDEOS, TRANSLATIONS
FREE CATALOGUES - MAIL ORDER

Now open till 4.00pm on Saturdays

55-57 Great Marlborough Street, W1V 2AY
Tel: 071-734 2012   Fax: 071-734 2013

Recommended Reading

Around Town, Art, Books, Cabaret, Children, Clubs, Dance, Film, Gay, Music, Politics, Sport, Student London, Theatre, TV and Radio

Time Out

London's best-selling weekly guide
to what to do and where to be seen

Money

substantial. The compensation will only be partial, as the funds are inadequate. As already stated, the Access Funds system is almost totally discretionary.

However, there are some conditions of eligibility. The three eligible groups of students are:
- Postgraduates: all full-time home students in higher education studying at levels above first degree;
- Undergraduates: all full-time and sandwich course home students in higher education, other than postgraduates;
- Further education students: all full-time and sandwich course home students in further education, aged 19 and over.

The term 'home' students as used here is that of the Student Loans Regulations; for a definition of home students, *see above* **Government-funded Student Loans**.

NUS believes that the restriction to 'home' students unnecessarily restricts the use of the funds. It means that overseas students will not be eligible for support from the Access Funds. NUS would like to see this aspect of the Access Funds system challenged.

Each college should also have a proper appeals procedure, whereby any student being refused a payment from the Access Funds is able to challenge the college authorities' decision. This is something that colleges should normally do, to check that the system is operating properly. Because the funds are limited, it is essential that a student applies as early as possible in the academic year.

Alternative Financial Assistance

NUS estimates that about 44 per cent of students do not receive their full parental contribution; some do not receive any. Unfortunately, education authorities do not have the power to waive the parental contribution.

Andrew Moore and Graham Roberts, in their book *The Student Money Guide* (*see below* **Further Reading**), advise you to discuss finances with your parent(s) well in advance of starting your course. This should give you a good idea of how much of the contribution you will receive, and so help you to plan ahead. The chapter on budgeting and dealing with debt provides more detailed information (*see page 116* **Basic Living**). The authors also suggest that you try to secure a holiday job and save some money to help during the course.

It's worth seeking alternative financial assistance. Information on educational trusts and charities can be found in the following publications – don't be put off by their prohibitive prices, as they should be in your local library:
Directory of Grant Making Trusts (Charities Aid Foundation, £49); *Charities Digest* (Family Welfare Association, £10.95 including postage and packing); *The Grants Register* (Macmillan Publishers Limited, £75); *Sponsorships* (Careers and Occupational Information Centre, Manpower Services Commission, £1.95 plus 60p postage and packing) – this gives information on employers and professional bodies offering sponsorships and supplementary awards for students following first degree, BTEC higher awards or comparable courses; *British Music Year Book* and the *British Music Education Year Book* (both Rhinegold, £12.95 and £9.95 respectively).

Students in need should also consult their local education authority, town hall and local religious bodies, as they might know of small local trusts. Colleges could have funds available for students in financial difficulties – both Access Funds (*see above*) and hardship schemes – so always consult the college authorities.

Banks, Building Societies, Credit Cards and Taxation

Statistics indicate that people are more likely to change their marriage partner than their bank, so it's not surprising that banks and building societies compete fiercely for the attentions of new students. In most cases it heralds the start of a long and profitable relationship. The initial offer of a free wad of fivers or an electronic gadget might seem attractive, but banks are often more concerned about the salary cheques you'll be depositing in your account when you graduate, and the interest rate and account charges they can land you with thereafter. NUS has a close relationship with the market leader in student accounts, the National Westminster Bank.

Choosing a bank account can be confusing when you're faced with claims and counter-claims from well-known high street names that seem to be offering a very similar product. However, there *are* some crucial differences between the banks and, whichever one you choose, it's the way you use the account that really matters. There are few ways of telling how a bank (or a branch manager) will treat you until you actually open an account, but there are a number of factors to consider that will help you to decide which bank to park your pennies with:
- Are there any branches in or near your college? If so, how many?
- What policy does the bank have on student advice?
- Is interest paid on the current account? If so, how much?
- How easy is it to get an overdraft?
- What rates of interest are charged on overdrafts? If so, at what levels?
- What will happen to your account and how you are treated when you graduate?

"As a rector of the University of St Andrews, I know how tough on students the introduction of student loans has been. The system is wrong in principle, and it encourages students to go into well-paid jobs rather than into the caring professions, where the monetary rewards are not as high. Students should continue to lobby against the scheme."

Nicholas Parsons Television personality (Engineering, Glasgow University, mid 1940s).

- Will they clobber you with bank charges and fees as soon as you finish your course?
- Do they offer preferential rates for graduate loans?

To open a student account, you'll need to prove that you're a full-time student by offering to pay in your first grant cheque, or showing a letter from your local education authority confirming that your tuition fees are being paid. There are incentives for all full-time students to open an account for the first time, although if you've already got an account, it's worth asking for the freebies when you pay in your first grant cheque.

Once you've opened your account, there are a number of things you can do to make sure that your money works for you or, if you've got an overdraft, at least that your bank manager doesn't work against you:

1) At the first opportunity, arrange a meeting with your bank manager, to introduce yourself. It gives you the chance to show that you're serious about looking after your account. Inform him or her of your plans to go into merchant banking or stockbroking when you finish your course.

2) Many banks and building societies have branches on or near campus. So, if your account is at home, transfer it. This will save you a lot of time (and money).

3) If you become overdrawn, or need an extension on your existing overdraft, contact your branch as soon as possible. Either write or, better still, phone and arrange a meeting with your bank manager. You'll appear more convincing if you turn up in person. Never run up an overdraft without being given the go-ahead beforehand

.4) If your bank or building society promises you free banking (within a certain overdraft limit), make sure the pledge is honoured. The staff often forget your student status and charge you. If they do, phone them up or go and see them and complain. They should refund any erroneous charges.

5) If you need an overdraft facility, always be prepared to bargain. Managers might be well aware of your current lack of funds, but they are also wide awake to your future earning potential.

6) Banks and building societies are not in the business of giving money away: they're out to make profits. So when the bank manager who likes to say 'yes' advances you the cash for a weekend for two in Albania, consider his or her ulterior motives.

Building societies & savings accounts

Most major building societies now offer current accounts with cheque books, guarantee cards, cashpoint cards and everything else you would expect from a bank. They also pay high rates of interest, but unfortunately have only a limited overdraft facility. People who rarely need to borrow money could consider these types of account.

One of the problems of managing money as a student is that there are times when you'll be relatively well off (because your grant cheque or parental contribution has arrived) and others when you'll find yourself penniless (the end of term). One way to overcome this cash-flow problem (and earn a little extra into the bargain) is to keep everything, except two weeks' spending money, in a deposit account, and transfer money to your current account only when you need it. If you also apply for your top-up loan at the start of term and keep it in a high-interest account, you'll find that you can earn yourself extra interest, without lifting a finger.

As a student, you're unlikely to be paying tax (*see below* **Taxation**). But most savings accounts deduct tax on the interest at source, and this is non-recoverable. The only place that doesn't is National Savings, run through the Post Office, which pays its interest gross. The Investment Account, which requires one month's notice to withdraw money, pays one of the highest rates of interest for a minimum investment of £5 and is tax-free. For building society accounts you will need to state how much interest you earned when you fill in your tax return.

Credit cards

Credit cards should be treated with care. The obvious temptation is to splash out and wait for the bill (and accompanying heart attack) at the end of the month. But credit cards do have advantages. If you're waiting for a lump-sum payment, such as your grant cheque or parental contribution, you can use a card to survive in the meantime.

There are also many disadvantages. Paying only the minimum amount every month, you will incur hefty interest charges – at time of writing, nearly 30 per cent a year (Annual Percentage Rate or APR). And, in addition to this, some banks have introduced an annual charge for their card (between £8 and £12); the rest of the banks are likely to follow suit.

Taxation

The cast of 'The Young Ones' may never have been seen procrastinating over P38s, P45s and P50s, or trying to tell their NICs from their PAYEs, but you will have to fill in a tax form sometime during your time in college.

The student grant, and now top-up loans, are not taxable. What's more, you don't have to pay income tax on any earnings from part-time and vacation work if your income is less than the single person's allowance. For the tax year 1990/91 the allowance was £3,005. If your earnings exceed the allowance, you are taxed at the basic rate of income tax (at time of writing, 25 pence in the pound).

If you think that your earnings in one tax year are going to be less than the single person's allowance, declare this by getting a P38(S) from your local tax office or your employer, and filling it in before you start work. You will then be sent a tax return to complete. This enables you to avoid Pay As You Earn (PAYE) Taxation, and you should be paid without tax being deducted.

If you know that you are going to earn more than your personal allowance, you can either opt to pay by PAYE or complete a P38(S) and pay tax on earnings above the pesonal allowance when you have completed a tax return. The leafet IR34 tells you more about the PAYE system.

If you're returning to education from full-time employment, you can claim any rebate available with the P50 form. If you have any queries, contact your local tax office or tax enquiry centre (listed in the phone book), or phone the Inland Revenue Enquiry Service (071 438 6622).

You will have to pay tax on building society savings accounts. The only savings accounts which you don't have to pay tax on are the Post Office National Savings accounts. If you open a savings account with a building society or bank, ask how much tax you will have to pay on your savings.

Further Reading

Grants for Students (DES booklet, free).
The Student Money Guide by Andrew Moore and Graham Roberts (William Curtis, £4.95).

Useful Addresses

Adult Education Bursaries c/o Ruskin College, Oxford OX1 2HE (0865 54331).
Department of Education and Science (DES) Publications Despatch Centre, Honeypot Lane, Canons Park, Stanmore, Middlesex HA7 IAZ (081 952 2366).
National Union of Students (NUS) Nelson Mandela House, 461 Holloway Road, London N7 6LJ (071 272 8900).
Scottish Education Department Gyleview House, 3 Redheughs Rigg, South Gyle, Edinburgh EH12 9HH (031 244 5869/5870).
Student Loans Company 100 Bothwell Street, Glasgow G2 7JD (0345 300900).
Teacher Supply and Training Branch Room 4/18, Department of Education and Science, Elizabeth House, York Road, London SEl 7PH (071 934 9000).

Choosing Accommodation 96

College Accommodation 97

Other Types of College Accommodation 106

Private Rented Accommodation 107

Tenancy Agreements 109

Tenants' Rights 112

Other Types of Accommodation 112

Useful Addresses 115

accom

modation

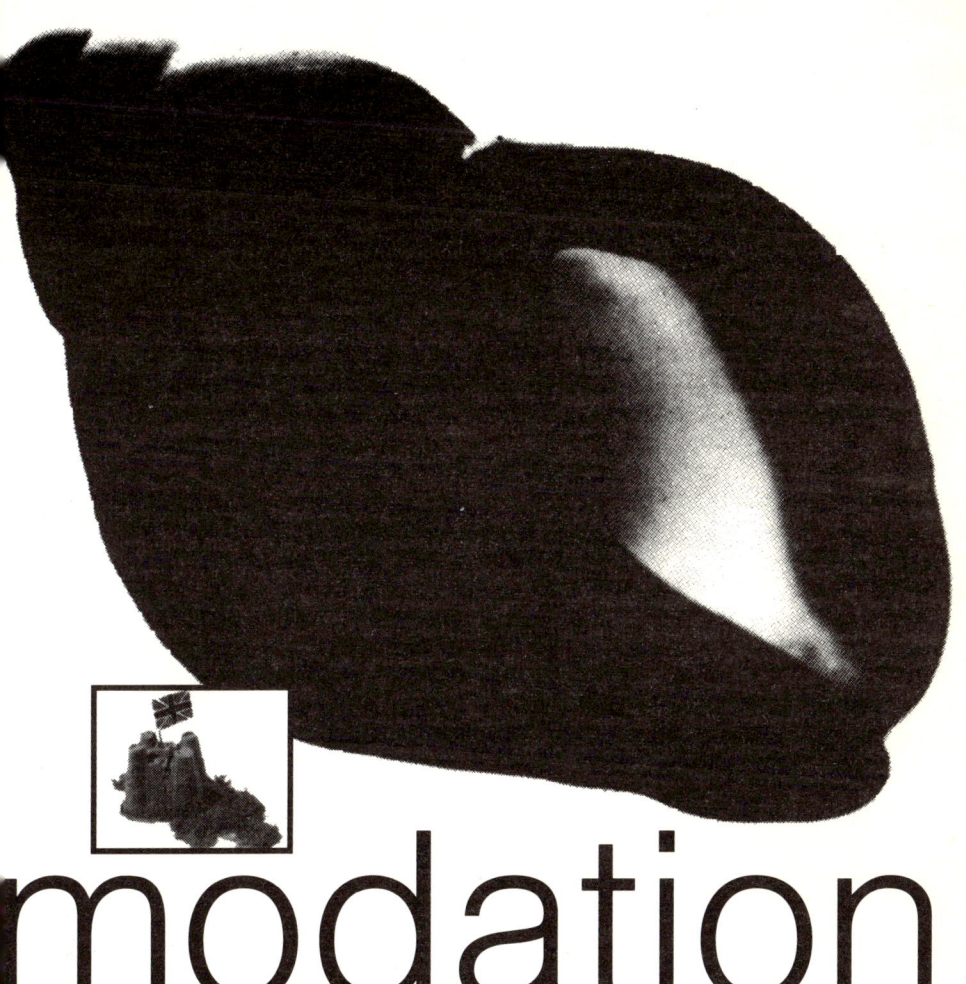

An Englishman's home is his castle, but try telling that to a student. **Tim Dawson** looks at the best ways of finding (and hopefully keeping) a roof above your head.

Wherever you go to college, you need a place to live. And wherever you live, the cost is likely to be between one and two thirds of your entire income, which is a good reason to take housing seriously.

Student housing problems are as old as this country's oldest universities. The first halls of residence were built in the early years of Oxford University in an attempt to contain the unruly behaviour of students. Today's problems are rather different. Many students have difficulty finding somewhere to live. Some colleges seem to think that it's satisfactory to put first-year students in sports halls and seaside holiday camps. In the private sector, some students face harassment from landlords; and high rents, and the poverty they cause, can drive some people to leave their courses.

Some student housing problems can only be solved by government and college authorities. Student unions have been running campaigns for decent, affordable housing provision, with some success, for years. Finding accommodation can be one of the greatest problems facing students, but it is possible to avoid the worst housing nightmares by thinking carefully about what you want, and planning how to get it. The golden rules are: seek advice when you are unsure, and deal with problems as soon as they arise.

This chapter explains the process by which most students are given rooms in college accommodation, and suggests what you can do if you are unable to find living space there. Each type of accommodation is evaluated, with all the information you are likely to need about your legal position and the ways in which different kinds of accommodation are organized and administered. At the end of the chapter are some useful addresses and phone numbers from which you will be able to get more help, should you need it.

Choosing Accommodation

Where you live as a student could well determine whether you get the most out of college. It is an opportunity to sample living with people who share your outlooks and interests, to live with close friends, and to stay in places you'd never otherwise have experienced. Living in accommodation you dislike will make you miserable, and could affect your academic performance.

The type of housing in which you will live as a student, and the sort of housing problems you will face, will be determined by where you choose to study. Some colleges (mainly campus universities) provide halls of residence for almost all their students, while others have no accommodation whatsoever, leaving students to rely on privately rented places. The price and availability of private rented accommodation varies dramatically from place to place, as does the rate of poll tax you'll be expected to pay. Students have to pay 20 per cent of the poll tax where they study. College authorities automatically register all students living in halls of residence, and are required by law to supply the local poll tax office with the names and addresses of all students enrolled on full-time courses. *See also page 116* **Basic Living**.

Most subjects of study are available at several colleges. Even if you find yourself looking for places through Clearing, there are often choices. Check the accommodation that is available, as well as the structure of the course, the recreational facilities and whatever else you are looking for (*see page 2* **How to Apply**).

Be honest with yourself. Finding a room in London, for instance, can take up a lot of time. Your rent might cost over half of your grant. On the other hand, being cosseted in halls can be suffocating, not to mention the strain of living

Accommodation

with hundreds of people you might not have much in common with.

The first guide to the type of accommodation that is available at a college should be the prospectus. This will tell you how many halls there are, how much they cost, and what the availability of private rented accommodation is. If you have the opportunity to visit a college before you make up your mind, ask about accommodation and visit it if you can. The college will paint a favourable picture of what is available, so bear this in mind.

You can also ask for information from the student union. Many produce alternative prospectuses, which should give you a better idea of what accommodation is available. Student union handbooks, usually produced for the start of each academic year, will give you a student's perspective of what it is like. Student unions also often produce more general packs on the housing situation and house-hunting in the area. You can write for information by addressing a letter to the student union at the college address. Always enclose a stamped addressed envelope (*see also page 2* **How to Apply**).

Students are no longer entitled to Housing Benefit, except in a few special cases (*see page 72* **Money**). The cost of your accommodation, therefore, directly determines the amount of money that you have left for other things. Already, applications to colleges in low-rent areas have increased. In addition to its offensive advert in *Viz* claiming to be the place where 'the men are men and the women are wild', Teeside Polytechnic in Middlesbrough has started advertising itself as the college with the cheapest private sector accommodation in the UK. When considering which colleges to apply to, and thinking about the sort of accommodation in which you might live, try working out how much rent you are likely to have to pay, and how much of your grant this will leave you with.

College Accommodation

The number of students studying at colleges in England, Scotland and Wales has risen considerably in recent years, in line with government plans to substantially increase the number of students in higher education by the year 2000. However, in the rush to get bums on seats in lecture theatres, colleges have not, so far, provided much new accommodation to cope with the influx of extra students. Building halls of residence and student flats requires capital expenditure which, in the current financial climate, most colleges cannot afford. Add to this the fact that more students are choosing college accommodation in preference to the high rents of the private sector, and the demands being placed upon colleges to provide accommodation are beginning to strain administrations' finances.

In September 1990, first-year students arriving at Lancashire Poly were put up in a Pontins holiday camp until they were found more permanent accommodation. Students at Staffordshire Poly were temporarily accommodated in a makeshift hall of residence in the college sports hall, while Leeds and Nottingham Universities have had to provide caravans for new students to stay in temporarily since September 1989. While these extreme situations are the exception rather than the norm, colleges are having increasing problems providing accommodation for their students. And that means that the better you know how to play the system, the easier it will be for you to get a place in college accommodation.

Average Rents Paid by Students

Below are the results of a survey of the weekly rent paid by students in private rented accommodation, carried out by NUS in January 1990. Prices will have increased since then, but probably by no more than the rate of inflation.
*only a selection of London boroughs is given

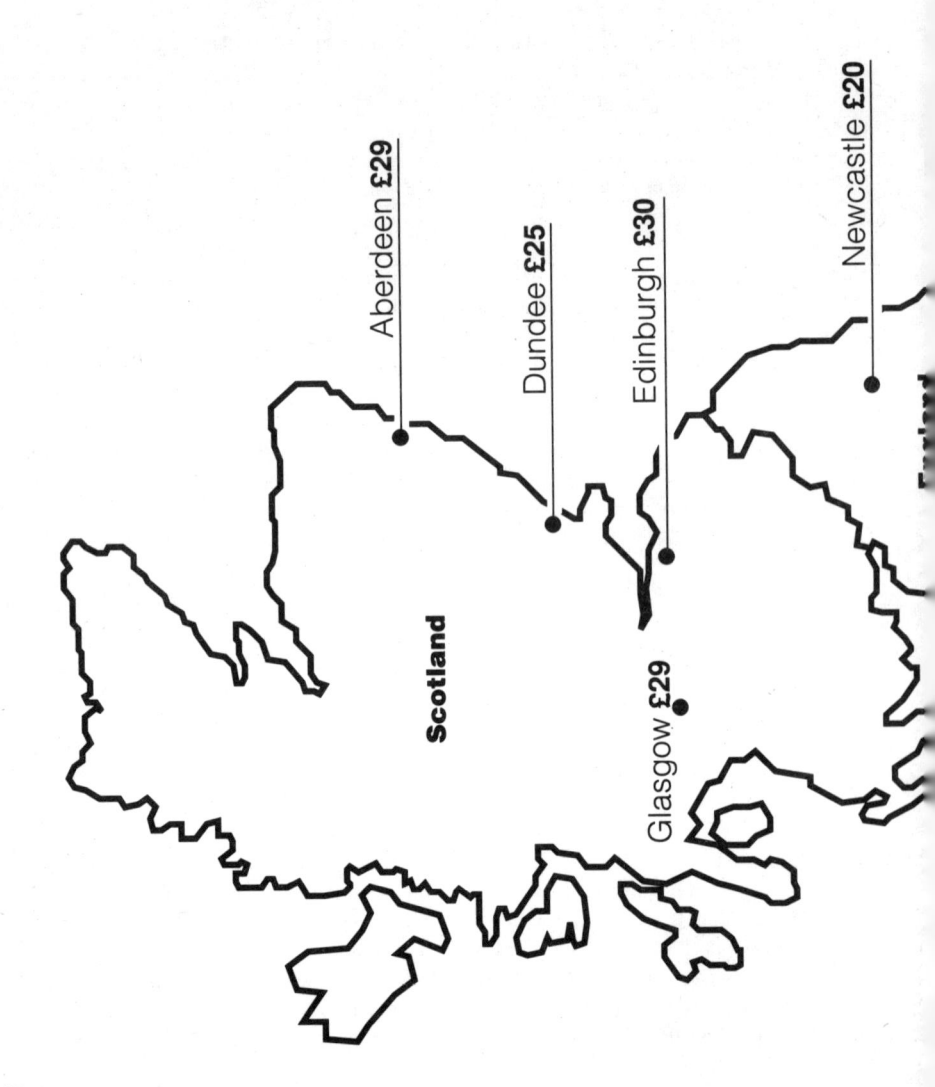

- Aberdeen £29
- Dundee £25
- Edinburgh £30
- Newcastle £20
- Glasgow £29

Scotland

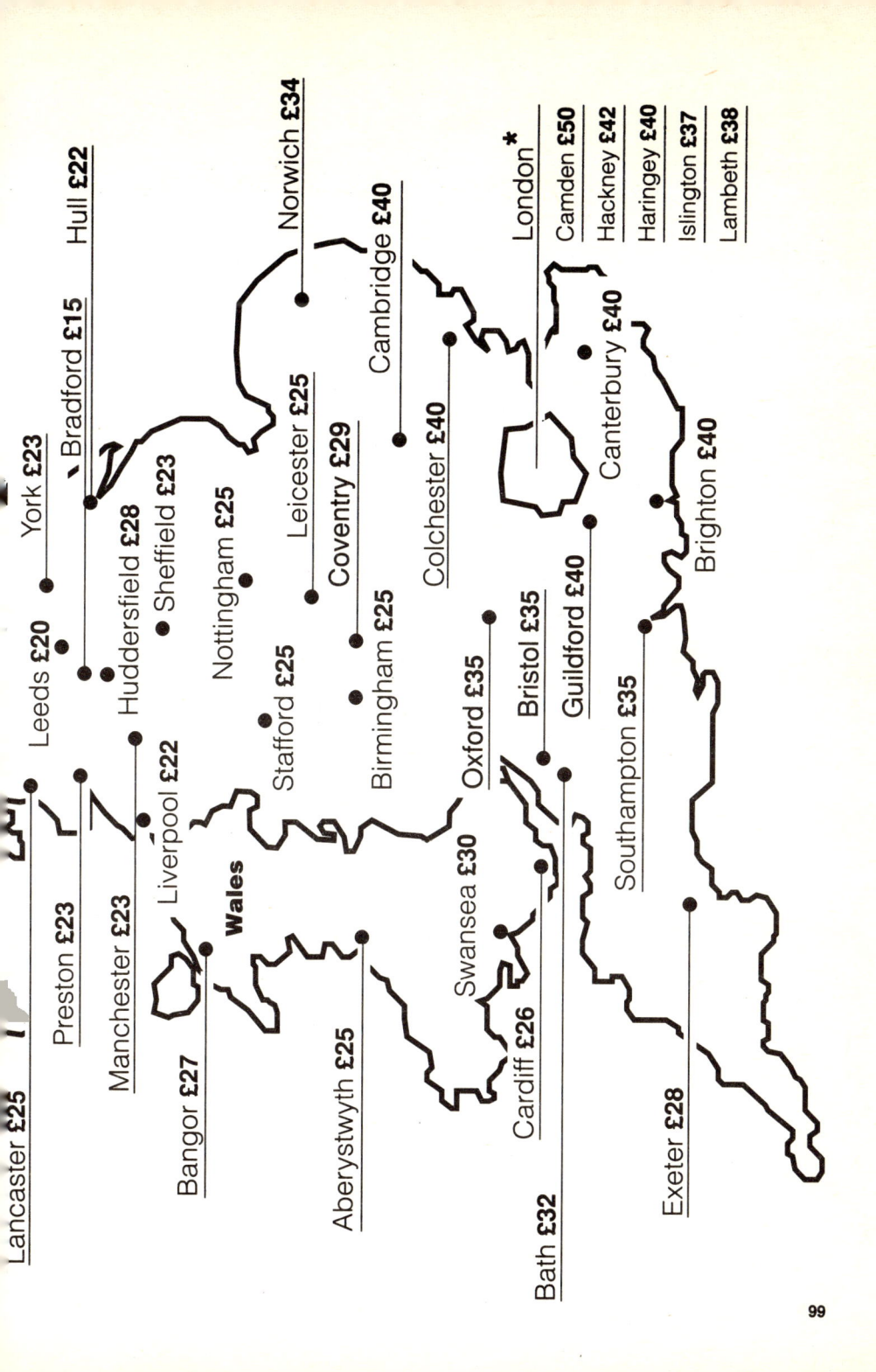

- Lancaster £25
- Preston £23
- Manchester £23
- Bangor £27
- Aberystwyth £25
- Cardiff £26
- Bath £32
- Exeter £28
- Liverpool £22
- Leeds £20
- York £23
- Hull £22
- Bradford £15
- Huddersfield £28
- Sheffield £23
- Nottingham £25
- Stafford £25
- Birmingham £25
- Swansea £30
- Oxford £35
- Bristol £35
- Southampton £35
- Leicester £25
- Coventry £29
- Cambridge £40
- Norwich £34
- Colchester £40
- Guildford £40
- Canterbury £40
- Brighton £40
- London *
- Camden £50
- Hackney £42
- Haringey £40
- Islington £37
- Lambeth £38
- Wales

College accommodation offices

College accommodation offices are responsible for placing students in halls of residence and for helping those students who don't get a place in hall (or don't want a place) to find private rented accommodation. Normally, you will be sent details of what accommodation is available when you accept a place on a course. If you are not contacted by your college's accommodation office, phone them immediately. If you cannot get through to them by using the college's main switchboard (colleges are frequently impossible to get through to on the phone just after A level and Highers results have come out), check with directory enquiries whether there is a direct line to the accommodation office, and if that doesn't work, write to them.

If your college can't provide you with a place in hall, staff should be able to put you in contact with landlords offering rooms for students. Some of the better-organized colleges, with little or no housing of their own, act as clearing houses for local landlords and will be able to find you a room directly. At the very least, your accommodation office should be able to put you in contact with accommodation agencies of good repute. Check with the student union to see if they can provide any help with housing – they sometimes have more up-to-date lists than accommodation offices.

In most cases, if your college is able to find you somewhere, it is sensible to accept it. Even if your college is only able to offer a room you don't like very much, or lodgings some way from where you will study, this will at least give you a base from which to search for something else. Colleges do sometimes suggest quite unsuitable types of accommodation, and one or two halls of residence are pretty undesirable. But most of the time, accommodation offered or recommended by colleges will be of a decent standard.

Halls of residence

Around 40 per cent of all students live in halls of residence. Halls of residence range in size from those with less than 100 students living in rooms in the same building, to those such as Pollock Halls at Edinburgh University which house nearly 2,000 students in a number of different blocks spread across campus. Surroundings and environment also vary: some are arranged in leafy quadrants, while others are tower blocks beside motorway intersections. Most fall somewhere in between and provide communal living facilities in purpose-built blocks of single-person study bedrooms, mostly for first-year students.

Meals are provided in many halls. Others are self-catering, with kitchen facilities on each floor or in each block. The better self-catering halls are divided into separate flats, each with its own kitchen. Nearly all halls have communal facilities which are likely to include a bar, a launderette, a TV room, a library and sports facilities, such as tennis and squash courts.

Halls provide simple, inexpensive accommodation, despite the occasional horror story. Crumbling blocks, with the heating turned off in the middle of February, have usually only been

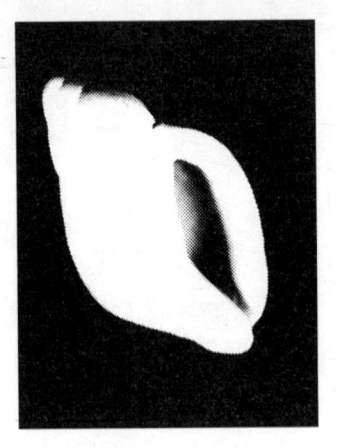

Accommodation

experienced by a friend of somebody's sister's boyfriend. They are rare indeed.

Promise of a room: Universities tend to have more halls than do polytechnics, and campus colleges have more halls than do colleges based in city centres. It is common for university and campus colleges with halls to guarantee accommodation to all first-year students. They consequently expect second years to live elsewhere, but they do offer some third years rooms. Liverpool University, for example, promises that 'the closest that you will come to sleeping rough will be dozing during lectures'. Others don't give such bold undertakings, and certainly not to students who have arrived through the UCCA/PCAS Clearing systems. Bristol Polyt-echnic, for example, has college accommodation for only ten per cent of its students. Polytechnics in London have particularly limited accommodation. Thames Poly claims to be the only poly in London which guarantees its first-year students a place to live.

Offers of hall rooms usually go out when you accept the offer of a place, in the summer before starting college. Check carefully when looking through prospectuses which halls are being promised to first-year students. If you are not offered a place in hall, find out from the college's accommodation office what the local private rental accommodation situation is.

If you have special needs – for example, if you have a partner with whom you wish to continue living, or you have children, or you are disabled – check even more carefully. Few colleges provide accommodation for students who are not young, single and able-bodied. Some make exaggerated claims about the accommodation they provide for people with special needs.

Living in hall

Halls vary enormously, although many of them now are made up of single rooms with shared kitchens and comprise entirely self-catering accommodation. You will be expected to pay your rent at the beginning of each term. At the very least, your rent will cover heating, lighting, hot water, cleaning of common areas, laundering your bedclothes and vacuuming around your room once a week. It used to be that most halls were either for men or for women, but single-sex halls are slowly disappearing. The character of single-sex halls is markedly different to that of mixed ones – men-only halls, particularly, have a reputation for being rowdy.

Rooms: In most halls of residence, the first thing that strikes you is the design, décor and size of the rooms. The furniture is stark and unimaginatively practical; the beds are small, uncomfortable and designed to promote celibacy; the décor is clinically institutional; and the rooms are tiny. There won't be much in your room to object to – because there won't be much in your room at all. There will probably be a bed, a desk, an armchair and a wardrobe. If you're lucky, there will be a washbasin and, along the corridor, a communal kitchen with a small fridge, an oven ring and a locker to keep your food in. You'll probably only be using the communal kitchen to rustle up beans on toast when you miss the evening meal or when you get up too late for breakfast in the hall canteen. You probably won't be able to afford to buy your own food when you're already paying for meals in your hall fees.

Washing and cleaning: There will be a wash-basin in most hall rooms, but you'll have to share bath and shower facilities. This can cause problems if everyone wants a shower at the same time – the cleanest people in halls are often the ones who get up first in the morning – or if the bathroom is on the ground floor and your room is on the second floor.

There can be other embarrassing moments. It's invaluable having your room cleaned every week, but only if you can remember which day of the week the cleaners come round. They will normally call mid-morning and will have a key to your room. So unless you put a note on your door asking not to be disturbed, they will enter unannounced. Even if you're still in bed, it won't bother them – they will just vacuum around you.

Sharing a room: Double rooms are still a feature of some halls, although few students like them. Sharing a room with someone you have never met before, and towards whom you have no romantic inclinations, can be a strain. You will need to be sympathetic to each other's needs and warn each other in advance of situations that are likely to cause tension: for example, when you've got friends coming round, when you're going to get leglessly drunk, or when you've got an exam for which you've got to spend the next week revising. If you don't work out any ground rules (and stick to them), it might not be long before you can't stand each other. People do move out of hall during the term, so if you put yourself on a waiting list you might be able to move into a vacated single room.

Food: Many halls include some catering in the rent. Some operate systems of meal tokens, while self-catering halls might have 'pay as you eat' canteens. Depending on your finances, you could find it a great luxury to have all your meals cooked for you, or, alternatively, an expensive and unhealthy bind. One advantage of paying for some or all of your meals in your rent is that it guarantees that you will still be fed at the end of term, when your money might have run out. However, in most halls, meals are served only at set times. So if you keep missing meals, it might be cheaper to live in a self-catering hall.

One or two halls, particularly at Oxbridge colleges and the more traditional, all-male halls, still have weekly formal dinners. Everyone is expected to wear gowns, and there is a top table of senior academics. However, most hall meals are far more informal. Where formal dinners are still held in less formal halls, they are usually only held once a term and, even then, they are no more than an excuse for dressing up and getting drunk.

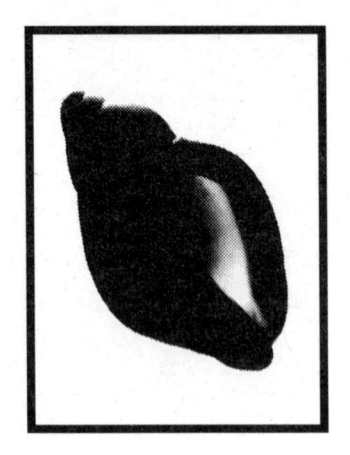

Accommodation

The rules: The legal terms under which you occupy a hall of residence room are unique to accommodation owned by educational establishments. You will be asked to sign a 'licence to occupy' agreement. Although this gives you few rights in law, most colleges are benevolent landlords. If you do think that you are being harassed, or not being provided with the level of services that you believe you are entitled to; or if you are told to leave the halls at some time other than that specified in your original agreement, there is plenty that you can do about it. The sections on wardens and hall committees *below* explain the avenues open to you in such circumstances.

When you pick up your hall keys, you will probably be given a set of rules stating what you can and cannot do. These can seem Draconian at first glance. They might prohibit anyone else from staying overnight in your room; the playing of musical equipment after 10pm; or even a gathering of more than three people. Such rules are rarely enforced with an iron fist. Most colleges tolerate occasional friends staying (with prior notification), and some couples manage to live in a single study bedroom. There are one or two places, however, where boyfriends and girlfriends are forced to clamber up drainpipes and to flee by leaping from windows.

After a few weeks you'll know which rules are important enough to break. Usually, anything that causes inconvenience to other people – loud music and parties – will be objected to most. And that's what people dislike most about living in halls – the lack of personal freedom: you want to play your music whenever you feel like it at whatever volume you want, but you don't want other people to play their favourite records at full volume when you want to sleep or write an essay. When you want to be alone, everyone comes round to see you. And when you want to see other people, they don't want to see you.

Most people are able to reconcile their differences and find that they are able to enjoy the many benefits of hall life. However, others find hall life unbearable and spend their time thinking of ways to move out. Most halls have procedures that enable people to move out before the end of the year. You will probably have to pay a 'severance fee' – which could be as much as £150 – to compensate the hall for the loss of hall fees. Alternatively, there might be someone who is desperate to move in to the hall where you are living (because they have friends there or because it's cheaper, for example). You might be able to arrange a swap with them, and avoid paying a severance fee.

If the hall is so bad that you want to get out, the chances are that there will be other people who feel the same way. Rather than trying your luck living with a bunch of strangers in student ghettoland, you could be better off getting together with other hall malcontents and looking for a shared house to rent.

Vacations: In most colleges, hall residents are offered the option of staying on during the Christmas and Easter vacations. Usually, you pay hall fees to cover the term-time weeks and then, if you want to stay for any additional days or weeks, you arrange to pay extra. Many first-year students who wish to return to their parental home during vacations opt for term-time lets only. This saves a good deal of money. You might be asked to clear your room during the vacations, as halls are often rented out for conferences during the vacation, but storage space should be available within the hall, so you won't have to cart your belongings home. Check that your course doesn't require you to come in during vacations to do project work or other necessary tasks.

Wardens: A system of wardens or resident tutors in halls is common, although precise systems and names vary from college to college. Wardens live in halls, oversee the administration and generally keep an eye on things. Most are helpful and can be very useful people to know, although, of course, there are a few tyrants. If you find yourself in difficulties of whatever sort, wardens can often point you in the right direction to find help. Wardens tend to be academic staff and have their own separate living quarters. Tutors tend to be post-graduates and live in hall rooms just like anyone else. They will be responsible for the 'welfare' of residents in a particular block or floor and should be the first people to talk to if you have any problems.

Hall committees: Some halls have committees of students who perform the function of a mini student union for that hall. They might organize social programmes, particularly if the hall is a distance from the main site. They also maintain day-to-day contact with the college officers administering the halls. If they are well supported, such committees can make a real difference to living in halls. Some have negotiated rent rebates when heating has been turned off, others have made sure that the catering service provided sufficient vegetarian food. The hall committee at Westfield Hall at Warwick University recently campaigned successfully for a minibus service to be set up between the hall and the university campus. Fifers Lane Hall committee at the University of East Anglia has achieved substantial improvements in the quality of the catering and sports facilities.

If you need to complain: Colleges usually have accessible administrative structures for halls of residence. If you have reasonable cause for complaint about your room, you should be able to get something done about it. As an individual, your first port of call is likely to be your nearest warden or resident tutor. If they can't help there will probably be a joint college and student union committee overseeing the administration of halls, which you can go to. In all cases, if you don't know where to turn, there will be someone at your student union (usually the welfare officer) who should be able to help.

Rents in halls: Hall rents are set each year by college committees. Students, elected though the student union, are represented on the committees which set the rents at most colleges in Britain. This means that each year, if the college wants to increase the rent, it must negotiate. Arguments usually rage about what should be included in the accommodation budget, and where extra money can be drawn from. Well-organized and supported student unions are often able to protect students from the worst rent rises.

A final tactic in rent negotiations is the rent strike, where everybody withholds their rent until the college backs down, or so the theory goes. Some have been highly effective, while

Accommodation

others have ended in a shambles. First-year students arrived at Bristol University in October 1990 to find that hall fees had been increased by 24 per cent on the previous year's. At £1,794, the fees took up 80 per cent of the full student grant and were the highest in the country. In the summer, the student union had taken an advert out in the *Independent* warning prospective students that they probably wouldn't be able to afford to study at Bristol University. It also wrote to all school heads around the country asking them to warn their pupils of the financial pitfalls of applying to Bristol. The University authorities failed to respond and students living in hall voted overwhelmingly, in a ballot, in favour of a rent strike. About £420,000, which would have been paid to the University in hall fees, was collected in a fund. A list of demands was drawn up which, only when met, would the money in the strike fund be paid to the University. In December, the University, faced with a deficit rumoured to be running at several million pounds, backed down and agreed to a number of the strikers' demands. Although rents would only be reduced if the University deficit was wiped out at the end of the year, future increases over the next five years were agreed to be no more than the rate of inflation; the date for setting future rent increases was brought forward to allow more time for consultation with students; and the University agreed to change its prospectus to reflect the true cost of living in hall. Fines imposed for non-payment of fees were waived and applications to the college access funds, denied to those students taking part in the rent strike, were finally accepted. Hall residents were happy with the result and voted by a large majority to end the rent strike.

Comparison of different halls around the country

(information based on academic year 1991-92)

Badock Hall, Bristol University
Mixed hall with 431 rooms, nearly all single, just over half with washbasins. Divided into 10 units. Communal bathroom and basic cooking facilities on every floor (12 people per floor). Breakfast and evening meals Mon-Fri, all meals at weekends. Bar, TV room, snooker room, library, launderette, tennis and squash courts. Car park. Distance from University: 2½ miles. Fee: £1,614 for 33 weeks.

Pollock Halls, Edinburgh University
Mixed hall with 1,794 students, nearly all in single rooms. Full board (breakfast and evening meal daily) or self-catering (for second, third or fourth years). Shop, sports hall, library, computer room. Distance from University: 15 minutes' walk. Fees: £41.30 per week full board single room; £24.60 per week self-catering single room.

Owens Park, Manchester University
Mixed halls (3/2 male/female ratio) with 1,000 single rooms, all with washbasins. Communal bathroom and small kitchen for every 10-12 people. Common room in each building (every 40-50 people). Breakfast and evening meals Mon-Fri; weekend meals available, cash only. Bar, library, launderette; next to university athletic grounds. Distance from University: 1½ miles. Fees: £1,316 for 33 weeks, plus four weeks Christmas vacation without meals.

Woodville, Sheffield Poly
Mixed hall with 173 single rooms, all with washbasins. Communal bathroom and basic cooking facilities for every 15 people. Breakfast and evening meals daily, lunch at weekends. Bar and social club. Sporting and social facilities on campus. Situated on campus. Fee: £1,660 per year.

Thomas Spencer Hall, Thames Poly
Mixed hall with 255 single rooms, all with washbasins. Communal bathroom and kitchen facilities. Breakfast and evening meals Mon-Fri. TV room, bar, launderette, squash courts. Situated on Woolwich site. Fee: £52 per week.

> "On a recent visit to Edinburgh University with my seventeen year-old daughter, I was amazed at how magnificent the halls of residence were – like Crest Hotels, with people cleaning all over the place. When I was at Trinity College Dublin, I was farmed out to digs in some district called Cabra, miles away from my best friend, where I shared a room with a stuffy girl who's now permanent under-secretary at the DTI, I think. Our beds were so close together you couldn't get a toothbrush between them.
> Mr and Mrs Gambol...

Other Types of College Accommodation

Although the hall of residence is the main type – often the only type – of student accommodation provided by colleges, some colleges do provide other forms of housing.

A small, but increasing number of colleges offer married and family accommodation. However, waiting lists for these rooms are long, so check availability before assuming that you will be able to get one. The colleges who have the best record of providing college accommodation to all their students are most likely to make special provision for married couples and students with children. Leeds University, for example, runs its own housing scheme where terraced houses owned by the University are leased out to families.

Other colleges set aside accommodation for particular groups of students. Sinclair House at Bristol University, for example, has ten self-catering flats solely for use by overseas students and 12 flats for second and third years. Linton House at Manchester University has 19 double rooms for married couples and five family rooms in which a baby or small child can be accommodated. Priority is given to postgraduate overseas students.

In addition to the lists of landlords and reputable accommodation agencies kept by college accommodation offices, some will also keep lists of local people who are willing to take in lodgers. Teeside Polytechnic recently tried to encourage lecturers and college staff to take in lodgers in an attempt to supplement its list of landlords.

Other colleges own 'student houses' which are essentially old houses converted into individual study bedrooms. The rent is likely to be lower than in a hall of residence, but you will not have the facilities of a hall available to you. Some colleges also have arrangements to house students in accommodation shared with other organizations. Thames Polytechnic, for example, has an arrangement with six local hospitals, including one mental health hospital, where students share accommodation facilities with nurses.

Private Rented Accommodation

The majority of students live in privately rented accommodation – such as flats, bedsits and shared houses – at some stage during their time at college. The quality of student accommodation in the private sector varies dramatically. Some students manage to secure fantastic flats for tiny rents, others are charged the earth for rooms that are small, damp and unclean. A few cities have plentiful, inexpensive private rented accommodation, for example, in shared terraced houses in Leeds. In other places, rented accommodation is either incredibly expensive or almost impossible to find, or both. Students in Oxford have experienced particular problems finding decent, affordable accommodation.

Until recently, the availability of Housing Benefit to students meant that landlords could get away with charging high rents because students were able to claim back a large proportion of their rent. However, with the withdrawal of entitlement to claim Housing Benefit from the vast majority of students, rents which were artificially high, but affordable, are now unrealistically high and many students find it difficult paying the sort of prices landlords are asking. Furthermore, just before the recent slump in property prices, a lot of landlords took advantage of high house prices and sold off

...charged £3.10s. a week rent, we had to be back at 5.30 each evening for a fry-up, and we got full-board on Sunday (yet more fry-ups). They were arch Protestants who only took us in because we weren't Catholic. Mrs. Gambol once said that if a viper landed on her face when she was walking in front of a Catholic church she wouldn't brush it off, lest someone think she were making a sign of the cross."
Sue Arnold *Observer* columnist (English Literature, Trinity College, Dublin, 1963-66).

many of their properties. Students are now competing to rent a declining number of properties at higher and higher rents, in a housing market virtually free from regulation following the 1988 Housing Act.

The cost of where you live will also vary considerably according to where you study. London is fantastically expensive; the south of England is generally dear, while northern England is reasonably cheap. However, generalizations can be misleading. You might think that rents in Hull and Aberdeen would be broadly similar. But, whereas Hull is one of the cheapest cities in the UK, the influx of oil workers to Aberdeen often pushes rents up to levels similar to those in Bristol or even London. *See* **Table: Average Rents Paid by Students**.

Finding a flat

Ideally, you should sort out private rented accommodation before you start at college and, in most cases, this is possible. If it isn't, at least be sure that you have a floor on which you can camp out for a week or two, until you organize something more permanent.

Some colleges – Leicester Poly and Sheffield Poly, for example – operate 'find-a-home' schemes, whereby first-year students who haven't been allocated college accommodation can come for a couple of weeks before the start of term to look for private rented accommodation. The students are put up in college accommodation and are given advice on how to find a flat, along with lists of local landlords and accommodation offices. Even if your college doesn't run such a scheme, it's worth phoning the accommodation office and asking if you can stay in college accommodation before the start of term while you look for a flat.

Plan ahead if you have to visit landlords before they will offer you a room. You are more likely to get a room if you are smartly dressed and polite. Plan your travelling carefully, and buy a street map to be sure that you know where you are going. You might have to visit some landlords in the evening. Phonecards are more convenient than a stack of ten pence pieces. Carry your cheque book and card with you, so that if you are offered a dream flat, you can sign up for it there and then.

Be prepared to be flexible. You might be offered a room by yourself, or a whole house, dependent on your finding three friends to live with you. If at any time you find yourself down to your last few pounds and have nowhere to stay, go to your student union welfare officer. He or she will refer you to the appropriate emergency agency.

Where to look: Accommodation offices will have lists of landlords and housing agencies, as will your student union. Properties are advertised in newsagents' windows and on notice-boards in the student union. Many flats and houses will be advertised in the classified columns in local newspapers. These tend to go very quickly, so find out at what time the first edition of the paper is published and get down to the paper's offices and pick it up before it hits the news-stands. Some estate agents also deal in rented property, though the rents charged tend to be quite high. If you see a flat advertised which takes your fancy, act quickly. Most landlords operate on 'first come, first served' basis.

Accommodation agencies make their money by charging a fee of up to two weeks' rent for finding you somewhere to live. However, it is against the law for them to charge for lists of flats or rooms. They can only charge you if you accept a property. Bear in mind that it is in their

Accommodation

interests to persuade landlords to charge the highest possible rent – agencies also charge the landlord a percentage of the rent. Your college accommodation office or student union will be able to recommend reputable agencies.

Word of mouth is an important way of finding accommodation. As quickly as new students are arriving, others are moving on. Most people stay in the same accommodation for no longer than a year and move to a new place during the summer or move away completely at the end of their course. Second and third years are the best people to talk to. Even if they can't let you have their place, they might know someone else who will. Similarly, a lot of landlords only let properties to students. So although they might have already let a property by the time you ring up, they could have others which they have not yet advertised. The earlier you start asking around, the higher the chance you will have of securing a choice bargain.

Rent

The level of rent, frequency of payment and means of paying (standing order, regular cheque or personal collection) should be made clear before you move in. If you pay your rent weekly, you are entitled to a proper rent book containing the name and address of the landlord or agent. If you pay your rent monthly, it is worth buying and keeping a rent book yourself (available from most large stationers), both to note down your own finances and to have a record in case of a dispute. Most landlords prefer termly payments so they can bank the cash.

Deposits

You will usually have to pay a deposit, and a month's rent in advance. Deposits are to cover any breakages and damages which you cause while you are in the property. It is important for both you and the landlord to agree a detailed list of everything that is in the flat and the condition that it is in. For example, if the internal paintwork is not up to much, make sure that he has confirmed this, and that it is down in writing. Some people go as far as taking photographs of the property when they move in.

Keep the receipt for the deposit and make sure that you retrieve it when you leave. The landlord can't deduct anything for normal wear and tear to the property, only for actual damage. You might also have to pay deposits to the gas, electricity and telephone companies, *see also page 116* **Basic Living**.

You are unlikely to be offered unfurnished accommodation, but check this. Find out who you will be sharing facilities with. Bedsits usually have shared bathrooms and kitchens. If your fellow residents are unbearably dirty, or unbearably clean, you might find living there difficult.

Tenancy Agreements

Renting any type of accommodation means entering into a legal relationship with the landlord. It is always best that the agreement between you and the landlord is in writing, in the form of a contract. But even if it is not, you are still protected by law. Many people are confused by the jargon and terms used in contracts. If you are offered a contract, and are at all unsure about the terminology used, get someone experienced to read it over for you before you sign it. Staff at your college accommodation office, or your student union welfare officer, should be willing to help.

The following applies only to England and Wales. The law is different in Scotland.

Assured tenancies

An assured tenancy lasts indefinitely. If you have an assured tenancy, your rent cannot be

Harriet Harman Shadow Health Minister (Politics, York University, 1968-71).

"I spent my first year in campus accommodation. My room overlooked the pathway to the Goodrick Gorilla Grill. I spent a lot of time looking out of the window at people having a better time than me and wondering why I wasn't going to the Goodrick Gorilla Grill too.
My second year was spent in a bedsit where it was impossible to keep warm without having two tons of blankets on the bed and a paraffin heater on. I was suprised I wasn't flattened to death by the blankets, burned to death by the heater or frozen to death by the cold.
It's important to live off-campus if you're at a campus-based college, although being in the House of Commons is a bit like being back on campus."

Accommodation

increased during the first twelve months that the tenancy exists. After a year the landlord can increase the rent. If you think that your rent is excessive compared to the average 'market level' (private sector rents) in your area, you can apply to the local rent assessment committee (listed under the council in the phone directory). If the committee determines that the rent you pay is 'excessive when compared to comparable local rents', it can instruct the landlord to reduce your rent to the going rate. Subsequently, the rent can't be increased for a further twelve months.

Reasons for eviction are divided into those which are mandatory and can't be contested, and those which are discretionary and can be challenged in court:
- **Mandatory grounds**: The landlord wants the accommodation back for personal use (two months' notice required); the landlord has defaulted on the mortgage and the building society wants to empty the property in order to sell it (two months' notice required); and the tenant has accumulated over three months' rent arrears (two weeks' notice required).
- **Discretionary grounds**: Deterioration of the home due to the tenant's negligence (two weeks' notice required); the furniture has deteriorated, and there is persistent delay in paying the rent (two weeks' notice required).

Assured shorthold tenancies

An assured shorthold tenancy is similar to an assured tenancy, except that it is for a fixed term (usually six months or a year), set at the time of your moving in. An assured shorthold must be in writing, as the tenancy agreement in itself gives tenants notice of when they must leave the property. It is the most common form of tenancy agreement, and you have the same rights in respect of rent as you do with an assured tenancy. A shorthold tenancy can only be terminated early on the same grounds as an assured tenancy, but landlords are also entitled to give tenants two months' notice to quit for no other reason than that they require possession of the property.

Licences

Licences are a device used by landlords to try and avoid the basic protection that the law affords tenants (with the exception of the type of agreement that you are likely to be offered if you live in a hall of residence, which is also called a licence). Put simply, tenancy confers on you the right to exclusively occupy a property. By contrast, a licence merely gives permission to be in the property. Licences are a controversial area in law, and in a number of cases students have successfully sued landlords who have issued them with licence agreements. To date, the courts have upheld that licences can't be used to limit statutory rights, and whether a licence has been signed or not, a tenancy is created with all the rights of a shorthold tenancy.

Don't sign a licence agreement if you can avoid it. However, if it's all that you can get, bear in mind that you probably have more rights than the licence agreement sets out. If you do have difficulties, seek advice from the college accommodation office, student union welfare office or Citizens' Advice Bureau (consult the telephone directory for your nearest branch).

Holiday lets

This type of let is aimed at tourists and gives you no protection whatsoever. You're entitled to rent the property for the purpose of holidaying in it. You can be evicted immediately after the agreement is up. Avoid at all costs.

Company lets
Though rare at the moment, this type of agreement is becoming more common among students. A company is the tenant. The people occupying the property pay rent to the company who is renting it, but do not have the rights of tenant. Some college authorities are using this type of agreement to make accommodation available to students.

Protected tenancies
If you started paying rent before 15 January 1988 (date of the latest Housing Act), you have considerably greater rights than otherwise. For example, you can have your rent fixed by the council's fair rents officer (tenancies taken up after 15 January 1988 are not covered by 'fair rent' legislation). This is likely to be considerably lower than free market rents.

Tenants' Rights
This section is based on the law in England and Wales. If you are the 'residential occupier' of a property, you can't be evicted without being given a 'notice to quit'. After that, a court must grant a possession order. If the court does this, the tenant will usually be given some time – perhaps a month – to leave. Only then can a landlord obtain a bailiff's warrant and have the tenant evicted. The conditions that must be satisfied before a court grants the order necessary to evict a tenant vary.

Some landlords try unscrupulous methods to evict tenants. If you unexpectedly receive a notice to quit, or any other obvious and unwanted attempt to remove you, seek advice immediately. Your student union welfare office should be able to help.

The law also protects tenants from harassment. It is an offence for a landlord to commit acts 'likely to interfere with the peace or comfort of the residential occupier or his household', or for the landlord to 'persistently withdraw or withhold services reasonably required for the occupation of the premises as a resident'. The 1988 Housing Act entitles tenants to compensation for illegal eviction – you can claim part of the profit your landlord gained by forcing you to leave. *See also page 244* **Rights.**

Most accommodation offices and advice centres try not to deal with any landlords who have a reputation for racism. However, if you do experience discrimination from landlords, contact your council's tenant-relations officer. Make sure that the people who referred you to the landlord know about the difficulties you have had. *See also page 236* **Black Students**.

Other Types of Accommodation
Council housing
Less than 5,000 students live in council houses nationally. However, if you can get in to property of this sort, it is usually very cheap. Councils operate waiting lists for their property. Points are awarded to people on the waiting list for things such as their current accommodation's overcrowding or disrepair, their ill health and so on. Whether someone is rehoused will depend on how many points they accumulate. Priority is given to families and people with children or to those over retirement age. It is unlikely that students without special needs will get to the top of a waiting list. However, councils have an obligation to put you on their list if you request it. Councils in London and in Scotland have to register you. Most other councils will normally only consider you if you have lived in the borough for more than a year. When students are offered council property it is

usually flats which other people are reluctant to live in, such as flats on the top floor of sixteen-storey tower blocks.

Your local town hall will be able to give advice on what is, and is not, available. Your student union will also know about any special schemes run by the council to house young people and people with special needs, such as disabled people.

Housing associations and co-ops

Housing associations aim to provide cheap housing, usually for specific groups of people who have housing problems, such as the elderly. A few housing associations do provide accommodation for single people, but most will have very long waiting lists. In one or two cities there are housing associations which were specifically set up to provide accommodation for students and other single homeless people. At Aston University, for example, there is a housing association, established by the student union, which houses 140 students just five minutes' walk from the teaching buildings. These, however, are exceptions – only about 3,000 students nationally live in housing association property. Most housing associations have waiting lists almost as long as those for council housing. Your college accommodation office or student union will know if there are any in your area it is worth putting your name down for.

A housing co-op is a group of people who manage and/or own property themselves. Properties range from those in which the occupants started squatting, and subsequently reached an agreement with the owners of the property, to more genteel, co-operatively owned premises. Co-op waiting lists are likely to be long, and most places are filled by word of mouth. Some people manage to find accommodation with them by getting involved in their meetings and helping with the properties they control.

Lodgings

A lodging is a room in someone else's household. It is common for some or all of your meals to be provided. Many students find the restrictions that this type of accommodation places upon them unacceptable, although it used to be one of the most common types of student accommodation. Some colleges with chronic accommodation problems have been trying to find more people who will take in a student, and to persuade students to live in lodgings. So don't be too surprised if your college suggests it.

If you are considering lodgings, make sure that you will get on with the people already living there. It is also important to establish from the start what the rules are and what you are actually paying for.

Lodgings are usually more expensive than other private rented accommodation, because the price includes bills and some food. You also have no protection against eviction if you are living with your landlord or their family.

Squatting

The abolition of housing benefit for students and the rise in housing shortages has made squatting an attractive option. Squatting is legal, but breaking and entering and criminal damage are not. The Advisory Service for Squatters (*see below* **Useful Addresses**) is the best place to start if you decide to squat, and it publishes a helpful introduction to squatting, *The Squatters' Handbook*. Squatting is illegal in Scotland.

It is advisable not to squat privately owned property, as the landlord is likely to hire bailiffs to throw you out. Council or government owned property is the best. When entering, choose daylight hours (so it doesn't look like you intend to steal), make as little noise as possible and try not to cause any criminal damage. If anyone questions you, tell them that you wish to squat and are doing nothing wrong.

Your first priority must be to connect padlocks and locks to the doors and windows and to place a notice on the front of the door saying that you intend to squat the premises until legally evicted. The London Electricity Board is obliged to provide you with electricity if you have identification and proof of a previous address. Visit your local LEB showroom. Water can usually be turned on from the mains or from the street.

The law on squatting is complicated. You cannot be removed without a Court Order of Possession, and you will be sent a court summons and an affidavit well in advance.

Squatting is not necessarily as cheap as it might appear. Depending on the condition of the house, it can get quite pricey. You will have to pay to get gas, electricity and water reconnected and if the place was easy to break into, you will have to spend a lot of cash on making sure that no-one else can break in. *See page 116* **Basic Living** for more information on getting gas and electricity connected.

Hostels

Hostels can provide useful short-term accommodation, especially in London. There are over 150 hostels in London, some providing night shelter accommodation, others short-term lodging (up to 28 days), and several which provide long-term accommodation. Some colleges have arrangements with hostels to provide places for students. For example, the YMCA in Portsmouth sets aside 68 places during term-time for students from Portsmouth Polytechnic.

College accommodation offices, student union welfare offices and local council housing departments will be able to give more details of hostels near your college.

Parental home

A large number of students choose to continue living with their parents for some or all of the time that they are at college. This is particularly common in Scotland.

The advantages are numerous. You can probably live more cheaply with your parents. Often it is easier to find a warm, quiet place to work than it might be in independent accommodation. It is possible to continue with your 'home' social life, mixing with your old school friends. And, in many households, meals are provided and the washing is done for you.

However, there are also plenty of disadvantages. You will receive approximately 35 per cent less grant. It is likely that you will have to spend more time travelling to and from college, since for most people even the college nearest to where they live is some distance away. Students who do choose to live at home frequently complain that it is difficult to get involved with college social life, since so much of it goes on after the last bus has gone, or at weekends.

In most cases, it all boils down to whether you can stand the idea of another three or four years with your parents, living within whatever restrictions that imposes, and being teased about your mother's apron strings; and whether you see living away from your parents, perhaps in a strange city, as an integral part of your (life) studies.

Accommodation

Buying a home
Few students can afford to buy their own home. Even if three or four join together, it is rare that their joint income is sufficient to secure a mortgage. Some people do manage it, and some financial institutions now put packages together for students.

It's more common for a student's parents to act as guarantors for a mortgage. This has certain tax advantages, and if the property market is buoyant, it is possible to make a capital gain when the property is sold at the end of the course. Taking in tenants in larger properties helps to reduce mortgage bills. If you are considering this option, bear in mind that you are likely to become landlord to your friends. It isn't easy dealing with someone who consistently pays their rent late.

National mobility and tenants' exchange scheme
This is a voluntary scheme agreed by most of the public housing agencies in the UK, to allow people who are already living in rented accommodation, or who are high on council waiting lists, to move around the country. To apply you must have a pressing need to move (some housing authorities accept a college course as pressing). For further details of this scheme, see the leaflet 'National Mobility Scheme', available from Citizens' Advice Bureaux (consult the telephone directory for your nearest branch). It is also possible for local authority tenants and housing association tenants to arrange a direct swap with someone from another area.

Useful Addresses
Advisory Service for Squatters 2 St Paul's Road, London N1 (071 359 8814). Advice on all aspects of squatting. Send for the excellent *The Squatters' Handbook* (60p plus postage).
SHAC 189A Old Brompton Road, London SW5 (071 373 7276). A voluntary organization giving free telephone advice on homelessness and private tenancies.
Shelter 88 Old Street, London EC1V 9HU (071 253 0202). A charity for homeless people. It has a number of useful publications and will put you in touch with a relevant local organization.

Home Improvement **118**	Shopping **130**
Living with other People **123**	Budgeting and Bills **132**
Food and Cooking **125**	Transport and Travel **140**
Cleaning **128**	Security **141**
Pets **128**	Insurance **144**
TV and Video Hire **128**	Further Reading **145**
Breakdowns **128**	Useful Addresses **145**

living basic

Being a student is not just about finding the right lecture hall at the right time. You'll also have to find somewhere to live and someone to live with. You'll need to decorate your home, keep it and yourself secure, struggle with rotas and recipes, and buy a seemingly endless amount of goods with a wholly inadequate grant. Gavin Hamilton **and** Hilary Hutcheon **describe how.**

Coping with coursework, essay deadlines and a new environment can be stressful enough, without having to worry about where your next meal is coming from, what your next bank statement is going to reveal and who's going to sort out the three-figure phone bill. If you're living away from home for the first time, getting to grips with matters domestic can be all the more problematic.

In this chapter, we give practical advice on how to cope with life outside the lecture theatre, and where to buy essential items (all prices are correct at time of writing).

Home Improvement

You can't do much to improve a room in a hall of residence. But a few posters, plants and rugs could at least hide the old Blu Tack and lager stains, and give the room character.

In lodgings and other rented accommodation, you usually have some degree of contact with the landlord, and any attempt to change your room will be subject to close scrutiny. You will be lucky if your landlord shares your taste in interior décor. How much you can change a place depends on how much money and time you can spare. Before you paint the walls black, rip up the floor and install a sauna, make sure the landlord won't object, or be prepared to do a lot of negotiating – and repainting – when you move out.

Doing it yourself

Your landlord might welcome the chance of some cheap redecoration, and might even pay for paint. But make sure you know what you're taking on: it's no fun living in a half-finished room because you didn't realize how long it would take to strip a wall.

When decorating, start at the top and work down. If the ceiling is stained, coat it with paint. If the existing paint is sound, all you need to do is wash it and let it dry thoroughly, before painting with a roller. Cracks should be filled flush with the surface; stains should be treated with the appropriate primer or sealer. Put old sheets or newspapers over the floor, or you could find magnolia splattered on the carpet.

Walls are more problematic, especially if they're wallpapered. If the landlord agrees, and if the walls are in a good enough state, you can paint over wallpaper. If the landlord doesn't agree, the paper must be stripped off, any holes or cracks filled and sanded down, and paint or new wallpaper applied. Painted walls can simply be washed down and painted over. Use pale colours to make small rooms look lighter and larger.

If you can't (or don't want to) make too many changes to your room or flat, cover the offending patterns with posters or pictures. Use Blu Tack on painted walls and drawing-pins on wallpaper. If you're hanging heavy pictures or large mirrors, and there's no picture rail, you need a drill, a few wall plugs and matching screws to drill a hole in the wall properly. Make sure you have the landlord's approval before you start.

If you can't live with the carpet, you must bargain with the landlord. Bare boards look couth but are cold, draughty and noisy. Paint floorboards if they are too decrepit to stain, and put down cheap rugs or carpet offcuts. Covering the original carpet with rugs and cushions is a warmer option.

Beg, borrow or steal old curtains from home, visit house clearances, or check the small ads in your local paper. If you can lay your hands on a second-hand sewing machine, then so much the better: you can create your own linen and curtains from cheap fabric remnants. Cheap slatted blinds made of cane or wood are sold at home furnishings stores such as Reject Shop and Habitat.

Basic Living

Painting Kit

Rollers Essential if you're painting a large area. Foam rollers are the cheapest, but are difficult to use and don't last very long. Synthetic pile, sheepskin or lambswool rollers are fairly cheap and easier to use. Do not apply gloss with rollers. A roller (with tray) will cost about £5.

Brushes The main sizes used for woodwork are 25mm/1in, 38mm/12in and 50mm/2in. You need a 100mm/4in brush for walls and ceilings. Brushes have either natural bristles or nylon filaments. The best brushes have more bristles. Check for loose bristles before buying or using one. Don't pay more than £5 for a medium-sized brush.

Paint Emulsion (used for walls and ceilings) is water-based, so you can clean your brushes or rollers in water. Glosses (for woodwork and metalwork) are normally oil-based, and brushes and rollers must be cleaned with white spirit or a brush cleaner. Trade paints are generally cheaper, but can only be bought in large sizes (5 litres/1.1 gallon minimum) and don't cover well. Don't pay more than £7 for 2.5 litres/about half a gallon of white emulsion; colour emulsion and gloss are slightly more expensive (don't pay more than £9 for 2.5 litres).

Sandpaper For sanding down woodwork.

White spirit or brush cleaner For cleaning gloss paint off brushes.

Old sheets or newspapers To cover the floor.

Rubber gloves and old clothes No matter how careful you are, you'll always drip *some* paint.

Furnished accommodation should have all the basics; if anything is lacking before you move in, ask the landlord to agree in writing to provide it before you sign the contract (*see* page 94 **Accommodation**). Second-hand furniture can be bought cheaply from junk or charity shops. Find out about auctions, which are often advertised in local newspapers. Large chain stores such as MFI sell cheap home-assembly furniture. All you need is a screwdriver and a lot of patience.

If you can't stand the heat...

Draught-proofing and insulation save on heating bills. Tack or tape polythene over the windows to create home-made double glazing; stick foam insulation tape around the doorways and fit draught excluders at the base of the doors, or lay 'sausage' cushions against them. There should be 10cm/4in of insulation in the loft; if it's not insulated properly, ask the landlord to apply for a grant to have it done. Check that the hot water tank is properly lagged; insulation should be at least 7.5cm/3in thick.

Your landlord should provide some means of heating the flat. Central heating is economical and effective, but, as it's the most expensive system to install, many landlords provide other forms of heating. If you have central heating, use the timer – leaving it on all day is very expensive. Fixed wall gas heaters, gas radiant or convector heaters and solid fuel room heaters are the next most economical. Electric storage heaters are economical if run on Economy 7 (*see below* **Budgeting and Bills: Electricity**). If your flat doesn't have any heating, bottled gas heaters are the cheapest portable heaters. Electric bar and fan heaters heat a room quickly, but are expensive (*see* **Table: Relative Costs of Heating Systems**).

Blocked loos This is usually caused by a blocked trap, and you can buy or hire special WC plungers to deal with the problem. Alternatively, use a mop with a polythene bag tied over the head. Bail out most of the water and plunge repeatedly. A gurgling sound will announce that the trap is cleared – flush the loo several times. Now wash your hands.

Burst water pipes If an indoor water pipe bursts, there's not much you can do other than turning the water off at the mains (usually outside the front door) or the indoor stopcock before phoning the landlord or plumber. Uninsulated pipes in the loft (leading from the water tank) are likely to crack in the winter – cover them in blankets, and during particularly cold spells open the trap door leading to the loft or storage area.

Iced fridges and freezers Defrost a fridge or freezer every couple of months, preferably before you can no longer close the door. Eat the food or store it in another freezer: it can be dangerous to let it defrost and then refreeze. Put cloths around and beneath the fridge or freezer to catch thawing ice and water, then turn the appliance off. You can speed the process up by placing a bowl of hot water inside. Don't mess around with boiling kettles and hairdryers, as it could be dangerous.

Plugs When you're wiring a plug, the earth wire is always yellow and green, live is always brown and blue is always neutral (*see* **diagram**). If in doubt, blue goes on the left, brown on the right. With wire pre-dating 1970, red is live, green is earth and black is neutral.
If a fuse in a plug blows, unscrew it and slot in a new one. Use 3-amp fuses for equipment rated at less than 750 watts, and 13-amp fuses for equipment rated at above 750 watts.

Blocked pipes First check that only one pipe is affected. If more than one is blocked, the problem is in the soil pipe or a drain. This is a job for the landlord. If only one is affected, check the trap – the device attached to the outlet pipe (*see* **diagram**).
In winter the water in the trap can freeze. Thaw gently with a hairdrier or rags soaked in hot water. If ice is not the problem, the trap could be blocked with waste (hair, tea leaves, congealed grease and so on). Press a plunger down over the plug-hole and pump quickly about a dozen times. Pull it off to break the seal, then have another go until the sink empties. If this doesn't work, put a bucket under the sink, remove the trap or open the access plug, and use a piece of wire to clear the pipes. If this still doesn't work, seek help.

Basic Living

Re-wiring a plug

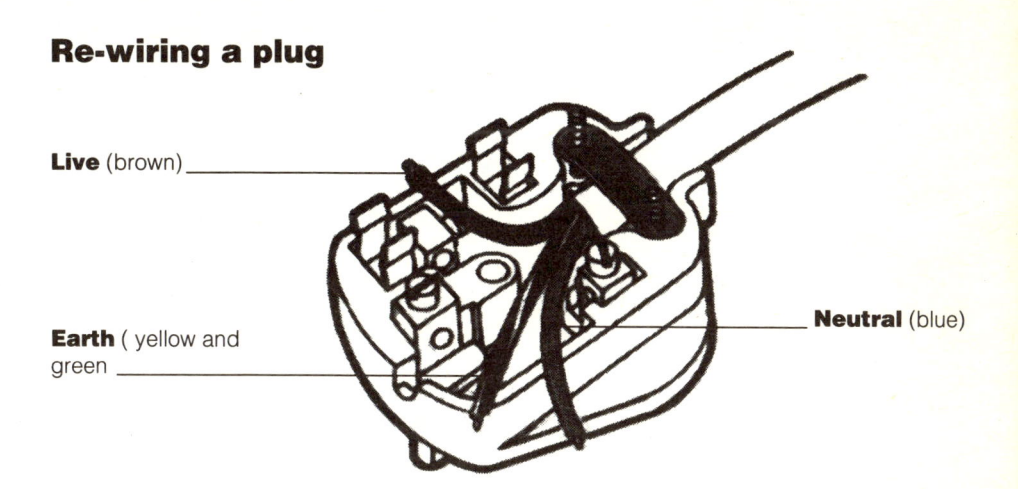

Live (brown)

Earth (yellow and green)

Neutral (blue)

Unblocking a sink

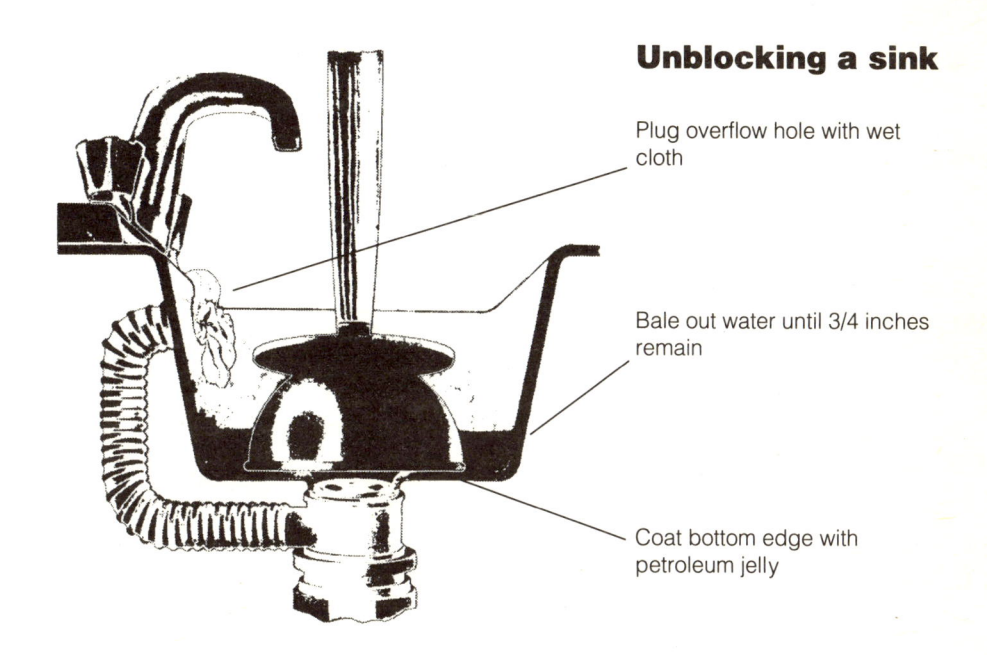

Plug overflow hole with wet cloth

Bale out water until 3/4 inches remain

Coat bottom edge with petroleum jelly

121

Intelligence service.

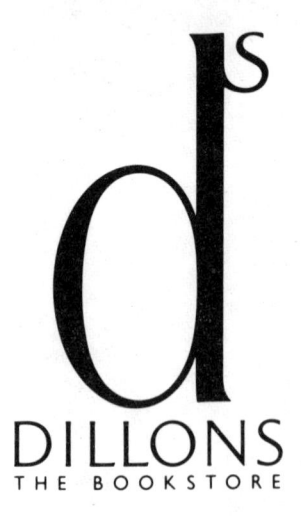

d's

DILLONS
THE BOOKSTORE

We've got every subject fully covered, so you'll find no shortage of information, both academic and general in Dillons Bookstores. And the service, you'll find continues until late on weekdays in almost all of our stores.

Europe's finest bookstore is at 82 Gower Street, London WC1.
Telephone 071 636 1577.

―――――― Dillons Bookstore Group ――――――

Dillons Bookstores are in Aberdeen, Belfast, Birmingham, Cambridge, Cardiff, Coventry, Exeter, Leicester, Liverpool, Manchester, Newcastle, Nottingham, Oxford, Southampton and stores nationwide.

Basic Living

Relative Costs of Heating Systems

Running costs for one kilowatt hour of space heating, based on average efficiencies for modern equipment.*

Electricity

Fan heater/bar fire	6.21p
Storage heater (Economy 7)	2.75p

Gas

Wall heater	1.89p
Radiant/convector heater	2.09p
Central heating radiator (conventional boiler)	1.94p
Central heating radiator (condensing boiler)	1.60p

LPG (bottled gas)

Butane room heater	5.54p
Central heating radiator (conventional boiler)	3.36p
Central heating radiator (condensing boiler)	2.76p

Solid fuel

Central heating radiator	2.31p
Open fire	4.02p
Room heater (Sunbrite)	2.30p

*Source: *Which?*, September 1989.

Living with other People
Flatmates

Most people never regret sharing a flat with other students at college. For some though, it can be a nightmare. It's not necessarily when flatmates dismantle their 500cc motorbike on the kitchen table as you're preparing dinner, or when they register you for the poll tax, that they drive you barmy. Usually it's the little oversights – not passing on telephone messages, not putting records back in the right sleeves, not cleaning out the bath – that make for the difference between domestic harmony and all-out war. Most people are blissfully unaware of their bad habits, so a polite complaint usually suffices to smooth out the problem.

Choose your flatmates with care. If the reason you want to live with someone is either because you think they're really cool, or you feel sorry for them because they've got nowhere else to live, or even because you want them to scivvy for you, forget it.

Honesty and tolerance are usually all it takes to ensure harmony. You need to be tolerant of your flatmates' needs but you also need to be honest enough to know when tolerance ends and irritation with, and resentment towards, your flatmates starts. If something really gets on your nerves, don't bottle all your feelings up inside you – voice your irritation.

Rotas

There's no better way to fall out with your friends than by arguing over domestic duties. What frustrates people most about sharing a flat is having to shop, cook, wash-up and clean for people who won't do their fair share of the communal chores.

"My student days? How the hell would I know? They were three totally lost years discovering how terribly good I was at drinking, how very useless I was at loving, and how very uninterested I was in studying. I probably had a very nice time, but I'm certainly not sure. Ask someone else who was there.
Somehow I did get a degree in English; my knowledge of the Elizabethan novel has stood me in tremendous stead over the years, although I've yet to find any single benefit from a whole obligatory year of Anglo-Saxon."

Chris Tarrant TV personality and DJ (English, Birmingham University, 1964-67).

If you try to do everything separately, you end up squabbling about the tasks that require co-operation (cleaning the cooker, scrubbing the floor) or about who buys the items that everybody uses (milk, loo roll). You'll have to co-operate on some things. A rota, detailing everyone's turns to shop, cook, clean or wash-up, is the best way to avoid friction. Rotas only work if they are fair, realistic, agreed to by everyone concerned and, above all, adhered to by everyone. *See* **Table: Examples of Different Rotas**.

Examples of Different Rotas
Everything: Sharing responsibility for shopping, cooking, cleaning and washing-up. This rarely works; and only exists in flats where there is someone who sees it as their God-given right to enforce the rota.
Cooking and washing-up: One person cooks an evening meal and someone else washes up afterwards. It only works if people are on hand to do their bit; and it places constraints on people to be home at meal times.
Shopping for everything: Doing a fortnightly supermarket shop for everything. This will only work if you all enjoy the same type of food and if everyone spends equal time in the flat.
Shopping for basics: Doing one big supermarket shop at the beginning of term for basics (toilet rolls, soap, toothpaste, tea, coffee, sugar, and so on). If you buy enough to last the whole term, you avoid arguments over whose turn it is to buy the loo roll.
Cleaning: As long as responsibilities are shared, cleaning rotas usually help to prevent flatmates from killing each other.

Boyfriends and girlfriends
If you move in with someone who has a steady boyfriend or girlfriend, the chances are that you will also be moving in with their partner. This

might not be a problem if you know your flatmate's partner well and get on with them.

But the nightmare scenario is this: you move in with someone who is unattached, and all is well in your shared abode. Flatmate then falls madly in love with a truly obnoxious person with many disgusting habits. The newly found love promptly moves in, and your flatmate's character is changed by passion. Your friendship with your flatmate rapidly deteriorates.

If it becomes increasingly clear that you have an extra (uninvited) flatmate who's not paying their way, say something. The worst thing you can do, as with any difference of opinion with flatmates, is to stay silent and let it stew.

Living on your own
You might prefer living alone if you're the sort of person who values privacy. If you want to be messy, you can be – no one will tell you to tidy up. You can socialize when you want to and you don't have to put up with other people's annoying habits. But it can be lonely and is likely to be more expensive than living in a shared flat.

Food and Cooking
On a diet of pie, chips, chocolate and beer, your body is likely to spend its time crying out for some decent nourishment rather than concentrating on next week's essay deadline. If you want a clear head, not to mention clear skin, you must eat well.

Fit to eat?
Fifty years ago, when people were hungry, they would reach out for a hunk of bread, a slice of cheese, or a piece of fruit. Now, their hands close on a Pot Noodle, Angel Delight or a Big Mac. A diet composed entirely of such processed, irradiated, tinned, dried, frozen, reconstituted and co-extruded food lacks vitamins and nutrients (*see also page 172* **Health and Stress**).

Increasingly, there is public concern that intensive farming has rendered once-healthy foods toxic. But despite alarming reports of salmonella in eggs and chickens, heavy metals in fish, Alar all over apples and pesticides on veg, these foods are integral to a healthy, low-fat, high-fibre diet. Even water, once prescribed by the pint to clear up a bad complexion, is gaining a reputation for being riddled with pollutants.

However, your diet would be pretty boring if you gave up all foods that have ever been the subject of a national scare. You can do a great deal to improve your health, and boost your immune system, by simply cutting down on fat, sugar and salt. Basic medical advice is that you shouldn't eat more than 80-85g/about 3oz of fat a day. Switch from butter and ordinary margarine to a low fat spread or a margarine high in polyunsaturates. Use low fat yoghurt instead of cream, and semi-skimmed or skimmed milk rather than ordinary milk. Buy cheeses containing the least fat, such as Edam and cottage cheese. When buying red meat, pick the leanest cuts you can find (and afford) and cut off any fat before cooking. Remove the skin from poultry before cooking. Eat as much white fish as you can afford, or plump for nutritious oily fish, such as herring and mackerel – they're cheaper. Grill, bake, boil, steam or microwave food; use a vegetable oil if you have to fry something.

According to the Health Education Council (*see below* **Useful Addresses**), the average Briton eats almost two pounds (about 900g) of sugar every week, in sweets, soft drinks,

THE ART OF LEARNING

A comprehensive list of titles on all aspects of the visual arts plus the complete Oxford University Press list.

Zwemmer Art Books
24 Litchfield Street
London WC2H 9NJ
Tel 071 379 7886

Zwemmer Media Arts
80 Charing Cross Road
London WC2H 0BB
Tel 071 379 7886

Zwemmer at the Courtauld Galleries
Somerset House, Strand
London WC2R 0RN
Tel 071 872 0217

Zwemmer at the Whitechapel Art Gallery
80 Whitechapel High Street
London E1 7QX
Tel 071 247 6924

Zwemmer / Oxford University Press
72 Charing Cross Road
London WC2H 0BE
Tel 071 240 1559

ZWEMMER
OXFORD UNIVERSITY PRESS
MUSIC & BOOKS

If it's notes you're after get all you need from London's leading music shop

Now open on two floors

26 Litchfield Street
London WC2H 9NJ
Tel 071 379 7886

Nearest underground station Leicester Square

Basic Living

biscuits and cakes, and in savoury foods such as soups, sauces and cheesy biscuits. Refined white sugar is entirely lacking in nutrients and adds only calories. Always check the labels on food and select the low calorie alternatives where possible. Eat healthy snacks of fresh or dried fruit, nuts, packets of corn chips or muesli. The British also put away far too much salt, almost ten times the recommended daily amount of one gram/0.035oz. Use as little salt as possible for seasoning.

You should try to eat at least 30g/1.05oz of fibre a day. Fibre is found in brown bread and rice, wholemeal pasta, potatoes, cereals and fresh fruit and vegetables. Eat fresh vegetables on the day you buy them: the fresher they are, and the less they are cooked, the more essential vitamins and nutrients they provide. Frozen vegetables are more nutritious than tired, limp greens and withered roots.

Markets and supermarkets

For cheap fresh fruit and veg you can't beat a good market. The best time to visit markets is when the stallholders are getting ready to pack up for the day and are eager to sell produce at cut price. Buy fruit and vegetables in season. Out of season, imported produce is much more expensive.

Buy tins and packets from the large supermarkets – their immense purchasing clout means they can extract good deals from manufacturers. Supermarkets are also cheap sources of booze and are often open quite late. And of course, some student union shops also sell cheap foodstuffs.

Visit your local health food shops for bulk purchases of pulses, rice, beans and dried fruit. An even cheaper alternative is to get together with like-minded eaters and visit a wholesaler – two or three people might chomp their way through a five pound bag of lentils in a term.

Meat and white fish is expensive. Save money by developing a taste for offal (liver, kidneys) and oily fish (mackerel, herring). Ask a local butcher or fishmonger to save you bones and offcuts for stews and soups.

In the kitchen

Take whatever basic cooking utensils you can beg from home; if two or more of you are sharing accommodation, you can pool resources. Junk shops are a good source of extra crockery and utensils. Take care if you acquire old cookware; it could contain cadmium or other potentially dangerous substances that can leak into your food if the dish or pan is chipped.

Basic items for an efficient, trouble-free kitchen include: a kettle; at least one saucepan and one frying pan; a tin opener, a bottle opener and a corkscrew; a sharp chopping knife and a bread knife; plates, bowls, cutlery, mugs and glasses; an ovenproof dish or bowl; a collander; a chopping board; a wooden spoon; and at least one dishcloth.

Before you start using new kitchen equipment, always read the instructions on the packet. Use a good cookery book until you're confident enough to create your own dishes (*see below* **Further Reading** for cookery books).

Getting out of the kitchen

Student union and college canteens are usually cheap, and the food on offer is also likely to be more varied than your own efforts. You're not restricted to your own college or hall – in London, for example, you can do the rounds of the student union and college canteens. All cities have cheapish eating places; art and alternative centres often provide healthy food at fairly low prices.

Cleaning

Housework cannot be avoided forever; you have to make an occasional effort. How regularly you clean is entirely up to you, but much depends on whether you clean up as you go along. The more regularly you do it, the less trouble it is.

To do it right, you need to buy a general-purpose cleaner and some bleach (for the toilet). Don't bother with air and carpet fresheners, or with fancy toilet flushes (the ones that make the water in the toilet go a funny colour). They're a waste of money and are often harmful to the environment.

The £800 million market in household cleaners is controlled by just six companies: Proctor & Gamble, Unilever, Reckitt & Colman, Colgate-Palmolive, Paterson Zochonis and SC Johnson. Consequently, there's little difference in the quality and effectiveness of each product.

Companies that make so-called environmentally friendly products claim not to use certain practices and harmful ingredients used by the established companies. However, many claims made on labels are wholly misleading. 'Environmentally friendly' is, in fact, a misnomer, as no manufactured product can have a beneficial effect on the environment. Some washing-up liquids are labelled 'phosphate-free'. In fact, no washing-up liquid on sale in the UK contains phosphates. Similarly, a 'no nitrates' label on a bathroom cleaner means nothing, since you can't buy one which contains nitrates. By law, detergents have to be at least 80 per cent biodegradable, so ignore products whose labels boast biodegradability. The *Green Consumer Guide* (*see below* **Further Reading**) recommends the Ecover range of cleaning products, sold at many supermarkets and health food shops. You should be wary of any products containing phosphates, bleaches, optical whiteners and enzymes.

Laundry

The cheapest launderettes are those in the student union or hall of residence. White fabrics should be washed separately from coloured clothes. Delicates (woollens and synthetics) need to be washed with care and at low temperatures, or by hand. If in doubt, read the label to see which temperature is suitable for the fabric. Washing programmes are listed on the side of most packets of washing powders. Most launderette machines have three programmes only. Whites should be washed at high/hot, coloureds at medium/warm and delicates at low/cool. If you're washing by hand, roll them in a towel or drip dry, but don't wring them.

Ironing is also an acquired skill – use a low heat on delicate fabrics and some synthetics. Most clothes give some indication on the label of the recommended ironing heat (*see* **Chart: Laundry Labels**). It's also a good idea to iron clothes inside out, as that will avoid crushing any delicate fabric and giving it a shiny, used look. Find out what the codes mean, or you could end up having to throw away your favourite shirt; a full list of label symbols is given in *The Home Expert* (*see below* **Further Reading**).

Pets

There's often someone in shared accommodation who has the bright idea to take in a pet cat or dog. If you are thinking of getting a pet, check that your landlord allows household fauna. Pet-owning only works if one person takes responsibility for feeding the animal and clearing up after it. The person who is in charge of the pet must also take responsibility for it when you all leave the flat. A pet is for life, not just the second year at college.

Basic Living

Laundry Labels

Washing symbol The number in the 'bucket' refers to the temperature of the water – from 95 (very hot) to 40 or 30. A hand in the 'bucket' means hand wash only. A cross in the bucket means do not wash (dry clean only).

Bleaching symbol 'Cl' in the triangle means that any household (chlorine) bleach can be used; a cross in the triangle means it cannot be used.

Ironing symbol One dot (cool) for acrylic, nylon, acetate, triacetate and polyester; two dots (warm) for polyester mixtures and wool; three dots (hot) for cotton, linen and viscose. A cross through the symbol means the item should not be ironed.

Dry cleaning symbol 'A' in the circle means that any solvent can be used; 'P' and 'F' mean that only certain solvents can be used. A cross means the item should not be dry cleaned.

Drying symbol A cross through the symbol means the item should not be tumble-dried.

Pets are expensive to keep. As well as their food, there's litter to buy, vets fees to pay, as well as miscellaneous items (flea spray, collars and leads) to invest in. Cats are a lot of trouble to look after, but dogs are even more. If you haven't got a garden, you shouldn't keep a canine friend. Dogs require a lot of attention and twice-daily exercise. Goldfish are much less trouble.

TV and Video Hire

Many video hire companies offer special packages for students. Radio Rentals reps even turn up at intro fairs to get people to sign on the dotted line. There's little variation in hire prices, but some dealers offer more in the form of back-up services and hire conditions. Expect to pay about £10 to £12 per month for a video recorder and around £18 to £20 per month for a basic TV and video package. Many companies ask for a deposit (up to three months' rental) and a guarantor and insist that you pay by standing order; all require you to take out insurance. And of course, when you hire a television (and when you buy one from a reputable shop), your name will go to the TV licensing authority.

Breakdowns

Wherever you live, things are bound to go wrong from time to time – fuses blow, pipes freeze up or get blocked, tiles fall off the roof. In rented accommodation, it is usually the landlord's responsibility to keep the premises in good repair and habitable (*see page 94* **Accommodation**). However, there are things that are easily dealt with without calling in (and paying for) outside help. A basic DIY book is invaluable (*see below* **Further Reading**).

TV & Video Rental Companies

DER A 21in colour TV and Ferguson VHS recorder system starts at £17.99 per month. One month's deposit is required plus six months' payment in advance. Insurance costs £30 per year.

Multibroadcast For £19.99 per month, you get a 22in colour TV with Teletext, a VHS recorder (various models) and a 14in portable colour TV. The 24in colour TV with long-play VHS recorder package costs £24.99 per month. Insurance is £2 per month. Students have to provide a guarantor and are required to pay by direct debit.

Radio Rentals A 21in colour TV with Baird VHS recorder costs £23.98 per month. You have to pay a three-month deposit and there is a minimum hire period of 18 months – any shorter period and the hire prices go up. Special student rates (£19.99 for the above package) are on offer at the start of the Autumn term.

Visionhire Visionhire offers a 21in colour TV with VHS recorder (various models) for £17.98 per month. A 21in colour TV with remote control and front-loading VHS recorder costs £22.98 per month. You pay one month's deposit; insurance costs £1.75 per month.

Shopping

Clothes

Second-hand clothes shops are hauling themselves up-market, selling reconditioned, high quality and, most importantly, clean clothes. Charity shops remain the best. Oxfam is particularly good, not just because there is at least one shop in every major town in the country, but also because some quality control is exercised over the clothes (only clean ones are accepted).

Jumble sales are another good place to search for bargains, although you might have to rummage through a lot of junk before you come across anything worthwhile. Look out for advertisements for jumble sales in the local paper and in shop windows. Some student unions play host to second-hand clothes dealers for a day. Prices, however, tend to be fairly high as there is a ready and willing market. Before shelling out for your 'bargain', check whether seams and stitching are intact; whether elbows, cuffs and the like are worn; and whether any stains or marks are likely to be ingrained.

If you're a dedicated follower of fashion, but find that finances won't allow designer labels into your wardrobe, don't despair. Most designer fashion shops hold end-of-season sales where the outgoing collection is sold at knock-down prices to make way for next season's gear. Combine designer items with purchases from the high street. Designers are also launching 'diffusion' ranges, such Gaultier Junior and Hamnett Active. The clothes are cheaper and aimed at a younger, less wealthy audience. If your college has a fashion course, many of the students will be selling their own designs at end-of-term fashion shows.

If you're handy with a needle, make your own clothes. If you haven't done it before, consult an expert or a fashion student before you start, and stick to easy patterns at first. Whether you're handy or not, you should invest in a basic sewing kit for day-to-day repairs (needles, black, blue and white cotton, buttons and a pair of scissors).

Books

Reading lists, given out by lecturers at the beginning of term, are intended to advise on how you should approach your studies. You aren't required to read every book on the list, let alone purchase all of them. You do, however, need to buy at least one course textbook.

Before you buy any books, seek the advice of a second- or third-year student. They can tell you which book is the most useful and might even be prepared to sell you theirs. In fact, many departments organize a day at the start of term when second and third years can sell off last year's course books. Many will try to flog you all the books that they rushed out and bought when they were first years and subsequently found to be useless.

The Net Book Agreement (NBA), which requires all booksellers to sell new books at the recommended retail price, means that there's no difference in price between small, independent shops and large chains such as Dillons and Waterstones. Dillons is campaigning with other large chains to get the NBA abolished. The service is more personal in the smaller shops and if they don't stock a book, they will order it for you. Try to support local bookshops – with the new Uniform Business Rate forcing many small businesses under, they need all the custom they can get.

A browse through the bargain basements in second-hand bookshops could unearth some unexpected delights, or you might find a newly-published hardback at half-price on display in the window.

> "Students are scruffy, weird and cry out for attention. I've been to talks with students and they take themselves too seriously. I know they're struggling for money but they should smarten up their image. I believe students should stick up for their rights, but sometimes they go over the top, what with Greenpeace and everything."
>
> **Vinny Jones** Captain of Sheffield United Football Club, has never been a student.

Best Buys

Iron Morphy Richards 42065 (£17). *Which?* Best Buy, July 1989.

Kettle Haden Clearview AJS24 (£15). *Which?* Best Buy, Dec 1990.

Reading lamp Bhs range (£7-£9). *Time Out* staff straw poll, Jan 1991.

Toaster Boots 21 (£18) or Swan 20436/7. *Which?* Best Buy, Nov 1989.

Radio cassette Panasonic RX-FT500 (£60) or Sony CFS201L (£45). *Which?* Best Buys, Dec 1990.

Household goods

Street markets should be the first (and cheapest) stop if you're looking for household essentials. For decent but reasonably priced crockery, you can't beat the Reject Shop, which has branches in most major cities.

MFI has plenty of cheap furniture and Bhs is the place for cheap reading lamps. John Lewis and Argos are the best stores for electrical goods such as kettles and toasters. Don't pay more than £10 for a reading lamp, £15 for a kettle or £18 for a toaster. If you buy a steam iron, don't spend more than £18. Basic irons can cost as little as £10.

Stationery

Student union shops are the best places to buy cheap stationery. Because most student unions buy in bulk through NUS Services (*see page 146* **Student Unions**), prices are low.

Free paper might be available from college computer departments or print rooms. Recycled paper is worth buying because the greater the demand, the cheaper it will be to produce.

Toiletries

The key to saving money on toiletries is to buy in bulk. Avoid fancy names and labels and choose the cheapest on offer. Many of the products on the market are manufactured by the companies that also dominate the household cleaner market. Mentadent P, Signal and SR toothpastes; Pears, All Clear, Timotei, Harmony, Cream Silk and Dimension haircare products; and Sure and Lynx deodorants are just some of the toiletries produced by Unilever. Supermarket brands are normally the cheapest and the difference in quality is negligible.

Consider the environment and look for the 'ozone-friendly' label. Do your bit for animal rights and avoid products that have been tested on laboratory animals. Many shops, including chains such as Tesco and Boots, stock cruelty-free products such as the range of Beauty Without Cruelty toiletries. The Body Shop's products are made from natural ingredients, are not tested on animals and are sold in biodegradable and recycled packaging. These products do cost more, but the more people buy them, the cheaper they will become.

Budgeting and Bills

Budgeting is a way of maximizing your spending power, not a way of cutting back on life's little extras. If you spend half an hour at the beginning of each term to draw up a spending plan and half an hour every month to review the state of your finances, you'll find that it is easier to set aside the cash for studying, resting *and* playing.

Basic Living

Drawing up a budget

There's no set way to budget – all we can do is provide some guide-lines on how to budget to suit your financial needs. This will depend on how many sources of income you have, when you receive your income, and how and when you pay your bills.

Start by working out what your total income for the term is going to be. If you don't intend to work during the holiday, this figure has to cover the period from the start of one term to the start of the next. For information on sources of student income, see *page 72* **Money** and *page 254* **Employment**.

Then calculate what your total expenditure on 'essentials' is going to be during this period.

Essentials:
- Accommodation (rent or hall fees);
- Food and household goods (including toiletries and cleaning materials);
- Bills (electricity, gas, phone, poll tax, water rates);
- Books, stationery and course equipment;
- Insurance;
- TV rental/licence;
- Clothes;
- Lunch at college;
- Transport to college (day-to-day and start/end of term).

Subtract your total expenditure for the term from your total income. Divide whatever you are left with by the number of weeks you're budgeting for. This is the amount you can spend each week on 'non-essentials' and everyday extras.

You might find it easier to budget if you share bills for food and household basics with your flatmates, particularly if you buy all basics at the start of term. You could even open a joint account with your flatmates to cover bills (*see below* **Bills**).

Complications begin if you don't take into account when and how you are going to receive, and spend, your income. That's why it's so important to review your budget every month to ensure you're keeping to your spending limits.

Keeping to your budget: The best way to keep to a budget is to always use the same method of payment for the same items of expenditure. Use your cheque book to pay for as many essentials as possible. Ask your bank to set your weekly cashpoint limit at the amount that you are left with after budgeting for essentials. That way, unless you go on a wild spending spree with your cheque book or credit card, your budget should work. It might be difficult for you to draw a line between essentials and non-essentials. Smokers, for example, probably count cigarettes among the former.

If things don't add up: Every time you write a cheque, make sure you fill in the stub. Keep a note of how much money you withdraw from the cashpoint each week. Many items of expenditure are fixed, such as rent, insurance and transport; others (food, clothes and bills) will vary according to your tastes and where you shop. These are the expenses you have to cut down on if you find you're overspending.

Sooner or later (probably sooner rather than later) you will have to ask your bank for an overdraft. Bank managers are aware of the erratic ways in which most students receive their income and are usually sympathetic to a request. Do not run up an overdraft without asking your bank manager first. That's when the letters demanding that you send back your cashpoint and cheque cards will arrive. If you don't have enough money to pay your bills, but have shown yourself to be in full command of your (inadequate) finances, you will be in a much stronger position when asking for an overdraft. *See also page 72* **Money**.

Eastern 6.5p per unit; £7.93 quarterly standing charge. Reconnection charge £60 (£90 for same-day service).

East Midlands 6.62p per unit; £8.40 quarterly standing charge. Reconnection charge £21.62.

London (London Electricity) 6.78p per unit; £10.27 quarterly standing charge. Reconnection charge varies according to circumstances.

Merseyside and North Wales (Manweb) 7.12p per unit; £9.85 quarterly standing charge. Reconnection charge £12.20.

Midlands (Midlands Electricity) 6.89p per unit, £7.69 quarterly standing charge. Reconnection charge £6.50; £18 if warrant required.

North Eastern 6.89p per unit; £9.94 quarterly standing charge. Reconnection charge £12.

North Western (Norweb) 6.61p per unit; £8.83 quarterly standing charge. Reconnection charge varies according to circumstances.

Southern (Seeboard) 6.62p per unit; £9.81 quarterly standing charge. Reconnection charge varies according to circumstances.

South Eastern 6.62p per unit; £9.81 quarterly standing charge. Reconnection charge £37.40.

South Wales 7.28p per unit; £10.25 quarterly standing charge. Reconnection charge £12.50; £30-£50 if warrant required.

South West (Sweb) 7.25p per unit; £10.20 quarterly standing charge. Reconnection charge £37.40.

Yorkshire 6.88p per unit; £8.60 quarterly standing charge. Reconnection charge £6.50; £15 if warrant required.

regional electricity charges

Scotland 6.24p per unit; £5.90 standing charge every two months. If landlord charges tenant for electricity supply, there can be an additional charge of 9.8p per day. Reconnection charge from £16, according to circumstances.

SKOOB

LONDON'S BEST
SECOND HAND BOOKSHOP

SKOOB BOOKS LTD
15 SICILIAN AVENUE pedestrian arcade
off SOUTHAMPTON ROW, HOLBORN,
LONDON WC1A 2QH
071 404 3063

Science Literature Humanities

SKOOB TWO
19 BURY PLACE near BRITISH MUSEUM,
BLOOMSBURY
LONDON WC1A 2JH
071 405 0030

Esoterica, Foreign Studies

10% DISCOUNT - STUDENTS & UB40'S
BOOKS BOUGHT
MON - SAT 10.30 -18.30

BOOKS

French's
THEATRE BOOKSHOP

for all plays
and books on theatre

Free mailing list to keep
you up to date with the latest
theatre literature

Free lists of theatre books

Call, write or telephone
World-wide mail order service

Open Mon-Fri, 9.30-5.30
52 Fitzroy St London W1P 6JR
Tel: 071-387 9373
Nearest tube: Warren St

BIRKENSTOCK

Made in Germany

CHOICE OF WIDTHS
FOR MEN & WOMEN

The Natural Shoe Store

325 King's Road SW3 Tel: 071-351 3721
21 Neal Street WC2 Tel: 071-836 5254 -
22 Princes Square, Glasgow

Dexter
PROUDLY MADE IN USA

BEEF ROLLS

CHOICE OF WIDTHS
FOR MEN & WOMEN

The Natural Shoe Store

325 King's Road SW3 Tel: 071-351 3721
55 Neal St, WC2 Tel: 071-497 8965
22 Princes Square, Glasgow

Basic Living

See also above **Home Improvement** for ways of keeping your heating bills down; and **Food and Cooking** for ways to economize on your food bills.

Deposit accounts

If you receive your income in one lump sum every term (ie your grant cheque or parental contribution), but pay most bills on a weekly basis, you should open a deposit account. Put your money in this account, transfer funds when necessary into your current account and you can earn some extra interest.

Bills

In a shared household, the worst thing you can do is to leave one person to pay all the bills. If that person isn't prepared to pay the bills and then get the money back from people afterwards, bills go from blue to red (final reminder) to dead (disconnection) faster than you can say 'it's not my fault – you said *you* were going to deal with it'.

You could open a joint account. Put the account in the name of the address of your flat, make everyone a signatory, but make sure that cheques need two signatories to be valid. If you each pay in a fixed amount every term to cover all eventualities, domestic bliss can be maintained. The bank might also give the account student status, saving you account and interest charges. You can also use the account to pay for supermarket trips, TV and video rental payments, and the milkman.

Don't panic if a bill seems absurdly high. Companies often make mistakes – particularly if the bill is an estimate because your meter has not been read – and you can write to the office which sent you the bill asking for a recalculation. If this fails to satisfy, or if you have any other complaint about the service you are receiving, contact OFFER, OFGAS, OFTEL or OFWAT, the official watchdogs for the electricity, gas, telecommunications and water industries respectively (*see below* **Useful Addresses** for all).

Electricity

Now that the electricity industry has been privatized, regional electricity boards have been replaced by regional electricity companies. However, consumers cannot 'shop around' for electricity – they still have to buy it from local sources. The lack of competition is likely to result in higher prices.

There's no connection charge for electricity – unless you were cut off for failing to pay a previous bill, in which case you must clear any outstanding debts. Most regional electricity companies encourage people to pay by standing order or direct debit; first-time accounts have to pay a deposit or pay by standing order.

One unit of electricity boils 12 pints of water in a kettle, toasts 70 slices of bread, allows two hours' ironing, or runs a 60 watt light bulb for 16 hours or a fridge freezer for 12 hours. Unit costs vary between different regions (*see* **Table: Regional Electricity Charges**). There are two sets of electricity charges based on units: the domestic general purpose charge per unit plus a quarterly standing charge; or Economy 7, under which you are charged a lower price per unit between midnight and 8am and a higher charge during the rest of the day, with a quarterly standing charge.

If you pay your landlord for electricity (you don't have an account in your name), your landlord cannot charge you more than the domestic standing charge plus the cost of units used.

Coin slot meters are used where electricity consumption is low, and they are being gradually replaced with electronic token meters to avoid the temptation to burglars. Many regional electricity companies have introduced prepayment key meters. Your meter is operated by a special key charged with the value of money you put in key-charge machines outside electricity showrooms, so you can pay for your electricity in small amounts every week.

Gas

If you're moving to accommodation with gas, ask the Gas Board to take a new reading. When you leave, have a last reading taken so you can receive your final bill. If you are cut off for non-payment you'll have to pay a reconnection charge (which varies according to circumstances), as well as clearing the outstanding bill. You will be disconnected if, 64 days after receiving the initial bill, you have still not paid.

The national domestic credit tariff for gas is 44.3p per therm, plus a standing charge of £9.40 per quarter. According to British Gas, one therm of gas will run a gas fire in a room for five hours, heat an oven at gas mark 5 for 15 hours or heat enough water for five baths, 25 showers or 72 washing-up bowls.

Telephone

Most households now have telephone connection, so you should be able to take over an existing telephone and line. If you take over a line without a break in service (no disconnection), it is free; otherwise you have to pay £36. If you've already been a BT customer, having a new line installed costs £127.40. For new customers, installation costs £148.65.

Deposits are at the discretion of British Telecom and depend on your locality as much as on you. If you're moving to an area with a high turnover of tenants, you are likely to be asked for a hefty deposit − but if you can show BT you're a good bill-paying customer the deposit might be reduced.

It costs £19.70 per quarter to rent a line or £31.92 for a line and phone. You could rent a coin box phone (£23 connection plus £37 quarterly rental). If you are served by a digital exchange (at time of writing, 25 per cent of BT customers and rising) it is possible to arrange to allow incoming calls only.

If you don't pay your bill after receiving a final reminder, you will be disconnected after seven days and sent a letter informing you of an 'expiry date'. If you pay the bill before the expiry date, you will be charged £35 to be reconnected. If you fail to pay before the expiry date, reconnection will increase to £60 and you might have to provide an additional deposit.

If you're sharing a phone it's a good idea to get everybody to make a note of the time, distance and length of all their calls. BT produces a free leaflet, Your Guide to Telephone Charges, which explains how much calls cost; it's available from your local BT district office (find the address in the telephone directory). Depending on where you live, BT can provide an itemized bill, at no extra cost, which gives full details of all calls costing 50p or more.

Telephone Charges

Unit fee: 5.06p.
Peak times 9am-1pm Mon-Fri
standard times 8-9am, 1-6pm, Mon-Fri;
cheap times 6pm-8am Mon-Fri;
24 hours Sat, Sun.

Number of seconds per unit:
local calls 60 peak; 85 standard; 240 cheap
national calls *(up to 35 miles/ 56.4km)* 26.25 peak; 35.1 standard; 81.8 cheap; *(over 35 miles/56.4km)* 23.25 peak; 31 standard; 51.5 cheap
international calls vary with country.

Water

During your stay in rented accommodation, you might receive a bill from the local Water Authority addressed to 'The Occupier'. You're unlikely to be responsible for paying this bill (check your contract), so pass it on to your landlord.

Poll tax

Full-time students are required to pay 20 per cent of the community charge to the council of the borough in which they live. It may or may not be the borough where their college is based. Part-time students have to pay the full amount, although they may be eligible for rebates on the grounds of low income.

To qualify for your 80 per cent discount, you should register as a student and might be asked to produce a certificate issued by your college confirming your student status. If you are living in a hall of residence, the hall authorities register you automatically. If you move to a new address in a new borough after the start of the financial year, the council should only bill you for the period you have been living there.

Your college is required to provide the names and addresses of all its students to the Community Charge Registration Officer and it's up to you to make sure that you are registered. It starts to get complicated when students change addresses during term-time, as inevitably happens. It's further complicated by the academic year (running from September to September) failing to coincide with poll tax bills covering the financial year (April to April).

In the short period of time since the poll tax was introduced, councils have experienced enormous problems registering, billing and recovering the money from residents. Hackney Council in London applied for 17 months of court time to prosecute non-payers for 1990-91 – it was allocated three weeks. The Audit Commission, the government's official financial watchdog, estimates that summonses for non-payment of the poll tax will have to be issued to six million people in England and Wales during 1991.

Many students have tried to avoid or delay registration in order to disrupt the system. Some students have not paid the poll tax either because they can't afford it or as a protest against this unfair tax; you'll have to make up your own mind whether to pay or not, although you're risking hefty fines if you don't. Non-registration and non-payment are civil offences and you could be taken to court. If, after a hearing, you still don't pay, councils have other powers, such as sending in the bailifffs. Most local authorities have been slow in chasing non-payers, and it is a very difficult process, especially with students who move house frequently.

Dealing with debt

Nearly all students get into financial difficulties at some stage during their time at college. Whether you're unable to pay a gas bill or are being threatened with legal action by your credit card company, it's very important not to panic: act quickly, calmly and responsibly.

If you can't pay your bills, contact your creditors as soon as a bill arrives, and explain why you cannot pay. Managers of banks, electricity and gas boards and hire purchase companies have contingency plans for people who can't pay the bills. Try to give some idea of when you will be able to pay (as soon as your grant cheque arrives or when you find a job, for example). Offer to pay in instalments, even if it's only £2 a week. Staff at gas and electricity showrooms can give you details of their payment schemes. If they agree to a delay in payment, or to payment by instalments, write to them setting out the agreement as you understand it, and keep a copy of the letter.

Don't, whatever you do, take out an 'unsecured loan for any purpose' offered by private finance companies. Loan shark companies advertise in national newspapers and prey on the vulnerability of people in debt. Don't be fooled by the speed and ease with which you can obtain a loan – the interest rates charged will be astronomical, forcing you further into debt.

If you are at all worried, seek advice. Debt counselling is readily available: many banks now have financial advisers specifically for students; and student union welfare officers and Citizens' Advice Bureaux (CAB) can also help. Many local authorities now have debt counselling services. Your town hall or local CAB will be able to give you more details. Alternatively, you can phone the National Debt Line (*see below* **Useful Addresses**) for support, advice and counselling. If the counsellors are not available to help you, leave your name and address on the answerphone and they will send you a self-help information pack which is free to individual callers. Two packs are available, one for people living in private-rented accommodation and one for people with mortgages.

For advice on how to cope with debt colletors, *see page 244* **Rights**.

Transport and Travel

Walking: Many people live within walking distance of college. A thirty-minute walk in the morning is one way of waking up for your nine o'clock lecture, but staggering home drunk at midnight can be neither fun nor safe. *See below* **Security**.

Cycling: The bicycle has many advantages. It's beneficial to health, it doesn't pollute the environment and it's cheap to run. But bikes are often stolen. The first safeguard against being left without a bike is to buy a good lock. A basic 'U' shackle bike lock costs £22 to £30, although prices rise to £40 and beyond for locks that are lighter and less easily picked. If your bike is very expensive, take off the front wheel and lock it together with the back one, or get another lock to secure it to the frame. In any event, always attach a bike to a fixed object.

Leave your bike in busy places where plenty of people are passing. New, smart bikes, particularly mountain bikes, are obvious targets, so make it dirty and cover up the maker's name. Never leave removable accessories on an unattended bicycle. Insurance is essential; *see below* **Security**.

Driving: It is possible to run a car at college, if you have sources of income additional to your grant. One way to reduce the costs is to offer people a lift into college and get them to

Basic Living

contribute petrol money. But charge passengers more than just the cost of the petrol, and they'll think you're running a taxi service and will start to expect lifts from you at all times.

Parking is usually a problem in city centre colleges because the best places are taken early (before 9am). Bicycles are not alone in being vulnerable to theft. Beaten-up rust buckets aren't usually nicked, but all cars are potential targets, and any car can be broken into. Buy the best alarm you can afford, and don't leave your car parked down dark, empty side streets.

Public transport: A recent 'manifesto for transport in the year 2000', supported by Friends of the Earth, the AA and the Town and Country Planning Institute, said that 'the Government's stringent attitude to public transport funding is affecting service quality and making public transport less reliable, punctual, clean and generally attractive than it could and should be'.

Despite underfunding, many local bus companies have arrangements with college student unions to run services between colleges and halls of residence. Your student union will be able to give you more details.

Nationally

If you haven't got a car, there are three main options for travelling around the country: trains, coaches or hitching. Rail travel is the quickest and most reliable, but also the most expensive. Coach travel is cheaper, but slower and less comfortable than travelling by train. Hitching is by far the cheapest, but can be unreliable and is potentially dangerous, particularly for women travelling alone.

Trains: The Young Person's Railcard currently costs £16 and entitles holders to a third off all rail fares for one year. Anyone aged between 16 and 23 or in full-time education can buy the card. It's available from major British Rail stations, BR-appointed travel agents and student union travel offices. BR also runs special offers at certain times of the year.

'Saver' tickets cannot be used during rush hours (times vary depending on the journey); 'Supersaver' tickets are not valid during rush hours, any time on Fridays throughout the year or any time on Saturdays in July and August.

Coaches: The National Express Young Person's Coach Card gives a 30 per cent discount on all National Express or Caledonian Express (Scotland) services. It's available to anyone aged 16 to 23 or in full-time education from National Express stations, travel agents and student travel offices. It currently costs £5 and is valid for twelve months. It's more expensive to travel on Fridays and it's always worth buying your ticket in advance, to avoid queuing at the coach station.

Hitching: Find yourself a good spot where drivers will notice you and, more importantly, where they can stop to pick you up without disturbing other drivers. Carry a card with your destination clearly marked. Try and stick to your intended route but be prepared to veer off it, and be willing to chat to your driver (or even buy him or her lunch) – many drivers pick up hitchers because they are bored and want some company.

Women should travel in pairs. If you don't like the look of a driver, just say no. Surprisingly, drivers are more likely to pick up a couple than a single person, although two blokes are less likely to be offered a lift.

Security

Despite numerous government initiatives and increased public expenditure on the police force, we still haven't cracked crime. In particular, violent crimes (rapes, muggings and stabbings) are rising at an alarming rate. According to Home Office figures, 176,965 violent crimes against the person (murder, manslaughter and so on) were committed in England and Wales in 1989, compared with 158,248 the previous year. Other crimes are also on the increase. There were 139,473 cycle thefts in 1989, a 28 per cent rise on the figures for 1988. The figures for students are proportionately higher, probably because many students live in run-down areas with high crime rates. But the chances of becoming another crime statistic are low, if you are aware of the dangers and the basic mistakes which people often make, and avoid them yourself.

Personal Safety

Avoid hassle: don't get drunk and stagger home on your own. Muggers see people who have had one too many as fair game. Arguing with people in pubs and clubs is another way of getting into trouble. When the police are called in to break up a fight, they tend to arrest everyone in sight, so you could end up in the cells overnight.

Most thefts of personal property take place because of carelessness on the part of the owner. Carry your wallet or purse in an inside pocket or firmly down inside your bag, and never keep your keys in the same place as anything bearing your address. Keep your cheque book and card separate and always ask for the carbons when you use your credit card as they carry both your card number and your signature.

Student unions often organize self-defence classes and your local council or sports centre might run courses. These can help to make you more aware of potentially threatening situations

"I spent three years at the Philippa Fawcett teacher-training college in Streatham and had the worst attendance record of any student who graduated. Next thing, I was elected to the Inner London Education Authority".
Ken Livingstone was Chair of the ILEA before becoming a Labour MP, and trained as a teacher from 1970-73.

Basic Living

and teach you to deal with a few of them. *See also* Workers Education Association *under* **Useful Addresses** *below.*

If you regularly receive obscene phone calls, ask British Telecom to screen your calls for you. However, the most effective deterrent is a blast down the receiver from a rape alarm or whistle. Keep one handy near the phone (*see page 228* **Women Students**).

Streetwise: By following a few basic rules, your safety on the streets at night can be more or less guaranteed:

- The best protection is to be with another person. Arrange to travel home with a friend and get to know your neighbours, as they might be able to give you a lift home.
- Avoid deserted, badly-lit roads or parks, especially in the dark.
- On busy roads, walk facing the traffic – drivers will have a clear view if anyone attacks you.
- Memorize a taxi firm number and always have a fiver for the fare on you. Even if you never resort to catching a cab, the option is always open to you.
- Steer clear of empty railway carriages and, when possible, sit downstairs on buses at night.
- Carry your keys in your hand so that you don't have to wait on the doorstep while you search for them. They can also make good impromptu weapons, but bear in mind that by law you're not supposed to carry anything that could be used as an offensive weapon.
- Don't flaunt money or expensive possessions. If you walk about with your bag slung casually over your shoulder, you are easy prey.
- If you are threatened, try not to panic. Look your potential attacker in the eye and attempt to talk your way out of the situation. If that fails, run as fast as you can, preferably to the nearest house or building with lights on. If in doubt, give your assailant your wallet and avoid a stay in hospital.
- If you are attacked, take a deep breath and raise hell – scream, struggle and generally kick up a stink. The advice often given on self-defence courses is to shout 'Fire!' because more people run to the defence of their property than to a stranger shouting 'Help!'.

Home security

Most burglaries happen during the day, and 25 per cent of burglars just enter through an open door or an unlocked window. In 1989, there were 825,930 burglaries in England and Wales, so beware of the 'it'll never happen to me' factor.

A good set of locks will deter the casual thief, so you must first find out whether your home is secure. If you want a professional opinion, call your local police station and ask for a visit from the Crime Prevention Officer, who can tell you if your existing locks could be picked without causing much external damage.

The front door needs more than the handy Yale-type latch which locks when you slam the door (and opens at the flick of a credit card), and you should consider buying a mortice deadlock. Brand quality is fairly consistent between Chubb, Yale, ERA and Ingersoll mortice deadlocks, but prices vary from around £30 for a Chubb to £50 for an Ingersoll. Downstairs windows need key-operated window locks. Locks for sash windows cost between £1.50 for an ERA and £5.50 for a Chubb and come in packs of two or more. The best lock for a casement window is a Chubb 8K106, which costs about £11 for a pack of two.

You can buy home security equipment from any large branch of DIY shops such as B&Q, Do It All, Homebase, Payless DIY or Texas Homecare, though it might be worth the £30 or more that locksmiths commonly charge to have the equipment fitted professionally. You should find a good selection of locksmiths in *Yellow Pages*; alternatively, the Master Locksmiths' Association (*see below* **Useful Addresses**) supplies information for contacting their members in your area.

When you leave your home, lock all external doors and windows, and either switch on a light at night or fit time switches to turn lights or a radio on and off at intervals. But use the timer with discretion – if all your lights are on at 4am, Joe Burglar won't be fooled.

There's some disagreement over whether Neighbourhood Watch schemes – where neighbours keep an eye on each other's properties and look out for potential burglars – have a consistent and lasting effect on burglaries, but it's a good idea to arrange with your neighbour to keep an eye on each other's houses.

Keep precious valuables in a safe deposit box at the bank. If you can't do this, mark items with your name and post code using ink that is visible only under ultraviolet light. The Crime Prevention Officer can do this for you free of charge.

Some crooks get in by claiming to be from the water board/gas board/poll tax office. Don't let anyone in unless you have been shown some identification.

Party tricks: If you have a party, lock away your valuables. Student parties in shared houses, when nobody knows who invited whom, let alone why, are heaven for light-fingered gatecrashers. Ask a couple of large friends to filter out the undesirables.

Insurance

The best way to protect your home and your possessions is to insure them. Endsleigh Insurance Services (*see below* **Useful Addresses**) was set up by the NUS in the sixties and still does much of its business with students. It is also the only insurance company recommended to students by NUS.

To make it easier to claim if something does get nicked, make sure you can prove ownership of the stolen goods. Keep receipts, note down serial numbers and take photographs of expensive items.

The Association of British Insurers (*see below* **Useful Addresses**) is the trade association for insurance companies. Contact them if you have a complaint about an insurer, or wish to check a company's status.

Bike insurance

However splendid your bike lock is (*see above* **Transport and Travel**), a determined thief can conquer it. If you take out a house contents insurance policy, pay the extra premium (about £10) for a bike: it's usually cheaper than taking out a separate policy. Most house contents insurance policies will only insure a bike up to £500. Keep receipts for all bike accessories you buy.

Life insurance

The British Investment and Insurance Brokers Association (*see below* **Useful Addresses**) says that an insurance salesperson is obliged by law to give the best possible advice to a potential customer, and that taking out a life insurance policy is hardly a top financial priority for a student.

As a student, any personal insurance policy may be a waste of time and money. Don't be talked into buying something you don't want, don't need or don't understand. If someone knocks on your door and tries to sell you insurance, tell them – politely – to go away.

Further Reading

Creditwise Office of Fair Trading (HMSO, free).
Food Facts by Carol Ann Rinzler (Bloomsbury, £5.95).
Food Fit To Eat British Nutritional Foundation (Sphere, £3.99).
Healthy Eating: Fact and Fiction (Which Books, Consumers Association and Hodder & Stoughton, £7.95).
Grub on a Grant by Cas Clarke (Headline, £4.99).
The Green Consumer Guide John Elkington and Julis Hailes (Gollancz, £3.95).
The Home Expert DG Hessayon (pbi Publications, £2.95).
How to be Green Friends of the Earth (Century, £4.99).
The Student Cookbook by Sarah Freeman (Collins & Brown, £4.99).
The Whole Health Manual by P Holford (Thorsons, £3.50).

Useful Addresses

Association of British Insurers Aldermary House, 10-15 Queen Street, London EC4N 1TT (071 248 4477).
British Investment and Insurance Brokers Association BIIBA House, 14 Bevis Marks, London EC3A 7NT (071 623 9043).
Endsleigh Insurance Services Endsleigh House, Ambrose Street, Cheltenham Spa, Gloucestershire GL50 3NR (0242 223300).
The Health Education Authority Health Information Centre, Hamilton House, Mabledon Place, London WC1H 9TX (071 383 3833).
Master Locksmith's Association Unit 4/5, Woodford Halse Business Park, Great Central Way, Woodford Halse, Daventry, North Hants NN11 6PZ (0327 62255).
National Association of Citizens' Advice Bureaux Myddelton House, 115-123 Pentonville Road, London N1 9LZ (071 833 2181).
National Debtline (021 359 8501).
National Express Enquiry Service (071 730 0202). Phone this London number for details of coach times and ticket prices throughout Britain, and for information on the Young Person's Coach Card.
Office of Electricity Regulation (OFFER) Hagley House, Hagley Road, Birmingham B16 8QG (021 456 2100).
Office of Gas Supply (OFGAS) Southside, 2nd Floor, 105 Victoria Street, London SW1E 6QT (071 828 0898).
Office of Telecommunications (OFTEL) Export House, 50 Ludgate Hill, London EC4M 7JJ (071 822 1650).
Office of Water Services (OFWAT) Centre City Tower, 7 Hill Street, Birmingham B5 4UA (021 625 1300).
Workers Education Association Head Office, Temple House, 9 Upper Berkeley Street, London W1H 8BY (071 402 5608). The WEA runs self-defence classes at its branches all over Britain. Call directory enquiries for your nearest one or contact the head office.

in distorting
frighte
of the summit,
indicated by
couldn't hear
some

Membership **148**

The Role of Student Unions **151**

How Unions Work **156**

College Services for Students **158**

Useful Addresses **159**

student
unions

The image of student unions as bastions of radicalism, revolution and rebellion has changed since the sixties. Political campaigns are still run, but more importance is now attached to providing services for students. **Tim Dawson** explores the state of the unions.

For many people, student unions conjure up an image of toytown revolutionaries plotting the overthrow of international capitalism. Others imagine student unions to be teeming with lager-swilling inebriates living it up at the taxpayer's expense in subsidized bars. Both these images are misleading and neither reflects the many activities of student unions.

Ideally, the structure of individual student unions should allow them to be whatever their members would wish, but there are financial constraints, as well as matters of central NUS policy to consider. Colleges differ greatly in the enthusiasm of their students for the union.

On the whole, student unions have excellent sport, leisure and welfare facilities. You should find someone with specialist training to help with your problems and, if you enjoy unusual, perhaps expensive sports, you are likely to find fellow enthusiasts, as well as equipment you could otherwise never afford. At no other time in your life are you likely to have such resources at your disposal.

Student unions vary dramatically in size, in the range of services they provide and in the different activities they fund. The smallest unions have access to just a small office and a common room and employ only a part-time administrative secretary. Some further education student unions don't even have that. But the largest unions own their building, employ upwards of 200 staff, have students working full-time for the union as sabbaticals and provide a multitude of different services, from bars and restaurants to launderettes and photographic dark-rooms. These facilities are run on a money-making basis. The profits are ploughed back into providing more and better services for students, such as cheap printing for theses and bigger shops, as well as subsidizing the other activities of the union, like campaigns and welfare provision.

In some colleges student unions are known by different names, such as the Guild of Students or Guild of Undergraduates. In Scotland most colleges have a Student Representative Council (SRC), which represents students on college bodies and carries out political and campaigning work, and separate bodies (sometimes called Student Associations) providing recreational, leisure and sporting facilities. Similarly, in some colleges the department providing student services is known by a slightly different name. For simplicity we will refer throughout to student unions and student services.

This chapter is intended to give you an idea of the range of facilities available in most colleges, how they are organized, and how you can make the most of them.

Membership
NUS

The National Union of Students (NUS) is a federation of 98 per cent of the student unions in this country. Student unions decide to affiliate to NUS by holding a referendum of all their members, or by voting at a general meeting, or other meeting delegated to take the decision. Every student union pays an affiliation fee to NUS. Students elected from all the affiliated colleges attend NUS Conference twice a year to decide the Union's policies and elect an executive.

NUS was founded in 1922 and is now one of the largest national student unions in the world. It employs nearly 80 staff and has over 800 affiliated unions.

Affiliation to NUS is often discussed in student unions. NUS is sometimes characterized as unrepresentative or too political, leading to

Student Unions

attempts to disaffiliate. However, out of the many votes that have taken place in recent years, only one student union (Royal Holloway and Bedford New College in London) has decided to disaffiliate. The decision was reversed six months later in a referendum of all students.

The main functions of NUS are to:
- Represent the interests of students to government and to other local and national bodies;
- Train student union officers to enable them to represent students more effectively;
- Advise student unions on aspects of welfare education and the law;
- Provide commercial consultancy for student unions, through NUS Services Ltd, and to negotiate bulk discounts of goods for resale. NUS also sells student goods, such as computers, cheaply.

Although NUS has its headquarters in London, it has a network of regional offices around the country, providing back-up services to individual student unions, such as advice and training for union officers. On a local level, NUS-affiliated student unions are organized into areas, co-ordinated by an area convenor. The area convenor is often a sabbatical and does everything from organizing local campaigns against the poll tax, to negotiating student discounts in local shops, clubs, restaurants and cinemas, to representing student unions to the local media and politicians.

College student unions

You automatically become a member of the student union once you register at college. You can use all its facilities, just as you can use the college library to take out books. However, in contrast to other college services, you can take part in the student union's decision-making process.

Union cards and NUS cards (usually the same thing) are issued at registration (*see page 60*

Glossary of Terms

AGM Annual General Meeting; **Constitution** The student union's governing rules; **Convenor** Student responsible for co-ordinating a particular group; **EGM** Emergency/ Extraordinary General Meeting; **Executive committee** The committee of elected student officers which runs the student union; **Executive officer** Student who is elected to the committee, and is still on a course (unpaid post); **General Secretary** Senior elected student officer in charge of union bureaucracy; **President** Senior elected student officer, often a sabbatical; **Sabbatical officer** Elected officer (either on leave during their course, or staying on after their course), paid by the student union; often referred to as 'sabbatical'; **Standing orders** Rules governing the conduct of student union meetings; **Treasurer** Elected student officer responsible for student union finances; **UGM** Union General Meeting, also known as General Meeting (GM) or Ordinary General Meeting (OGM); **Welfare officer** Elected student officer responsible for student welfare issues.

NUS Achievements

The following are just some of the successful campaigns run by NUS over the years:

1964 — In 1964 NUS campaigns helped to establish the grants system.

1970 — In 1970 NUS achieved a government guarantee of student representation on the governing bodies of every college.

1976 — In 1976 NUS ensured that all fees to home students were abolished, and headed off a government attempt to increase overseas students' fees.

1988 — In 1988 NUS persuaded the Government to reduce students' liability to the poll tax from 100 per cent to 20 per cent.

1990 — In 1990 NUS stopped EEC regulations that would have forced all minibus drivers to hold special licences; this would have severely restricted the activities of union sports clubs and safety minibus schemes.

Arrival at College). When you pick up your card, ask what discounts the student union has negotiated with local shops, clubs, restaurants and cinemas; there may be a booklet with details of the various discounts on offer. If in doubt, enquire about student discounts whenever you pay for something. Nationally, the NUS card is the most widely recognized form of student ID, along with the International Student Identity Card (ISIC, *see page 278* **Travel**). The ISIC is the only document which is internationally accepted as proof of student status, and entitles holders to additional discounts under the worldwide Countdown Card scheme.

Funds and resources

Student unions are funded by the college administration, in the form of a block grant paid to the union each year. The amount of the grant varies, depending on the size and type of college. For 1989/90, the student union at Edinburgh University received a staggering £1,049,951 (or £88.51 for every full-time student), while Dorset Institute of Higher Education's union (now Bournemouth Poly) received only £51,000, or £16.06 per student. A medium-sized university or polytechnic union will receive a block grant of around £200,000 a year. Once it has received its grant, the student union is free to spend it as it wishes, as long as the expenditure falls within the aims and objects of the union. Every student union has a constitution in which its aims, rules and regulations are set out.

Student unions also make money from retail, and in recent years trading has accounted for an increasing part of their incomes. Many unions are huge commercial concerns; the University of Warwick student union, for example, has a turnover of nearly £3 million a year.

Not all the income received by student unions is spent directly on their members. Some have to pay maintenance costs for the union building. In 1990, the University of Bristol Union received a £570,000 grant from the University but had to pay £263,000 in maintenance costs and £193,000 in wages.

The Role of Student Unions
Commercial services

Because of the recent cuts in government spending on higher education, student unions have turned to running bars, shops, restaurants, nightclubs and travel centres to boost their dwindling resources, often with considerable success. The student union at Leeds Polytechnic made a net trading profit of £184,919 in 1990, on top of a block grant from the Polytechnic of £242,378, and has an annual turnover of about £1 million. Very few unions lose money on trading, although some use profits from one operation to subsidize another. The extra revenue can be used to pay for union campaigns, or for funding clubs and societies.

While some unions own little more than a coffee machine and a photocopier, others run small shopping malls, bars and restaurants, nightclubs, even Jacuzzis and saunas. Cardiff University student union's nightclub, The Hanging Gardens, is extremely popular with both students and locals. The shopping mall at the University of London Union (ULU) has a large general shop, a sports shop, National Westminster and Barclays banks, an Endsleigh insurance office and a printing and photocopying shop.

Union bars have always been considerably cheaper than pubs outside college, but you'll also find the refectories, snack bars, union shops and launderettes good value. Student unions pool their buying power through the National Student Services Organisation (NSSO) so that they can purchase products cheaper. NSSO is the second-largest bulk purchaser of alcohol in the country. There are now plans to bring NSSO together with NUS Services as one merged student services company, wholly owned by student unions.

Space in union buildings is often rented out to banks, shops and building societies. The majority of the larger student unions run travel agencies, or let space within their buildings to a specialist student travel company. *See also page 278* **Travel** and *page 116* **Basic Living**.

Entertainment

Extensive entertainment (ents) programmes of concerts and discos are provided by most student unions. These are usually co-ordinated by a sabbatical social secretary or entertainments officer, although increasingly, in the bid to become more commercial, unions are employing full-time staff members to run ents. Students are still involved in decisions about what events to put on: there will probably be an ents committee. Ents organizers always need students to help run concerts and discos, to produce posters and leaflets, to sell tickets, and even as DJs. While some of the jobs are hardly glamorous, at least you get into the gig for free, and will probably be paid a few quid into the bargain. You should also gain an insight into how the entertainments industry works: the college ents scene has spawned countless roadies, DJs, concert promoters and music agents.

The bands playing at the union might not be to your taste, but social secretaries don't just put on the bands they like. A lot will depend on which bands are touring, whether the union can afford to pay them and whether there are any alternative venues in the town which offers the band more money. If you are appalled by the quality of the bands appearing at your union, you can always complain to the social secretary. Many ents committees hold open meetings where people can voice their opinions. If you have a particular taste in music which you feel is being ignored, go and complain. You could even offer to organize your own specialist music night, for instance a heavy metal night, a Kylie Minogue party or a cultural evening.

Most student unions have drama societies which cater for all thespian tastes. Some will be closely linked to the drama department, but most welcome anyone. Productions are staged throughout the year and the more successful shows are taken to the Edinburgh Fringe Festival in the summer. Drama societies won't just be looking for aspiring actors; they will also need stage and lighting technicians, set and costume designers and people to organize the publicity.

Clubs and societies

Most new students become involved in clubs and societies of one sort or another. There are societies catering for every imaginable pursuit, from hang-gliding to hockey, role-playing to roller-skating.

The intro fair will be the societies' main recruiting ground. Every club, and students trying to start new ones, will have a stall. You can wander around letting members of various groups try to persuade you that this society or that club deserves your membership. Costs will vary: gliding will be more expensive that fell walking, but all activities will receive some subsidy from the student union.

Think carefully before you sign up with every society in sight: many students join groups and then never go to a single meeting. Also, be realistic about what you can afford: diving, parachuting and rally driving require considerable expenditure throughout the year. *See also page 60* **Arrival at College.**

Political: Most political groups and parties recruit members through college societies. The Labour Club, the Liberal Democrats and the Conservative Association are well known political groupings, but the Socialist Workers Party, the Fabians and the Tory Reform Group will also be among the clubs jostling for your attention.

There are plenty of single-interest groups which are active in colleges, such as CND, Greenpeace, the Anti Apartheid Movement and animal rights groups.

Political clubs and societies are usually affiliated to national organizations – the Socialist Workers Students Society to the Socialist Workers Party, the Labour Club to the National Organisation of Labour Students – and if you join one of these clubs, you will have the chance to become involved in the heady world of national student politics. Party political groups are also linked with their parent organizations at a local level, and student canvassers are often crucial to winning marginal wards at election time.

Cultural: Groups of students, such as Chinese, Arab and Jewish students, usually organize societies which hold social events and campaign about issues that affect them. Most welcome members from outside their community who are interested in their culture and want to join in with the social events. Sometimes an issue arises which the society's members want other students to hear about. After the 1989 massacre in Tiananmen Square, Chinese societies organized demonstrations in the UK which successfully publicized the plight of Chinese students afraid to return to China. Many had their visas extended as a result.

Academic: Some academic departments, such as law, languages, business studies and the sciences, have societies where students and academics can mix socially, and which organize events linked to courses. Some exist for purely social reasons and are concerned with nothing more than the study of alcohol abuse; others are more serious, with lectures and guest speakers on subjects relevant to the department.

Sport: Sporting societies are either directly funded by the student union or by an athletics

Student Unions

union. Either way, sports clubs cater for the widest variety of tastes.

Championships are organized in traditional sports between college teams, but polytechnics rarely compete against university teams. The British Polytechnics Sports Federation and the Universities Athletic Union (*see below* **Useful Addresses** for both) arrange fixtures for the different sectors. Matches are played on Wednesday afternoons and so college timetables should be arranged so that there is no compulsory teaching then. On courses where this doesn't happen students have campaigned successfully to persuade lecturers of the need for time to play sport.

If you don't want to play competitive sport against teams from other colleges, there will probably be an 'intramural' league where departmental teams or anyone else who can get a team together play regularly. Although the games are still competitive, the atmosphere is a lot more friendly. More students play intramural than inter-college sport.

When you are looking through prospectuses, check what sporting facilities are available. Some colleges have magnificent sports centres, swimming pools and pitches; some will share facilities with other colleges; others can only point to the nearest municipal facilities. If you can, use open days to visit sports facilities. Prospectuses rarely undersell the college's facilities.

Starting your own society: Student union constitutions make it easy for members to get together with a few friends (usually ten to twelve) and start a new club; your student union will probably have an officer with special responsibility for societies, often the treasurer. He or she will be able to tell you what money is available and how you can get hold of it.

> **"Leeds University between 1978 and 1982 was a branch of Butlin's. I had a sensational time promoting concerts for two and a half years. We got our priorities right in those days – these days, I hear that students work. I'd apply now to become a postgraduate, but I never graduated."**
>
> **Andy Kershaw** Radio 1 DJ (Politics, Leeds University, 1978-82).

Help and information
The welfare office: All student unions provide welfare advice. Some employ professional advisers and some use elected officers who receive training before they start. There is usually a welfare officer on the executive committee, or there may be a welfare sub-committee. The welfare officer runs campaigns on health issues and produces welfare manuals. Some student union welfare services lend small sums of money to students who are in financial trouble because their grant cheques are late.

Your student union welfare office should be able to help with health, financial or academic problems. You can visit the office to look at some of the leaflets and booklets on display, or to have a confidential chat with someone. You can also ask to be referred to an advice agency specializing in your particular problem.

Safe transport for women: Some colleges run special transport facilities for women. Ask at your student union to see what is available. *See also page 228* **Women**.

Nightlines: These are confidential phone lines provided for students by students. Student volunteers are given crisis training, often by the local Samaritans, and always need more trainees. Nightline staff are available for telephone calls and usually for chats in person through the night, and some nightlines also have people on call during the day.

Campaigns
A survey in 1988, undertaken by the government after pressure from right-wing Conservative MPs eager to show that student unions spent their time funding left-wing causes, found that most student unions spent less than one per cent on political groups.

However, student unions do run various political campaigns, as well as more prosaic ones on college issues – extortionate refectory prices or the lack of condom machines in the college toilets. Campaigns on national issues such as the poll tax or student loans are usually run in conjunction with NUS, and include publicity stunts, radio phone-ins and, if the mood is right, occupations of college buildings, as well as demonstrations and rallies.

Many of the student demonstrations in the sixties successfully argued for student representation on college committees. Nowadays, the first step in any campaign is through official college channels, and only if this strategy fails are more traditional campaigning tactics employed.

The student union will have representatives on the highest decision making bodies of the college. Committees vary from college to college but are likely to cover all aspects of college life. Although student reps on committees are always in a minority – often only one or two on a 30-strong committee – they usually get support from staff reps and their views are taken seriously because, for many desk-bound college administrators, committees are the only opportunity they have to talk to students and to get an idea of student opinion in the college.

Unions also make representations to local MPs and councillors on behalf of students. Usually, the views expressed to politicians, college governors and the media are in line with union policy, but sometimes opinions are given for which the person will be asked to account at a future union meeting. *See below* **How Unions Work**.

The student media
Thousands of students work on college papers, radio stations and television to gain insight into

Student Unions

how the media work, and countless journalists have started their careers in the student media.

Almost every college has a student paper. Some are poorly produced drivel, others are stylish and daring. All are produced by students with little or no previous experience. Usually they have more space to fill than they have copy to fill it: anyone who expresses an interest in writing, production or photography is welcome. The publications also need designers and layout artists, cartoonists and people to sell advertising. The best time to get involved is at the start of term when papers are short of staff.

Just as common as regular student publications are one-offs. Student unions often provide cheap printing facilities and some have computers suitable for desk-top publishing. Students themselves provide a ready market for interesting looking cheap publications. Cartoon books, political polemics, poetry collections and newssheets regularly appear on most campuses.

Some colleges have their own radio and television stations; those that do exist are under constant financial threat of closure. Most are entirely managed and run by students on a voluntary basis, and are usually crying out for people to help. Check college prospectuses and student union handbooks to see what is available. Exeter University has a well-established student radio station – it won the *Guardian*/NUS Student Media Award in 1990 – and University College London operates one of the very few successful student television stations. In total, there are 20 student radio stations and 10 student television stations in the UK.

It is also possible for students to gain experience of the professional media. Many local radio stations accept ideas from people writing in and, with tenacity, students have negotiated regular spots on local radio. Newspapers and magazines are sometimes willing to give students a week's work experience if you don't mind working for nothing; *see also page 254* **Employment**.

Keep an eye open for the *Guardian*/NUS Student Media Awards. Prizes are given for the best college radio stations, newspapers, magazines and journalists. Details are available from the NUS Press Officer throughout the year; entries are accepted between May and July, and the results are published each year towards the end of October.

Community action

Student community action (SCA) groups exist in most colleges and offer students who are prepared to give up a little time each week the chance to help disadvantaged local people. In some places this means visiting homes for the mentally ill or physically disabled, or visiting and helping old people in their own homes. At other colleges SCA groups are involved with local youth groups and schools projects, or arranging holidays for people who would otherwise have little chance to have one.

SCA work provides endless opportunity for involvement in a world a little wider and less cushioned than college itself; it is a side of student unions' work which is all too often overlooked. *See also page 254* **Employment**.

Rag weeks

In most colleges there is an annual rag week, when students make a concerted effort to raise money for a range of charities. Many student rags divide their proceeds between a campus appeal (such as a South African Scholarship Fund or a nursery fund), a local charity and a national charity.

Fundraising activities generally involve getting dressed up and doing lots of wacky

155

"When I was President of NUS I thought I was fantastically important. Students now have a much better grasp of reality. I think that television has played a big part in creating a generation of people who are much more clued in and want answers very quickly. The downside of this is that a lot of students think that on very big questions there are very simple answers."

Trevor Phillips Presenter, The London Programme, LWT (Chemistry, Imperial College, London, 1975-78; President of NUS 1978-1980).

stunts, like three-legged races around the town centre and 'rag raids' to other colleges. Social activities often include a rag ball, and a rag mag will be sold.

Rag mags gained a reputation for being offensive, but recently many rag organizers have brought in rules that jokes for inclusion in rag mags must be non-racist and non-sexist.

In one or two colleges rag is a massive event, involving all the students in raising hundreds of thousands of pounds each year. The students at University College of Wales in Aberystwyth and at Loughborough compete to hold the biggest and best rag week in the country. Few students at these colleges are not involved in one way or another, and the rag organizers are very good at motivating every student to work as hard as possible to raise money.

How Unions Work

Student unions are often huge operations, but they are controlled and run by their members. Criticism is often levelled at student unions for being undemocratic and unrepresentative, but the problem can be that too few students are involved. Decisions about how to spend the union budget, what services to provide, what campaigns to run, what entertainments to put on and which staff to employ are all taken by students, but because of the different decision-making structures, action is often bogged down in bureaucracy.

Executive officers

Once a year student unions elect officers to carry out their work. Some elections are furiously contested, with the candidates producing glossy manifestos, staging publicity stunts to get themselves noticed and persuading anybody who looks remotely like a student to vote for them. In other contests, candidates are unopposed and the elections pass unnoticed by the vast majority of students at the college.

An executive committee will have, at the very least, a president, a treasurer, a secretary and a welfare officer. Depending on the size of the union, they may be complemented by a social secretary, a clubs and societies officer, a campaigns officer, a community action organizer and executive members responsible for representing a particular site or department within a college. An 'executive' usually meets once a week and is responsible for putting into practice the policy passed at union meetings (*see below*), as well as overseeing the day-to-day running of the union.

Sabbatical officers

Some of the officers of your union will be 'sabbaticals'. Although they have been elected from the student membership, they are paid (about as much as the annual grant) to work for the union, full-time, for a year. This gives them time to do their jobs properly without jeopardizing their studies. Other officers of the union, non-sabbaticals, do the job part-time while they are studying. Most unions also have numerous other committees, to oversee the executive's work and to administer union's work. Any student can stand for these offices.

Union meetings

At several points during your time at college you're likely to hear various students babbling that 'the Union General Meeting (UGM) is the sovereign body of the union'. This means that whatever decisions are taken about union activities, the buck stops at the UGM. All students at a college can attend a UGM and although not all decisions are taken there – some, for example, are taken at executive committee meetings – the UGM has the power to reverse any decision taken by any other body in the union's structure, as well as the power to order an executive officer or staff member to carry out a particular policy.

Most of the political action takes place at UGMs. Representatives of the various political groups will usually submit motions for discussion and use the debates as an opportunity to score points off each other. Meetings are held every three or four weeks, and there are likely to be debates on both topical and long-running issues. Clubs and societies often submit motions on issues that they are concerned with: Friends of the Earth might argue for paper recycling to be introduced into the union building, while the Islamic society might call on the union to force withdrawal of *The Satanic Verses* from the college bookshop. Occasionally, there will be a motion calling for the union building to be renamed The Kremlin or mandating the union executive to all wear silly hats for a week for charity, but usually the motions discussed will be of a fairly serious nature. UGMs also provide individual members with the opportunity to question the executive members, particularly the sabbaticals, about their work.

Although some people pop up at meetings again and again to shout and roar their views, the chairperson should give preference to first-time speakers. You'll also find that once a meeting starts, the chairperson starts talking in a strange dialect with references to standing orders, taking the motion in parts and votes on whether to take a vote on the move to vote on the amendment to main motion. Don't panic. There will probably be a guide to the various terms used and what they mean.

Student Representative Councils (SRCs)

Political and social activities are sometimes dealt with by separate bodies, particularly in Scottish unions. The Student Representative Council represents students on college bodies and carries out political and campaigning work. Separate student and athletics unions provide leisure and sporting facilities.

College Services for Students

There will be a department at your college dedicated exclusively to providing student services. This is where you should find those services that are not provided by the student union, such as accommodation, careers and possibly overseas student offices. In smaller colleges where the student union is unlikely to have the funds to run a comprehensive welfare service, it is likely that the college itself would organize counselling and welfare. It is also likely to run a student health centre (*see page 172* **Health and Stress**).

Facilities within each college can be divided between those provided by the college and those provided by the student union. In most colleges, if a service is not provided by the college, it will be available in the student union, and vice versa. The set-up is slightly different in each college: in some, all the bars are run by the college, in others, they are all run by the union. Sometimes a facility or outlet changes its administration. At the University of Hull, for example, the student union took over the sports and leisure facilities in August 1989.

While the student union welfare office will be able to advise on how to look for a flat and how to spot a dodgy contract, the college accommodation office will be able to provide lists of local landlords and reputable accommodation agencies (*see page 94* **Accommodation**). The student union may organize a careers fair, while the college careers office will be able to tell you how to find out more about a particular career (*see page 254* **Employment**). Similarly, the student union can help overseas students if they have problems with social security benefits, but the overseas students office will have to be called in to deal, for example, with a dispute over a student's right to remain in this country (*see page 28* **Overseas Students**).

Religion

There is usually a cleric for each major religion at college, and their names and addresses are given to students as they register. If you can't find them, the student union welfare officer should be able to help. Many colleges have a chaplaincy building shared by the various religions practising on campus, as well as separate societies for the various faiths. Prayer rooms are available on large campuses for those religions where frequent prayer is necessary. Christian societies often provide a social focus on campus, although some of them are battlegrounds for evangelical faction-fighting.

College chaplaincies play an important welfare role and often run counselling services. They can help in alerting students to the dangers of religious cults. Three religious sects in particular – the Unification Church (also known as the Moonies and the Collegiate Association for the Research of Principles), the Church of Scientology (also known as the Scientologists) and the Central London Church of Christ – have been accused of taking financial advantage of their members and often try to recruit students.

Crèches and nurseries

Unfortunately, college childcare provision is poor. Some colleges and student unions run nurseries, but there is always tremendous pressure on places, which are especially difficult to find for very young babies. Check availability when you choose a college. Prices of college-run nurseries are often so high that only college staff are able to use them. Despite this, many colleges are starting to realize that they cannot hope to attract mature students and women returning to education if they do not provide childcare. Many of the crèche campaigns run by student unions have started to have effect in recent years. At some colleges there are also half-term playschemes, often run by the student union, to help parents with children of school age.

Useful Addresses
British Polytechnics Sports Federation/British Universities Sports Association 11 Alcock Street, Birmingham B9 4DY (021 766 8855).
National Student Services Organisation (NSSO)/NUS Services Ltd Bleaklow House, Howard Town Mill, Mill Street, Glossop SK13 8PT (0457 868003).
National Union of Students (NUS) Nelson Mandela House, 461 Holloway Road, London N7 6LJ (071 272 8900).
Universities Athletic Union London Fruit Exchange, Brushfield Street, London E1 6EU (071 247 3066).

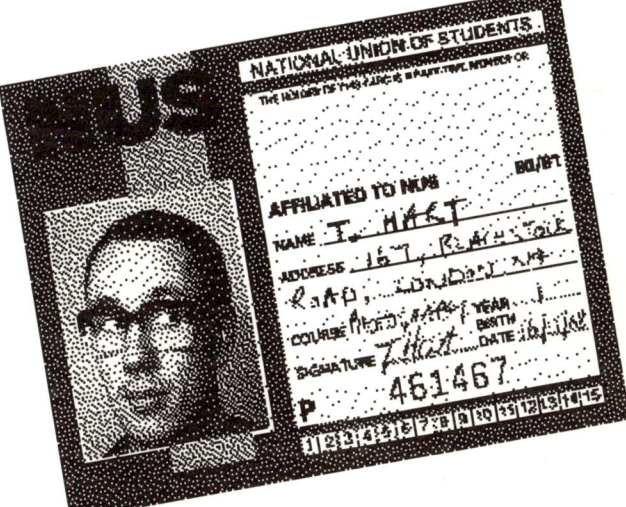

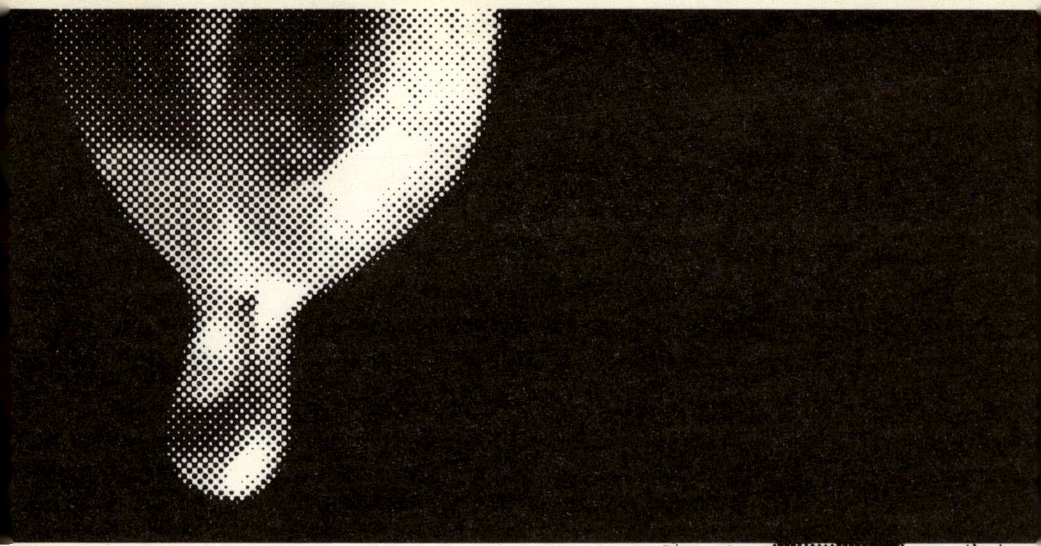

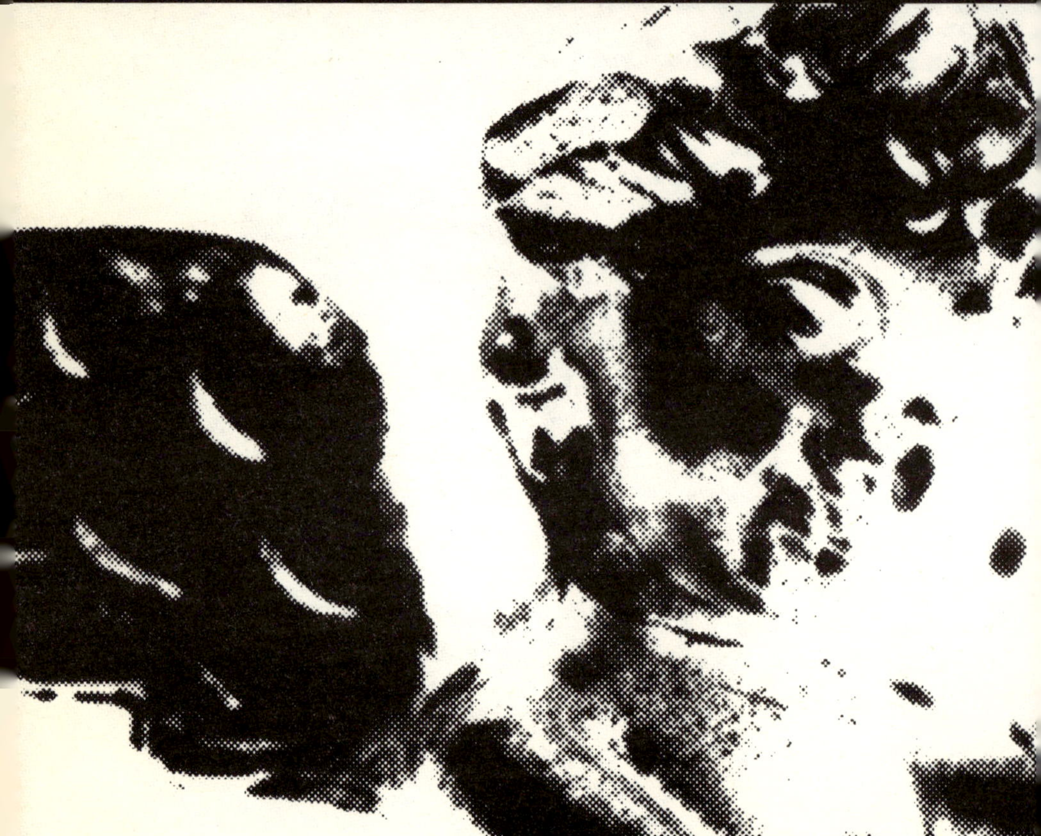

Meeting a Partner **162**

Sexuality **163**

Sex – Some Suggestions **163**

Sexual Difficulties **164**

Diseases **165**

Contraception **165**

Abortion **170**

Further Reading **171**

Useful Addresses **171**

sex and relationships

College provides the opportunity to make many new friendships. It may be where you establish your first long-term relationship, or have your first sexual experience. **Tony Balacs** and **Hilary Hutcheon** set out some facts and explode some myths.

You're likely to meet an awful lot of people over the next few years. As your tutors will never tire of telling you, college is a time of discovery and learning, immensely important and formative. Indeed, many new students feel that going to college marks the first time they are truly able to live as they would wish, despite work and exam pressures. Forming relationships, including sexual ones, can obviously be part of this freedom; but the sheer number of new faces you'll meet and the limitless experience they promise, although exciting, can also sometimes be daunting.

After the mass media coverage of Acquired Immune Deficiency Syndrome (AIDS) in the eighties, attitudes towards sex are none too clearly defined at the start of the nineties. The position is now somewhere between that of the permissive sixties and the prudery of earlier times, and many present-day sixth-formers have opinions about sex which appear very conservative to their free-loving parents. But today's students are likely to be far more open and responsible than their predecessors, while having to cope with uncomfortable new realities.

Who is this chapter for?

Among first-year undergraduates there will be students with widely differing attitudes and experiences. Some will have arrived straight from school, having had the same close-knit group of friends for a long time and perhaps no experience of sexual relationships. Some will be eagerly awaiting their first sexual encounter and others will have passed this milestone several years back; while for some, sex will be something for which they are perfectly content to wait, maybe until marriage or co-habitation.

None of these situations is the norm for first-year students. As far as possible, we'd like this chapter to be relevant to every first-year student, whatever their sexuality, but of course you should make use of whatever information is important to you.

Meeting a Partner

Many student handbooks suggest ways to meet people. When there are hundreds, if not thousands of new students eager to socialize, there's no lack of opportunity to make friends and meet a potential partner. But it's still hard to find someone who suits you out of the vast number who don't. Take your time and trust your instincts; when you see the same people every day the atmosphere can become claustrophobic, making it difficult to know what you really do feel. If you make an idiot of yourself early on, whether by declaring your heart's true love on the front steps of the college or by insulting the Dean, it is likely to become common knowledge, and perhaps an embarrassing memory to be wheeled out at every drinking session. Don't be pressurised early on to do anything you're not perfectly happy with. But equally, have some fun exploring your new-found freedom.

Meeting people will not be hard. Your friends will introduce you to their friends; you'll sit next to someone gorgeous at a seminar or you'll catch somebody gazing at you in the library. By all means, do what you fancy with the person you fancy, but just make sure it's safe and make sure it's your choice. What other people think is far less important than what you feel is right for you – if that means staying in with a good book, then that's fine.

Sex versus the essay

Who wants to sit through a lecture after a night of tempestuous sex? Wouldn't a walk by the river be more romantic? There's a temptation to postpone work when passion strikes. A relationship can swiftly assume far more importance in your life than studying, especially if you start bunking off lectures and falling behind with your essays. Relationships are important, but so is work. You have to decide how much one is going to impinge on the other. It's no good pleading unrequited love to the finals examiners; you can end up with lousy results and resent it for the rest of your life.

Sexuality

You may believe that sex should take place only within a monogamous relationship, or even only within marriage. Alternatively, you may want to find out what you like best before making any kind of permanent commitment (always assuming you think permanent commitments are a good idea). Most people's views lie somewhere in-between. Exploring your sexuality can be a heady liberation as well as a painful process and it can take a lifetime. Leaving home is often an escape from pressures and expectations, and the college environment is generally more tolerant, and more supportive, than the outside world.

Whatever your viewpoint, and whatever your preference, the same rules apply. Don't do anything you don't want to, don't make anyone else do anything they don't want to, never assume you know better than someone else what they want, and don't be persuaded that anyone else knows better than you what you want. And be safe.

Obviously the more partners you have, the higher the risk of infection will be. The only way to avoid sexually transmitted diseases (STDs, including AIDS) is to know all the risks and how to avoid them: by practising safer sex, you can reduce the risks. For detailed information on safer sex *see page 172* **Health and Stress.**

Sex – Some Suggestions

• It takes two to have good sex in a relationship. Some people forget this, and concentrate on their own pleasure to the exclusion of the other person. Others think their role is solely to give pleasure. Being able to ask for what you want is important, although it can take quite a while for this not to be embarrassing.

• Communication is important. You probably don't know what your partner is feeling or thinking: ask them. They don't know what's going on in your head: tell them. And if you find this difficult, say so.

• Other people tell us how to feel and what to do in bed. Magazines, films, trashy romances – most portray a stereotypical version of sex and sexuality. Sex (almost invariably heterosexual) is done under sheets with the man on top, and after a lot of serious moaning and bumping they both come. Together. Fade to black.

• Real sex is rather more prosaic. Films never show you struggling with the condom or frantically flipping your cap around the bathroom. They don't usually portray the shyness of the inexperienced or the fear that you won't live up to your partner's standards. And for most of us, simultaneous orgasm only happens once in a blue moon.

• You don't have to have intercourse: you can have loads of fun without it. Only about a third of women come solely through intercourse, which isn't surprising, given that only the lowest part of the vagina contains nerves, and the clitoris (which is positively buzzing with nerve endings) will only be stimulated by straightforward penetration if both partners' anatomies happen to match up.

• Sex doesn't necessarily mean penetration. For sexual pleasure and fulfilment, lips, tongues, hands and even sex toys may well do very nicely.

• Looks are by no means everything, whatever Hollywood and the glossy magazines would have us believe. And beauty is very much in the eye of the beholder. Media stereotypes have nothing to do with you enjoying your own and others' minds and bodies.

- It's not a contest. Notches on the bedpost are not a sign of maturity. Be honest, be sensitive and have respect both for yourself and for other people.
- Enjoy sex, but be safe: always use a condom. For information on AIDS and STDs, see page 172 **Health and Stress**.

There's no reason why awareness of AIDS and other sexually transmitted diseases should spoil sex. But in an environment where there are many potential new partners, it's essential to take responsible, informed decisions about who you sleep with. As a cover-all piece of advice on penetrative sex: if you're a man, wear a condom; if you're his partner, insist on it. And remember, HIV is everyone's problem; don't believe the tabloid-inspired propaganda.

Sexual Difficulties

Although the cause is occasionally physical, most problems stem from poor communication, pressure to conform to male and female role models, ignorance, a lack of trust and commitment, or unresolved conflicts in the relationship. Guilt, shyness and fear can all block our sexual responsiveness. So, what can the symptoms be?

Men may find themselves unable to get an erection when they most want to, or they may come too quickly, most likely just before penetration. Women may find it hard to relax, resulting in tightness, or a vagina which is too dry for penetration to be comfortable. Don't attempt penetration if this is the case. It may well be due to nerves, so don't get acrimonious – that will only exacerbate things – and, as a way of reducing the anxiety, try to forget penetration for a while. Just concentrate on getting to know what you each find pleasurable.

External factors can interfere as well. If you're exhausted or pissed, you may have a good time, but don't count on it. Cold rooms, squeaky beds and the thought of what can be heard through thin walls are definitely acquired tastes, and a recurring problem in draughty old halls of residence.

The assumption that sex means penetration, and that anything else isn't the real McCoy, is not particularly helpful. Labelling kissing and touching 'foreplay' suggests that they are leading up to something more important; it doesn't have to be like that. Oral sex, self- or mutual-masturbation, massage, and simply cuddling are all part of making love – pick what you enjoy and do it. Penetration is also the least safe option.

If you still have sexual difficulties, consult one of the books listed at the end of this chapter, or seek professional, sympathetic advice, such as a student counsellor or a doctor, via your student health service (or *see below* **Useful Addresses**). Dealing with difficulties in a spirit of patience, good humour and understanding can often be the surest way of overcoming them.

Women's sexuality has for centuries been defined by men: from Aristotle, who claimed that the female state was a deformity; to Freud, who said that women were driven by penis envy. In Victorian times women were expected to be virginal and passive; the permissive sixties demanded that women have multiple orgasms all over the shop. What actually goes on between the sheets has also, to a great extent, been defined by men, which means that they will get off on it. As a woman, it's important to find out what suits you, and communicate it to your partner. These days it is easier to say yes, or no, to what you like. But it's not easy to sort out what you want while you are still hedged about with demands and expectations from other people.

The most common symptom is not being able to relax, and finding that the man comes too quickly. Tension makes this worse, as men tend to come quicker and women slower. Perhaps you feel that things are moving too fast, or that you want more of a say in what's going on. If you do, say so. Don't rely on your partner to automatically know how you feel. Sometimes, an involuntary contraction of the muscles around the vagina makes penetration impossible (vaginismus). Again, getting used to your partner can help enormously with this, but if the problem persists, a visit to a counsellor is a good first step. And if your partner is unsympathetic, remember that it's their own insecurity talking, so don't let it make you feel bad.

Diseases

There's always a risk that you're going to catch something nasty when you get into bed with someone other than teddy (*see page 172* **Health and Stress** for the details). But there is one basic precaution which should always be taken:
- Insist on using a condom – it is without doubt the best insurance against sexually transmitted diseases (STDs), including HIV, an advantage which far outweighs any of the claimed disadvantages (*see below* **Contraception**). You should use a condom with *all* partners, even if they've only ever had sex with one person or even no-one before. Remember:
- You can never be sure that the person is telling the truth about their sexual history;
- People have been known to become infected with HIV the very first time they have sex;
- A condom will help prevent passing on any diseases *you* might have.

It's also possible that there is a link between forms of sex which can allow transmission of the human papilloma virus and cervical cancer. For accurate information about AIDS and HIV *see page 172* **Health and Stress**. But do note that both HIV and the papilloma virus responsible for cervical cancer are most easily passed on through penetrative sex.

Solutions to painful sex

It's important to be sure that infection is not the reason for painful sex. If: there's pain even when you're not having sex; the pain during intercourse is severe; there are sores of any kind; pain is associated with passing urine; and if it doesn't feel like a pain you might get when the entrance to the vagina is too tight (this can hurt men too), a visit to a GP, whether the college's or your own, would be advisable. It's likely to be a reassurance rather than anything worse, and there will certainly be female doctors available for women students.

Tightness of the vulva or dryness in the vagina may be not only painful, but the way an infection starts. If this is the case and you try to have penetrative sex, the vagina is likely to suffer small abrasions in which an infection can easily take hold. This need not necessarily be serious, but any vaginal infection is unpleasant and worrying. It's always best not to rush things, and perhaps to use lubricated condoms. It is vitally important only to use water-based lubricants, such as Durex Lubricating or KY Jelly (available at chemists' counters). Note, though, that neither of these lubricants are contraceptives. Do not use vaseline or similar petroleum-based jellies or baby oil: they can provoke allergies and erode condoms within minutes.

Contraception

Deciding what contraception to use is not just a matter of sexual methods. It's about health, responsibility and how we structure our relationships. Who buys the condoms, who pops the pill, who takes the risk? Being able to share the responsibility makes it that much easier; two people prevent conception better than one.

Types of contraceptive used by students.
38% of students use condoms
30% use the Pill
25% occasionally or usually use no contraception or rely upon natural methods
68% say AIDS has altered their attitude to sex
82% approve of sex before marriage
25% claim to have had no sexual partner in the past year
44% claim to have had one partner in the past year
15% claim to have had two partners in the past year
14% claim to have had three or more partners in the past year.
Source: National Student Magazine in conjunction with Durex.

The Condom: An ancient invention (the Romans used pigs' bladders) that can provide a good five minutes' entertainment to break the ice. Used properly, a condom offers protection against unwanted pregnancy and helps reduce the risk of cervical cancer and STDs; and the ribbed ones can add an extra thrill to the occasion.

Allways use a high quality brand such as Durex or Mates which has been awarded the British Safety Kite mark. They are highly effective *among people who use them properly.* They should be handled gently and rolled on well before penetration, lubricant-side out. It's important to squeeze the end of the condom while putting it on the penis, as this expels any air, and make sure any bubbles are squeezed out under the rubber along the shaft of the penis. Air in rubber makes a balloon, which it only takes a little prick to burst....

The man should withdraw his penis immediately after ejaculation since the condom is likely to slip off a penis which is getting smaller. It should be held around the base of the penis during withdrawal, for the same reason. The open end of the condom should be tied before it's thrown in the bin and the penis shouldn't touch the woman's genital area until all the semen has been washed off.

Although condoms have much to recommend them, they can sometimes split if used incorrectly (one reason why they must never be re-used, no matter how small your grant). Using a water-based lubricant reduces this risk but, if a condom does split, visit a doctor and ask for a 'morning-after pill' (*see below*).

Some men find it difficult to maintain an erection with a condom on, while others complain that they reduce sensitivity (which some women would consider a boon). Some people are allergic to the latex or spermicide. Shop around – hypo-allergenic brands, such as Durex Allergy, are available.

Putting a condom on can certainly interrupt the flow of things and nobody seriously suggests that unrolling a bit of rubber over your dick is a sexy thing to do. But it can be done with an eye to the entertainment value, and it can be done with a caring hand.

Finally, unprotected anal sex holds a very high risk of getting or giving HIV. British condoms are neither tested nor manufactured for use in anal sex, but used properly can minimise the risk of HIV transmission. If you are going to have anal sex it's best to use one of the stronger condoms on the market with plenty of added water-based lubricant such as Durex or KY.

The Pill: Although most types are extremely effective, there are clearly doubts about the wisdom of stuffing your body full of hormones for years on end, and various health risks have been identified, especially for women who smoke or have high blood pressure. Use of the Pill slightly increases the risk of thrombosis or cardiovascular problems, and the risks are further increased by age, obesity and cigarette smoking.

The combined Pill contains progesterone and oestrogen, which work together to prevent ovulation. Triphasic and biphasic pills vary the amounts of hormones over the month, to reduce the overall dosage. The mini-pill contains only progesterone, which thickens and alters cervical mucus so the sperm can't get through, and changes the uterine lining so it won't receive the egg if it is fertilized.

If you want to go on the Pill, visit your doctor or a family planning clinic. They will advise you on whether to take it, and what to take, and give you all the information you need. If you are at all confused, ask. It's your body and any mistake means that you are risking pregnancy or possible ill-health.

Advantages of the Pill include sex free from the fear of pregnancy and a regular menstrual cycle. Some women also report fewer menstrual cramps, a reduction in flow and less premenstrual tension (PMT, also known as PMS or pre-menstrual syndrome). But it doesn't guard against HIV transmission or other STDs, and tends to increase the temptation not to use condoms. Some women taking the Pill experience nausea, depression, breast tenderness, changes in weight, and very rarely, liver tumours; these effects can often be countered by trying a different formulation. However, if you are experiencing nausea or vomiting, or are taking anti-epileptic, anti-fungal or anti-biotic drugs, the effectiveness of the Pill can be lessened. Be sure to use another form of contraception and consult your doctor for advice. But if you want safer sex, use a condom too.

Diaphragms and caps: The diaphragm is a dome of rubber a bit smaller than the palm of your hand. It fits across the cervix to prevent sperm getting into the womb and it must be used with spermicide. The cap is smaller, looks rather like a bowler hat and is held snugly onto the tip of the cervix by suction. Both are available in different sizes and must be fitted by a doctor.

When properly inserted, neither of you should feel a diaphragm or a cap. Put a diaphragm in no more than three hours before intercourse – if the time is longer you'll need more spermicide, or a new pessary. Leave the diaphragm or cap in for six hours afterwards to make sure all the sperm are dead, but don't leave them in for more than 24 hours or you'll risk infection. Before further intercourse, check that it's still in the right position and add more spermicide. Used properly, these methods are very effective.

The IUD or intra-uterine device: Or coil. Or loop. IUDs have weird names like Copper-7, Lippes Loop or Multi-load.

Because they are more likely to cause serious problems than other methods of contraception, IUDs are unlikely to be prescribed for younger women or for women who have not yet had a child. The following information is therefore mainly for reference.

IUDs don't prevent ovulation, they prevent implantation, which has concerned some women opposed to abortion. (An IUD can be inserted within five days of unprotected intercourse if you think you may be pregnant and it will prevent a fertilized egg from implanting.) Copper IUDs also kill sperm; these need to be replaced every few years because the copper slowly disintegrates. Some women are allergic to copper.

"I was the same at university as I am now. Contrary to what everyone else was doing, rutting like rabbits, I had the sexual track record of a panda. I think I was still sorting it all out. Sussex University was a really good place to be then; liberal in the best sense of the word. One day I was lying in the bath, and my best friend and flatmate was shaving. 'I think I'm gay', I said. 'Oh really', he said, and carried on shaving. I loved the fact that at university everybody talked about...

A doctor will insert an IUD for you. A thread hangs from the IUD into the upper part of the vagina where it can be felt. If it disappears, it may be coiled inside the uterus, or the IUD may have fallen out. Some women have had problems with IUDs; pelvic infections can occur and may be a threat to fertility. The device is unlikely to turn up in your armpit or fall out of your nose, but in a few cases one has passed through the wall of the uterus and ended up in the body cavity, apparently as a result of unskilled insertion. Another problem is that the IUD can be expelled through the mouth of the womb, especially during menstruation. The chance of this happening drops rapidly after a few months; check with your doctor or clinic if you are worried, and use extra contraception until you've had it confirmed that the coil is still in place.

The sponge: A soft, circular sponge impregnated with spermicide is inserted high into the vagina before intercourse, rather like a diaphragm. It must stay in place for at least six hours after intercourse. Sponges have a relatively high failure rate, so they are not recommended.

Injectables: Progestogen is injected in the woman's buttock or arm and is released slowly into the bloodstream, preventing ovulation. The contraceptive effect lasts for two to three months, although the drugs can affect your body for much longer.

Both Depo Provera (DMPA, or DP) and the less commonly used, depression-inducing and masculinizing Noristerat, have been the subject of controversy in a number of countries, particularly the United States. DP may delay the return of fertility for up to two years and frequently plays havoc with the menstrual cycle. Studies with animals on high doses of DP have revealed cancer-promotion, though as far as risks to women are concerned, studies are inconclusive. DP is licensed in the UK as a last-resort method only; Noristerat for one-off use. They are not a routine option.

Implants: Capsules containing hormones used in some brands of the Pill are implanted under the skin inside your upper arm, and gradually release their contents into the body. They can be left in place for up to five years. A lot of the hormone is released at first, dropping to about the same level as one Pill a day after 18 months. Implants can be removed by a doctor at any time. Side-effects are similar to the Pill's, but these preparations are unlikely to be authorized for use in young women.

Morning-after pill or Emergency pill: This should not be treated as a contraceptive and should be used in an emergency only. It can be taken any time up to 72 hours after unprotected sex (so the term 'morning-after' is not strictly accurate) and is effective in preventing pregnancy. It is rather like a heavy dose of the standard contraceptive Pill. Although some women report only minor side-effects (nausea, cramps or just a heavy period), the hormone dose is very large and you can feel lousy for a couple of days.

The Male Pill: Research hasn't yet put it on to the chemists' shelves, although trials of a weekly injectable have been very successful. It looks promising for people in a stable relationship, so long as there aren't any long-term side-effects, but for casual sex two problems arise. Do you trust a man who says he's on it? And, as it won't provide protection against AIDS and STDs, why not just use a condom anyway?

The Safe Period: Reliable only if you have a *very* predictable cycle and it should be a first choice only for those who object to contraception. If you'd rather not have a baby, but feel that pregnancy would be no disaster, maybe these methods are for you.

...relationships and feelings; it was the norm. It's absolutely crucial that people express their feelings. University gave me the sense that it was all right to talk about it.

Things have changed of course – in the old days I used to go out every night, try and get laid and fail; I used to call it sexual frustration. Now I go out every night, try and get laid and still fail. But these days I call it a healthy lifestyle".

Simon Fanshawe Comedian and broadcaster (Law, Sussex University, 1975-78).

The idea is to work out when the woman is fertile and to abstain from sex or use contraception during that time. Ovulation may be detected by careful measurement of the woman's temperature or by examining her cervical mucus – some women use these methods quite successfully.

The rhythm method, on the other hand, is perfectly capable of precipitating a disaster all on its own. It relies on predicting when ovulation will occur on the basis of several previous menstrual cycles. As these can easily vary according to stress, illness or nothing in particular, it is unreliable at best, and utterly unsuited to a typical student's lifestyle. Forget it.

Coitus interruptus or withdrawal: Not a good idea. The man secretes lots of sperm-containing fluid even before ejaculation. Once this has entered the vagina, withdrawal will make no difference, and in any case, 'I promise I won't come' is an utterly untrustworthy line. If you have had unprotected sex, you should visit a doctor the next day and ask for a morning-after pill *(see above)*.

No sex: Very effective and highly recommended, if it's what you want.

Other things that don't work: Douching: you're more likely to give sperm a helping hand, or to irritate the vagina. Coitus reservatus, or holding back, is more likely to turn into coitus interruptus (*see above*). American tips (short rubber sheaths that cover the head of the penis) tend to fall off. Standing up during intercourse, going to the loo afterwards, jumping up and down, swearing profusely and extreme panic are all useless.

Family planning

If you want family planning, your first stop might be your family doctor. If you don't want to talk to him or her, you can see any other GP or visit a family planning clinic (*see below*

Useful Addresses). Contraception is free at any family planning clinic.

Abortion

The circumstances in which women decide to end a pregnancy vary enormously. The decision is rarely free of internal conflict, and for some it may be particularly painful. But it has to be a personal decision, based on what's best for you; don't be pressurised by your partner or family. If you think you might be pregnant but don't want to be, seek advice from a doctor, a family planning clinic or a counsellor immediately: modern pregnancy tests can show positive results within a week of a missed period. You will also be given access to counselling.

Should you decide on an abortion, you might be entitled to a free NHS abortion. You can be referred by your doctor or a family planning clinic to a NHS hospital. Alternatively, you can pay to have an abortion at a private clinic. An initial consultation with a counsellor and two doctors (required by law) costs £40. Private abortions are charged according to how advanced the pregnancy is, from £180 (up to 12 weeks, no overnight stay) or £205 (up to 12 weeks, overnight stay), up to £425 (between 19 and 22 weeks). Whether or not you pay, the legal requirement is the same: two doctors must agree that pregnancy would be physically or psychologically harmful to you.

Early on, abortions cause only minor physical discomfort, although the emotional experience can still be very painful and long-lasting. Before 12 weeks, abortions are carried out by the vacuum aspiration method, which is safer than having your tonsils out, and about as painful. This method does not generally require an overnight stay in hospital. Thereafter, abortion becomes more complicated, involving what is effectively an induced miscarriage, delivered vaginally and generally involving a

Sex and Relationships

stay in hospital. If you feel in need of counselling after an abortion, contact your local family planning clinic. The British Pregnancy Advisory Service, for instance, has 21 branches around the country, and post-abortion counselling for BPAS patients is available free, with a £25 fee for non-BPAS patients.

Ignore any tales you may have heard about self-induced abortions. Trying to do an abortion yourself by any means whatsoever, with or without someone else's help, will almost certainly be unsuccessful and is extremely dangerous. Don't do it.

You should be wary of organizations such as Life, which offer free pregnancy tests, but are vehemently anti-abortion. If you're in any doubt, it's best to contact one of the organizations we list under Useful Addresses.

Further Reading

Our Bodies, Ourselves – A Book by and for Women by Angela Phillips and Jill Rakusen, 1989 (Penguin, £15.99).
Women's Experience of Sex by Sheila Kitzinger, 1985 (Penguin, £7.95).
The Well Woman's Self-Help Directory by Nikki Bradford (Sedgewick, £12.99).
Pat Dew: a story of disability, pregnancy and birth (Seal Press, £7.95).

Useful Addresses

Association of Sexual and Marital Therapists PO Box 62, Sheffield SI0 3TS. Write for a list of qualified specialist psychotherapists.
British Association for Counselling 37A Sheep Street, Rugby, Warwickshire CV21 3BX (0788 78328/9). The Association keeps a list of counsellors, including those specializing in psychosexual problems.
British Pregnancy Advisory Service Austy Manor, Wootton Wawen, Solihull, West Midlands B95 6BX (0564 793225). Non-profit-making charitable clinics offering contraception, abortion, pregnancy testing, donor insemination and low-cost counselling. There are 21 offices around the country; phone the above number for your local branch.
Brook Advisory Centres 153A East Street, London, SE17 2SD (071 708 1234). Offer free pregnancy tests, counselling, contraception advice and abortion referrals for people up to the age of 25.
Durex Information Service for Sexual Health North Circular Road, London E4 8QA. Offers a wide range of leaflets about safe sex, contraceptives, cervical cancer and HIV and Aids.
Family Planning Information Service 27-35 Mortimer Street, London W1N 7RJ (071 636 7866). This is not a clinic. It offers free advice over the phone, or by sending an SAE, on contraception. It also helps with sexual problems, and puts people in touch with other organizations for abortion referral.
Pregnancy Advisory Service 11-13 Charlotte Street, London W1P 1HD (071 637 8962). This service offers walk-in pregnancy testing, with results available two days after a missed period. Staff also give advice on birth control, including the morning after pill, plus abortion advice and referral. Not free.
National Abortion Campaign Wesley House, 4 Wild Court, London WC2B 5AV (071 405 4801). Contact the Campaign for information on abortion and reproductive rights.
Women's Health and Reproductive Rights Information Centre 52-54 Featherstone Street, London EC1Y 8RT (071 251 6580). The Centre offers information and advice on birth control and women's health; there's a nominal charge for leaflets.

NHS Treatment **174**
Complementary Therapies **175**
Women's Health **177**
Men's Health **179**
Sexually Transmitted Diseases **179**
Aids **183**
Drug Misuse **186**
Smoking and Drinking **188**
Sports Injuries **191**
Skin Problems **191**
Psychological Problems **193**
Self-Help **196**
Further Reading **197**
Useful Addresses **197**

health and stress

Staying healthy at college should be your first priority. And the antidote to stress is not eight pints of lager and a lungful of nicotine. Doctors **Anna Graham** and **Ann Robinson** suggest ways of preventing illness and tell you when to seek medical advice.

173

Most civilizations have come to the conclusion that a healthy mind in a fit body is the basis for happiness. *Mens sana in corpore sano* was the Roman view. But in the modern world, we don't seem so sure. All too often we find ourselves relying on a diet of cholesterol (chips), alcohol (beer) and nicotine (cigarettes). These foods and stimulants, taken in excess, lead in later life to coronary heart disease, strokes and, in the case of cigarettes, cancer and other diseases. All such diseases are avoidable.

A health-conscious lifestyle is the answer; and prevention is always better than cure. Of course, some things you can't always avoid: stress, exhaustion, colds, flu, stomach upsets, migraines and conjunctivitis, are among the most common student complaints. But a lifestyle which includes time for nutritious food, regular sleep and exercise, study, decent accommodation and an active social life will help to make you feel and look fit and healthy.

NHS Treatment

Doctors: Colleges will often have their own health centres, and sometimes resident or visiting doctors. Details are available at registration (you should be given the relevant forms to fill in) or from your student union welfare officer.

If you want to sign on with a local doctor under the National Health Service (NHS) you'll need your medical card. If you can't find it, ask the GP with whom you want to register for a Lost Medical Card form. Lists of NHS doctors are available in libraries and post offices or from your local Family Practitioner Committee or Citizens' Advice Bureau (consult the telephone directory for your nearest branch). NHS doctors who practise within a mile of your college or where you live should accept you as a patient, unless they are already oversubscribed. Women who prefer to be treated by a woman doctor can insist on this; again, phone your local Family Practitioner Committee for a list of GPs or look for a list in your local library.

Overseas students can also register with NHS doctors and those on a course lasting more than six months qualify for NHS treatment from the first day they enter the country. If you are here for less than six months, it's best to take out health insurance. *See also page 28* **Overseas Students**.

Health benefits & Income Support: The new student loans system has serious implications for students' claims for health benefits, reduced-rate prescriptions, dental treatment and glasses. Students used to qualify for these on grounds of low income; however, the student loan is now treated as 'notional income' – ie students are assumed to have taken out a maximum loan regardless of whether they have or not. A weekly 'disregard' of £10 is applied only if the student meets the conditions for entitlement to Income Support (*see page 72* **Money**). The rest, the vast majority of students, will have the loan included as income and, as a result, might not receive any help at all.

Prescriptions: Pick up leaflet AB11 from your doctor, post office or social security office for more information about help with NHS costs; and leaflet P11 from doctors, social security offices or chemists for facts about NHS prescriptions. You can claim on form AG1 from any social security office, dentist, optician or hospital. The DSS will then send you an AG2 certificate (for full help) or an AG3 (for partial help). If, when you pay prescription charges, you think you might qualify for free prescriptions, ask the chemist for receipt form FP57 (EC57 in Scotland). The back of the form tells you how to claim a refund.

Dentists: A list of dentists is available from your local Family Practitioner Committee, library or Citizens' Advice Bureau.

Opticians: Find out if you are entitled to help with costs before you visit an optician, because they don't give refunds. Leaflet G11 from the Department of Health will tell you all you need to know. You'll find the discount form AG1 at any optician, who should also fill it in. Any registered high street optician will test your eyes and provide and sign form AG1. You will automatically get full-value vouchers for glasses if you are a student aged under 19.

Complementary Therapies

If popping a pill or prodding up a pessary isn't your cup of tea, there are more natural alternatives. As well as the tried and tested DIY remedies for various ailments – ingesting vast quantities of vitamin C to fight against colds, for instance – there are many ways you can keep your general level of health high, or fight off infection when it takes hold. Therapies should usually be used to complement orthodox medicine – not as alternatives; and it's best to ask therapists for proof of qualifications. For associations of registered practitioners of therapies mentioned below, *see below* **Useful Addresses**.

Homoeopathy is the only alternative system of medicine that is fully recognized by the NHS. Most homoeopathic remedies are made from herbs and other natural substances, which help the body to help itself. Homoeopathy can treat or prevent both acute and chronic conditions, and is one way of detoxifying the body. Some NHS doctors practise homoeopathy: consult the local Family Practitioner Committee for details, or the Institute for Complementary Medicine, which has a computerized referral system to put people in touch with practitioners.

Shiatsu and acupuncture are techniques based on a system of energy-channels, or meridians, that run through the nervous system. Trauma or suppression of emotion affects the balance or the flow of energy, and massage of the meridians (shiatsu), or the insertion of needles into specific points along them (acupuncture), can unblock and rebalance the flow. Acupuncture is also thought to be effective in treating some ilnesses which respond poorly to orthodox methods, such as asthma, migraines and ulcerative colitis.

Osteopathy (a system of healing based on the manipulation of bones or other parts of the body) is an increasingly recognized method of treating long-standing aches and pains which are sometimes not helped by conventional treatment, such as backaches.

The Alexander Technique is commonly misrepresented as being about no more than lying on your back with your knees up and a telephone directory under your head. The reality is quite different. On the physical side, it's about unlearning bad habits in standing, moving and breathing. But connected with this is how we let our bodies take the strain of our emotions. By learning to deal with emotions directly, we can stop off-loading life's anxieties and pressures on to our bodies.

Hypnotherapy can be used to treat problems like smoking, insomnia, phobias and eating disorders. Most hypnotists will tell you that all hypnosis is self-hypnosis, so there's no possibility of being made to do something that you don't want to do. A hypnotist can put you into an extremely relaxed state, when you will be more susceptible to suggestion.

Other forms of relaxation – aromatherapy, yoga, t'ai chi, meditation – can all be effective in helping you to cope with the various stresses and strains of being a student. Check in your local newspaper, wholefood shop or health centre for people or groups providing the right alternative therapy for you.

AND THEY DON'T KNOW EACH OTHER WELL ENOUGH TO DISCUSS USING A CONDOM?

A condom can help stop you getting HIV, the Human Immunodeficiency Virus that leads to AIDS. So never, ever, feel shy about asking your partner to use one.

HEALTH EDUCATION AUTHORITY

AIDS. YOU'RE AS SAFE AS YOU WANT TO BE.

FOR MORE INFORMATION OR CONFIDENTIAL ADVICE ABOUT AIDS, FREEPHONE THE 24-HOUR NATIONAL AIDS HELPLINE ON 0800 567 123.

Women's Health

Regular breast examinations will help you to spot any lumps at an early stage, when chances of recovery (if there is a problem) are much higher. Pick the same time each month, preferably just after your period when breasts tend to feel less lumpy. First, check in a mirror for any obvious change in shape, size, skin texture or nipple discharge. Then lie flat and, using the pads of your fingertips, rotate them in small circles, starting at the nipple and working outwards as you move round the breast. Also check under your arms for swollen lymph glands, which will feel like firm, discrete lumps.

It is notoriously hard to assess oneself, so a yearly visit to a Well Woman's Clinic is advisable. And visit the doctor if you find any changes that are worrying you. The chances are that it's a blocked duct or a swollen gland, and will disappear in a few weeks or months. Get it checked, just in case. If you're in your teens or early twenties, it's unlikely that you'll suffer from malignant cancer – but benign lumps are quite common, so it's important to start self-examination young.

All women should have a cervical smear test at least every five years, and some doctors recommend testing every three years. Women in high-risk categories (those who've had an STD, multiple partners, cervical abnormalities, several children, and whose partners have had STD) should have more frequent tests. Contact a Well Woman clinic, Family Planning clinic or STD clinic if your doctor refuses you a test or if s/he is ambiguous about the result. Always make sure you get the result in writing, even if the surgery staff say someone will ring you if it is positive.

PMS

For three weeks of the month you are good-tempered, helpful, even charming. Then one morning you wake up under a grey cloud and everything is wrong. Not all women are affected by PMS (pre-menstrual syndrome) and for some symptoms may not be severe, but many women feel clumsy, tired and irritatable.

Meanwhile, there are men who have been heard to opine that PMS is used as an excuse for bad behaviour, or that women go crazy and aren't responsible for their actions. Ignore them, and get to know your own menstrual cycle together with the emotional changes it brings.

Remedies for PMS abound, from regular evening primrose oil and vitamin B6 to massage. So long as you eat a balanced, varied diet, get enough sleep, take gentle exercise and try to visit your local health food shop for herbal teas or your local chemist for aspirin or paracetamol, you should survive the PMS blues. If symptoms are severe, medical help should be sought as there may be problems that require diagnosis. You could also contact PMS Relief for advice (*see* **Useful Addresses**).

Cystitis

Cystitis is a common and painful affliction, caused by inflammation of the bladder, usually because of an infection which spreads up the urethra. Women are more vulnerable to this than men because their urethras are short, so bacteria don't have to travel far to get into the bladder. Sex is frequently a trigger to a painful attack. The symptoms are: a strong need to pass urine very frequently (up to every five minutes if you're unlucky); a painful stinging or burning sensation on urination; small amounts of urine passed, which may smell different (often fishy); and traces of blood in the water. Some people experience low abdominal pain.

Guide to Vaginal Discharge

All women secrete moisture and mucus from the membranes that line the vagina. It is perfectly normal to have a discharge, and it is also a good way of telling if something is wrong. There are several kinds of discharge:

Normal: Transparent or milky, possibly slippery, yellowish when dry.

Thrush (yeast infection): Thick, white, rather like cottage cheese, coupled with itching. Easily treated but extremely easily transmitted, see a doctor. *See also below* **Sexually Transmitted Diseases**.

Vaginitis (inflammation of the vagina); **Cervicitis** (inflammation of the cervix); **Anaerobic vaginosis** (bacterial infection): White, yellow, bloody or greyish, with bad smell after sex. All are easily treated, see a doctor. *See also below* **Sexually Transmitted Diseases**.

Trichomoniasis (parasitic infection): Yellow or yellow-green, thin, foamy, smelling of fish. Easily treated, see a doctor. *See also below* **Sexually Transmitted Diseases**.

Early gonorrhoea; Chlamydia (both bacterial infections): Normal at ovulation (roughly, in the middle of the menstrual cycle), but thin, transparent at other times. They are both easily treated, but can spread to other parts of the body; see a doctor. *See also below* **Sexually Transmitted Diseases**.

Cervical erosion (changes to developing cervical cells): Some traces of blood in otherwise normal discharge; see a doctor.

'Easily treated' as used above does not mean that the symptons should be ignored; get advice as soon as possible. Any treatment should also include sexual partners. The above are only guidelines; if you are at all worried, always consult a doctor.

Initially, you can treat cystitis yourself by drinking at least four pints of water a day, with a teaspoonful of sodium bicarbonate in each pint. Avoid coffee, tea, alcohol and sugary or heavily spiced foods. A hot water bottle held over your aching belly is very comforting. If symptoms do not improve after 24 hours, or if you have a temperature of over 37°C and are shivering, or if your back just below the ribs on either side becomes painful (a sign of kidney infection), go straight to your GP who will probably prescribe antibiotics and take further action if necessary.

Men's Health

Young men often neglect their health. They tend to drink more, take more recreational (not medically prescribed) drugs, are less concerned about healthy eating and have less consideration for their own psychological needs than women. This no doubt has a significant impact on well-being and physical health over the years and partly explains why men's life expectancy is almost ten years less than women's. It is important to start good habits young. See below **Smoking and Drinking** and **Psychological Problems** for advice.

Like breast cancer in women, testicular cancer can be picked up early through self-examination; and early treatment can make a successful outcome more likely. Monthly examination of both testes is recommended. First check for any obvious changes in size, shape, consistency and postion of each testis. Then feel the back where the epididymis is (it's a thickening attached to the back of the testis) and again feel for swelling or changes in consistency. Then check up the spermatis cords (running up the back of the scrotum towards the body). If you do find any change, make an appointment to see your doctor. Most lumps and bumps are benign, but it's important to get an expert opinion.

Sexually Transmitted Diseases

Anaerobic vaginosis or gardnerella

See treatment for thrush *below*. The infection should be cleared if you are planning a pregancy, as some links between this condition and prematurity and post-partum complications has been made.

Chlamydia

The most common STD in the West, chlamydia is a bacterium which acts more like a virus, which may cause secondary problems elsewhere in the body. It's very infectious. If left untreated it can lead to infection of the cervix, urethra, womb lining and fallopian tubes; chlamydia is thought to be the most common cause of pelvic inflammatory disease, and can also be passed on to a baby during delivery, causing a serious eye infection. Only one third of infected women display symptoms, which are increased vaginal discharge, soreness, frequent and painful urination, lower abdominal pain and fever. In untreated women it may be apparent for the first time only when they fail to become pregnant. Men will generally have a discharge and a burning sensation when peeing.

Both partners require diagnosis, and condoms should be used until the infection clears. Treatment with antibiotics is easy and effective when chlamydia is caught early enough. If you suspect that you or a partner might have it, go to an STD clinic, where a full range of tests is available.

Genital warts

The umbrella term for the group of viruses that cause warts is human papillomavirus (HPV). Recently, genital warts have been linked with an increased incidence of cervical cancer. Warts are sexually transmitted, via penetrative or oral sex. The symptoms are – well, the warts themselves. But it's difficult to spot internal warts (inside the vagina as well as the cervix), especially in the early stages when they tend to be microscopic. The only other symptom may be some abnormal vaginal discharge. Men can get warts anywhere on the penis and around or inside the anus. These may itch.

Warmth and moisture may encourage growth. Warts can be removed with laser treatment, frozen off with liquid nitrogen, or burned off with chemicals. If you think you might be pregnant, make sure the doctor knows, as some treatments have been linked to miscarriage and birth defects. Remember to have a regular cervical smear.

Gonorrhoea

Gonorrhoea is a problem, since it can be caught and carried unknowingly. It can be spread through genital, genital-oral and genital-rectal sex. The eyes can become infected by contact with infected discharge, and gonorrhoea can also be passed on to babies during birth. Half of the women and some of the men who have gonorrhoea display no symptoms; other women may experience a slight increase in vaginal discharge and possibly pain when peeing, while men may produce a thick yellowish discharge and experience intense pain when peeing. If untreated, it can block the fallopian tubes and lead to infertility or ectopic pregnancy; nearly a fifth of all women known to have gonorrhoea develop pelvic inflammatory disease. Early detection and treatment is crucial. Treatment is with one shot of penicillin.

Hepatitis B

Hepatitis B is spread through blood, semen and saliva. Symptoms do not always appear. There is a danger of irreversible liver damage and the disease can last for months.

Herpes

Whereas cold sores are caused by one type of herpes simplex virus, HSV1, genital herpes is caused by HSV2, although there is some crossover mainly because of the increase in oral-genital sex. Herpes is caught through vaginal, anal or oral sex with someone who has an active infection; it can be spread via the genitals, mouth or fingers.

The symptoms usually arrive two to 20 days after infection. Itching or tingling in the genital area, pains in the legs, or burning sensations in the buttocks or groin may precede small clusters of red spots which subsequently change to white blisters. Within a few days the blisters burst and form open sores. Then a scab appears and the sores heal themselves. Men may experience pain in the testicles, followed by sores on the penis, and sometimes also on the scrotum, buttocks, anus and thighs. They can also have sores without knowing it, hidden up inside the urethra, together with a mucous discharge.

The virus can be transmitted from just before the blisters erupt and while the sores are present. It gets in through breaks in the skin, or through mucous membranes in the genitals or eyes. But it's not that easy to catch: there is only a 15 per cent chance of catching it if you have unprotected sex with someone who is shedding the virus at the time. There is virtually no risk when the carrier has no sores.

The first attack is usually the worst. Only about ten per cent of sufferers get frequent attacks after that. About half have attacks every few months for no more than a year, and most find the attacks decrease in frequency and severity with time. They seem to be triggered by stress, illness, menstruation or pregnancy.

Health and Stress

There is no cure, but it is possible to control very severe and frequent recurrences. You can significantly improve syptoms with Acyclovir, but you must go to your doctor immediately after infection, as it only works if applied early. It doesn't kill the virus, but greatly alleviates it. A vaccine is currently being developed to provide immunity. Self-help remedies include stress control, frequent baths with baking powder, and wearing loose cotton underwear.

Scabies

Mites dig in under the outer layer of skin to lay eggs, causing itching over the buttocks, armpits and thighs. If scratched, the holes dug by the mites can be infected by bacteria and cause a rash. You can get scabies from sex or just from sharing a bed, but the most likely form of transmission is skin contact. It can be spread without the carrier being aware that s/he is infected, but can be easily treated with lotions.

Syphilis

Henry VIII had it, but these days syphilis is fairly rare. It's caused by a bacterium which infects the lips of the vagina, the clitoris and the opening of the urethra, and sometimes also the cervix in women; and the penis in men. Once infection takes place, there are three major phases – each phase may or may not be accompanied by symptoms. In order to treat syphilis successfully, diagnosis in the first phase (a hard, usually painless spot or ulcer in the infected area, with a possible inflammation around the affected area) is vital. The second possible sign is flat, warty growths on the vagina and white spots on the tongue. With all this, there's also fever, fatigue and aching joints. If untreated, the symptoms may disappear and the infection become latent. It can stay that way, or come back again to haunt you. Treatment is with two weeks on penicillin or other drugs. Syphilis during pregnancy is extremely serious as it may lead to foetal deformity and death. Blood tests should be repeated if you think you may have been exposed during any stage of pregancy.

Thrush

Candida albicans, a yeast fungus, is normally found in the intestines and vagina. If your system is knocked out of balance (for example, through being pregnant, being on the Pill, suffering from stress, illness or allergies, and taking antibiotics) the acidity of the vagina may be reduced, and the fungus can then take hold. Alternatively, you might get infected through having sex with someone who has thrush.

The symptoms are a white discharge, which can be as thick as cottage cheese, and which usually itches. The short-term solution is a trip to the doctor and a handful of pessaries or a tube of cream (Canesten). This should deal with it. Any sexual partners should go for a test to check whether they also have it, or you could find yourselves passing it back and forth between you. If you do manage to clear it up and then find it comes creeping back, you probably need to stabilize your system.

Try to omit high high levels of sugar, fats and refined flour from your diet, and to avoid fungi and yeasty or mouldy foods, such as blue cheese, leavened breads and mushrooms. Natural (live) yoghurt is the standard cure – eat it, insert it, douche in it – the live acidophilus cultures fight the candida in the intestines Eat as much garlic as you like – it's a natural antibiotic. Other possible remedies range from vinegar baths to acidophilus lactobacilli capsules from the chemist. Pick the one that works best for you.

ABORTION

For advice and help
Confidential, Caring — Individual Attention
London 071-388 4843   Leeds 0532-440 685
Manchester 061-832 4260
24 hours info service all week
114 Whitfield Street, London W1P 6BE

MARIE STOPES
CARING CLINICS SINCE 1925

ABORTION
Advice and Help
071-580 9001
Weekdays, Sats
available in London at
our own nursing home
after consultation
EARLY PREGNANCY TESTING
PRETERM
40 Mortimer St, London W1.
near Oxford Circus
SMALL IS FRIENDLY

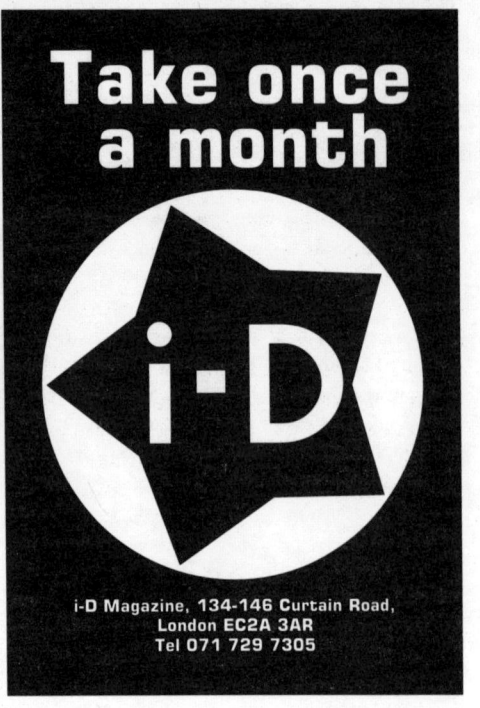

ABORTION
Advice & Help
071-580 4847
* Immediate Consultations
* Pregnancy test while you wait
* Open 6 days a week

Personal care and attention
MPCC
Metropolitan Pregnancy
Control Clinic
40 Mortimer St, London W1.
near Oxford Circus

Take once a month

i-D

i-D Magazine, 134-146 Curtain Road,
London EC2A 3AR
Tel 071 729 7305

Recommended Reading

Around Town, Art, Books, Cabaret, Children, Clubs, Dance, Film, Gay, Music, Politics, Sport, Student London, Theatre, TV and Radio

Time Out

London's best-selling weekly guide
to what to do and where to be seen

Trichomoniasis, trich or TV

TV is a parasitic infection which may lead to urinary tract infections. It gets active in the vagina and causes a thin, foamy, yellow-green discharge which is both itchy and smelly. Soreness and painful peeing are also common symptoms. It can also cause cystitis. Men tend to display no symptoms except occasionally a thin, whitish discharge, and pain when peeing.

Treatment is usually with metronidazole. You should avoid drink and sex while taking it. TV may be spread through objects such as towels, underwear, and bathing suits. If you have recurrent attacks, ask your doctor about having the vaccine. It has been noted that there is often a relationship between TV and the more serious gonnorhoea. If you have one of these conditions, it might be wise to be treated for the other.

Vaginitis, vulvitis

If you itch or hurt Down There, and are worried that you are over-discharging, you could have a vaginal infection. This condition can be sexually transmitted or due to bacterial/yeast overgrowth. In either case, both partners will require treatment. If you've recently given birth, had an abortion or any other gynaecological procedure, symptoms may be an indication of infections in the womb. Have it investigated.

If the above does not apply, eliminate any chemicals you are using (creams, lotions, talcs, deodorants, scented soap). Then eliminate tampons, caps, sponges and anything else you insert regularly. You might simply be allergic to, or irritated by, one of these. It's best to avoid sex, all chemicals and tight clothing, and to use gentle creams to relieve itching or soreness. A few days of handling with care should see the symptoms clear up. If they persist, you must see a doctor.

Prevention

Prevention is better than cure – always practise safe sex. The more people you have sex with, the higher your chance of catching something. Just because s/he looks relatively symptom-free on the night, that doesn't mean there isn't something unpleasant to avoid; men suffer from less symptoms (often, none at all). Take precautions.

Barrier methods of contraception make sense, and a condom is the best one. A spermicide that contains nonoxynol-9 offers some protection against herpes, HIV and some STDs. Avoid Intra-Uterine Devices or coils (IUDs), since these increase susceptibility to infections. Hygiene is also important, as some conditions are not just sexually transmitted. Linens, underclothing, toilets and cosmetics are possible sources of infection.

STD clinics

If you think you have a problem, it's best to visit an STD clinic immediately. The experts there may well be more alert to the possibilities and dangers of STDs than your doctor. You don't need to be referred, and everything that takes place in the clinic is confidential.

There's no reason to be shocked or dismayed to discover that you have an STD. Don't worry. It can happen to anyone with an active sex life, and also to some without one. At a clinic there is usually someone available for counselling on how to deal with STDs.

AIDS

AIDS stands for Acquired Immune Deficiency Syndrome. The disease is a possible consequence of infection with HIV (Human Immunodeficiency Virus), which can attack the body's self-defence system, leaving it vulnerable to common infections which may be life-threatening to people with AIDS. However, most peole with HIV remain perfectly healthy for many years – indeed, they might never become ill – and the majority are probably unaware that they are infected.

HIV is present in the blood, semen and vaginal fluids of an infected person, but is only transmitted if those fluids get into someone else's bloodstream. This most commonly happens in the following ways: through sharing drug injecting equipment; through unprotected anal or vaginal sex (which is a risk for both partners); and from a mother to her baby before or during birth.

HIV cannot be passed on in the same way that you can catch chicken pox or flu, and is not transmitted in saliva, sweat or tears. Everyday social contact, such as shaking hands, kissing, coughing, sneezing, sharing kitchen or toilet facilities and so on, is perfectly safe.

Don't believe the hype

In November 1989 *The Sun* ran a story with the headline 'Straight Sex Cannot Give You Aids: Official'. A number of politicians, mostly in the House of Lords, have also been peddling the idea that you are only likely to develop AIDS if you're some kind of 'weirdo' (in other words, a gay man or an intravenous drug user). Everything these ignorant buffoons have said flies in the face of all the research which has been carried out into AIDS and HIV.

Don't believe anyone who tells you that the number of new AIDS cases is decreasing or that the risk of infection to heterosexuals is negligible. The leading AIDS charity, The Terrence Higgins Trust, says that 'the epidemic in the UK is increasing'. Although the majority of those known to have been infected so far have been injecting drug-users and sexually active gay men, heterosexual men and women represent an increasing percentage of those with AIDS and HIV. Indeed, the number of cases of AIDS and HIV among heterosexuals is doubling every year and shows no sign of decreasing.

Official figures up to the end of January 1991 show that 4,228 people in the UK have been diagnosed as having developed AIDS; while the number of people with HIV has been estimated at 100,000. The World Health Organisation reckons that there are 600,000 people with AIDS world-wide and a further six to eight million infected with HIV. What is also very worrying is that many of the people recently diagnosed as HIV positive have been found to have contracted the virus in the seventies or early eighties, when no-one even suspected that it existed.

Although gay men have been disproportionately affected by the epidemic in the UK, because the virus was widely transmitted in the years before it was discovered, the rapid and widespread adoption of safer sex by gay men has drastically reduced the incidence of new infections. Worldwide, the majority of people with HIV or AIDS are heterosexual and, by contrast with gay men, heterosexuals have been slow to take the threat seriously. Surveys among young people indicate that while most heterosexuals have a very high awareness of the medical and scientific aspects of HIV infection, attitudes towards safer sex and sexuality remain remarkably complacent.

'It'll never happen to me' is the view still held by many people. But with the increased likelihood of the disease spreading to epidemic proportions, anyone who takes this approach is openly flirting with the risk of infection. You can't tell if someone is infected simply by looking at them, talking to them or even being in love with them. But by having safer sex and not sharing needles, it makes no difference whether we or our partners are HIV positive or not.

Safer sex

Although there have been significant medical advances in treating HIV and the opportunistic infections of AIDS, the prospects for a vaccine against HIV or drugs to restore HIV-related immune damage are still remote. The best option is to avoid getting HIV in the first place. That means having safer sex with every person you have sex with, every time.

Safer sex is any form of sex which reduces or eliminates the chances of your partner's blood, semen or vaginal fluids getting into your bloodstream. That means using condoms and added water-based lubricant for penetrative sex, or sticking to non-penetrative forms of sex such as massage, masturbation, rubbing bodies together, sex between the thighs, in armpits, between the breasts, playing with nipples, ears, feet – the list is limited only by your imagination.

Some people use sex toys such as dildos and buttplugs; don't share these without using a new condom for each person. Oral sex is probably safe as long as the person doing the sucking doesn't have cuts, sores or ulcers in their mouth. To be even safer, use dental dams (squares of latex) or condoms with flavourings or foods added. Information on dental dams can be had from the Women's Development Officer at the Terrence Higgins Trust (*see below* **Useful Addresses**) or from the London Lesbian and Gay Switchboard (*see page 220* **Lesbian and Gay Students**).

Safer Sex does not mean no more sex, but it does mean changing the ways you have sex. If you and your partner enjoy experimenting you will find new pleasures and satisfaction in your sex life. Be adventurous, use your imagination and don't be afraid to talk it through with your partner. See *also page* 160 **Sex and Relationships**.

HIV and drugs

Anyone who shares needles, syringes or other equipment to inject drugs – even just once – risks also injecting HIV directly into their bloodstream. Always use your own equipment, or in an emergency clean used equipment by washing thoroughly several times in hot water or with bleach.

There are a number of needle exchange schemes operating throughout the UK which offer free counselling and exchange services. Some are attached to hospitals; others are attached to youth and community projects. For information about schemes in your area, look in your phone book, ask at your student union or contact one of the organizations listed under **Useful Addresses**.

HIV antibody tests

Blood tests are now widely available from doctors or through STD clinics. They test for antibodies to the HIV virus, and so can tell you whether you are infected and infectious to others. They do not, and cannot, tell you whether you have AIDS, or will ever develop AIDS. Antibodies to the virus take on average three to six months to develop, so that a negative test result could still mean that you've been infected in the recent past, but not yet produced antibodies. If you think you might be infected, wait at least three months before going for the test. One in every 300 tests gives a false result, but positive results are always double-checked. You really can't use the test to find out whether you should be having safer sex. If you are negative, you need to have safer sex to avoid getting infected in the future; if you are positive, you need to have safer sex to avoid infecting anyone else, and to avoid getting re-infected, which could be harmful to your health.

Make sure that you are given full counselling before and (if you decide to have it) after a test. You need to consider fully whether you really need to know your antibody status, and what the effect of the information will be. The Terrence Higgins Trust urges people to first consider the possible consequences in terms of problems getting insurance. STD clinics are the best places to have a test: they have a better record than doctors on confidentiality and most provide a proper counselling service.

Certain countries – Saudi Arabia, China, USSR – have compulsory testing, which applies to students wishing to study there for extended periods. Some companies insist on prospective employees being tested.

Drug Misuse

This broadly refers to the taking of drugs for non-medical reasons. A wide range of drugs can cause physical and psychological dependence, both a craving for more of the drug and a debilitating pain if denied it. Valium (a prescription drug) and nicotine (a legal drug) are addictive. 'Hard drugs', such as heroin, are both addictive and potentially lethal.

'Soft drugs', such as cannabis, are fairly common at many colleges. It's essential to avoid all drugs if you have had psychological or psychiatric problems in the past; or if your family has a history of psychotic illnesses, such as manic depression or schizophrenia. Drug-taking can increase the risk of becoming mentally ill: sometimes in the short term only; but also triggering latent psychiatric problems which could handicap the rest of your life. *See also below* **Psychiatric Problems**. Many student unions produce literature and give advice on the misuse of drugs.

Effects
Benzodiazepines (valium)
Benzodiazepines are most likely to be prescribed by your doctor. They are highly addictive (after two weeks in many cases) and are also available on the black market. Up to five per cent of users suffer from withdrawal fits. If you've been taking them for over two weeks and want to stop, seek medical advice.

Cannabis
Cannabis is usually smoked, sometimes eaten, and induces a 'high' or a sense of relaxation, as well as altering sensations and judgement. Drowsiness and confusion are other likely effects; high doses can cause hallucinations. Although it's the safest of the illicit drugs, short-term use of high doses can cause psychosis and paranoid ideas; the long-term effects can be apathy, dulling of personality and reactions, and decreased motivation. Driving under its influence can be fatal.

Designer drugs (Ecstasy, Ice)
'Designer drugs' is an American term which means a new, abusable hallucinogenic compound which has been synthesised to avoid prosecution, as it's not yet named on the US illegal drug list. UK drug laws are not the same, so most are illegal here.

Ecstasy is a stimulant which also produces a pronounced feeling of serenity. Because of dubious manufacturing techniques, different doses can have different molecular compounds and thus be of variable quality: some has been very dangerous, causing terrifying hallucinations which cannot be treated.

Hallucinogens (LSD, Magic mushrooms)
A trip on hallucinogens usually lasts several hours. The experience can be exhilarating, but also very, very disturbing, since every normal feeling is intensified several times over. A bad trip can be accompanied by abdominal pain, a sense of being unwell and, sometimes, irrational and possibly destructive behaviour. It can also cause psychosis, when your sense of reality is lost in a very threatening and frightening way. Psychosis can last for weeks and needs urgent medical attention. Flashbacks may occur for years after.

Management: If you are with someone who is having a bad trip, stay with them: it shouldn't last more than 12 hours. If it does, or if your friend appears to be very disturbed or frightened, call a doctor.

Opiates (Heroin, Morphine, Codeine)
Opiates can induce a feeling of relaxation and euphoria. Other effects are nausea, vomiting and drowsiness, commonly followed by constipation, impotence and depression. Opiates are highly addictive, to the extent that even mild dabbling can get you hooked. Addicts have to keep taking opiates to ward off withdrawal symptoms. Injecting an impure opiate causes inflammation of veins, abscesses, heart problems and blood poisoning. Hepatitis B and AIDS (*see below* **AIDS**) can result from the use of unsterilized needles.

Management: Withdrawal symptoms resemble a savage bout of flu: fever, aches, runny nose, diarrhoea, insomnia. They start about 24 hours after tailing off the drug, and last up to five days. After two days, the symptoms start to abate. It is very difficult to withdraw on your own, so seek medical advice from your GP or the local drugs dependancy unit. Doctors may prescribe methadone, a long-acting opiate syrup which is taken in gradually reduced doses to stagger the effects of withdrawal. Short-term use of tranquillisers and sleeping pills can help the addict; or you could be referred to a self-help group.

Stimulants (Cocaine, Amphetamines, Crack)
Stimulants create a sense of wellbeing, but they can cause abdominal pain, paranoid suspicions, insomnia and irritability. You will experience an upsurge of energy and talkativeness, but the morning after you can feel depressed and miserable. Regular use of stimulants leads to tolerance, a craving for larger doses and depression when the body is denied these drugs. Some people can become psychotic if they use stimulants in high doses, sometimes showing symptoms of schizophrenia and losing all contact with reality.

Crack is widespread in the USA, but relatively new in this country. It's highly addictive (some people are addicted after using it once) and severe depression follows its use.

Management: You may not realize that you're addicted to a stimulant. If you are, be reassured that the tiredness and depression that you feel when you stop using the drug will go after a few days. A self-help group is a good idea. If a friend is psychotic or disturbed, it's important to contact a doctor (*see below* **Psychological Problems**).

Overdose
Overdoses are mostly due to deliberate self-harm rather than to too many recreational drugs.

Aspirin or paracetemol overdoses are the most common. If you find someone unconscious, follow the ABC of resuscitation, and call an ambulance.
- **Airway**: Firstly, make sure that they can breathe. You should loosen clothing and remove any objects from their mouth. Place them on their side in the recovery position (draw their legs up to their chest in the foetal postition), to ensure that they do not inhale vomit.
- **Breathing**: If they aren't breathing, lay them flat on their back and gently push the jaw back so that the head is bending back and the neck is exposed. Place your mouth over theirs and breathe into their mouth until you see their chest rising and falling rhythmically. You can place a handkerchief between your mouths if you're worried about infection.
- **Circulation**: Feel for a pulse in the neck, just under the angle of the jaw. If there's no pulse, lay one of your hands across the other and push down on the unconcious person's breastbone 60 times a minute. Break off to breathe into the person's mouth every ten compressions of the breastbone.
- Try to find out what drugs, if any, have caused the loss of consciousness.

Smoking and Drinking
Alcohol
Have you ever woken up and wondered how you got home the previous night? Do you ever open a pair of bleary eyes, with no recollection of where you were and what you said or did? Do you ever roll over only to encounter a stranger in your bed, without any idea of who they are? Even if you have never experienced the trauma of 'the morning-after', you may well sometime during your stay at college. And if it's already a regular feeling, the chances are that by the evening, you're at it again, knocking back the vodkas, throwing up on the kebab shop steps and being wheeled home in a shopping trolley.

The pressure to conform can be enormous, particularly during the first few weeks of term, when the general attitude seems to be 'fill the freshers up with loads of drink and they'll just adore college life'. This attitude continues throughout college and, if anything, gets worse as the pressure to be a social and academic success increases. In 1985, a survey at Newcastle University found that one in eight first-year male students were heavy drinkers. However, by the third year, the proportion had risen to one in three.

Make mine a large one
Alcohol is the UK's most popular drug – it's socially acceptable, widely available and, in most cases, it causes no harm. But for those who drink excessively (more than the recommended weekly limits – *see below* **What's in a drink?**), the long-term physical and emotional effects can be horrendous:
- Your liver can only burn up one unit of alcohol an hour. If it has to deal with more than this, it can suffer long-term damage;
- Alcohol can be a contributory cause of high blood pressure. Excessive drinking causes fatty deposits in the heart, increasing the likelihood of cardiac failure;
- Alcohol increases production of the gastric juices which eat away at the stomach lining, and can result in stomach ulcers;
- Excessive drinking over a long period of time can cause sexual impotency by making testicles shrink (in men) and vaginal lubrication decrease (in women);
- Alcohol attacks brain cells and reduces the memory-span, leading to nerve damage and memory loss;

Health and Stress

- Alcohol can make you overweight. Your liver (which burns up ordinary food calories and stores excess ones) cannot store calories which come from alcohol – it has to burn them up immediately. This means that alcohol calories push aside food calories, which are then stored as fat;
- Alcohol is a depressant drug – it acts as a tranquillizer for people who are very anxious. When alcohol is removed from the body, the nervous system 'rebounds' and the opposite effects of the drug appear – tension, restlessness, nervousness. These effects can continue for hours, days or even weeks. If excessive drinkers don't drink for a day or two, they may experience rebound;
- Alcohol suppresses 'rapid eye movement' (REM) sleep, or 'dream sleep'. Dream sleep is necessary for a good night's rest. If you stop drinking for a day or two, the brain rebounds with increased REM sleep, leading to bad dreams, nightmares and restlessness.

Drinking and driving

On 5 December 1984, David Ronald, a 20-year old student at Brunel University, had an accident. A driver, who had been drinking, smashed head-on into David's car, while overtaking on a bend. It was entirely the fault of the drinking driver, who escaped unharmed. But David was killed.

By slowing reflexes and the capacity to deal with the unexpected, alcohol reduces the ability to concentrate. At the legal limit – a blood alcohol concentration (BAC) of 80 – people under 25 are four times more likely to have an accident than if they had not been drinking.

On average, it takes your body an hour to get rid of one unit of alcohol. So, after a lunchtime drinking session you could still be over the limit

"Try and look at it in a philosophical way and realise that there is a whole world out there apart from the student world. As you arrive at college, you must realize that any change is disturbing: student life is not a bed of roses. Be prepared to use every service, such as the many counselling services that are available. For God's sake don't be too proud. Of course stress exists in student life – if anyone tells you that student days are the best days of your life, tell them to get stuffed."

Claire Rayner Agony aunt and writer (former student nurse).

in the evening. Similarly, six pints in the evening could put you over the limit the next morning. If you drink quickly and on an empty stomach, alcohol will have a more rapid effect.

Hangovers

Whatever weird and wonderful remedies people may put forward, there is, unfortunately, no miracle cure for hangovers. The only way to solve the problem of hangovers is to drink less. However, drinks with high additive levels (cheap red wine, for example) are more likely to leave you hungover than others (gin, vodka).

Alcohol draws water out of the cells in the bloodstream, causing dehydration. By drinking a pint of water before you go to bed, you can limit the morning-after feeling. Only if you're sober enough to remember, though. If you do need painkillers, avoid aspirin, which will only irritate your stomach further.

What's in a drink?

Doctors advise that you stick to recommended weekly limits:

Women No more than **14 units** a week.
Men No more than **21 units** a week.

A unit of alcohol is equivalent to half a pint of ordinary strength lager or beer, a glass of wine or a single measure of spirits. Drinking within the above limits should not cause any long-term damage to your health – provided you don't drink it all in one session. If you drink between 15 and 21 units (women) or 22 and 35 units (men) a week, the risk to your health is increased. You should be watching your drinking with a view to cutting down.

Drinking more than 21 units (women) or 35 units (men) a week is likely to cause long-term damage to your health. You should be cutting down now.

Cutting down

Accepting that alcohol is, or could become, a problem in your life is the first step towards cutting down and adopting a healthier lifestyle. If you are concerned about someone else's drinking, you might try convincing them of the need to cut down.

Try keeping a drinking diary. Make a note of how many drinks (in units) you have each day, together with when and where. If you do this over a number of weeks, you will soon be able to spot the situations which lead to heavy drinking, and so be in a position to adapt your lifestyle accordingly.

Set yourself limits for an evening's drinking (eg no more than six units). Try to avoid buying rounds – you may end up drinking more than you want to. Combine your drinking with other activities, like eating or dancing. Try non-alcoholic or low alcohol drinks occasionally – everyone has the right to choose whether or not to drink alcohol, including you.

Alcohol dependence

Drinking regularly and heavily may lead to physical dependence. You can tell if this is a problem if you get the shakes on waking, sweat at night, vomit regularly in the morning and (more seriously) have fits. If your dependence is very severe you may get delirium tremens and hallucinate. If you suffer from any of these symptoms you will need medical help if you want to stop drinking. Similarly, if you are finding cutting down or stopping difficult, you may be psychologically dependant on alcohol. Seek advice from your doctor.

Smoking

The list of smoking-related illnesses is long and most smokers are well aware of them. There's also growing evidence that passive smoking is harmful. Many students start smoking at college and stay addicted for the rest of their (shortened) lives. Try and give up – the longer you put it off, the harder it will be to kick the habit.

There's really no best way to break the addiction, and people tend to give up for different reasons. You must really want to give up. Not being able to afford the habit isn't a good enough reason, since as soon as you do have enough money, you'll start again. However, the realisation that you're likely to die from lung cancer could be the best incentive to stop.

A lot will depend upon your own situation. If you're sharing accommodation with 40-a-day addicts, your chances of giving up will be a lot lower than if you're surrounded by rabid anti-smokers who break out in a violent sweat at the sight of a packet of Silk Cut. Going down with the flu, and being physically incapable of taking caffeine, let alone nicotine, will be a good time to try. But again, you really have to want to give up.

If you decide to give up, it's no good allowing yourself to have the occasional drag – that's how you probably started in the first place. Be positive. Tell people about your decision and stick to it, no matter how strong your urge to hit the packet again. Willpower is the key. Self-help groups, hypnotherapy and acupuncture have all proved effective.

Sports Injuries

Recurring sports injuries may occur as a result of poor technique, poor equipment or inadequate training. In order to prevent sprains and muscle tears it is best to build up fitness gradually, choosing correct shoes and being coached in high impact sports like squash, rather than developing potentially dangerous habits.

Athletes are particularly prone to pulled muscles (which means a partial tear of the muscle fibres). Rugby players and boxers often suffer a direct blow to a muscle. Muscle injuries may cause bruising, while the muscle itself frequently goes into spasm and feels very tight and lumpy.

Tennis players and golfers commonly get tendon injuries. Tendons connect muscles to bones and don't have much stretch in them. Overuse causes pain, swelling and restricted movement. Sudden pain and loss of movement usually indicates a ruptured tendon.

Squash players and joggers often get knee complaints, whereas footballers tend to suffer from sprained ankles. Ligaments (which are bands of tissue around joints) get pulled, the surrounding muscles go into spasm and the joint swells up with protective fluid, consequently feeling hot and tender.

Self-management: We recommend following the RICE principle for the first few days after a minor injury:

- **R**est, to minimise the damage;
- **I**ce, or a bag of frozen food, held over the injury;
- **C**ompression. You can buy a Tubigrip bandage (£2) from the chemist;
- **E**levation, to allow the swelling to go down.

After 48 hours you can start gentle exercise, massage or local heat treatment. It's best to take anti-inflammatory painkillers (aspirin or ibuprofen preparations are available over the counter) while the pain persists. If the injury doesn't settle, you should see a doctor for stronger painkillers or referral to either a physiotherapist or orthopaedic surgeon.

Skin Problems

Skin problems are very common. About one quarter of all adults have significant skin problems at some time. However, that may not be much of a comfort when your face breaks out in acne.

Acne

Acne may appear in your teenage years or develop for the first time in your early twenties. No one knows why acne develops. It's certainly not inherited, infectious or related to your diet. Its appearance is a combination of bad luck and your skin type.

Self-management: Acne should be treated vigorously. Untreated or squeezed spots may form scars which will not then go away. If possible, you should avoid hot and humid environments. Tropical countries and hot kitchens won't do your complexion any good. Try to avoid heavy, oil-based cosmetics, but light, tinted moisturisers can be useful to conceal spots. Ultraviolet rays from sunshine or sunbeds may help to remove acne, but long-term overexposure is a cancer risk, so don't overdo it.

Over the counter: Acne soaps and face cleansers which contain at least five per cent benzoyl peroxide are useful. They should be applied over the acne affected area, not to individual spots, and left on for two hours before being rinsed off. They may make your skin red and dry at first, but this will stop once tolerance builds up, at which stage you can use the preparation twice daily.

Prescribed treatment: Doctors may prescribe antibiotics to be taken orally over three to six months. By killing skin bacteria, antibiotics allow spots to heal. If spots recur after the treatment, it's possible to stay on a low dose for a longer period. The potential side effects are diarrhoea and thrush; and if you are also taking the Pill, its effectiveness can be lessened (*see page 160* **Sex and Relationships**).

Women who have acne and are taking the Pill can combine two remedies by taking Dianette, an anti-acne contraceptive pill. Ask your GP or student health doctor to refer you to a dermatologist (skin specialist) if you have very severe acne which doesn't respond to these treatments.

Sunburn

The best way to avoid sunburn is to stay out of the midday sun and to use a cream with a Sun Protection Factor (SPF) suitable for your skin. The higher the SPF, the stronger its blocking powers.

If you do get burnt, avoid the sun, place towels soaked in water over the burnt area and dab soothing calamine lotion on the burn. Use painkillers such as paracetemol (maximum eight tablets a day) and, for short-term use, one per cent hydrocortisone cream, available over the counter. Daily application of moisturiser goes some way towards preventing peeling, while antihistamine tablets such as Piriton will relieve that irritating itch, but leave you sleepy, and shouldn't be taken if you're planning to drink or drive.

You should seek medical help if you have sunstroke (vomiting, dehydration, delirium), deep burns which have stripped off the uppermost layers of skin, or pain which needs stronger painkillers.

Skin cancer

Visit a doctor if you notice a skin patch which is:
- Newly acquired;
- Itchy;
- Increasing in size;
- Changing in colour (usually getting darker);
- Developing an irregular border;
- Bleeding or ulcerating spontaneously;
- Developing a bumpy surface.

Any worrying skin lesion should be removed by a GP or dermatologist for detailed examination to ensure that it isn't cancerous. Most skin patches turn out to be harmless, but it's best to get them checked. Protecting your skin from the sun is really the best way to avoid getting skin cancer.

Psychological Problems

Student life can be a stressful business, sometimes unbearably so. Leaving home and having to make new friends at college is often uphill work. Add to that the pressures of finding accommodation, managing on a grant, keeping up with coursework and preparing for exams, and the picture is far from rosy. Students are an underprivileged group, with low income, poor diet, substandard accommodation and a great deal of stress.

The difficulty is recognising when stress is building up to unbearable levels. Some students don't seek help early enough and end up with severe psychological illness. If you can see that a friend is not coping you should urge him or her to confide in a tutor, the college doctor (or a counsellor attached to the college) or a local GP.

For some people, some degree of stress is necessary in order to perform well: a surge of nervous energy before an exam is normal. A fast pulse rate, pounding headache and rushing to the toilet every few minutes are normal reactions to stress.

Depression

Warning signs that suggest abnormal levels of stress are poor concentration and appetite, isolation and impaired enjoyment. True depression, as opposed to just feeling pissed off, can develop if these warning signs are ignored. Depression means that your mood is flat and you find it hard to respond to anything, you suffer from insomnia and recurrent guilt feelings. As depression deepens you may start to feel so hopeless that you consider suicide.

Professional help is essential. Counselling could help you to discover the origins of your depression. Drug treatment might be necessary and can be remarkably effective.

Eating disorders

It is ironic (perhaps inevitable) that with a plentiful and readily available supply of food, so many people in the western world should suffer disorders of eating. The most common are obesity, anorexia nervosa and bulimia nervosa. Obesity is the most common nutritional disorder in the UK and unless there is a rare endocrinological cause is usually due to eating more calories than are expended. Obesity, which is, after all, a culture-specific term, may not even be a problem for some people. However, if you are unhappy with your weight, and if self-regulated dieting has not worked, you could join a local group (such as Weight Watchers) or go to your GP, who will recommend behavioural therapy or psychotherapy.

Anorexia nervosa is a common complaint, more frequently affecting high academically-achieving middle-class females, but also reaching young men. Features are a dramatic weight loss following fastidious dieting, over-estimation of body size and, in women, a disrupted or arrested menstrual cycle and self-induced vomiting. Psychological problems, often related to the family, may be a root cause. Treatment is often difficult because the sufferer doesn't want to change and their lifestyle is frequently one of isolation and defensiveness. If you would like advice or know someone you think needs support, either contact your doctor

When to Seek Medical Advice

In the following circumstances, GP consultation is recommended: (For all the below, see relevant sections within this chapter for further information).

- Colds and flu;
- Cystitis and urinary tract infections;
- Gastroenteritis, abdominal pain, nausea, vomiting and drowsiness;
- Cuts and grazes;
- Stress and insomnia;
- Unexplained weight loss;
- Long-standing fever (over three days);
- Unusual bleeding from: rectum; vagina; bladder; coughing;
- Loss of sensation/weakness in the body;
- Menstrual problems: missed/extra periods; bad PMT; painful periods;
- Unexplained lumps and bumps;
- Pregnancy: unwanted or wanted;
- Anxiety, depression, etc;
- Unprotected sexual intercourse – for morning after pill – within 72 hours;
- Overseas travel. Visit doctor at least two months before for advice on vaccinations and prophylactic medication.

In the following circumstances, emergency treatment at the nearest Accident and Emergency department is strongly recommended:

- Loss of consciousness/change in conscious level;
- Overdose;
- Shortness of breath;
- Severe chest pain;
- Fitting or seizures;
- Extreme pain;
- Continuous vomiting;
- Sudden loss of use of a limb/part of body;
- Trauma: fractures; severe laceration; penetrating injury;
- Loss of vision/immovable object in eye;
- Allergic reaction: swelling of face and lips; shortness of breath; tightening of chest;
- Severe burns;
- Uncontrollable bleeding.

or one of the advice centres listed under **Useful Addresses**.

Bulimia nervosa is even more common than anorexia. Sufferers are equally preoccupied by body shape but tend to remain a constant size in spite of frequent diets, binges, self-induced vomiting and laxative abuse. They often socialize more and are likely to drink heavily and take drugs. Relationship problems and depression may be the cause, but can also result from this disorder. Again, a visit to a doctor or advice from eating disorder associations will provide good support.

For more information on nutrition and healthy eating, see page 116 **Basic Living**.

Manic depressive illness

Contrary to popular usage of the term, manic depression is an illness where you might be very elated, over-optimistic, hyper-energetic and quite unrealistic for a spell; and then become extremely depressed, slowed down, negative and withdrawn. Some people are high or manic when they become ill, some alternate between mania and depression and some are mainly low. It is possible to be ill once and then never again. In common with schizophrenia, it is often friends and family who notice that someone is high, low or saying bizarre things. If you know someone who appears to be suffering, suggest that they go to their doctor. If this is a first attack, you will be referred to a psychiatrist for treatment.

Nervous breakdown

'Nervous breakdown' is a meaningless term usually applied to people who aren't coping with life. Often, the person is severely depressed and may well need counselling and possibly antidepressant drugs in order to fully recover. Depressed people 'retain insight', in that they know what is happening to them.

Panic and generalised anxiety disorders

Between two and four percent of the adult population suffers from anxiety disorders at any one time. You might find that you are persistently worried or on edge, that you feel tense, your heart is beating faster, you're sweaty or your sleep is interrupted. Perhaps there are certain predictable situations (crowds) which make you feel frightened, that something awful is about to happen and you get palpitations, chest pain, the sensation of choking or sometimes a feeling of being completely out of control. This is a panic attack.

College life can be very stressful and you might suffer from these feelings for the first time. It's best to go to your GP, who will recommend relaxation exercises, behavioural therapy, drug treatment, or a combination of all three.

Phobias

The fairly widespread fear of spiders is not always a problem. But a phobia about enclosed spaces which leads to a panic attack whenever you to go to a supermarket is more worrying. When a phobia starts to interfere with your life, you should seek help. Behavioural therapy, which gradually teaches you to control the panic, is usually successful within a few months. Phobias may arise for the first time when you are depressed and anxious.

Schizophrenia

Schizophrenia affects one in 100 people and may be precipitated by the stresses of student life. It is up to friends to recognise the symptoms, because someone in the throes of a schizophrenic breakdown will not see that they are behaving abnormally. Signs to look out for are strange, disconnected speech with streams of words that don't make sense; delusions that the TV set is broadcasting direct to the person and that his or her thoughts and actions are being controlled by outside forces; and general paranoia. Long-term schizophrenia makes the sufferer withdrawn, suspicious and prone to alcoholism. A psychiatrist is essential both for the initial diagnosis and the subsequent treatment. Self-help groups and complementary therapies are advisable once the person has stabilised. Unless expert help is sought at an early stage, the schizophrenic may attempt suicide.

Self-Help

If you do fall ill, make sure you take time off and stop studying so you can get a good rest. It is also a time to ask for help from your friends, flatmates or neighbours. Help with preparing food and running errands, or simply popping in to make sure you have everything you need is invaluable.

The following are conditions which can usually be treated at home without medical help. If you are at all concerned at the outset of an illness, you should visit a doctor immediately. Similarly, if after two to three days there is no improvement or if you are not happy coping by yourself, do not hesitate to go to your doctor.

Cold/influenza: If you have the familiar combination of a runny nose, sore throat, cough, headache and, in the case of flu, aching muscles, fever and malaise: rest at home; go to bed if you feel it's necessary; drink plenty (hot lemon and honey is good for sore throats); and take aspirin (if you don't suffer from stomach ulcers) or paracetamol tablets to ease your symptoms. Powdered preparations such as Lemsip are soothing.

If you start coughing up yellow/green sputum, you may have a chest infection and should visit your GP who will prescribe a course of antibiotics. If your sinuses (forehead and cheekbones) ache and are stuffy, you may have sinusitis – again, visit a doctor.

Meningitis/Glandular fever: A severe headache, neck and back stiffness, drowsiness, irritability and pain in the eyes when in the light are all symptoms of meningitis: visit a doctor at once. Meningitis can kill if it is not diagnosed and treated early and its symptoms are easily confused with those of flu.

If you have a sore throat, feel weak and exhausted and don't seem to get any better after a week, you may have glandular fever. Visit your GP, who will take blood tests.

Stomach upsets/gastroenteritis: If you have severe abdominal pain, continuous vomiting and/or bad diarrhoea, you should go to your doctor immediately.

A heavy drinking session or unusually rich food can make you feel nauseous, give you diarrhoea or make your guts ache. It could be that you've picked up a gut infection, in which case your symptoms will be more troublesome. The best course of action is to stop eating for the day and drink plenty of water while resting at home. If you feel better the next day, reintroduce bland, non-fatty, light food in small quantities: toast, porridge, rice, boiled vegetables. If symptoms do not improve after two days, visit your GP.

Cystitis: *see above* **Women's Health**.

Cuts and grazes: If you have a small, superficial cut or graze which does not gape open, you should clean the affected area and apply antiseptic. Plasters and bandages are an effective way of keeping wounds clean and preventing infection. If your cut is deep and/or gapes open you might need stitches and should visit the local hospital's Accident and Emergency (A & E) department. You should also visit a doctor if you last had a tetanus booster more than ten years ago (or have never had one). Also visit a doctor if your wound becomes red around the edges and starts to ooze pus. Go to the A & E department if you think there's glass in the wound.

Bee stings and insect bites: Although these can be troublesome and nasty, they rarely require expert treatment. Bee and wasp stings are helped by applying vinegar and taking antihistamines (Triludan, Piriton, and so on), available from all chemists. Some people are allergic to stings and find that the affected part swells to an excessive degree and feel a tightening in their chest, have shortness of breath or find that their face, lips and mouth swell. This is a medical emergency and you must go to your local A & E department immediately.

Foreign bodies in the eye: Usually, natural tears are enough to remove anything from the eye. You might also need to use an eyebath and eye-washing solution. If this doesn't work and your eye is still irritated, or if you suspect a piece of metal or glass is in your eye, go to your local A & E department.

Burns: If you have a small burn, the best treatment is to put it under a running cold tap as soon as possible. This will relieve the pain and minimise tissue damage. Once you feel some relief, cover the affected area with a loosely fitting bandage. If a large area of your body is affected, if the pain is very severe or if the burnt tissue is painless and white, you should go straight to your local A & E department. Smaller burns which become infected, red and ooze pus should be inspected by your GP.

Further Reading

Food and Nutrition: *Anorexic Experience* by Marilyn Lawrence (Women's Press, £4.95); *Below The Belt* by Denise Winn (Optima, £3.95); *Candida Albicans: Could Yeast Be Your Problem?* by Leon Chaitow (Thorsons, £2.99); *Dieting Makes You Fat* by Geoffrey Cannon and Hetty Einzig (Sphere, £1.95); *The Politics of Food* by Geoffrey Cannon (Century, £6,95); *Fat is a Feminist Issue* by Susie Orbach (Hamlyn, £3.50); *Our Bodies, Ourselves* by Angela Phillips and Jill Rakusen (Penguin, £12.99).

Sex and Health: *The AIDS Handbook* by Carl Miller (Penguin, £4.99); *Contraception – The Facts* by Bromwich and Parsons (OUP, £5.95); *Understanding Cystitis* by Angela Kilmartin (Arrow, £4.99); *Self-Help With PMS* by Michelle Harrison (Optima, £7.99); *Herpes, AIDS and Other Sexually Transmitted Diseases* by Derek Llewellyn-Jones (Faber, £3.95); *Sexually Transmitted Diseases – The Facts* by David Barlow (OUP, £2.95).

General Health: *Symptoms – The Complete Home Medical Guide* by Dr Isadore Rosenfeld (Bantam, £14.99); *A Dictionary of Symptoms* by Joan Gomez (Paladin, £4.95).

Complementary Medicine: *The Alexander Principle* by Wilfred Barlow (Gollancz, £4.99); *Aromatherapy* by Patricia Davis (Daniel, £9.95); *The New Holistic Herbal* by David Hoffman (Element, £9.99); *Homoeopathy* by George Vithoulkas (Thoirsons, £3.99); *The Complete Book of Massage* by Clare Maxwell-Hudson (Dorling Kindersley, £8.99); *The Complete Yoga Book* by James Hewitt (Rider, £9.99).

Useful Addresses

Action on Smoking and Health (ASH) 5-11 Mortimer Street, London W1N 7RH (071 637

9843). Send a large stamped, addressed envelope for an information pack on how to stop smoking by yourself. This is not a counselling service.
Alcohol Concern 305 Gray's Inn Road, London WC1X 8QF (071 833 3471). A referral agency for people with drink problems. Callers are put in touch with a suitable local day or residential group. It runs a library (visits by appointment only) and publishes leaflets and a bi-monthly journal.
Alcohol Concern Wales/Gweithgor Alcohol Cymru Brunel House, Fitzalan Place, Cardiff CF2 3BA (0222 488000). The Welsh equivalent of Alcohol Concern. (There is also a Northern Ireland Council on Alcohol and a Scottish Council on Alcohol.)
Alcoholics Anonymous 11 Redcliffe Gardens, London SW10 (081 352 3001). A support organization for all alcoholics who want to give up drinking. Counsellors will give advice and support over the phone (10am-10pm daily, answerphone outside these hours), put callers in touch with local members, or arrange for someone to visit. Everyone who operates the phones is a recovered alcoholic.
Anorexia Anonymous 24 Westmoreland Road, London SW13 (081 748 3994). If you're worried about an eating disorder (anorexia, bulimia), contact this confidential advice agency. You can book an appointment at their clinic. Helpline open 8am-9pm Mon-Fri.
Body Positive 51B Philbeach Gardens, London SW5 9EB (office 071 835 1045/helpline 071 373 9124). A self-help group for all people affected by HIV anti-body positive and AIDS. Provides an informal drop-in facility, weekend training sesions, a free fortnightly newsletter and some grants. Helpline open 7-10pm daily.

Eating Disorders Association National Information Centre, Sackville Place, 44 Magdalene Street, Norwich, NR3 1JE (0603 621414). Offers help and information for sufferers from anorexia or bulimia and their families. Staff will put callers in touch with local self-help groups. Members receive a list of guidelines for sufferers and their families, a magazine, *Signpost*, and information on the state of local services.
General Council and Register of Osteopaths 56 London Street, Reading, Berkshire RG1 4SQ (0734 576585/566260). Contact the GCRO for the name of your nearest registered osteopath.
The Haemophilia Society 123 Westminster Bridge Road, London SE1 7HP (071 928 2020). Provides advice and information to haemophiliacs.
The Health Education Authority Hamilton House, Mabledon Place, London WC1H 9TX (071 383 3833). This organization produces literature on a wide range of health topics, but does not give advice on health matters.
Herpes Association 41 North Road, London N7 (071 609 9061). A 24-hour recorded message gives you the number of a volunteer on duty who will explain genital herpes and suggest ways to avoid passing it on. Write for an information pack, enclosing five 20p stamps and a self-addressed envelope.
International College of Oriental Medicine Green Hedges House, Green Hedges Avenue, East Grinstead, Sussex RH19 1DZ (0342 313106). Write (enclosing a stamped addressed envelope) or phone for a list of qualified acupuncturists who have completed the College's three-year course.
International Federation of Aromatherapists 4 Eastmern Road, London SE21 8HA. Send a

Health and Stress

stamped, addressed envelope for a list of aromatherapists in your area.
London Food Commission 88 Old Street, London EC1V 9AR (071 253 9513). A consumer watchdog body which provides up-to-date information about food, and publishes *The Food Magazine*, quarterly.
National Association for Mental Health (MIND) 22 Harley Street, London W1 (071 637 0741). A useful starting point for anyone with general enquiries about mental health. Callers are referred to one of MIND's many local groups. MIND's legal service advises on maltreatment, wrongful detention and sectioning.
National AIDS Helpline (0800 567123, 24 hours daily).
Northern Ireland Council on Alcohol 40 Elmwood Avenue, Belfast BT9 6AZ (0232 664434). A support organization for people with drink problems. Counsellors offer information and advice.
PMS Relief 6 Beech Lane, Guildford, Surrey (0483 32573). PMS Relief offers one-to-one counselling and aims to make people more aware of help available.
Positively Women 5 Sebastian Street, London EC1V OHE (071 490 5515). Information, advice and support for women who are HIV positive.
QUIT 102 Gloucester Place, London W1H DA (071 487 2858/helpline 071 487 3000). Offers advice and information on how to give up smoking, provides 'QUIT Packs' and refers enquirers to local stop-smoking groups.
Standing Conference on Drug Abuse (SCODA) 1-4 Hatton Place, Hatton Garden, London EC1N 8ND (071 430 2341). Free advice and counselling service for groups or individuals with drugs-related problems, including HIV and AIDS.

Scottish Council on Alcohol 137-145 Sauchiehall Street, Glasgow G2 3EN (041 333 9677). Provides information, advice and referrals to local counselling services. Produces leaflets and a quarterly paper, *Alcohol Update*.
Society of Teachers of the Alexander Technique 10 London House, 266 Fulham Road, London SW10 9EL (071 351 0828). Send a stamped addressed envelope for a list of approved teachers and schools.
Terrence Higgins Trust 52-54 Gray's Inn Road, London WC1X 8JU (office 071 831 0330/helpline 071 242 1010 (3-10pm daily)/legal line 071 405 2381 7-10pm Wed). Counselling service for anyone worried about AIDS, HIV or Hepatitis B. Leaflets and information are available from the office, counselling through the helpline or face-to-face (by appointment).
UK Training College of Hypnotherapy and Counselling 10 Alexander Street, London W2 5NT (071 221 1796/071 727 2006). Phone or write for a register of qualified hypnotherapists.
Women's Health and Reproductive Rights Information Centre 52-54 Featherstone Street, London EC1Y 8RT (071 251 6580). Information and support on all aspects of reproductive health, and help for women who want to change their GPs. There is a reference library specializing in literature on women's health. Send a stamped, addressed envelope for publications.
Women's National Cancer Control Campaign Suna House, 128-130 Curtain Road, London EC2A 3AR (office 071 729 4688/helpline 071 729 2229 9.30am-4.30pm Mon-Fri). This organization provides information and education on cancer prevention and early detection.

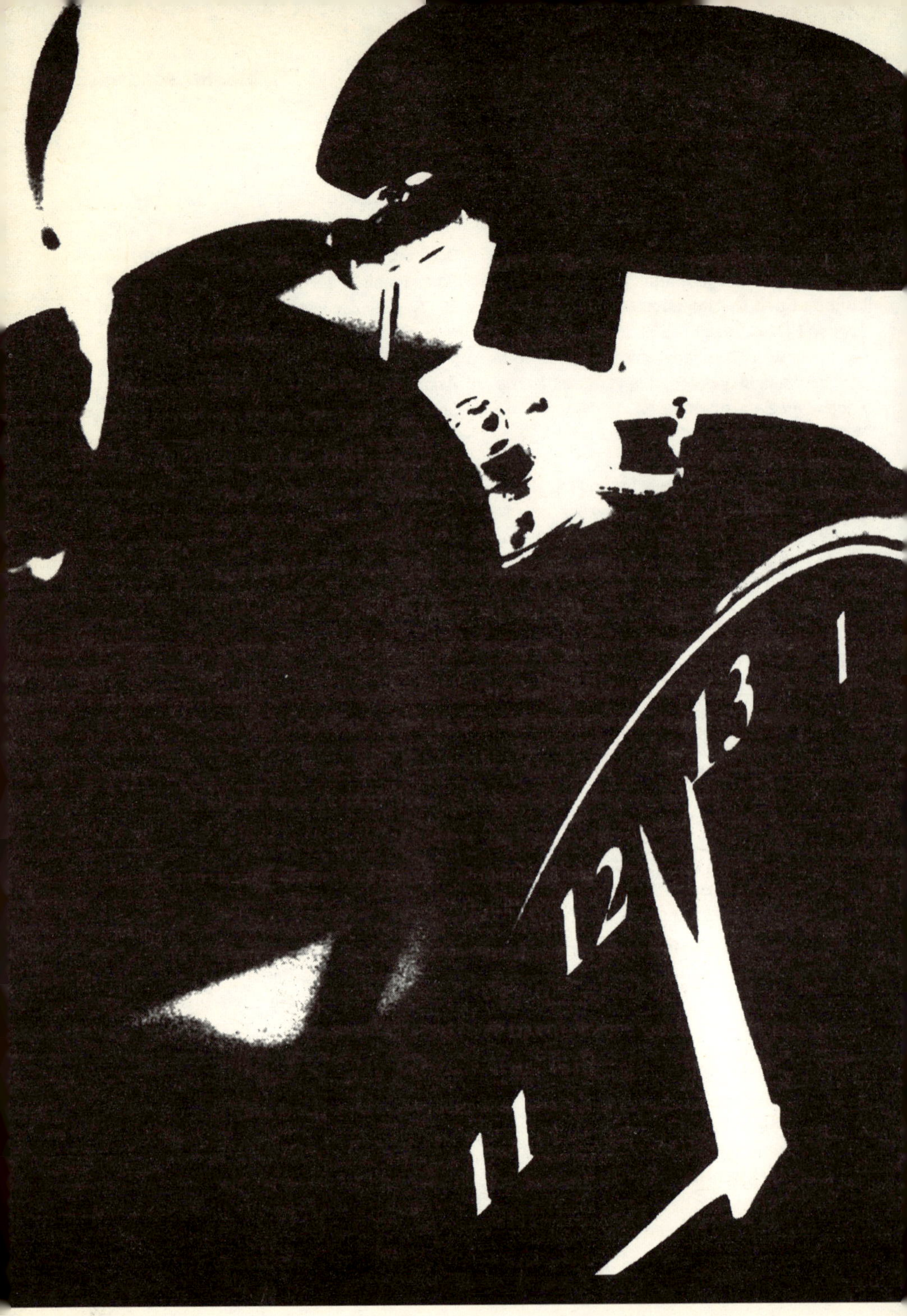
11
12
13
1

When and How to Work **202**

Libraries and Resource Centres **203**

Seminars and Lectures **204**

Essays, Reports and Dissertations **206**

Revision and Examination **207**

Failing Exams **208**

Changing Course or College **209**

Further Reading **209**

study techniques

Few people starting college will be familiar with seminars, tutorials and dissertations. **Judith Horsfield**, Manchester Poly's Learning Skills Co-ordinator, explains how to organize your time and get the most from your course.

One of the first things you'll discover as a student is that time is very precious and there's never enough of it. Nobody expects you to work all the time – you'd be a very one-sided person if you did. You must make time for socializing and relaxing, activities which will help you to unwind and work better. But in order to fit it all into your week, you're going to have to organize your time carefully. What you're aiming for is an acceptable balance between work and pleasure, and an even spread of your study sessions throughout the week.

The first thing you should do when you arrive at your college is to find out all you can about your course: times of your classes; number and dates of your assignments; months of your examinations; dates of holidays. These will give you targets around which to organize your workload. Once you've done this, you can plan your time on a weekly basis.

There's no single right way of organizing time: it's up to you to decide what will work best. But you will have to sort out some system of deciding *when* you're going to work and *what* work you're going to do.

When and How to Work

You know the times of day when you work best, so, as far as possible, organize your work schedule around these. Try to keep your study sessions short. Except when we're writing, most of us cope better with short and frequent work periods of about one and a half to two hours than with lengthy marathons of three to four hours.

If you find it really difficult to get down to work, try studying in even shorter sessions – perhaps half an hour to three quarters of an hour. You'll find this less daunting and should manage to concentrate better. Many students find that they have to do most of their work in short periods. Provided you have enough of them, that's fine.

Before you start, set yourself a definite task for each study session. This will stop you wasting time deciding what to do, give you a goal to work towards and provide you with a sense of achievement. Promise yourself some sort of reward at the end of a session so you've got something to look forward to: time with your friends, a television programme or a favourite sport, for example.

It's a good idea to take a few minutes' break in the middle of a working session to do something relaxing and different: have a cup of coffee, read the paper, take a short walk. It doesn't matter what you do, so long as you restrict it to about ten minutes. Then you'll come back refreshed and ready to start again.

Don't overlook all those odd snatches of time during the day when you find you've got ten to fifteen minutes on your hands. These moments are ideal for working. Because they're short and therefore limited, concentration isn't a problem and you'll be surprised at how much you can get through. So keep a few tasks handy for these occasions.

Making lists: At the beginning of each week, draw up a list of the work you need to do that week. Try to prioritize it:

- Got to do;
- Ought to do;
- Would like to do.

Then work at it in that order. Don't worry if you don't get around to the 'would like to do'; you can always carry those tasks over to the following week and you could even have to accept that they won't get done. After all, you can't do everything – so you're going to have to learn how to select and make decisions about what to leave out.

It's important to accept that there's no point spending hours trying to achieve perfection on one piece of work; you never will. You'll have to settle, like all of us, for the best you can do in the time available, and aim to spread your efforts evenly over all your work.

Libraries and Resource Centres

Something else you need to do early in your course is to become familiar with the library. Most colleges provide some form of library induction programme, but it's still worth spending a couple of hours in there on your own, walking around, reading notices, picking up leaflets and seeing what's on offer.

Although you have probably used public libraries before, you might not have seen them as a place to study and as a main source of reference. Outlined below are some basics about college libraries to help you find your way around.

Classification system

The materials in a library are arranged according to a classification system so that they can be easily found. The most usual is the Dewey Decimal – a numerical system which arranges material according to subject. But some libraries arrange books by author, for example, so you need to learn which system your library uses, and then how to use it.

The catalogue

The key to the library is its catalogue. This tells you exactly where you'll find the book you want. But in order to use the catalogue you'll need some information about the book: the title, the author or the specific subject it's about. Many libraries now have on-line catalogues, which allow you to check whether a book is actually in stock (ordinary computer databases and microfiche catalogues just tell you which books the library holds). You'll find instructions on using these by the terminals; they're not difficult, and you'll soon master them.

Sources of information

In addition to books, the college library will offer many other sources of information:

Periodicals: Do get into the habit of using these. Their articles have the advantage of being short and up to date. Most libraries display the current issues and keep back copies on shelves;

Pamphlets: They can contain valuable information: reviews of topics or reports of research work;

Audio-visual material: Video tapes, audio tapes, records, posters, slides and film are all increasingly used in higher education. You'll be able to borrow them, but the rules for doing so could differ from those for borrowing books;

Examination papers and theses: Your college library should contain sets of past examination papers and copies of dissertations and theses. It's worth looking at these to get an idea of what's expected of you.

Special facilities

Your library will also offer a range of special facilities:

Reservations: If the book you want is not on the shelves, you will be able to reserve it by completing an application form;

Short-term loan: Most college libraries have a short-term loan system – books which are heavily in demand can only be borrowed for a very limited time. This is to enable more people to have access to them;

Inter-library loans: If your college library does not have the book you want, staff should be able to arrange for you to borrow it from another library;

Photocopying: You might find that you want to make a copy of some material which cannot be removed from the library. Most libraries now provide coin-operated photocopying machines for this purpose;

Study space: Your library will provide study space where you can work. It's a good idea to use it, in order to avoid distractions. Have a wander round and find a place that suits you.

Don't restrict your hunt for material to your college library. It's often surprising what you can find in local libraries. You might also be able to use the specialized libraries in your area.

Computer centres

Most colleges have a drop-in computer centre with computing and word processing facilities. If you're not familiar with using these, you will have the opportunity of learning how to during your time at college. You'll find them an enormous help.

Language laboratories

Many colleges have open-access language laboratories which you can use to develop your skills in a particular language. The advantage of these laboratories is that the study programmes are individually based, so you're able to work at your own pace and in your own time.

Other students

One other very important resource is your fellow students. You can get a great deal of help and support from them if you discuss your work in a group. You could even consider organizing a self-help study circle. It can be much more pleasant working with others than always on your own.

Seminars and Lectures
Lectures

The lecture is the most traditional teaching method in higher education. Lectures are given to groups of 20 to 200 students; and everyone attending is expected to listen and take notes. It's not easy to co-ordinate listening and writing, but you'll quickly improve. The lecture topic will have been announced beforehand, so try to do a little preliminary reading; you'll then be taking notes from an informed position.

Your concentration is bound to wander at times – everybody's does. But do listen carefully to the beginning and end of the lecture. Before they start, most lecturers will outline what they plan to cover and the order in which they'll do it. This should provide you with a structure for your notes and, perhaps, your main headings. The end of the lecture will probably contain a summary of it, so you can use this as a check on your notes.

Try to take very brief notes: think in terms of key words and phrases rather than full sentences. You can always expand the notes later. It's a good idea to spread your notes out and to leave plenty of 'white space' on the page. This makes it easier for you to add things later, and to read your notes when you're revising.

If you tire very easily when taking notes, think about note-sharing with a friend. You could arrange to cover half the lecture each. Of course, if you note-share, you'll have to make sure you can read one another's handwriting.

As soon as possible after the lecture, check through your notes. This is when you can expand them if you wish – while the topic is still fresh in your mind. You could also highlight the important points in colour. Don't feel you're wasting time. It will only take about ten minutes, and working with your notes in this manner is one of the best ways of learning them. It will save you time when you come to revise.

There will be some lecturers who will be more interested in postgraduate research and talking about their own pet subjects than teaching first-year undergraduates. As a result, they won't pay much attention to ensuring that their lectures are informative, structured and relevant to the course; they could just be plain boring. If you feel that you won't get anything out of attending their lectures and that your time might be better spent working in the library, there's no obligation to go, nor is there anything to stop you from walking out of a lecture if it is terminally dull.

Seminars

Seminars are discussion sessions with your tutor and about eight to fifteen other students. They will be much more informal than lectures and you will be encouraged to take an active part in them. The more you contribute, the more worthwhile you'll find them, so be ready to share your ideas. You'll know the topic of the seminar in advance, so you'll be able to do the required reading and preparation.

If you like speaking in group discussions, you're lucky. But don't hog all the space. Learn to listen and respect the views of others, even if you don't share them.

Don't worry if you find it difficult to speak in a seminar discussion. Nobody wants you to suffer agonies just because you feel you've got to speak. You can contribute equally by being an active listener: encouraging others with your attention and asking questions.

It's not easy taking notes in a seminar, since writing can hold up the discussion, but you'll want to remember what has taken place. So, as soon as possible after the seminar, write yourself two or three 'take home' points: the most important issues raised in the seminar. You might even consider sharing and exchanging these with a friend.

Seminar paper

You might be asked to give a seminar paper, which you write in advance and then present to a small group of students for discussion. There's no cause for alarm: you're not expected to provide a scholarly lecture; rather, it's an opportunity for you to share your ideas with others and get some feedback.

The research and planning of a seminar paper is much like that of an essay or report, but the presentation is different. You're giving a talk to an audience, so you'll need to look at people and interact with them. You'll find this much easier if you plan to talk from notes rather than read your paper. By all means, use hand-outs and other visual aids. They can give you something to talk about while making things easier for your audience, too.

You might feel a little nervous when you begin to speak. We all do, but the nervousness soon disappears. Just relax, speak slowly and pause from time to time. Your audience needs time to absorb what you're saying before you move on to the next point. At the end of the seminar, don't forget your 'take home' points. Your paper will have generated some interesting ideas which you'll want to record.

You and your fellow students can help each other a great deal by being responsive, so do make an effort to be a good listener when someone else is giving a paper. You'll want them to listen to you – so you should listen to them.

Group work

An important part of most students' learning experience is working in a group with other students. Tasks will vary, but will include some kind of problem-solving subject or investigation. During this time your tutor will take more of a back seat and the group will be responsible for its own organization and working methods.

You will have to learn how to work in a group, which means being committed and involved in the task, reliable (turning up at meetings and so on), responsible in taking an active part, and tolerant of other people's working methods. You'll also need to be patient. At times you might feel you could do the task more quickly on your own, but then you wouldn't be developing the important group skills you'll need throughout your working life. Remember too, that all groups start slowly until they get organized and establish their working methods. Once you've got used to working in a group, you should find it both satisfying and effective.

Essays, Reports and Dissertations

As part of your course you will be required to do some writing: essays, reports and dissertations. Written work allows you to explore a topic in depth, and to use your initiative in deciding both how to structure the material and what to include.

Allow yourself plenty of time: last minute, all-night writing sessions can lead to panic and mental block.

Understanding the question

The first thing to do is to make sure you understand what you're being asked to do. Try highlighting key phrases or re-writing the question in your own words. Make sure you're very clear about the instruction words – those which tell you what to do with the topic.

You also need to consider whom you're writing an essay for. It's not a good idea to write as though only your tutor will read the work, as you risk assuming too much knowledge from the reader and perhaps leaving out something important. Try writing for a fellow student who's interested in the topic and has not thought about it in depth.

Reading and research

Map out your areas of research before you start. You can't afford to waste time gathering irrelevant information, so draw up a list of the questions you need to answer or the topics you want to investigate, and use these as guidelines for your reading.

As you read, make a careful note of authors, titles and publication details. You'll want these later on for your bibliography. It's wise, too, to make notes in your own words. This not only ensures that you've understood what you've read, but also means you'll guard against plagiarism.

Plagiarism is when you either intentionally or unintentionally try to pass off someone else's words as your own. It's a serious offence, and you'll be heavily penalised for it. Whenever you quote or refer to someone else's work you must acknowledge and identify it.

You'll never feel you've done enough reading; there's always more you could do, but you've got to give yourself a cut-off date. Try to allow a 24-hour gap between research and planning. This will give you a chance to mull over and assimilate the information you've gathered.

Planning

This is an important part of writing. It's the stage when you select your ideas to make a logical, tightly-knit whole, so it takes time. It's a good idea to draw up a preliminary plan in which you just write out your ideas as you think of them.

Then you can select the best ones and put them down in order. At this stage, it often helps to work out the conclusion – the direction of your work and where it will end up in terms of:
* Judgements;
* Arguments;
* Conclusions;
* Recommendations.

This will clarify your thoughts; you can then order your material to lead logically to this conclusion.

Writing

We all put off writing, but sooner or later we've got to get down to it. Start with a rough draft which you write fairly quickly. Don't worry about expression, just get something down. You can always change it later, whereas you can do nothing with a blank page.

Begin writing where you find it easiest. A paper doesn't have to be written in the order in which it will be read. So, if it helps, leave the introduction until last: it's often the hardest part and, as it should introduce your writing to the reader, it makes sense to write it when you're sure about the paper.

When you've produced your first draft, you can edit and revise it. It's at this stage that you begin to be concerned about expression as well as content and structure. You'll also have to check your references; you must identify any books or articles you've read or referred to. There's a recognized way of doing this, using footnotes and a bibliography. If you're not sure about it, ask your tutor for help. You need to get it right.

When you've finished your final draft, leave it a while before checking it for the last time. After all this effort, you really have finished – so reward yourself!

Revision and Examination

Most courses still retain 'unseen' written examinations. The thought of these can be frightening, but remember that the examiners really are on your side: they want you to pass.

Revision

The first thing you need to do is to form some idea of possible topics for each examination. Past papers are usually a reliable guide, particularly if you look back over several years. Look at your lecture notes too; the more emphasis a topic has been given, the more likely it is to form part of the paper.

Once you've identified possible topics, choose those on which to concentrate. You can't cover everything, so you have to be selective. Drawing up a timetable of when you plan to revise each topic can be an enormous help. This way you make sure that you allocate a space for everything. Try to keep your revision sessions short, to make concentration easier.

It's very important to make time for relaxation when revising. This will not only help you work better; but, if you're in the habit of cutting off and relaxing, you'll be far less likely to panic.

Everybody finds revision tedious, especially if it just consists of reading and re-reading notes. So, try active revision:
* Condense your notes to a series of headings;
* Draw up some answer plans to possible questions;
* Revise with a friend.

Examinations

Expect to feel nervous. A certain amount of worry can encourage you to give your best. However, if anxiety gets out of hand and you're not coping, tell someone. Help is available: talk

to your tutor or student counsellor. There are also ways you can help yourself:
- Allow enough time for your revision;
- Make sure you know the time and place of the examination;
- The night before the exam, check you've got all the necessary equipment;
- Arrive in plenty of time.

You'll know well in advance the number of questions you should answer for each paper. So work out how long you should spend on each. You'll need to divide your time equally between all the questions you're supposed to answer. An unanswered question earns no marks, and even a first class answer elsewhere can't compensate.

When the exam starts, take your time, read the paper through slowly and choose your questions. Answer your best question first. This will calm you down and give you confidence. If you do get stuck and can't remember something, don't panic. Leave a gap, and move on. You can always go back later, and if you don't, it doesn't matter. It will only be part of an answer.

It's worth trying to allow time for reading over your paper at the end. It nearly always pays off.

After the exam is over, you'll of course want to talk about it with fellow students. But don't let their claims upset you and make you dissatisfied. Just get away and relax for a while.

Failing exams

Many students fail one or more exams during their time at college. Exam regulations vary from college to college and from course to course, but in most cases there are options open to you, from academic appeals to resits. However, if you feel you are unable to complete your course for whatever reason, talk to your personal tutor, a careers adviser or a counsellor before making any firm decisions. If you leave without completing your course, your LEA will only require you to pay back any grant which you have received after the date of your leaving college.

Appeals

On most courses there is a formal structure for appealing against exam results, which lays down the conditions for an appeal and how to go about it. If you believe the result is not a true reflection of your ability, and if there were exceptional circumstances which affected your studying or exam performance, talk to your personal tutor or student union about appealing. The first thing to do is to establish whether you have failed on purely academic grounds, or:
- whether the failure was linked to personal or medical extenuating circumstances of which the examination board was unaware; or
- that your results were adversely affected by procedural or organizational irregularities in the conduct of the exam.

Resits

Resits are quite common, particularly in the first year. However, the prospect of a resit at the end of the summer can quite ruin your holiday. If you have to resit, you will have to take the exam again, usually before the start of the next term, and if passed, the student can carry on with the course. If you fail a resit, you may not be allowed to continue your course.

Re-taking a year

If you are offered the chance to retake a year, you might have the choice of full or part-time attendance, or you may even be able to retake the exams without attending the college, if you have satisfied the coursework requirements. LEAs will not fund students to retake a year (neither the course fees nor a grant). However, with medical evidence and support from the college, an extra year's grant might be awarded. See your student union welfare officer for advice.

Changing course or college

Some students find, particularly during the early part of their academic career, that they are dissatisfied with their course and would prefer to change to another subject or institution, or both. If you are contemplating a change of course, be sure not to delay beyond the first term of the second year, otherwise you could lose your eligibility for funding for the new course. If you withdraw from your course before you have attended for one term and seven weeks of the second term, your LEA will accept that the course was a wrong choice, and this period will be disregarded if you apply for a mandatory award for another designated course (*see page 72* **Money**).

The main factors governing such transfers are personal, educational and financial.

Personal: It is important to establish your real motives for seeking a transfer. If you have embarked on what proves to be the wrong course for you, seek professional advice from a counsellor or a welfare officer before making a move.

Educational: If you decide to change your course after you have attended for one term and seven weeks of the second term, then you need the endorsement of the academic staff to secure the transfer of your grant, as well as (obviously) a place on the course onto which you wish to transfer.

Financial: Students wishing to transfer from one degree (or equivalent) course to another during or at the end of the first academic year may be able to retain their LEA award for the duration of the new course, so long as there is academic approval for the transfer.

If you are transferring to another college, you must have two letters of approval. The reason for your transfer must be purely on academic and educational grounds, and you must have an offer of a place on a new course.

One final word. Everyone has their own way of working. This chapter is not a fail-safe recipe for studying – it only offers some ideas for you to think about and, subsequently, to modify as you see fit. The essential thing is that you *enjoy* your work. So, if at any time worry outweighs fun, don't be afraid to ask for help.

Further Reading

Studying for a Degree in the Humanities and Social Sciences (PJ Dunleavy, Macmillan, £6.99).
Learn How to Study (D Rowntree, Macdonald Orbis, £4.99).

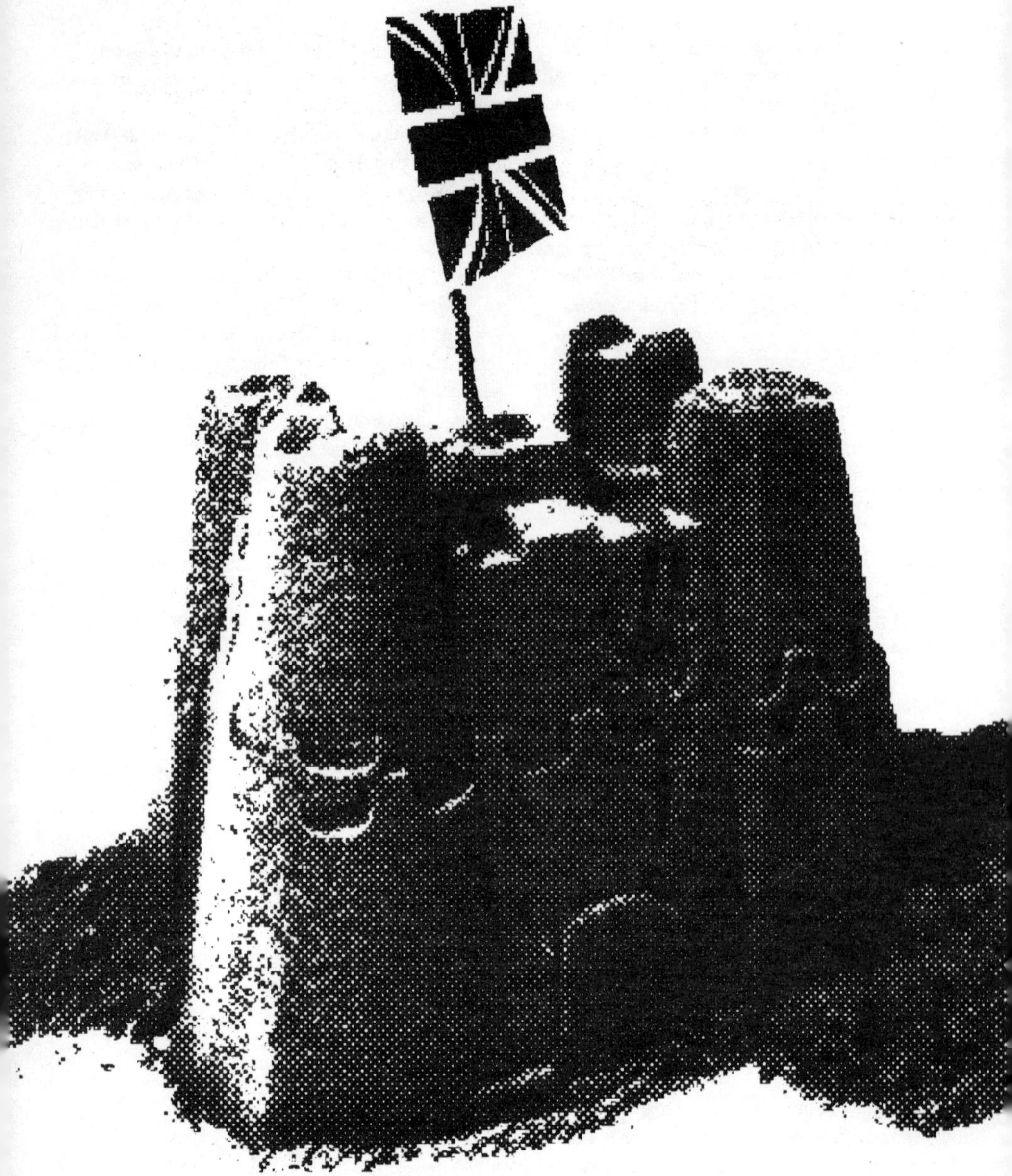

Studying abroad

These days, it's not so rare to study outside of Blighty: many countries welcome British students to their shores. **Jane Woolfenden**, from Middlesex Poly's International Student Office, looks across the waves to opportunities abroad.

First Thoughts **212**

Options **212**

Making a Decision **215**

Further Reading **218**

Useful Addresses **219**

The chance to study abroad is no longer the prerogative of language students. Recent years have seen a wide and fast-expanding range of educational opportunities in other countries.

It is the short-term periods abroad which are increasing in popularity and which are the concern of this chapter. Postgraduate students, and those wishing to investigate the possibility of longer-term study abroad, should consult the following publications: *Study Abroad (UNESCO)*, *Higher Education in the European Community*, and *Commonwealth Universities Year Book* (see below **Further Reading** for further details).

First Thoughts

Once you have decided to spend some time as a student abroad, you can narrow down the options by choosing between:
- Enrolment on a course which requires a period spent overseas;
- Participation in an exchange or study-abroad scheme arranged by your college;
- Making independent arrangements.

Ideally, you should make these decisions when you are applying for further or higher education. What prospective colleges have to offer by way of foreign study may be a deciding factor in your choice of both course and college. If you are still at school, you will have the option of taking a year off between school and college and using that time to study abroad. There will, however, be some of you who do not have the luxury of choice and for you, the range of options will be narrower. You may, for example, be enrolled on a course already, in which case you will have to:
- Investigate whether your college is involved in any exchange schemes and find out if you can participate;
- Wait until you have finished your course;
- Obtain permission to take a term or a year off in the middle of your course;
- Study abroad during the vacation.

Then there is the question of time and, more to the point, money. How much time can you spare? Can you afford the expense? While some of the options may cost little more than a return ticket, and in some cases not even that, other options will be dearer.

Options

The European Community and ERASMUS

Many more opportunities to study within the EC have emerged since the setting up of ERASMUS – the European Community Action Scheme for the Mobility of University Students (note that ERASMUS uses the word 'university' to refer to all higher education institutions). ERASMUS offers a programme of financial support to colleges, students and staff for the promotion of student mobility and institutional co-operation throughout the Community. In many cases this has resulted in the setting up of Inter-university Co-operation Programmes (ICPs) – joint study programmes where students divide their time between two or more participating institutions and which often lead to dual qualifications.

If you are not enrolled on an ICP you may still be able to apply for an ERASMUS grant. The grants enable students to spend a recognized period of study in another member state. To be eligible you should be in at least your second year of higher education and must be able to provide written approval from your home institution. ERASMUS student grants contribute towards: travel; foreign language preparation; and extra expense incurred through higher cost of living in the host country. While you are abroad you should continue to receive any other student grant or loan to which you are entitled (*see page 72* **Money**).

If you are currently applying to college, you should contact the admissions office to enquire about any Inter-university Co-operation Programmes. If your college is not involved in an ICP but you wish to find out more about ERASMUS grants, you should contact UK ERASMUS Student Grants Council (*see below* **Useful Addresses**).

TEMPUS

TEMPUS (Trans-European Mobility Scheme for University Studies) is a companion scheme to ERASMUS designed specifically for countries in Central and Eastern Europe. It is still in its pilot phase. Further details can be obtained from EC TEMPUS Office (*see below* **Useful Addresses**).

Exchanges

Student exchanges can take place when a college has links with an institution abroad or is a member of an international exchange scheme. The concept of an exchange is simple. A specified number of students from one college exchange with an equivalent number from another. The tuition fees you have paid pay for the student taking your place, and vice versa. In many cases accommodation is dealt with in the same way – you each leave behind enough money to cover the costs of the incoming student. If you are on a grant you may be eligible for a higher rate to cover increased living expenses. Check this with your local education authority. The only major expense will be your fare and in some cases this may be covered by a grant (*see above* **The European Community and ERASMUS**).

Some colleges may restrict exchange opportunities to students on specific courses. In others, the exchange programmes will be open to anyone. As the finer details of programmes vary so much, there is no alternative to approaching individual colleges to discover what links they have and how their particular exchanges work. To make matters more difficult, the information cannot always be found in the general prospectus. Some colleges issue a separate publication dealing with their overseas programmes. Try your college's international office, if it has one. Alternatively, the relevant faculty office will at least know about course-specific schemes. Usually, you can only take part in an exchange if your college has the necessary links. You could always encourage your faculty to establish links with a similar one overseas, or persuade the college to participate in a programme administered by a central body. However, by the time the terms and conditions have been negotiated, you will probably have graduated....

Courses which require some study abroad

If you are taking a language degree you will almost certainly be required to spend time in a country where that language is spoken. Time spent abroad may be an integral part of an American Studies or French Studies course. The joint study programmes set up under ERASMUS (*see above* **The European Community and ERASMUS**) normally stipulate time abroad. Some of the courses offered may be sandwich courses, in which case the required period of work experience can be spent overseas. All such courses will be listed in the UCCA and PCAS handbooks or in individual college prospectuses. If the course is one which has been set up under ERASMUS, then it will also appear in the list produced by the ERASMUS Bureau (*see below* **Useful Addresses**).

Direct enrolment

You may be called a visiting student, an occasional student, a semester- or a year-abroad student; the name changes but the concept is the same. It involves taking a year, term or semester out from your studies in the UK and spending the time at a college abroad. You make your own arrangements and need not rely on your college having overseas links. Your studies there will not normally form an integral part of your course, although they may be related, nor will they necessarily count towards your final qualification, although you may be able to negotiate some form of recognition for your time overseas.

Entrance requirements will vary but it is usually a condition that you are enrolled on a degree programme in your own country and you will normally need to provide a letter of support from your home college. As a visiting student, you may simply join pre-existing courses or enrol on a course specifically designed for students from overseas. The concept of the semester or year abroad is a commonplace in the USA, and many countries (for example Japan, Korea, Egypt, Mexico and Brazil) now offer Junior Year Abroad programmes designed for American students but open to students from the UK as well.

To find out what is on offer to visiting students, you should approach individual colleges directly. You will be able to obtain names and addresses of likely institutions, and in some cases more detailed information, from:

- The Education or Cultural Department of the embassy or High Commission of the country concerned (a list of these can be found in the *Education Year Book*, *see below* **Further Reading**);
- The British Council, either in the UK (*see below* **Useful Addresses**) or overseas (a list of overseas offices can be obtained from the London office);
- Fulbright Commission (formerly the UK/US Education Commission) for advice on studying in America (*see below* **Useful Addresses**);
- Various publications such as *Applying to Colleges and Universities in the United States – a handbook for international students*; the *Commonwealth Universities Year Book*; the *European Council of International Schools Higher Education Directory*; *Higher Education in the European Community – a student handbook*; and *Study Abroad (UNESCO)* (*see below* **Further Reading** for details of all the above).

The drawback of direct enrolment is the cost. You will need enough money to cover tuition fees, accommodation, travel and living expenses. The organizations listed above will advise you of any available scholarships.

Language courses abroad

A short language course can be taken at virtually any time: in the year between school and college, in the vacation, at the end of your course, or when you'd long since thought you were finished being a student. As long as you can afford it (good language courses are not cheap) you will have a bewildering range to choose from. There are many reasons why you might want to learn a language and as many different courses to match. The following are just a few examples:

Studying Abroad

- Language for pleasure;
- Language for academic purposes;
- Language for a specific purpose, for example French for engineers, Spanish for doctors, Italian for business;
- Courses which combine the study of language with a hobby, for example Italian and the History of Art, Spanish and horse-riding, Greek with tennis.

In addition to pre-sessional courses intended, and often compulsory, for their own foreign students, many colleges abroad run language courses during the vacation. However, the majority of courses on offer will be in private language schools. As is the case in the UK, there will be genuine, reputable schools and there will be disreputable schools. For reliable information, contact the Cultural or Education Department of the relevant embassy, or the British Council in the UK or in the country concerned. Some courses, particularly in Eastern Europe, might attract a scholarship. For information on this contact the Specialist Tours Department at the London office of the British Council.

In addition, many of the large language teaching organizations in the UK have branches overseas; for example, Berlitz, Eurocentres, International House (*see below* **Useful Addresses**). Some national tourist offices provide packages which include language tuition, and details of language schools in Europe appear in *Study Holidays* (*see below* **Further Reading**).

International summer schools

Summer schools may be hosted or run by colleges, national institutes and academies overseas. Some are organized by colleges in the UK. There are many different courses on offer, ranging from pottery or peace studies, to opera appreciation or architectural renovation. Good sources of information on summer schools and available scholarships are:

- Education and Cultural Departments of embassies and High Commissions;
- Extramural Departments of colleges in the UK and overseas – many have their own summer school offices;
- The British Council Specialist Tours Department.
- The following publications (*see below* **Further Reading** for details): *Study Abroad (UNESCO)*; *Study Holidays*; and *Time to Learn*.

Making a Decision

Before you decide where, what and how to study abroad there are a number of important considerations.

Language

In theory, you could study abroad virtually anywhere in the world, but for obvious reasons most students choose colleges in Europe, the Commonwealth and the USA. Proficiency in the language of instruction is essential if you are to gain the most from your time abroad, and most colleges will require you to take a language examination before admitting you on a course. Knowing how to hold a simple conversation is not enough. Neither is it just a question of vocabulary: you need to know how to use the language. Taking an exam or writing an essay in a foreign language exacerbates problems of appropriate language use, and many students studying abroad have come unstuck because they were unable to express their knowledge in the required way. Many colleges will offer pre-sessional language courses and some may also include sessions on study skills. Check to see if language courses are included in the fees.

Teresa Tinsley Author of *How to Study Abroad* and *Time Off in Spain* (Spanish and Linguistics, Essex University, 1975-79).

"What's most important? Do your research. Be clear about your objectives but don't be limited by them. If you're not on a language course, get to grips with the language before you go. Don't assume that your qualification will be directly useful to you when you get back: your wider experience may be the best justification for having gone abroad. Potentially, the most exciting development is the new EEC Joint Study Programme, intended to bring all European first degree courses of four or more years' duration into line. Exactly where this will leave the UK, with its predominantly three year degrees is unclear (in Spain a first degree takes five years)."

Coursework, credit and qualifications

Before you go, be clear about the extent to which the course taken abroad will count towards your final qualification, if at all. In some cases, your coursework marks will be taken into account, in others you will be required to take exams in the host institution. Find out whether it is possible for visiting students to take examinations in their own language. You should also find out the form examination will take; it may be by thesis or project which can in some cases be written in English. If you are going to the USA it would be advisable to learn how to type (handwritten assignments are not accepted).

If you are going to obtain a foreign qualification, make sure that it will be recognized back home. You can check this by contacting the National Academic Recognition and Information Centre (*see below* **Useful Addresses**). Your home institution may operate a modular system, based on the principle of cumulative transferable credit. You build up your own programme by selecting from a range of subject units, then while you are away you simply amass credits towards your final qualification.

Final considerations

Immigration: Make sure you are clear about visa and immigration requirements. These will vary from country to country and according to your proposed length of stay. Host colleges should provide the necessary information, but if you are unsure about what is required, contact the relevant embassy or High Commission.

Vaccinations: Proof of vaccination against certain diseases may be necessary. The embassy or High Commission will be able to give you the details. As some vaccinations make you feel ill, don't leave them till the last minute – give yourself time to recover before you travel. *See also page 278* **Travel**.

Insurance: Some countries have reciprocal health agreements with the UK which entitle you to free or cheaper medical treatment. If you are travelling to a country which does not have such an agreement, take out medical insurance before you go. Endsleigh Insurance (*see below* **Useful Addresses**) offers a special student insurance service.

Money: Whether your fees are being paid via your college in the UK or directly to a college abroad, make sure that you are clear about what is included. Are you paying for tuition only? Is accommodation included? Who pays examination fees? You should also think about how you are going to receive money abroad, particularly if you are going to be away for some time. Ask your bank about ways of transferring currency, about whether you are going to a country which has foreign exchange controls and about opening a bank account abroad. If you are travelling to Europe, you can draw money from your British bank account by using Eurocheques, but this can be an expensive way of getting at your money; in some countries extra charges are incurred each time you use a cheque. You will also need to order some local currency for your journey and your first few days abroad.

Accommodation: Will the host institution provide accommodation, help you to find somewhere, or leave you to your own devices? Don't leave the UK without having arranged at least temporary accommodation. If you are offered the choice, it is advisable to take accommodation provided by the college. Unless you have contacts, it is difficult to organize private accommodation abroad while you are still in the UK. You may dislike the idea of halls of residence, but they do provide a ready-made social life and a base which you can use while finding your feet and looking around for something else. You may not feel up to negotiating with landlords, electricians and plumbers in a foreign language.

Dates: Different countries arrange their academic year in different ways. Find out exactly when you have to arrive and whether you will be met. Try not to arrive very late at night or on public holidays and try not to miss any orientation sessions which are organized for new students. If you are going to be taking exams, find out when they will be held and make sure that you will still be around. You should also ensure that you do not miss any important exams being held back home.

Loneliness and culture shock: Moving home, starting at a new college and going abroad can all be traumatic at the best of times, and you will be doing all three in the space of just a few days. Once the initial excitement has worn off, you may well be left feeling disappointed and lonely. You will be surrounded by people but there will be few familiar faces. Simple things which you once took for granted, like getting money from a bank, catching a train and using a telephone, could leave you angry and frustrated. You will regularly make a fool of yourself because you are unsure of the system. Part of the answer to this is knowing what to expect, and that includes expecting to be disappointed, depressed, unhappy or lonely.

Before you go, read as much about the country as possible, avoiding promotional literature. Talk to people who have been there, and don't let them only tell you how wonderful it was; get them to tell you all about the problems and the disappointments as well. When you are there, try to join in as much as possible, particularly the events organized especially for new students. Above all, try to be positive, flexible and receptive to different ways of doing things. Don't isolate yourself, and try not to take it out on your fellow students; they might be able to help you if you let them.

Reverse culture shock: No sooner have you become used to life abroad than it will be time for you to return to the UK, and that adjustment can be just as problematic. The key is to keep in touch. Telephone and write to friends and family, keep up to date with local and national news, and make sure you don't miss any new developments in your field of study. Finally, once you are back home, don't forget to keep in touch with the friends you will have made while you were away.

Further Reading

Applying to Colleges and Universities in the United States – a handbook for international students (Peterson's Guides, Princeton, New Jersey).

Commonwealth Universities Year Book (Association of Commonwealth Universities, 36 Gordon Square, London WC1H OPF).

Directory of Work and Study in Developing Countries (Vacation Work Publications, 9 Park End Street, Oxford OX1 1HJ).

ECIS – European Council of International Schools Higher Education Directory (21B Lavant Street, Petersfield, Hampshire GU32 3EL).

Education Year Book (Longman Group UK Ltd, 4th Avenue, Harlow, Essex CM19 5AA).

Higher Education in the European Community – a student handbook (Kogan Page, 120 Pentonville Road, London N1 9JN; or from HMSO bookshops).

Studying Abroad

Scholarships Abroad (The British Council, 10 Spring Gardens, London SW1A 2BN).
Scholarship Guide for Commonwealth Postgraduate Students (Association of Commonwealth Universities, 36 Gordon Square, London WC1H OPF).
Study Abroad (UNESCO) (UNESCO, 7 place de Fontenoy, 75007 Paris; or from HMSO, PO Box 276, London SW8 5DT).
Study Holidays (Central Bureau for Educational Visits and Exchanges, Seymour Mews, London W1H 9PE).
Time to Learn (The National Institute of Adult Continuing Education, 19B De Montford Street, Leicester LE1 7GE).
Year Off, Year On (Hobson Publishing, Bateman Street, Cambridge CB2 1LZ).

National Academic Recognition and Information Centre c/o The British Council, 10 Spring Gardens, London SW1A 2BN (071 930 8466).

Useful Addresses

Berlitz Schools of Languages 321 Oxford Street, London W1 (071 408 2474).
British Council 10 Spring Gardens, London SW1A 2BN (071 930 8466).
EC TEMPUS Office rue de Trèves 45, B-1040 Brussels, Belgium.
Endsleigh Insurance Services Endsleigh House, Ambrose Street, Cheltenham, Gloucestershire GL50 3NR (0242 36151).
ERASMUS Bureau rue d'Arlon 15, B-1040 Brussels, Belgium; **UK ERASMUS Student Grants Council** The University, Canterbury CT2 7PD.
Eurocentres 21 Meadow Court Road, London SE3 9EU (081 318 5633).
Fulbright Commission (formerly the UK/US Education Commission) 6 Porter Street, London W1M 2HR (071 486 7697).
International House 106 Piccadilly, London W1V 9FL (071 491 2598).

Coming Out **222**

Student Union Lesbian and Gay Societies **224**

The NUS Lesbian and Gay Liberation Campaign **225**

Dealing with Harassment and Prejudice **226**

Further Reading **227**

Helplines **227**

Useful Addresses **227**

Lesbian and Gay Students

The first year at college is a time of unprecedented freedom for most students. **Steve Clamp** and **Nikki Greenway** from the NUS Lesbian and Gay Committee show you the way to friendship, support, and feeling happy with your sexuality.

Starting college and coming to terms with being lesbian or gay can both be traumatic. Yet for many young lesbians and gay men leaving home for the first time, the initial year at college can be their first chance to explore their sexuality. Being at college leaves you free to live your own life, to be honest about yourself and your sexuality, and to become involved in issues and campaigns that interest you. If you're lesbian or gay, the information, advice, support and contacts you need to make the most of college life are part of the student scene, making it a sympathetic climate in which to come out.

This chapter aims to help you get the most from your time at college, giving advice and information on coming out, feeling positive about your sexuality and dealing with any problems you may have.

Coming Out

Attending college often entails living away from home and learning to adapt to a different environment. You're starting a new course, mixing with new people and making new friends. This may be a little daunting, but it does mean that you can make positive decisions about who you are and who you socialize with.

The first thing to realize is that you are not alone. You're neither the only lesbian or gay man at college, nor the only person making new friends. The next step is often admitting to yourself that you're a lesbian or a gay man, and feeling proud and happy to acknowledge the fact. There's nothing bad or embarrassing about lesbianism or homosexuality. Both are as valid forms of sexuality as heterosexuality.

Coming out – to people you live with, people who are on your course, or to new friends – can seem worrying. This is where your lesbian and gay society fits in, because you can use the friends and contacts you make in the society for moral support if or when you decide to tell your heterosexual friends. *See below* **Student Union Lesbian and Gay Societies**.

Bear in mind that you have the power to decide when, where and how to come out. Students are usually an easy-going bunch, so you shouldn't get too much hassle. If anyone is ignorant enough to give you a hard time about your sexuality, take comfort in the fact that their prejudice is their problem, not yours, so don't accept any blame for it.

It's best not to procrastinate and decide to come out 'next term' because, more often than not, next term turns into next year, you become worn down with the indecision and deception, and you miss out on a lot of fun. Being an 'out' lesbian or gay man at college should mean being honest with yourself; so the sooner you're free to be you, the better.

Family and friends

Coming out is a major step in your life. There's always a risk of rejection when telling people that you are lesbian or gay. Informing members of your family and close friends is perhaps the most difficult task, so it's important that the decision is your own, and that you believe what you're doing is right.

There are so many advantages to being out; countless difficult situations can be avoided once you're honest with yourself and with other people. If you don't have to lie about where you go and what you do, you avoid the stress that accompanies deception. And if you make sure that you're the first to tell friends and relations, they won't feel let down as they might do if they found out by chance.

Gay & Lesbian Students

Many students are dependent on other people for various reasons, whether financially, physically or emotionally. And dependency on others makes it much harder to come out, particularly to parents, guardians or spouses, who are usually heterosexual and have always assumed that you are too. Therefore, coming out to the family might constitute a direct challenge to the ideas they have about you. Be prepared for the various different reactions from family members: they might be totally accepting, sad or openly hostile. But even if people take the news badly, their attitudes will often change in time.

If you're unsure of parental reaction, consider telling other family members who are closer to you and may be more sympathetic. These could be brothers and sisters, or more distant relations. There are a number of preparations you can make to ease the situation. It's wise to try and build up a network of supportive lesbian and gay friends, just in case things go wrong. Collect literature and contact numbers for support groups; prepare answers to any possible questions (particularly in answer to the common myths that it's your fault, that you've done something wrong, that you've been influenced by someone); and phone Lesbian Line or Gay Switchboard for expert advice (*see below* **Helplines**).

It's likely that you will be the one broaching the subject when you do tell your family, so it might be useful to try and gauge their reaction to lesbianism and homosexuality beforehand. Choose the best time to tell them. If you announce your sexuality during the heat of an argument, reactions are more likely to be hostile. Be positive about what you are telling them, and be honest. Whatever happens, try not to become aggressive, as this will only make matters worse in the long run. Most importantly, speak to them face-to-face, if you feel you can. It might be more difficult, but they'll respect you for it. You can always follow up the conversation with letters and phone calls. Once you've told them, give family and friends the space and time to adjust, bearing in mind that your news has probably come as something of a shock.

If it's your friends or family who bring up the subject first, try not to worry. Although you might be caught by surprise, it's very probable that they've thought carefully about the situation before approaching you. Stay calm and answer any questions openly and honestly. If you're sure of your sexuality, but deny it because of embarrassment, you can make matters more difficult in the long term.

Don't despair if the worst happens and your family or friends reject or disbelieve you. There are people who can help: contact Gay Switchboard or Lesbian Line (*see below* **Helplines**), both of which provide counselling and can put you in touch with other useful organizations. The friends that already know and accept you should be very supportive, so approach them. If you want to mend any rifts between yourself and your family, try asking relatives who feel sympathetic to your situation to mediate on your behalf. It's the people who can't accept the facts that have the problem, not you.

Older lesbian and gay students, who are married or co-habiting with a heterosexual partner, with or without children, are in a difficult position. Coming out in this situation takes strength and firm resolve. Groups such as Lesbian Mothers' Custody Project (*see below* **Useful Addresses**) advise not telling a spouse or partner until you've contacted an established organization, which will be able to counsel you in greater depth.

223

Coming out to children might be even more difficult. Only you can be the judge of when your children are old enough to understand what being lesbian or gay means. In these circumstances it's best to take the initiative, be positive and consider any possible questions they might have. Explain your feelings about your sexuality, taking into consideration that your children may have heard only negative comments about lesbianism and homosexuality.

As with family, it's difficult to have an open relationship with your friends if you can't be yourself, so consider coming out to them too. By keeping quiet and withholding the truth, you might eventually lose friends. Sometimes your friends will have suspected anyway. If this is so, make sure that you have the answers prepared to any questions they are likely to ask. Some might be negative towards you at first, but change their attitude over time – give them the space they need. Identify those who are more likely to accept your news, and tell them first; this will make matters easier, and boost your confidence about coming out to other people.

Student Union Lesbian and Gay Societies

Lesbian and gay societies, usually set up in college unions by the students, have several important functions. They provide a safe place for lesbian and gay students to meet and give each other mutual support and strength; they form the focus of a fulfilling social life free from harassment; and they represent the views of their members to the student union, and campaign for lesbian and gay rights. Lesbian and gay societies naturally form the focus for friendships, campaigning and partying at college.

Lesbian and gay societies vary in size from union to union, but they all have one thing in common: they're fun, supportive and friendly places. And, like any group, what you get out of it depends on what you put in.

If your student union has an intro fair, there will almost certainly be a lesbian and gay society stall. Some students have no trouble walking up to the society's stall and joining immediately. Others find it difficult to come out in this direct way, but when they finally take the plunge, they

When I got to college, I still thought I'd give heterosexuality a try: after all it's much easier to be heterosexual. Coming out on my degree course was a major preoccupation: it took up a lot of my time and was a very exciting period of my life. I had my first relationship with a woman just before my degree course began. It was such a relief to find that I wasn't the only one, as I thought I would be. When the relationship finished after almost three years, it was a positive thing: I discovered the lesbian and gay scene.

Even though art schools have a tradition of acceptance – of race, gender, class, sexuality – I found it was the opposite,

Gay & Lesbian Students

end up wondering why it took them so long to do something so natural. The world won't collapse around you if you walk up to the stall and say you'd like to join; on the contrary, you'll feel great that you've done it.

If, however, you don't feel up to joining the lesbian and gay society at the intro fair, you could either meander around nonchalantly, sneaking looks at the stall to try and make out when the first meeting is, or phone your student union's Nightline service and ask them for details of the society. Alternatively, go to the student union when there aren't many people about, and look at the society's posters to find out where and when their meetings are.

In colleges that don't have a society, arrangements often exist with other colleges, whose lesbian and gay societies will always welcome new members from other colleges and the local community. The local Gay Switchboard or Lesbian Line, or the NUS Lesbian and Gay Liberation Campaign (*see below*) will be able to put you in touch with local groups and student union societies at other colleges. Alternatively, ask your student union why there is no lesbian and gay society. The union officers, particularly those in the welfare office, should make it as easy as possible for you to start one. It could just be the case that one used to exist, but folded when its most active members left the college. Clubs and societies funded by student unions are required to have a minimum number of members before they receive funding. However, this requirement is usually waived for lesbian and gay societies. *See also page 146* **Student Unions**.

The NUS Lesbian and Gay Liberation Campaign

Over the years, lesbian and gay students have argued for the same rights and liberties as heterosexual students, and against discrimination and hostility based on ignorance. Their case has been won, and it is now recognized that, just as NUS represents the views and demands of its heterosexual members, so it must fight for its lesbian and gay members. NUS official policy now binds it to campaign for equal rights for all

particularly with the staff. But at the end of the day, the support of friends outside the college and the novelty of discovering the lesbian and gay scene made up for the negative aspects. And it also gave me the courage to tell my parents.

The biggest focus in my life at the time was coming out and being out – being myself. When you've spent so many years not being true to yourself and to other people, and you suddenly can, it's a major breakthrough.
Ritu Black Asian lesbian DJ, voted DJ of the Year 1990-91 by *Pink Paper* readers (Fine Arts painting, Wimbledon School of Art, 1983-86).

lesbian and gay men, on terms determined by lesbian and gay students.

The NUS Lesbian and Gay Liberation Campaign was founded to marshal support for the cause by organizing national conferences and providing NUS with resources and input from lesbians and gay men to back up its policy. These resources vary from posters and leaflets for campaigns to ideas and discussions on the needs of lesbian and gay students. The focus of the Campaign is its two annual conferences. These conferences allow lesbian and gay students from around the country to meet, discuss issues and determine the direction and policies of the Liberation Campaign.

Another of the Campaign's aims is to promote a positive profile of lesbians and gay men and to support their societies and campaigns in student unions. The Campaign Committee consists of eight annually elected lesbian and gay students, and at least two lesbian or gay convenors, whose job it is to assist the Campaign Committee in its work.

As well as helping individual student unions to set up lesbian and gay societies, the Campaign also encourages unions to have lesbian and gay officers on their executive committees. The promotion of lesbian and gay awareness weeks in colleges is another important priority; these promote positive images of lesbians and gay men, and help students either to come out, or to support demands for equality and liberation.

You can contact the Lesbian and Gay Liberation Campaign at NUS head office or through your student union.

Dealing with Harassment and Prejudice

One cruel fact of life for lesbians and gay men is that they have to endure other people's prejudices, which all too often lead to open harassment. Most prejudices stem from ignorance and stereotypical images of lesbians and gay men (for instance, that all lesbians are butch and all gay men are effeminate). Sometimes they are deeply-held views or opinions, but still they're far from objective. These prejudices are subjective, opinionated and born of the belief that heterosexuality is somehow superior or preferable to lesbianism and homosexuality. Many of these prejudices are an attempt to stir up guilt about lesbian and gay sexuality.

Prejudice can be unspoken thoughts or verbal insults. Harassment, which has its roots in prejudice, might take the form of a series of verbal assaults, taunts or physical intimidation. If you are harassed, don't fall into the trap of blaming yourself in any way. You're the one who suffers at the hands of ignorant persecutors; there's no reason to feel guilty. Instead, direct your energies towards getting something done about the situation. Tell supportive friends and don't bottle up frustration and anger.

To take further action against your harassers, inform someone in your student union: either the lesbian and gay officer, or the welfare officer. Depending on how your student union is organized, there are a variety of ways in which the harassment can be dealt with. These range from a quiet word to the harasser from your union's president, to a full disciplinary hearing at college level.

Lesbians and gay men can feel unable to rely upon the law for protection, since all too often the law is on the side of their oppressors, or is silent on lesbian and gay rights. The situation is different at college and your student union is more likely to make a stand against homophobic behaviour.

If you are harassed, bear in mind that – as the victim – you have the right to define what harassment is, so don't be swayed by false charges of over-sensitivity or pettiness by your

Gay & Lesbian Students

attackers. You're entitled to stand up for yourself. Never let the bigots get you down; their prejudices are their problem, not yours. Always tell your friends what's going on and get some support from them.

Your time at college is, after all, a time for personal development. By being true to yourself and being proud of who you are and what you are, you can only feel better for it in the long term. And you might even inspire other lesbian and gay students to come out.

Further Reading

Being Lesbian by Lorraine Trenchard (Gay Men's Press, £3.95).
How to be a Happy Homosexual by Terry Sanderson (Gay Men's Press, £3.95).
Gay Times (monthly) 283 Camden High Street, London NW1 7BX (071 267 0021).
The Pink Paper (weekly) 13 Hercules Street, London N7 (071 281 8615)
Scene Out (monthly) 23 New Mount Street, Manchester M4 4DE (061 953 4045).

Helplines

Black Lesbian & Gay Centre Project (081 885 3543). Open 6-9pm Thur.
Edinburgh Gay Switchboard (031 556 4049). Open 7.30-10pm daily.
Edinburgh Lesbian Line (031 557 0751). Open 7.30-10pm Mon, Thur.
Jewish Lesbian & Gay Helpline BM Jewish Helpline, London WC1N 3XX (071 706 3123). Open 7-10pm Mon, Thur.
London Lesbian & Gay Switchboard (071 837 7324). Open 24 hours daily.
London Lesbian Line (071 251 6911). Open 2-10pm Mon, Fri; 7-10pm Tue-Thur.
Manchester Gay Switchboard (061 274 3999). Open 4-10pm daily.

Manchester Lesbian Link (061 236 6205). Open 6-9pm Mon-Thur.
Parents & Friends of Lesbians and Gays (081 523 2910). Open 24 hours daily.

Useful Addresses

This is by no means a comprehensive list. For other useful contacts, check the listings in the lesbian and gay press or call your local Lesbian Line or Gay Switchboard (check in the front of the phone book or with directory enquiries for their number).

Black Lesbian & Gay People of Faith (BLAGPOF) BM Box 4390, London WC1N 3XX.
GEMMA (Lesbians with/without disabilities) BM Box 5700, London WC1N 3XX.
Lesbian & Gay Christian Movement (LGCM) Oxford House, Derbyshire Street, London E2 6HG (071 739 1249).
Lesbian & Gay Fostering and Adoptive Parents Group c/o London Friend, BM Friend, London WC1N 3XX.
Lesbian Mothers' Custody Project c/o 52-54 Featherstone Street, London EC1Y 8RT (071 251 6576).
NUS Lesbian & Gay Liberation Campaign c/o National Union of Students, Nelson Mandela House, 461 Holloway Road, London N7 6LJ (071 272 8900).
SHAKTI (South Asian Lesbians & Gay Men) BM Box 3167, London WC1N 3XX.
SIGMA (Support for Spouses of Married Gays) BM Sigma, London WC1N 3XX.
Parents Enquiry (Advice for parents of lesbians and gays) c/o Rose Robertson, 16 Honley Road, London SE6 2HZ (081 698 1815).

Teaching theTutors **230**
Campaigning for Childcare **231**
Safety **231**
The Women's Press **233**

NUS Women's Campaign **234**
Women's Groups **234**
Further Reading **235**
Useful Addresses **235**

women
students

A woman's experience of college life will be different from that of the male majority. **Hazel Bathie** and **Julie Emery** give their advice on how to deal with prejudice and sexism, and how to enjoy the company of other women, free from the attentions of hairy-knuckled neanderthals.

While women account for 57 per cent of the population, it's still the other 43 per cent that get their bums on the most influential seats. There are more women studying in higher education than ever before and many people will tell you that second-class citizenship is a thing of the past. Nevertheless, there's still plenty to be angry about. Sexual harassment and sexism are as common in higher education as anywhere else. Year after year, thousands of women enter colleges with the expectation that they will be judged on their academic ability, not their appearance; and that they will be treated with equal respect to their male peers. A lot of these women are destined to be disappointed.

Some women's experiences of college life will be dictated to a certain extent by their choice of course. More women are enrolling each year on traditionally male-dominated courses, such as engineering, as opposed to traditionally 'female' courses, such as arts and humanities. However, stereotyping still persists, and much careers advice goes along with outdated notions of what women 'should' and 'should not' study.

Women currently represent 45 per cent of the student population but colleges, in common with just about any organization you can think of, are predominately male in their hierarchy. Look at the members' list on any board or committee that's around, and you'll find men dominate.

Although you're unlikely to be swooped upon by a bunch of misogynist lecturers and administrators, reading this chapter may prepare you for problems that can arise. It's especially useful to know about the organizations and groups that women students can approach for help about anything, from sexism and sexual harassment to problems such as the lack of tampon machines in the building.

Someone to talk to

Most colleges have women's officers, either sabbatical (the minority) or non-sabbatical executive members (the majority). If your college has no officer who specifically represents women, and you need to talk to someone, speak to a union officer who is a woman, or the welfare officer. And while you're there, ask them why there isn't a women's officer. For example, if you have any problems with a lecturer consistently downgrading your work, being sexist, or sexually harassing you, the women's officer or the welfare officer can help. They will also have information on health matters, rape crisis centres and counsellors, and which DSS benefits you can claim as a student (don't hold your breath).

The women's officer will also welcome your involvement in the activities and campaigns that she is organizing, and any suggestions or ideas you might have. If you want to get organized to demand your rights, the student union is the forum in which to do it.

Teaching the Tutors

Issues relating to sexism, sexual harassment and women's safety on campus – both in and out of the classroom – are among the most important student union campaigns. These issues must be tackled if women are to have equal opportunities in education.

The first thing to recognize if you find yourself being treated in a sexist way or being harassed, is that it cannot be your fault. There is no such thing as 'asking for it'. Women have the right to be treated as serious students by male tutors and students. If an incident or a remark makes you feel uncomfortable because you are a woman, it is sexism or sexual harassment. Whatever we wear and however we look, we have the right to be treated with exactly the same respect as men.

There *is* something you can do about it. Tell other women what is happening: you're probably not the only one. Speak to the student union women's officer or welfare officer in confidence. And go along to the women's group and talk to the women there.

Some colleges have procedures which enable women to complain in confidence if the problem is with a male tutor or lecturer. One of the women tutors or the student counsellor may be the first point of contact; your student union can advise you. Even if you choose to take your complaint no further, it's important to let your student union know what's happening, and it may help you to talk about it.

Student unions can take action against sexual harassment by demanding that effective procedures are introduced, and that the college takes the issue seriously. It is *not* just a bit of fun – it affects our lives and our studies.

Campaigning for Childcare

One problem for women is the pitiful lack of childcare facilities. Student union campaigns over the past few years have done much to highlight the problems and inadequacies of childcare provision in colleges. Waiting lists for college and union-run crèches and nurseries are horrendously long, sometimes as long as two years. The costs of places in these nurseries are often far too high for students to afford, although some colleges do offer subsidized places to students. If women on a compulsory residential course have children they may be obliged to fork out for a crèche worker (about £30 per day), insurance and materials. If the course has been properly thought out, allowances for these extra costs will have been made, and the college board will have either approached the local education authorities to include these additions in your grant, or made its own arrangements for the extra funding.

Before you apply to a college, check the course details to see if allowances are made for childcare, and look for any loopholes or practical problems that would prevent you from attending classes or completing the course. If you discover any such problems, inform the course organizers to see if anything can be done about them. Tell your student union and encourage them to start a campaign. College authorities should be taking their equal opportunities policy statements seriously, and putting them into action. *See also page 44* **Mature Students** *and page 72* **Money**.

Safety

Women's safety on and around campus should always be high on the list of priorities for student unions and college authorities, although more often than not this is not the case. There are many simple measures that authorities could take to make colleges safer for women students. Money is often cited as an excuse for inaction – money that always seems to be there for new corporate logos and entertaining VIPs. Get together with other women students in your union to demand better lighting, free self-defence lessons, secure accommodation and so on. Be careful, but don't let fear rule your life.

If you live alone, put only your initials on the doorbell, along with those of some fictional flatmates. Obscene phone callers are rarely dangerous but can be very upsetting. Don't let them know you are harassed or bothered: just put the phone down. Also, BT can be very sympathetic and will screen your calls for you if you ask them to.

Aim not to be out alone at night. Some unions organize a safe-women's transport

Jo Richardson, Shadow Minister for Women; her first job after school was in the administrative office of a steelworks factory.

"When I first went to work, I didn't have many opportunities – and often still don't have enough. I went out to work straight from school partly because I wanted to, and partly because I failed my exams. I've sometimes regretted not going on to higher education, because it does two things for you. One is that you are involved in student life and meet people from different backgrounds. I think it's important for women to have contacts with other students – I kind of leapt from being a schoolgirl to being a wage earner. The second is that the discipline of studying does help you to think and gives you confidence, whatever you study. I have found that it's sometimes more difficult to grasp things which frighten me, like economics".

service after college events; if your union doesn't operate such a scheme, investigate how to go about establishing one. Others may have a deal with a local taxi company, giving concessionary rates. If no such arrangements are made for women students at your college, it's worth campaigning for some kind of travel service. Whatever the situation, don't take chances when travelling at night; licensed black taxis are always the best bet if you're alone. If you do have to take a minicab, ask for some form of identification from the driver, and always sit in the back. And if you must catch a train alone late at night, try to find a carriage with other women in it.

Go along to a self-defence class: check if your local council has any. Look in the union shop for rape alarms. If they don't sell them, take the union to task, then try a large department store. Rape alarms are either gas or battery operated and make a most ungodly noise. Gas alarms cost about £5: Alarmagrip, Feel Safe, Talisman Continuous 805 and Walk Easy are all good examples. Battery alarms (Attackalarm and Chubb PA01, for example) are more expensive because they last longer; they cost between £11 and £16. Better still, your union should distribute subsidized or free alarms, and the college authorities should be prepared to meet some, if not all, of the cost.

If you are attacked, it's your decision whether or not to tell the police. If you do, you will have to undergo an internal physical examination, so go to the police as soon as possible after the attack, without changing, washing or having an alcoholic drink. Take a woman friend, and ask to be examined by a woman doctor. Whether or not you go to the police, you should go to your doctor or to an STD clinic to check whether you are pregnant or have caught a sexually transmitted disease (*see page 172* **Health and Stress**).

And contact your local Rape Crisis Centre (*see below* **Useful Addresses**).

The Women's Press

As you settle into your course and into college life, you may want to find out more about feminism, or about aspects of your course that relate to women. A lot of good work has been done on women's hidden history, and the part women have played in art, literature, political struggle, historical events and so on, although you might find that little of this has percolated through to the reading lists. Speak to your women's officer or find out about women's centres in your area. Students in London can visit the Feminist Library and Information Centre (*see below* **Useful Addresses**), a voluntary body with a collection of 5,000 books and periodicals and around 1,000 pamphlets.

The newsletters, newspapers and magazines published by various women's organizations can also provide answers to some questions you might have, such as the differences between radical and socialist feminists or why some groups of women prefer to organize autonomously. For instance, *Spare Rib* (monthly, £1.40) lists events such as women's bands and theatre groups as well as covering topics and issues relevant to women. Other publications include *Everywoman* (monthly, £1.40), a news, current affairs and general interest magazine; the quarterly *Feminist Review* (£8.50), encompassing feminist culture and politics; and *Trouble and Strife*, which is published around three times a year (£2.50), and covers mostly radical feminist and lesbian politics and culture.

Women's publishing houses such as Virago and the Women's Press put out works exclusively by women, from established classics to new manuscripts.

"Having enormously enjoyed and benefited from my time at an all-women's college, I strongly recommend women to make the most of women-only groups and activities while at college. The rewards last a lifetime."

Harriet Spicer Managing Director Virago Press (English, St Anne's College, Oxford, 1969-71).

NUS Women's Campaign

The Women's Campaign (an autonomous section of NUS) was established to fight for women's rights by co-ordinating and assisting the activities of women students, women's groups and women's officers in colleges throughout the country. The Campaign is headed by the NUS Women's Officer, who is elected at the annual women's conference (to which any student union is entitled to send a delegate). There is a Women's Committee whose members are students or student union sabbatical officers.

Members of the Women's Committee are available to speak at meetings in colleges, and all can be contacted through the Women's Campaign (*see below* **Useful Addresses**). They also run a number of national events, including Women's Aggregate (an informal meeting for debates and workshops held early on in the academic year), the Women's Campaign Conference and Women's Officers' Day. The Campaign exists as a resource for all women in colleges; it can be called upon for advice and support, campaign materials, speakers, and other practical help. The Campaign strives to involve women students in campaigns around important issues. Recent priorities have included women's reproductive rights, the poll tax, childcare and the Gulf War.

Women's Groups

Joining the women's group is a more direct way of getting involved in women's issues. If there isn't a group where you are, you could set one up yourself. You should be able to get funding from the union – this money can be used for activities such as women-only events in union venues, commissioning speakers or publicizing campaigns. The group should be accessible to all women. Advice on setting up a women's group is available from the Women's Campaign.

Being a woman student in a male-dominated college may have its drawbacks, you do have recourse to the NUS Women's Campaign and to your student union, if problems arise. But student life is supposed to be a laugh as well as hard work. It will be more fun if you take full advantage of your student union and its events and facilities. There will be times when you'll feel threatened or harassed just because you're a woman; but remember you're not alone. There are people and organizations that can help. And the fact is, apart from anything else, women find each other good company.

Further Reading
Current Issues in Women's History edited by A. Angerman (Routledge, £9.99).
Don't: A Woman's Word by Elly Danica (The Women's Press, £3.95).
Learning to Lose: Sexism & Education edited by Dale Spender and Elizabeth Sarah (Writers & Readers Publishing, £5.95).
Sex Roles and the School by Sara Delmone (Routledge, £8.99).
Sexual Violence: The Reality for Women by the London Rape Crisis Centre (The Women's Press, £4.95).
Sweet Freedom by Anna Coute and Beatrix Campbell (Blackwell, £8.95).
Woman's Consciousness, Man's World by Sheila Rowbotham (Penguin, £4.99).
A Woman in Your Own Right by Anne Dickson (Quartet, £4.95).
Women, Race and Class by Angela Davis (The Women's Press, £5.95).

Useful Addresses
Feminist Library and Information Centre 5 Westminster Bridge Road, London SE1 7XW (071 928 7789).
London Rape Crisis Centre PO Box 69, London WC1N 9NJ (*helpline* 071 837 1600; open 24 hours daily).
National Childcare Campaign c/o Wesley House, 4 Wild Court, London WC2B 5AV (071 405 5617).
NUS Women's Campaign Nelson Mandela House, 461 Holloway Road, London N7 6LJ (071 272 8900).
Women Against Sexual Harassment 242 Pentonville Road, London N1 9UN (071 833 0222).
Women's Health and Reproductive Rights Information Centre 52-54 Featherstone Street, London EC1Y 8RT (071 251 6580).

All students are equal but some are more equal than others. For some students from ethnic minorities, racism at college can be a familiar but unwelcome problem; while for others, college is a liberating experience. **Patrick Younge** tells you how to break down the barriers of bigotry and ignorance to get the most from college life.

black students

Making Contact with other Black Students **238**

Racism on and off Campus **239**

Racism Abroad **239**

Dealing with Racial Harassment **240**

Making a Stand against Racism **242**

Further Reading **242**

Useful Addresses **243**

Britain's colleges are among the most vibrant institutions in the country, bringing together predominantly young people of varied backgrounds and races from across the UK and the rest of the world. Many black students find college a more liberal and supportive enviroment than that of the 'outside world'; and some who find the cultural constraints of their homes restrictive feel a sense of liberation at being able to mix freely with students of different cultures, races and religion. Unfortunately, this mix does not insulate colleges from the rest of society and racial discrimination is as much a fact of college life as it is of society at large.

In this chapter, the term 'black student' is used to refer to all students who consider theselves to be 'non-white': for example, Afro-Caribbeans, Asians and Orientals. This chapter is not meant to exclude you from the other chapters in this book, aimed at all members of the student population, but to provide advice that you might find useful.

Reports from the Commission for Racial Equality (CRE, *see below* **Useful Addresses**) between 1987 and 1990 show that black students are still getting a raw deal, both when they apply for courses and for jobs after graduation. This isn't to say that as a black student, your college life will be dissimilar from that of your white counterparts in many respects. Lack of money, too many essays and sub-standard housing are universal crosses that all students, whatever their colour, have to bear. But you will experience many differences in college life which are unique to black students.

In most cases, a good look around your college will show that black students are few and far between, and initial feelings of personal and cultural isolation are not uncommon – especially for first-year students. You could be the only black person on your course, or one of a small number; even if you are lucky, there's unlikely to be more than 20 per cent black students doing your subject (figures for the ratio of black students in British colleges are difficult to come by, but PCAS figures for 1990-91 indicate that black students form 23.3 per cent of polytechnic admissions). But one of the few advantages of being in a minority is that, should you want to, you can be on first name terms with many, if not most, of the black students in your college.

Making contact with other black students

One easy way to become acquainted with other black students is to join the Afro-Caribbean society or Asian society as soon as you get to college. Many colleges also have Indian, Arab, Pakistani and Islamic societies, for example. These societies, usually funded through the student union, are an easy way to meet people who share your background and experiences. They usually organize social, sporting and cultural activities, many of which will also involve people from the local black community.

Occasionally, these societies organize political activities. But increasingly, political issues are being taken up by the National Black Students Alliance (NBSA; *see below* **Useful Addresses**). The NBSA is made up of college-based black student groups and provides them with a national voice. It plays an active role in the NUS, and has a number of representatives on NUS's Anti-Racism Committee. With the support of NUS, it has been active in a variety of campaigns against injustice, such as the Broadwater Farm Defence Campaign, as well as campaigns against racist attacks and racist violence. They are now giving a high priority to making students, black and white, aware of the race equality implications of 1992 and the single European market.

If your college doesn't have an Afro-Caribbean or Asian society, or a black student group, you could approach your student union and ask about how you and your friends can start one. The process is usually very simple and you should be well supported.

Racism on and off campus

You will find that the presence of black student groups is useful if you face racial prejudice or harassment. Overt prejudice is relatively unusual on campus; casual racist remarks from fellow students, or prejudice from lecturers who scorn the black contribution to their subject area, are not uncommon. Many white students will not have mixed with non-white people before, and a great deal of prejudice stems from ignorance alone.

The graduate recruitment process is one aspect of campus life where widespread discrimination is still rife. Surveys carried out by the CRE in 1987 and 1990 have shown that black graduates are almost twice as likely to be unemployed one year after graduation as white graduates with the same qualifications – despite the fact that black graduates write more application letters and attend more interviews. In the CRE sample, a larger proportion of Asians – 16 per cent – than any other ethnic group were continuously unemployed during the year following graduation.

Action to ensure racial equality in the graduate recruitment process is now being taken by college careers services and the Association of Graduate Recruiters (*see below* **Useful Addresses**), but many aspects of discrimination still remain. If you feel that you have been discriminated against in the graduate recruitment process, either by your college careers service or by a prospective employer, complain to your college authorities, and to the senior personnel officer in the company to which you applied. If you're unhappy with their response, you can take the matter up with the Employment division of the CRE.

There are a large number of off-campus situations in which you can encounter racism. For example, although it's highly unlikely that you will face discrimination when applying for college-owned accommodation, applying for a private flat can subject you to the irrational whims and prejudices of landlords. Stories of white students being offered flats that black students had previously been denied are still common.

There's little you can do in these situations, because it's so difficult to prove that you have been discriminated against because of your colour. All the action you can take is to present whatever evidence you have to your college accommodation service, to the CRE or local race equality organizations, such as the local Race Equality Council (*see below* **Useful Addresses**) and ask them to act on your behalf.

Racism abroad

You might be confronted with instances of racial prejudice, ignorance, insensitivity and bureaucratic apathy if your course involves studying abroad. A number of recent cases show that colleges aren't aware of the racism facing black people in the foreign countries where they're sent to continue their studies.

For example in 1988, Mandy, a black student from Cambridge, was due to be sent to Nice, France, to complete her year abroad. Nice is the political centre of the French National Front,

'I left my degree course at Heriot-Watt early over their racist agreement with South Africa to send only white students for training as mining engineers (the SA government did not allow black British students to study there). In some respects, things have changed – I was amazed on a recent visit to my old Technical College at Tottenham to see that almost all the students were black – but I don't know how much people's personal attitudes to black people have changed since I was a student in the sixties... black students generally are still getting a raw deal. College authorities still don't take black students' needs into...

and has elected a National Front MP to the French parliament. In 1988 there had been a number of reports of young blacks in the city being beaten up and, on a couple of occasions, murdered. Mandy was worried by these reports and requested an alternative placement. Her college put up fierce resistance to her request placement, although eventually Mandy was successful.

Andrew, who studies French and Russian in Scotland, has been warned that when he undertakes the Russian part of his year abroad he is not to be seen 'going out with white women', lest he provokes a violent response from xenophobic Russians. But it must be remembered that all students going abroad need to be aware of cultural differences in the country they are visiting, and should be given advice on how to behave and react to the new environment.

Situations such as these illustrate the problems that you can face if you are going to study abroad. Make sure that you check any foreign placement well in advance, so that if you have any reservations, you can present them to your course tutor and college authorities before the placement process is set in action.

Dealing with racial harassment

Racial harassment is rapidly becoming the main problem facing black students. Although there are no accurate nationwide figures, it is widely accepted by police and politicians that racist attacks are on the increase and that the level of violence used by hard-line fascists against black people is escalating.

Unfortunately, harassment isn't confined to members of neo-Nazi groups; student behaviour cannot be isolated from that of society at large, and with harassment on the increase generally,

Black Students

...account and foreign students have a particularly hard time. They get no proper counselling but their money is taken all the same.

The loan scheme may cause enormous problems for black students. In the US, banks have been refusing them loans because they are more likely to come from poor families and so be a bad risk. That could happen here and is the reason for the 'poverty conscription' into the US army we have seen; it's the only way many black people can get higher education.'

Bernie Grant Labour MP (Mining Engineering, Heriot-Watt University, Edinburgh, 1967-69).

it's also becoming one of the more unsavoury features of college life. Nor is it simply a problem in the big cities; reports of harassment are recorded in both small-town and inner city educational establishments. For years college authorities have pretended that racial harassment simply didn't happen on 'their' campus. But now, partly in an attempt to attract more black students, college authorities are taking the issue more seriously.

The Committee of Vice-Chancellors and Principals (CVCP) (*see below* **Useful Addresses**) has recently published its guidelines for dealing with racial discrimination on campus. The free publication, called *Racial Harassment: Guidance for Universities*, includes a definition of racial harassment as treatment that any 'reasonable' person would regard as 'offensive and intimidating to the recipient'. Racial harassment is said to be 'the behaviour that creates an intimidating, hostile or offensive environment for study and social life'. Such behaviour includes 'derogatory name calling, insults and racist jokes, racist graffiti, verbal abuse and threats, physical attacks and ridicule of an individual for cultural differences'.

If you feel you're being subjected to racial harassment there are a variety of ways in which you can seek help and advice. At all times it's important to realize that it's not your fault and that you do not have to tolerate it.

Cases of harassment can be dealt with by your college, the police or the CRE, depending on the degree of harassment you have suffered. You should record the events that are causing you distress, and keep a note of how the incidents have changed the pattern of your academic or social life. Make it clear to the people causing you offence that their behaviour is unacceptable to you. This may, in some instances, be sufficient to stop it. But an inability to tackle your oppressor in this way does not constitute consent to harassment, nor should it prejudice any complaint that you may wish to bring.

If you are unable or unwilling to tackle your harassers directly, you should raise the issue with your head of department, personal tutor, student union, college counselling service, chaplain or any other responsible person or friend you feel you can trust. These people should be able to advise you on a course of action, or possibly take the matter up on your behalf. They may even suggest a way of dealing with the problem that you hadn't thought of yourself. You should make sure that any discussions you have at this stage are confidential, and that no action will be taken by anyone without your consent.

If the problems cannot be resolved by these informal means, you (or someone acting on your behalf) should make a formal complaint to the college which could lead to disciplinary action being taken against your harasser.

In the case of a physical attack, or harassment outside the college's jurisdiction, you should seek immediate help, and you should report the attack to the police, either in person or by writing to them. Despite the history of police inaction on cases of racial abuse, it's important that the harassers are dealt with legally. If you're unsure about the police, take a friend or relative to the station with you. If you believe that there is a racist motive behind the attack, make sure that the police record this when you report the attack to them.

If you're dissatisfied with the response of your college or local police force to your complaint, you should take the matter to the CRE and ask them to act.

Making a stand against racism

When discrimination is a routine part of daily life it's difficult to know on which occasions to make a stand. Being at college is no different. But you shouldn't have to put up with a second-class experience of college life just because you're black.

In one recent case, black students who alleged that they were being marked down in their exams on racial grounds had their claims vindicated by a college enquiry, and subsequently had their degrees upgraded. It's clear there can be much to gain from making a stand, if you think you have a case.

But if the prejudice and intolerance is too great, and you decide to quit, don't think that it's the end of the world. In 1966 a black student left his college in disgust at its links with South Africa. He went on to become Britain's first black council leader and, at time of writing, one of only four black MPs. He is Bernie Grant, MP for Tottenham.

Further Reading
Black and White Britain: Third PSI Survey by Colin Brown (PSI).
Britain's Black Population: 2nd edition by Ashok Bhat (Vertical Statistics Race Group).
The Golden Thread: Asian Experiences of Post-Raj Britain by Zerbanoo Gifford (Grafton, £7.99).
Racial Inequality in Education by Barry Troyna (Tavistock Publications).
Staying Power: The History of Black People in Britain (Pluto Press, £12.95).
A Tolerant Country? by Colin Holmes (Faber, £5.99).

Useful Addresses
Association of Graduate Recruiters
Sheraton House, Castle Park, Cambridge CB3 OAX (0223 356720).

Black Students

Commission for Racial Equality Elliott House, 10-12 Allington Street, London SW1E 5EH (071 828 7022). Contact the Commission for a list of useful publications, including: *Code of Practice for the Elimination of Racial Discrimination in Education* (1989, £1.50); *Words or Deeds? A Review of Equal Opportunity Policies in Higher Education* (1989, £2).
Committee for Vice-Chancellors and Principals (CVCP) 29 Tavistock Square, London WC1H 9EZ (071 387 9231).
Greater London Action for Racial Equality St Margarets House, 21 Old Ford Road, London E2 9PL (081 983 1122).
National Black Students Alliance c/o Masoud Hedeishi, Manchester University Student Union, Oxford Road, Manchester M13 9PR (061 275 2930).
National Association of Race Equality Councils (NAREC) 8-16 Coronet Street, London N1 6HD (071 739 6658). Contact the head office for details of your local Race Equality Council.
Scottish Asian Action Committee 73 Robertson Street, Glasgow G3 (041 248 5033).

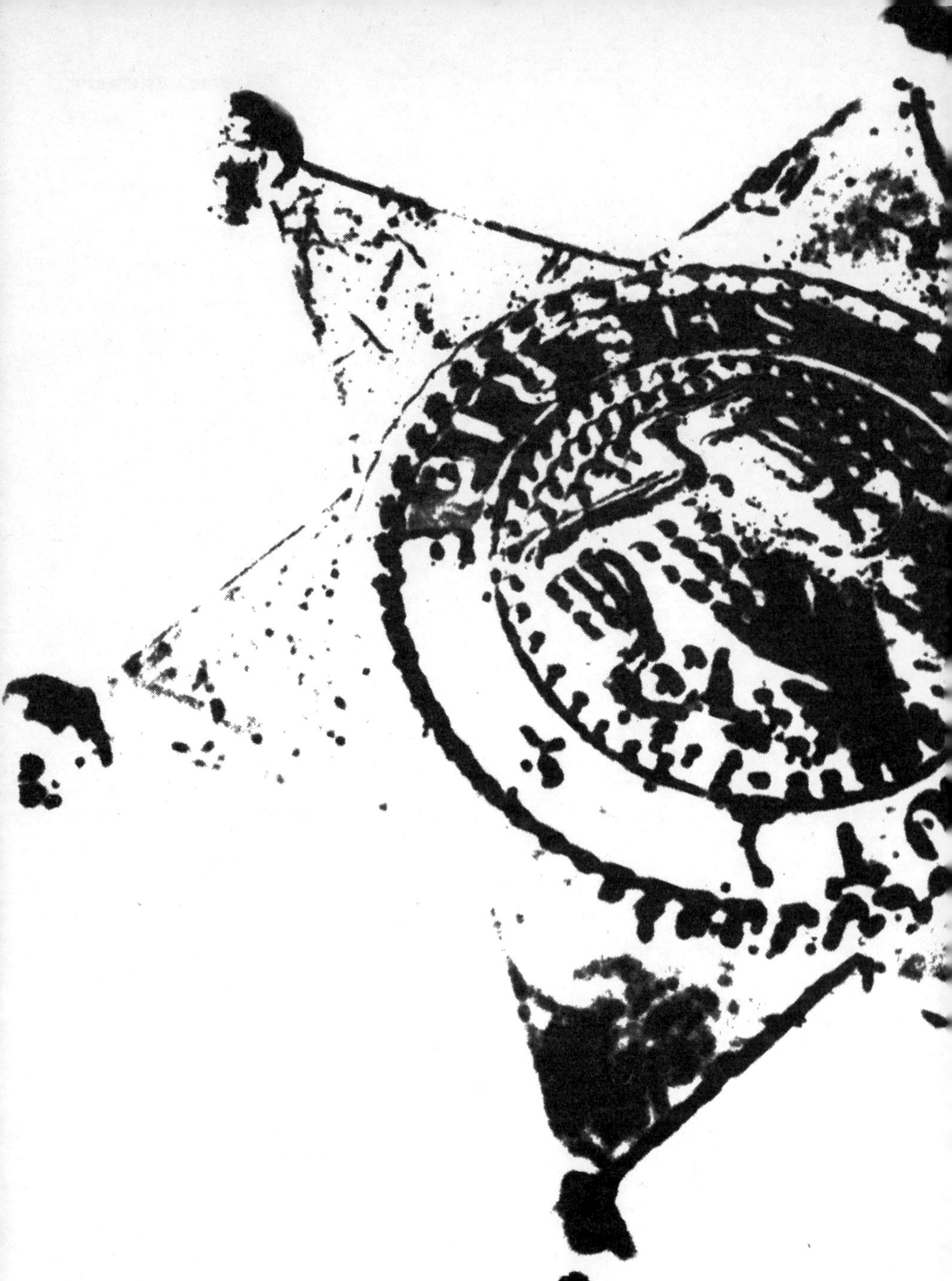

Legal Rights **246**
Consumer Rights **249**
Electoral Rights **252**
Ombudsmen **253**
Further Reading **253**
Useful Addresses **253**

rights

Irrespective of your status as a student, you have rights. And you don't have to be a lawyer, a political activist or a High Court judge to understand what they are. **Gavin Hamilton** outlines your basic rights as a citizen, a consumer and a voter.

You won't forfeit your rights as a citizen the moment you become a student. But if you don't know what your rights are, or how they can be upheld, you can still find yourself at a disadvantage. All too often, in any situation which involves the law or official authorities, the individual concerned feels exposed and defenceless, with nowhere to turn for help and advice. And in any spot of bother with the boys and girls in blue – or even just a squabble with a stroppy shopkeeper – awareness of your rights (and how to use them) is vital. In this chapter we outline the basic rights held by all UK citizens.

See also *page 28* **Overseas Students**; *page 94* **Accommodation**; and *page 254* **Employment**.

Legal Rights

There is a clear distinction between civil offences (such as non-payment of bills) and criminal offences (theft or drink-driving, for example). The main difference is that you cannot be sent to prison for a civil offence, nor can you pick up a criminal record.

Don't despair if you do become embroiled with the law, because there's plenty of advice and support available. You will not be treated as a criminal by the advice agencies, nor will you be the only person in the world in your situation, although it may feel like that if you don't seek help.

If you are arrested

Behave intelligently if you're stopped by the police: control your aggression and try to remain polite. Give your name and address as soon as you're asked and without fuss – you are obliged to by law if the police have any reason to believe you have committed an offence; if you refuse, you'll end up being held longer than necessary. You have the right to remain silent after identifying yourself. If you are arrested by plain-clothes police, ask to see some identification. If you can, note the police officers' names, numbers and descriptions. This is important if you want to make a complaint later.

Don't start informal conversations with the police or try to make deals with them. Since the tape recording of interviews was introduced to end oppressive interrogation, lawyers have reported instances of interviews on the way to the station, which are not recorded. Only make a statement if you're sure it will help. A damaging statement signed by you is difficult to explain away and many judges are not swayed by pleas of undue pressure. Write down everything about the incident as soon as possible. The police are obliged to provide writing materials for anyone under arrest at a police station. Your notes will make it easier for you to explain what happened to a solicitor or to a court.

You are allowed to make one phone call – use it to let someone know where you are and what has happened. You have the right to consult a solicitor: do so. If you don't have your own lawyer, the police must give you details of the duty solicitor scheme (*see below* **Legal Aid**).

Legal advice

If you have any sort of legal problem and need advice, before you rush out and sign up the services of the first solicitor you come across, seek help from a legal advice centre or a Citizens' Advice Bureau (CAB). The CAB specializes in giving advice to people on low incomes, including students. Staff can advise you on the best course of action for your particular case, refer you to a solicitor, and advise you on how to apply for Legal Aid. Your nearest legal advice centre or

Rights

CAB will be listed in the local phone directory. The National Association of Citizens' Advice Bureaux (*see below* **Useful Addresses**) can also tell you where your local centre is, but it does not give out advice. Alternatively, you can try to get the information or advice you need from your student union or college law department.

Legal Aid

The statutory Legal Aid scheme is intended to help people with the cost of legal advice, assistance and representation. Eligibility is dependent upon your financial status and as most students are on low incomes, you will probably be entitled to full costs. Even if you are not entitled to the whole amount, you may qualify for partial assistance.

To apply for any of the three types of Legal Aid (*see* **Types of Legal Aid**) you will need to see a solicitor. Not all solicitors deal in Legal Aid cases, so ask at your local CAB or legal advice centre for a list of Legal Aid solicitors. Consult the Solicitors' Regional Directory for names of local solicitors and the sort of work that they do (copies are kept at all libraries and town halls and at most advice centres). Alternatively, visit any solicitor's office where you see the Legal Aid sign. You will have to fill in a form declaring your income and savings. You will then be means tested to see whether you are eligible.

If the police question you about an offence, you are entitled to free legal advice, for which there is no means test. If you have to go to the magistrate's court on a criminal case, there will often be a duty solicitor available at the court or on call to give you free advice and representation on your first appearance. Again, there is no means test.

The Legal Aid Board publishes a useful booklet, the *Legal Aid Guide*. It's available from Citizens' Advice Bureaux, legal advice centres, libraries, or direct from the Legal Aid Board (*see below* **Useful Addresses**). The Scottish Legal Aid Board (*see below* **Useful Addresses**) gives information about Legal Aid in Scotland, which is administered separately.

NUS Legal Aid Fund

NUS operates a scheme to which affiliated student unions can apply for legal aid for themselves and their members (but only if the latter do not qualify for ordinary state legal aid). If you have tried all the other options open to you without success, you may be able to get help from this fund. Your student union can give more details.

Types of Legal Aid

1. **Legal Advice and Assistance** (also known as the **Green Form** scheme). Covers advice and help with any legal problem and, in some cases, through Assistance by Way of Representation (ABWOR), going to court.

2. **Civil Legal Aid** Covers civil court proceedings, whether being brought or defended.

3. **Criminal Legal Aid** Covers criminal court proceedings, but only for defending (and not bringing) a criminal prosecution.

247

"The UK needs to make a vocabulary of rights part of the legal vocabulary – no such concept currently exists. We need people to be more rights conscious – students play a part here – and we would do well to integrate European Council law into the British mainstream."

Paul Boateng Labour MP (Law, Bristol University, 1969-71).

Making a complaint against the police

If you think that the police have behaved improperly or illegally, you can make a complaint. The complaint must be against a particular officer or officers and it's best to first seek advice from a law centre, CAB or Legal Aid solicitor (*see above* **Legal advice** and **Legal Aid**). A complaint can be made verbally or in writing (though preferably in writing) to the chief constable of the force employing the officer concerned, to the Commissioner of Police (in London), or to a local police station. Your initial statement should be brief and you should keep a copy of it. You have three main options open to you.

An 'informal resolution' is the quickest and simplest option, but even if upheld, no formal entry will be made in the record of the officer or officers concerned. Although the procedure is informal, an officer of the rank of chief inspector will oversee an investigation and you will be required to give further statements and provide witnesses (if there were any). If successful, it's possible to receive an apology on behalf of the chief constable or force but, as there is no specific procedure laid down, not necessarily from the police officer concerned.

If a complaint is formally investigated, it can be supervised by the Police Complaints Authority (PCA, *see below* **Useful Addresses**), a body made up of civilians appointed by the government. The PCA must supervise any complaint alleging that the conduct of a police officer resulted in death, serious injury or actual bodily harm to another person, corruption or a 'serious arrestable offence'. There will be a lengthy process of investigation and you will be interviewed and asked to provide statements and witnesses. Always have someone with you when you are interviewed, preferably a solicitor. Disciplinary proceedings may then be brought. The PCA also has the

Rights

power to refer the complaint to the Director of Public Prosecutions (DPP) who can prosecute the officer concerned. In reality, very few officers are ever prosecuted by the DPP.

Alternatively, you can take out a civil action and sue the police for wrongful arrest, imprisonment or assault. If you win, you will receive a sum of money in compensation. Many civil cases succeed where formal complaints fail. If you are considering a civil action, take legal advice as soon as possible.

The National Council for Civil Liberties (*see below* **Useful Addresses**) publishes a free booklet, *Complaints against the Police.*

Consumer Rights

Anyone who spends money on goods and services is a consumer. And students, as consumers, have rights just like anyone else. Consumer law is a complex (and often confusing) subject, and while there may be no need to understand all its complexities, it is worth bearing in mind that even when you buy a loaf of bread or use a credit card, you have rights. The most important are outlined below.

Returning faulty or damaged goods

You can return and claim your money back on goods which don't match the description on the packaging, label, brochure, advert, or what the retailer told you about them. It's also illegal for retailers to sell goods that fall short of their description, be it in size, weight or measure. Anything you buy must be of saleable quality; defects that are clearly obvious or would show up on reasonable inspection won't entitle you to a refund. However, defects you can't see or faults which develop later will almost always entitle you to a refund.

Don't be put off asking for a refund by difficult retailers or shop assistants who may try to say that it's not their fault, but that of the manufacturer. In fact, the retailer is legally obliged to provide a refund, even though the merchandise may have come from the manufacturer pre-packed and the retailer has not checked it personally.

Credit cards and hire purchase

If you pay by cash or cheque and something goes wrong, your only come-back is against the retailer. But if you pay by credit card the lending facility will be liable for the faulty goods or services as well as the retailer. The sum paid must be over £100. You'll also be able to claim compensation from the credit card company if the contractor or retailer goes bankrupt or can't be found.

If you buy something on hire purchase (HP), you do not technically become the owner until you have paid the final instalment. You are simply hiring it and are therefore not covered by the law regarding bought merchandise. However, you are afforded protection by another law which allows you to return and claim a refund on defective or faulty goods bought on HP. You can also insist on a replacement, or alternatively, claim the cost of repair from the shop or finance company.

Credit sale agreements differ from HP as the goods become your property immediately. Because the finance company is lending you the money for the goods, your consumer rights are the same as if you had paid cash for the goods.

Contracts and clauses

When shopping, ignore any notices which seek to limit or reduce the consumer's rights, such as 'the management does not accept responsibility for damaged goods' or 'we retain the right not to give refunds for faulty goods'. *See above* **Returning faulty or damaged goods**.

The law with regard to service contractors, such as builders, is much the same as for retailers. You can ignore any clauses in a contract which refer to injury and death, such as 'any injury caused as a result of the work being carried out is hereby excluded.' So if a light, put up by an electrician, crashes down on your head, you can claim compensation. However, a contractor's liability can be excluded in other cases. If, for example, it is stated clearly in a contract that a contractor's liability for loss or damage to goods while in his or her care is limited to £50, you will be bound by it.

The law regarding clauses, contracts and small print is a minefield. The best advice is to read a contract – particularly the disclaimers and exclusion clauses – very carefully before signing anything and if there is anything you don't understand, ask.

Debt collection

If you leave a bill unpaid for too long, you are likely to be contacted by a debt collection agency, which will attempt to recover the money through the courts, on behalf of your creditors. Official letters from debt collection agencies often increase panic and uncertainty, particularly if you have never had to cope with repaying debts before.

You can't be prosecuted in the criminal courts or sent to prison for non-payment of debts. Harassment by collection agencies is illegal. They can't threaten you with criminal proceedings, repossession of property or force you to sign documents that allow repossession of goods. They cannot make threatening visits or phone calls, nor can they impersonate court officials in an attempt to recover the money. If you work, they cannot contact your employer to get the money, or wait outside your workplace on pay day.

If you receive a letter from a debt collection agency, contact the agency as soon as possible and inform the staff that you intend to pay. If you ignore the letter, it will be taken as an indication of your intention to avoid paying and the agency will intensify its efforts to recover the money. The fact that you have received a letter from a debt collection agency is an indication that your creditors intend to recover the debt no matter how hard you try to avoid it.

Make them an offer to pay in instalments. No matter how small these are, it will let them know that you intend to pay. Draw up a repayment schedule and always keep copies of correspondence that you send. Make sure you keep up the payments. If you don't, you will be 'surcharged'.

Misleading or offensive advertising

Anyone has the right to complain about an advert that they consider to be misleading or offensive, or both. The first step is to contact your local council's Trading Standards Department. Alternatively, you can register a complaint with the Advertising Standards Authority (*see below* **Useful Addresses**). If this fails to achieve anything, you can appeal to the Director General of Fair Trading, who is based at the Office of Fair Trading (OFT, *see below* **Useful Addresses**). The Director General has the power to take out an injunction to prevent the publication, or continued publication, of an advert.

Getting help

Although the law and the threat of court action is ultimately the most effective way to resolve an issue or deal with a claim, legal action is slow, often complicated and there is no certainty that the outcome will be successful. Going to court should therefore be seen as a last resort. There are a number of alternatives to pursuing legal action, any one of which can be successful. They should be considered before any legal avenues are explored.

"I can vouch for the importance of political activity – I can count among my achievements the lowering of the voting age to 18 in the sixties, extending pub opening hours, legalising indie radio stations and, I hope, the appointment of a minister of pop music, as in France."
Screaming Lord Sutch Musician and politician (History and Economics, Harrow College of Further Education, 1954-57).

On a local level, the Trading Standards Departments of local councils play an important role in the enforcement of consumer protection. A complaint to them can often be enough to force a local shop into ending illegal trading practices. Some councils also have Consumer Advice Centres which advise on consumer matters and negotiate on behalf of the consumer. Citizens' Advice Bureaux and Law Centres often have advisers who specialize in consumer law.

Nationally, the Office Of Fair Trading does not handle individual cases, but does receive feedback from Trading Standards Officers and Citizens' Advice Bureaux. A complaint to the OFT may contribute to an unfair trading practice being exposed. A complaint to the relevant trade association to which a trader belongs may also bring results. Such associations exist to promote standards among their members and are therefore keen to uphold standards.

Electoral Rights
The electoral register

As a student you can register to vote at both your term-time and home address. You can vote at both addresses in local elections, but only at one in a general election. If you are 16 or 17, your name can be included on the electoral register and you will able to vote as soon as you are 18.

Electoral registers are compiled each year. Forms will usually be sent to your address during the summer of the previous year (August or September) and should be returned by the date specified on the form (normally mid-October). If you don't receive a form, you can pick one up from your student union or town hall. A draft register will be published and there is then a period of about three weeks during which you can check the draft register to see that you have been registered. Many student unions keep copies of the draft register and copies are also kept at town halls. If you have not been included, you can have your name added to the register by contacting the electoral registration office at your local town hall. If you live in a hall of residence, the hall authorities should have included you automatically on the register. However, it is your responsibility to ensure that you have been registered.

If you going to be unable to make it to a polling station on polling day (if you're on holiday or are ill, for example) you can arrange to vote by proxy (you appoint someone to vote on your behalf) or you can apply for a postal vote. For either of these, forms can be picked up from, and need to be returned to, the electoral registration officer at your local town hall; they must be returned at least two weeks before polling day.

MPs and councillors

MPs hold regular surgeries where their constituents can voice their concerns on any issue under the sun, be it the poll tax, pollution or parking on the pavement at the end of their street. Surgeries are held at least once a month and sometimes as often as every week. For some you will need an appointment; for others you can just turn up on the day. Although most MPs follow the party line on national political issues, on local issues they are very sensitive to local opinion and your views do carry weight.

Local councillors also hold surgeries for their constituents and these obviously deal exclusively with local issues. Councillors have the power to get things changed through the council and will also, if they are in the same political party as the local MP, be able to have a quiet word with your MP.

Details of MPs' and councillors' surgeries are available in local libraries and town halls.

Rights

Ombudsmen

Statutory provisions have been made by Parliament for dealing with bad administration – be it serious delay, discrimination, mistakes in the handling of claims or failing to follow recognized procedure – in government departments and public bodies, in local authorities and boards, and in the National Health Service. Ombudsmen (sic) have powers to examine files and documents, interview people involved in the matter and, when the investigation has been completed, to report and pronounce on whether the complaint has been upheld. They do not have any power to enforce any change, or remedy any mistake, but they can publicize a matter and, if need be, refer it to Parliament.

Before contacting the Ombudsman (*see below* **Useful Addresses**), you should first take up your complaint with the relevant person or body, who should then pursue it on your behalf. For the Parliamentary Ombudsman, this is your MP; for the Local Ombudsman, the council department; and for the Health Service Ombudsman, the Health Authority or Family Practitioner Committee. Students have used Ombudsmen in the past to pursue complaints. A number of students have, for example, contacted the Local Ombudsman to complain about late grant cheques.

Further Reading

Civil Liberties Guide by Malcolm Hurwitt and Peter Thornton (Liberty, £4.99).
Complaints against the Police (Liberty briefing, £1).
Legal Aid Guide (Legal Aid Board, free).

Useful Addresses

Advertising Standards Authority Brook House, 216 Torrington Place, London WC1E 7HN (071 580 5555).
Consumers' Association 2 Marylebone Road, London NW1 4DX (071 486 5544).
Law Centres Federation Duchess House, 18-19 Warren Street, London W1P 5DB (071 387 8570).
The Law Society 113 Chancery Lane, London WC2A 3PL (071 242 1222).
Legal Aid Board Newspaper House, 8-16 Great New Street, London EC4A 3BN (071 353 7411).
Local Ombudsmen *England* 21 Queen's Gate, London SW1H 9BU (071 222 5622)/29 Castlegate, York YO1 1RN (07904 30151); *Scotland* 5 Shandwick Place, Edinburgh EH2 4E9 (031 229 4472); *Wales* Derwen House, Court Road, Brigend, Mid-Glamorgan CF3 1BN (0656 661325).
National Association of Citizens' Advice Bureaux Myddelton House, 115-123 Pentonville Road, London N1 9LZ (071 833 2181).
National Council for Civil Liberties (Liberty) 21 Tabard Street, London SE1 4LA (071 403 3888).
Office of Fair Trading Field House, 15-25 Breams Buildings, London EC4A 1PR (071 242 2858).
Office of the Parliamentary Commissioner for Administration (Parliamentary Ombudsman)/Health Service Ombudsman *England* Church House, Great Smith Street, London SW1P 3BE (071 212 6271/7676); *Scotland* 11 Melville Crescent, Edinburgh (031 225 7465); *Wales* Pearl Assurance House, Greyfriars Road, Cardiff (0222 394621).
Police Complaints Authority 10 Great George Street, London SW1 3AE (071 273 6450).
Scottish Legal Aid Board 44 Drumsheugh Gardens, Edinburgh EH3 7SW (031 226 7061).

254

employment

Barwork and busking, grape picking in Gloucestershire and supervising spoilt brats in Santiago: there are plenty of ways you can boost your income and gain valuable career experience. **Julie Emery**, **Jefferson Hack** and **Gavin Hamilton** sidestep the government cuts.

Supplementing your Income **256**
Working Holidays **260**
Careers **267**
Other Options **273**
Further Reading **275**
Useful Addresses **276**

The financial restrictions of student life need not commit you to a life of drudgery. If you're using your years at college as an elaborate tax dodge, then read no further; but if, like hundreds of thousands of other students, you have no set career plans and need to work to supplement your income, it's time to consider part-time work and work experience. In this chapter, we recommend ways to earn extra cash, suggest ideas for working holidays at home and abroad and consider the options that will be open to you when you leave college.

NUS does not believe that students should have to work while at college and campaigns for a proper grants system. However, because of the inadequacies of the current situation, many students are forced to work; investigate joining the relevant trade union if this is the case.

Supplementing your Income

It may not be the most exciting way to spend the few weeks away from lectures, but casual work is often available throughout the Christmas and summer holidays. Start looking well before term ends.

Many large department stores take on students over the summer as replacement staff, as well as at Christmas and sale time to cope with the extra work. Local councils also employ seasonal workers: as playleaders and helpers at playschemes and crèches; as park assistants, care and catering assistants. If you're a strong swimmer and have qualifications, you could spend the summer as a life-guard at your local pool. Check in the local paper or free council publications for details of vacancies, or phone the town hall personnel department to ask about temporary jobs.

Hospitals employ students as porters (steel yourself for the morgue-run now and again) and, where qualified, as lab assistants to cover for staff on summer holiday. Apply to the hospital personnel offices by April. Helping out with the Christmas mail at the post office can get you extra cash at an expensive time of year: ask early at your local head office. Sporting events organizers are major casual employers, but most of the work is advertised by word of mouth.

Using your subject

Tutoring a couple of evenings a week, either privately or at a tuition school, is good experience if you're interested in teaching, at home or abroad, and can be a lucrative way to keep your brain ticking over during the holidays. If you're on a fashion or dressmaking course, you can make money designing or altering clothes. Catering students may be able to earn pocket money by cooking for private parties, washing up in professional kitchens, working as a kitchen assistant, or gaining useful experience as a commis chef. Designers and artists can look for work pasting up, or designing letterheads, shop signs, record covers and so on.

If you have a flair for designing T-shirts, jewellery or postcards, think about starting your own business. This needs proper planning and a great deal of energy and determination; your local Job Centre can provide you with guidelines.

Temporary & part-time work

Part-time work is often the only way out of an awkward financial situation. For temporary work, look on the notice-board in Job Centres, employment agencies, college unions and newsagents. Check the 'situations vacant' columns in local newspapers and magazines. Shops and businesses often advertise for staff in the windows of their premises. Ask to see the

Employment

managers, or leave a contact number and address. Avoid managers when they're clearly too busy; approach them at a quiet time.

Bar & catering work: The bar and catering industry has always attracted students, since much of the work is unskilled and usually readily available. For work in major high street chains such as McDonald's and Pizza Hut, contact the branch you wish to work for and fill in an application form. Don't expect to earn much more than £2 per hour initially. It's unrewarding work and certainly not a post to put at the top of your job list. However, despite the small returns, a certain camaraderie is often built up between workmates, and the experience of dealing with the public and having to work fast and efficiently will be always be useful.

Busking: Most major cities have at least one site that is a legal busking place; there are three in London, for instance. Busking is good musical practice and can be fun. If you're considering busking, try to be different, not necessarily in what you play, but more in how you play it; incorporate pavement art into your act – draw a banner or flag and try to get someone to collect money for you. Don't busk if you can't play, unless your ineptitude is part of the act – one member of the *Student Book* team profitably played outsized cardboard instruments to a tape. However, any buskers operating without a permit are acting illegally and face stiff fines.

Car-window cleaning: A popular summer occupation in the major cities, car-window cleaning at traffic lights is harder than it seems. It's best to work in pairs, one person sponging and one person wiping. Don't ask for money; for every driver who doesn't pay there's another whose generosity makes up for it. Try to work in an area with a minimum of three traffic lanes. It's important to have fun while doing such a gruelling job. Dress up, take a water pistol, hand out sweets and always smile. Average earnings for a four-lane stop in central London is £8 to £9 per hour. Take care when doing this work – it can be obstructive and possibly dangerous.

Dispatch-riding: Motorbike dispatch messengers must own their wheels; a fearless and masochistic streak will also help. It's best to find out from riders how much it costs to work for the various agencies before phoning dispatch companies to ask for work. Most companies charge 'circuit fees', which are either worked out as a percentage of earnings, or are charged as a flat rate of about £50 a week, plus about £10 per week for radio hire (to communicate with the head office). You have to deduct from your earnings various expenses, such as parking tickets, police fines, full third-party insurance (£40-£45 a week) and £35 to £40 per week for bike running costs. You must have the full gear, including waterproofs and boots. Most professional riders earn about £200 per week and the best riders can earn between £300 and £350, but as a new recruit, expect to be given the worst jobs, and to earn £100 per week or less, increasing to £140 in good weeks. You're paid by the job, so you lose money if you're ill or if the bike breaks down.

For bicycle dispatch-riding, a push-bike and full third-party insurance are required (it's extremely difficult for bicycle couriers to get insurance). Average weekly earnings are £100 to £120, although it takes about a month to get used to the roads. Car fumes can be very unpleasant but, in the summer, you get a great tan and the excuse to show it off in dayglo cycling clobber. Motorbike and bicycle dispatch agency names are listed in the *Yellow Pages* under Couriers or Dispatch.

ARE YOU LOOKING TO MOVE UP OR OUT?
PROMOTION?
CAREER CHANGE?
POSTGRADUATE STUDY?

Whether you're considering going for your boss's job or getting out completely **The Graduate Post** has been re-designed with you in mind. As well as all the usual - jobs, news, features, comment and postgraduate update, **The Graduate Post** now carries a Job Changer section, so if you're looking to move up, on or out, you'll find **The Graduate Post** is the newspaper for you.

Regardless of your degree discipline, geographical location or career area, **The Graduate Post** is the only newspaper to bring you the latest in graduate jobs every fortnight.

Make those changes today with a personal subscription to **The Graduate Post**.
Subscribe for 12 months @ £16.50, 6 months @ £9.90

- simply call **0800 282589** with your ACCESS details or send cheque/PO made payable to Newpoint Publishing, at Newpoint Publishing, Graduate Post Subscriptions, Dept GP, 76 St James Lane, London N10 3DF.

THE GRADUATE POST

THE PENGUIN BOOKSHOP

puffin CHILDREN'S BOOKSHOP

Recently we were involved in a Management Buyout and are now proud to call ourselves Phoenix Bookshops Ltd, a small, but expanding, chain of independent Bookshops.

In our Penguin Bookshops we aim to stock most of the Penguin titles together with a rich and varied selection of books from other publishers. Our Puffin Bookshops boast what is probably the largest range of children's books and merchandise anywhere in Britain.

We are always delighted to hear from anyone interested in a career in bookselling. Applications should be sent to our Personnel Officer at 93 Fortess Road, London NW5 1AG.

Penguin Bookshops in London:
- Camden High Street
- Covent Garden Market
- 157 King's Road

Also at:
- 41 North Street, Guildford
- 54/56 Bridlesmith Gate, Nottingham
- 21 Coppergate, York
- Cathedral Square, Peterborough
- The Pallasades, Birmingham

Puffin Bookshops at:
- Covent Garden Market
- 14 Coppergate, York

Employment

Domestic & childminding work: Early-morning or evening cleaning only takes a few hours of your week. Look in newsagents' windows or the local press for ads. *The Lady* (weekly, 50p) has columns of vacation work for mother's helps and au-pairs, and local papers carry ads for domestic help of all kinds. Also, look out for domestic agencies in your area which might need people to childmind, house-sit, cat-sit, dog-walk or spring-clean. *See also below* **Working Holidays**.

Drugs trials: We don't recommend drugs trials as a way of supplementing your grant. The NUS guidelines, drawn up in conjunction with the Association of Independent Clinical Research Contractors, state, 'for all students taking part, the study must involve no more than minimal risk' and 'no financial inducement or coercion should colour your judgement and payment must never be offered for risk'. However, lack of official legislation on this subject in the UK gives overseas drugs companies *carte blanche* to use British students in tests that are illegal in the USA.

Those companies offering the largest sums of money are likely to be the ones whose drugs trials represent the highest risk. Such trials can be deadly: two students have died since 1984 after undergoing drugs trials and it is believed that their deaths were directly related to the experiments they took part in. All the medical school student unions have policies against drugs trials and won't allow companies or schools to advertise for student volunteers in their publications or on their premises. The lure of taking part in a trial is the money, but if you're considering it as an easy option, think about what you're doing to your body.

Market and social research: Telephone market-research companies are good for part-time work at weekends and in the evenings. They tend to be staffed by students and resting actors. Self-confidence is essential if you're to elicit information over the phone from unsuspecting members of the public, some of whom are less than pleased about being disturbed by a nosy stranger.

Social research usually means spending time on pavements or going from door to door, asking people to answer questions for a questionnaire. Survey subjects range from housing to health, and it's useful work for those studying sociology and associated subjects. Training is usually thorough, and you're well briefed before being let loose. Be prepared to go out in all weathers.

Market trading: Entrepreneurs can try setting up their own market stall. It's common practice to buy cheap second-hand clothing from charity shops and resell it to market traders, or peddle it at a profit from a market stand. Some markets have a separate administration office which you will need to contact in advance before you set up a stall. Others work on a first come, first served basis on the day. There's usually a fixed noticeboard on which you write your name, to be read out along with your allocated stall.

Modelling for students: Reputable life drawing and photography course organizers often hire models to pose nude for classes. Expect to earn about £4 per hour. There are very stringent guidelines laid down by local authorities which cover the procedure and conditions under which the work can take place. Ignore all advertisements in newsagents' windows.

Office work: Temping skills, such as typing, shorthand and basic computing, are often essential for office work (*see below* **Careers: Gaining skills**). If you have them, get your name down at one of the several large national agencies, such as Reed or Brook Street.

"I think university newspapers are the best way to get an idea of how both the university and a newspaper ticks: I missed more deadlines for essays than for the newspaper. I also performed 'conjuring cabarets' at the university. I had been a magician and a member of the Magic Circle before going up to Oxford and we took part in cabarets at college.
One evening, two colleagues and I were doing a well-known cabaret directed by Dudley Moore. On our cue we came...

'Unskilled' work: The large cinema complexes, rather than the independents, are likely to have vacancies for jobs such as ushering or selling tickets and refreshments. For retail work, local shops, especially the ones you visit regularly, are good places to start. Many students look for Saturday jobs, and local shops are ideal for this, as are supermarkets for cashiering or shelf-stacking work. Hotels are also good places to work part-time during the term, as kitchen staff, cleaners and receptionists. Generally speaking, councils are among the best sources of unskilled work, particularly for labouring work during the summer vacation. The posts offered by local authorities depend on the region you live in. Get in touch with your local council and ask them to send you a job list and application form.

Student union work: Many of the large unions take on students as bar staff, security officers, cloakroom attendants, general helpers, and even DJs, particularly during special events. Alternatively, ask at your college library if there are any vacancies for assistants.

Working Holidays

A good way to earn money (however little) and to gain valuable experience at the same time, is to go on a working holiday, here or abroad. For example, working as a group counsellor on a children's adventure holiday or, if you want to feel the sun on your back, picking grapes in Western Europe or parts of North America. Anything, in fact, if it means you avoid pulling pints in the pub at home. You're unlikely to make a fortune, but you should earn enough to pay your way and to have a holiday afterwards. For details of all the organizations mentioned in this section, consult the **Useful Addresses** at the end of the chapter.

Archaeology

Beginners get board and lodging and a little pocket money; more experienced volunteers may be offered travel expenses and wages. You can get work on excavations abroad only if you have previous experience on digs in this country. Be prepared to work hard in all weathers and to stay in very basic accommodation. You should also get an anti-tetanus jab. Details of UK digs can be found in *British Archaeology News* (£10 per year on subscription), published by the Council for British Archaeology (112 Kennington Road, London SE11 6RE). Digs abroad are often advertised in *Archaeology Abroad*, available on subscription (£4 per year) from 31-34 Gordon Square, London WC1H 0PY. *Current Archaeology* is another publication which advertises for volunteers for digs; an annual subscription costs £12 a year from 9 Nassington Road, London NW3 2TX.

Au pairing/domestic work

Au pairs, in return for board, lodging and pocket money, live with a family to help with household duties and look after the children. All too often, au pairs are exploited by families looking for a full-time nanny on the cheap. You should establish the nature of your duties, and how much free time you can expect, before you accept a job. It's wise to look for au pair work through a specialist employment agency. The Federation of Recruitment and Employment Services can provide a list of reputable agencies. Try to get hold of the *Au Pair and Nanny's Guide to Working Abroad* (Vacation Work, £5.95) which has a comprehensive list of agencies. Lists of situations vacant for au pairs and nannies are published in *The Lady* (weekly, 50p).

...out in synchronisation with the music to perform the trick of sticking pins into balloons without bursting them. Unfortunately, it was so frigging cold in the hall that the liquid inside the balloons to stop them bursting froze. The three of us stood there like pricks frantically popping balloons while the director looked on, tearing his hair out. After that, I decided I should retire from magic shows and I took up journalism."

Peter Preston Editor of *The Guardian* (English Literature, Oxford University, 1957-60).

WORK IN LEISURE

PGL offer opportunities to work with children or families for long or short periods as activity (outdoor, sports, creative) instructors, Group Leaders, or in a wide range of supporting domestic and administrative roles at residential activity centres.

Details from:

Application Department,
PGL Young Adventure Ltd,
Alton Court,
Penyard Lane (855),
Ross-on-Wye, HR9 5NR.
Tel: (0989) 764211

PGL ADVENTURE

Camp America

Spend nine weeks putting your skills to the test in the exciting atmosphere of an American Summer Camp – an experience of a lifetime!

CAMP AMERICA is looking to recruit Youth Leaders/Specialist Counsellors with skills in child-care and/or specialist activities such as sport, music and drama, or arts and crafts, working with American children over a nine week programme.

CAMP AMERICA also has high demand for their Campower programme. We have many positions available for people with skills in areas such as secretarial, kitchen and laundry work, driving, landscaping and many more.

If a camp full of kids isn't for you, our FAMILY COMPANION programme could be your ticket to a summer Stateside. Family Companions provide childcare for an American family, for a 10 week programme, with responsibility for child supervision and light household duties.

CAMP AMERICA provides you with a FREE London-New York return flight, J1 Cultural Exchange visa, pocket money, board and lodging at camp/family, and time for independent travel after your placement.

So if you're interested, 18 or over, and free from June 1st, 1991 – APPLY NOW!!! Send a postcard with your name and address to **CAMP AMERICA**, Dept (ANR18A), 37A Queens Gate, London SW7 5HR.

SUMMER WORK IN THE STATES

GO FOR 90,000 MORE JOBS!...

Would you like to be able to pick and choose from over **90,000** jobs in more than **2,000** companies? Or select your postgraduate course from over **1,400**? Well you can with the new 1991 edition of Graduate Opportunities.

GO 1991

Pick up your personal copy from your careers service today. Only limited numbers available!

NEWPOINT
The Newpoint Publishing Company Limited

PART OF REED INTERNATIONAL P.L.C.

Employment

BUNAC

The British Universities North America Club (BUNAC) operates student work-exchange programmes in North America through its BUNACAMP, Work America, Work Canada and KAMP schemes.

BUNACAMP places people as 'counsellors' on children's summer camps in the USA. Children are packed off to the camps by their parents for anything from one to eight weeks, and the resident counsellors teach them activities ranging from tennis and water-skiing to photography, first aid and typing. It helps if you have suitable experience or qualifications (such as previous work with young people); but a genuine regard for, and understanding of, children's needs is more important. For a registration fee of £50, BUNAC places you at an approved camp, organizes and pays for a return flight and work papers (including the J-1 visa, which legally entitles you to work in America), and pays for accommodation and food while you're there. The camps are open from mid-June to mid or late-August. At the end of your contract, you get about $400 in wages, as well as the opportunity to travel around the country for six weeks, with advice from BUNAC on how to go about it. You have to be aged between 192 and 35 to apply. The scheme is intended for students, but other people are welcome to, and do, apply. Unfortunately, there are limited opportunities for people with disabilities in camps in the US.

The Work America and Work Canada schemes, sponsored by the US Council on International Educational Exchange and the Canadian Federation of Students respectively, enable full-time degree and HND students to combine travel with virtually any summer job in North America. For £64 (Work America) or £55 (Work Canada), BUNAC arranges your visa (valid from June to early October) and flight (which you pay for) and offers suggestions for employment. To apply, you must provide proof of a definite offer of employment or sponsorship, or show that you have sufficient funds ($600 US travellers' cheques or $1,000 Canadian travellers' cheques) if you're planning to look for a job when you get there. You're obliged to attend an orientation course in the UK before you go; and, if your placement is in Canada, a medical examination. The organization rejects applications from people who have previously taken part in the schemes.

The Kitchen and Maintenance Programme (KAMP) is a fare-paid package offering employment on children's summer camps. The work is usually in the kitchen, but laundry and outside maintenance jobs are also available. The cost is £59 and, as well as having your return flight paid, you get free board and accommodation together with wages of at least $500 when you finish. You work from mid-June to the end of October. Only full-time UK degree or HND students are eligible. BUNAC also runs Work Australia and Work Jamaica schemes.

To apply for any of the BUNAC schemes, you must join BUNAC. Membership costs £3 a year; there are branches in most UK colleges. For more information on travelling to the USA and Canada, see page 278 **Travel**.

Children's activity holidays

Camp America is a similar programme to BUNACAMP *above*. Successful applicants are offered work on a children's summer camp and live either in a camp or with a family nearby. You are given full board and lodging for up to nine or ten weeks. The air fare is free and the package includes up to ten weeks' independent travel time, with advice on where to stay and go. The wage is somewhere between $150 and $450, depending on your age and what job you're allocated on the camp. Like BUNAC, the organization secures you a J-1 visa; *see below* **Useful Addresses** for Camp America's British offices.

Children's activity holidays, such as those run in the UK by PGL Young Adventure, can provide a fun-filled holiday job. You can apply to be a group leader, or opt for behind-the-scenes work, as a kitchen assistant, for example. Helpers receive board and lodging and around £30 per week in wages. Contact the personnel departments of any of the companies listed in *Working Holidays* (*see below* **Further Reading**).

Conservation Work

Projects designed to contribute in a practical way to the conservation of the countryside, or to protect and restore buildings of historic interest, are run throughout the UK. The work may be drystone walling, cleaning polluted rivers and ponds, maintaining footpaths and bridle-ways, or restoring old agricultural buildings; whatever it is, you must be fit and prepared to work long hours. Basic self-catering accommodation is usually provided, although you're generally expected to pay for it. The British Trust for Conservation Volunteers runs more than 500 different projects every year.

Couriers

Camping companies, especially those operating in the South of France, usually advertise for summer couriers in the *Guardian* and *The Times*. Although you have to work long hours for very little money, being a courier is a cheap way of getting some summer sun. Overland expedition companies (*see also page 278* **Travel**) often need couriers, drivers, cooks and mechanics. You have to be over 26 and an experienced traveller or driver to apply. Mainstream travel companies also employ couriers to escort people from the UK to holiday destinations abroad, and as representatives (reps) in foreign hotels. Competition for courier jobs is intense, so contact companies months in advance.

EC jobs

The European System for the International Clearing of Vacancies and Applications for Employment (SEDOC) is a European-wide scheme that enables people to find work in any EC country. Your local Job Centre can access a central computer for information on job vacancies throughout Europe. Most of the jobs available through the SEDOC system are permanent rather than temporary.

If you're aged between 18 and 28 and are no longer in full-time education, you may be able to take part in the EEC Young Workers Exchange Scheme. Short-term schemes (three weeks to three months) take in a programme of meetings and visits to a particular local firm or industry, while long-term schemes involve up to six months' practical work experience with two months' language tuition provided beforehand. Participants get 75 per cent of their transport costs paid, as well as all accommodation costs. For more information, contact the Vocational and Technical Education Department of the Central Bureau for Educational Visits and Exchanges.

Farmwork

Working on the land demands patience, energy and endurance. Fruit-picking is particularly hard, and tedious to boot. Pickers are normally paid according to the quantity of fruit or veg gathered. Consequently, if the weather prevents you from working, or if it ruins the crop, you don't get any

Employment

money. Prospective pickers should therefore take sufficient funds to keep them going in the event of rain stopping pay. Work in the UK is available from June to October (depending on the crop grown) at a number of farms and farmcamps. *Working Holidays* (*see below* **Further Reading**) has a comprehensive list of employers. Workers' accommodation is usually under canvas, although you may be lucky and get a self-catering hut.

Abroad, the French grape harvest takes place between mid-September and mid-October. The pay is reasonable – there's a national minimum wage of about £3 per hour – but you have to compete for work with many other students, as well as French seasonal workers. Apply in writing (and in French) to the Centre de Documentation et d'Information Rurale which acts as an official clearing house for seasonal agricultural employment. *See also page 278* **Travel**.

Work is also available to agriculture and horticulture students via Farm Experience Programmes in Australia, Canada, Denmark, Finland, Germany, Hungary, Israel, The Netherlands, New Zealand, Norway, Poland, Switzerland, Sweden and the USA. Details can be obtained from the International Farm Experience Programme. If you aren't eligible for the scheme, you can still get information about other organizations which might be able to help you.

Kibbutzim and moshavim

A kibbutz is a communal society in Israel, whose members own the means of production and share all communal facilities. Members, or kibbutznik, don't receive wages but, in return for their labour, have their basic needs provided for. There are over 250 kibbutzim in Israel. Volunteers are welcomed for periods of more than one month. You must be prepared to abide by the rules of the kibbutz and to accept the work you're asked to do. It could be picking bananas and dates, working in the factory, cowshed or chicken house, or in the kitchens. You work for eight hours a day, six days a week (with Saturdays off) and receive food and accommodation, monthly pocket money (about £20) and, in some kibbutzim, cigarettes and toiletries. Work often starts as early as 5am, to leave afternoons free. Volunteers, aged between 18 and 32, and in good health, are accepted.

Moshavim are collectively run, but privately-owned farms, where volunteers are welcomed. There are nearly 1,000 such farms in Israel. Overseas visitors usually live on the farm with individual families. Moshavim differ from kibbutzim in that, although you have to work, you're paid more than just pocket money. The work is often tougher than on a kibbutz and the pay is still relatively low, but you should be able to save enough money to travel afterwards.

To find work on a kibbutz, you can either travel to Tel Aviv and approach one of the kibbutz offices directly, or you can apply in advance through an agency in the UK. Kibbutz Representatives sends volunteers to kibbutzim throughout Israel. They charge a £30 registration fee and require applicants to undergo a medical examination. Project 67 offers a kibbutz or moshav package. For between £230 and £300, depending on your length of stay and the month you leave, you receive your flights, registration, transport, accommodation, board and pocket money. If you decide to go directly to Tel Aviv, make sure that you have enough money to support yourself while you look for work, because the airport officials at Tel Aviv can make life very difficult for travellers with nowhere to stay. Project 67 also arranges straightforward holidays on kibbutzim and moshavim. *See also page 278* **Travel**.

"I arrived at college determined to act. I also told the college principal that I admired those involved with the student union but could not find students' problems interesting enough to do anything about them myself.

My acting career failed miserably after taking the lead in my first play. Deciding it was easier to make up my own lines, I turned back to the student activists who, somewhat to my surprise, put me forward as a candidate for the student union; for a year, I was the only Alliance member of a Labour-dominated SU. The next year, we...

Ski resorts

Skiing holidays are notoriously expensive, but working as a barperson, cleaner, porter or ski instructor should give you enough spare time (and funds) to ski. The Jobs in the Alps agency provides domestic and catering work (an agency fee is charged). For work as a ski instructor, get some brochures from a ski tour operator, and write to their personnel departments asking for work. It helps if you speak the appropriate language.

Voluntary & community work

There are hundreds of possibilities for voluntary and community work in the UK. Although you are unlikely to be paid, you should gain valuable experience which will impress future potential employers. Your student union may have a Student Community Action programme, which always needs new volunteers. The Royal Association for Disability and Rehabilitation (RADAR) publishes a leaflet, *Volunteers for Holidays*, that lists organizations requiring volunteers to help people with disabilities. Vacation Work publishes the useful *International Directory of Voluntary Work* (£6.95). Voluntary work overseas is diffcult to secure on a short-term basis. Organizations such as Voluntary Service Overseas (VSO) now only take professional people with specific skills or qualifications. Workcamps (*see below*) are your best bet if you haven't got these.

Workcamps

Workcamps, where young people come together to work on a particular project, are a form of short-term voluntary service. The type of work undertaken depends on the area or the country the camp is in. It might involve providing roads and water supplies to a rural village, building a children's adventure playground or helping people with disabilities. Camps are run for two to four weeks from April through to September. The Quaker camps are particularly popular (contact them at Friends House) and the International Voluntary Service runs camps around the world (*see below* **Useful Addresses** for both).

Sort yourself out

If you plan to work abroad, sort out a job before you leave the country. Language schools, au pair agencies, holiday companies and voluntary organizations all advertise in the press, so scour the *Guardian*, *The Times* and the Sunday papers. If you apply and are successful, the organizations take care of all the paperwork. Vacation Work arranges working holidays abroad (and at home), as well as publishing a series of guides, including the *Directory of Summer Jobs Abroad* (£6.95).

Outside the EEC, you need a work permit or visitor's pass to find a job legally. For the USA, Canada and Australia, this should be no problem; for other countries it's more difficult, as you may also need a residence permit. Contact the embassy of the country you're planning to visit for the relevant information. If your employment abroad is being arranged through an organization based in this country, such as BUNAC or Camp America, you should be able to get the information you need before you leave. The Department of Employment publishes information on working abroad in the leaflets *OW5* and *OW21*. They are available from Job Centres and Department of Employment offices. For details of visa requirements, *see page 278* **Travel**.

Careers

Choosing a career (or even just thinking about what you might be doing twelve months after leaving college) is a dilemma that you probably don't want to give much thought to right now. But leaving it to the last minute can be a mistake. Most companies recruit students in the autumn and spring terms of their final year; applications for postgraduate courses should be considered during the summer vacation before your final year starts; and even voluntary work has to be thought about months before your

...made it an Alliance student union and finally, I finished my college days as its full-time President.

Within six months of leaving college, however, I was the new MP for Truro. I had gone to work for the MP David Penhaligon as his researcher in the House of Commons, but he died in a car crash just before Christmas. In some ways, the job is the same as SU President – plotting in corners, helping those I represent, debating the issues of the day – but as a backbencher I have less power, a far smaller budget, and work with a largely male, middle-class and middle-aged set of MPs who behave as though they are back at prep school. Oh – and the acting comes in handy too."

Matthew Taylor MP (PPE, Oxford University, 1982-86).

finals. If you haven't spent any time contemplating what your future holds, you may regret it when all your friends find careers. Whatever you decide to do, you need to act on your decision at least a year before you finally emerge from the security of college life.

Getting involved

Prospective employers like to see evidence of enthusiasm, commitment and extra-curricular activity at college. Involve yourself in college activities and organizations; you can take your pick of the clubs and societies at your college's intro fair.

Most employers are interested in people who have held a position of responsibility in a college society, whether it's on the Rag or the Ents committee, or a more caring organization, such as Community Action Groups or Nightlines. They see this type of college activity as an indication of initiative. The director of the University of London Union's Careers Service told us: 'Employers don't want to employ someone who's spent three years at college sitting in his or her room.' At most colleges there are course-related clubs and societies, whose members organize trips, talks and social activities relevant to your field of study. If you're elected to the club committee or offer to help out, it all helps to make a curriculum vitae (c.v.; *see below* **Drawing up a c.v.**) more interesting.

Employers also like to see voluntary or community work of any sort. For anyone thinking of a career in the social services, voluntary work is often an essential requirement. Furthermore, working as a volunteer for a worthy cause can be immensely satisfying and enjoyable. Almost everyone has something to offer and, because the commitment is optional, you can give an hour a week or more, depending on how much free time you have. For more information on the different options open to you, *see above* **Working Holidays**. No matter what career you intend to follow, working for voluntary organizations never fails to impress on a c.v.

Your c.v. is an advertisement for you, so be sure to include in it anything relevant to the position you're applying for. Of course, some employers turn straight to your education and experience, but if they spot an activity on your c.v. which is pertinent to the job you want, it could make the difference between being offered an interview and receiving a rejection letter.

Making contacts

Whatever job you apply for, you need to sell yourself. Be prepared to stick your neck out and make contacts in your chosen field. Unfair though it seems, it's often not what you know but who you know that gets you ahead in the career race. Your tutor may be able to help you here, especially if you're thinking of going into a field directly related to your course of study. Tutors may well have specialized knowledge of the job market your course leads to and be able to put you in touch with 'the right people'. If you're willing to go out and meet people in the line of work you want to enter, you might be able to organize some work experience (*see also below*).

If you aren't applying for formally advertised jobs, selling yourself is extremely important. If you have an idea of what career you want to pursue, but are not sure how to get a job, you have to try to persuade people to offer you a place when they don't actually have a vacancy advertised. Use any contacts you have, even if it's just a friend of a friend whom you once met in a pub.

Employment

Careers fairs/the Milk Round

There are many more options open to you than just the Milk Round, the traditional route for graduates and college-leavers into employment. Virtually all colleges hold careers fairs in one shape or form. Some are organized by the student union, others by the college careers service or student careers society, and still others by external organizations. Companies and organizations from many different areas, including industry, commerce and the public sector, take part. At these fairs, you have the opportunity to talk to people about working for their organization, and most companies have people on their stalls who have been students recently, and whose memory of the whole business of receptions, applications and interviews is still fresh. Use the fairs to ask questions and to get the information that you think you need to help you make the right decision.

However, don't be too concerned or surprised if you find that you're none the wiser after attending a fair than you were beforehand. Most of the stallholders will be from individual companies trying to pursuade you to join their company rather than attempting to convince you of the benefits of pursuing a particular career. So if you go to a fair with no real idea of what you want, you're not likely to get much out of it.

College Careers Services

Careers officers cannot choose your career for you – and they shouldn't have to – but they can point you in the right direction. They can usually come up with suggestions and ideas about your future that you hadn't thought of, and can help you decide on a plan of action, both for supplementing your income and getting on the right track for a future career. While you're in the office, have a look at the library, where the reference books and job leaflets are a useful starting point. Many careers offices now have computer programmes which match your strengths and weaknesses with job areas. These have become more sophisticated in recent years, so you shouldn't be blandly assured that the two job areas for you to explore are accountancy and Antarctic ice-sculpturing.

Work experience

Work experience can be the key to success. It gives you the opportunity to get on-the-job training and to find out if you would be happy in the career you've chosen. Not only do you become acquainted with the everyday workings of the business, but your c.v. looks all the better for the evidence that you made the effort to learn more.

If you get on well, the company bosses may act as referees for you – they may even hire you when you leave college. Bear in mind that although you gain useful experience, in some cases you may not be paid. However, if you don't know what field you want to break into, only first-hand experience can help you decide. Some courses, such as media studies, have periods of work experience built into them. In the majority of cases, it is up to the student to arrange the placement, but the college will ask the employer to give an assessment of the student.

There are more work experience opportunities for science students than for arts students. However, persistent letter writing and phoning should eventually yield results, so don't hesitate to sell yourself. Some college careers services keep a list of companies that offer work experience or job shadowing schemes, so this may be a good place to start. If your careers office fails to cover the areas you're interested in, find out who does and contact them. Explain that you're eager to learn about the business, and would like to work for repayment of expenses. It's best to go for a minimum of two weeks, since the first week is often rather hectic and disorientating. The longer you stay, the more you benefit and learn.

The major points to bear in mind during work experience placements are listed below. Some of them might seem rather obvious, but they're all equally important when it comes to doing well and making a good impression.

1) As soon as you get to your place of work, find out when to take lunch, where the type writer, photocopier and stapler are, how to use the phones and other basic details.
2) Make sure you understand what you're supposed to do. You must ask if you're uncertain or else you will waste both your time and that of your employer.
3) Act professionally. This work can influence your future career. Don't arrive late, take too long for lunch or leave early.
4) Always let people know what you intend to do. If you're going to be late, phone in or, better still, explain the day before. If you decide not to show up one day, for whatever reason, don't bother coming the next. You definitely won't get a reference.
5) Don't be offended if you're given routine or boring jobs to do – just do them efficiently and quickly. More responsible jobs may come along. No matter what task you're given, you will learn. Everything counts as experience, and you can pick up a lot just by being at work and observing what goes on.
6) People may not speak to you very much for your first day or two. Don't be upset by this. Just work quietly and listen to what's going on around you.
7) If you want to learn about something, it never hurts to ask. Let your employers know your interests, so they can try to give you suitable work.
8) Whatever you do, don't walk out – even if you hate the work and the people. Make it your aim to create a good impression. You only have a short period of time in which to do this.
9) Employers are often very busy and liable to forget they have a student in their office. It's up to you to show them that you're willing to learn new skills and to play an active part in the company. The more interest you show, the more experience you're likely to get, so ask for work if you have nothing to do.
10) Finally, enjoy your work experience. You should gain a great deal from your place ment, even if it's a resolution never to go near a publishing, advertising or catering company again.

Gaining skills

Even while you're still at college, there are a number of things you can do to improve your chances of avoiding graduate unemployment, without attending hundreds of company receptions, without spending hours going round recruitment fairs and without filling in endless application forms.

Learning to type, for example, could prove invaluable. Most jobs involve some form of administration, and an ability to type puts you one step ahead of the rest. Most careers offices run typing courses, normally over a period of ten weeks, which tend to be cheaper than courses run by private colleges. Alternatively, sign up for an evening class (you can get information from any local library). With all classes, you need a degree of self-discipline. Set aside a time each week for attending the class and for practising.

"**Nowadays, students are being trained for the old British job machine. Education should be an ongoing process for life, providing a broad and flexible set of skills that can be re-used and re-cycled throughout life, so that you don't spend two thirds of your life working and the remaining third waiting to die**".

Sarah Parkin Green Party speaker (student nurse in Edinburgh, early sixties; tutor in nursing research at Edinburgh University).

Computers and word processors are now a familiar sight in offices. Their prominence tends to put a lot of people off applying for vacancies, because they think that anything less than a degree in computer science renders their application useless. If you get any opportunity whatsoever to use computers on your course, take it. Better still, try to attend an evening class in the subject. Even if you just learn about the basics, an employer will be impressed by your willingness to learn and by the fact that you have proved yourself to be computer-friendly. You can buy cheap personal computers from NUS Services.

Drawing up a c.v.

It's not just a case of sitting down for five minutes and quickly jotting down a few details on the back of an envelope about your A level grades, the summer job you did in 1987 and the fictitious position you have held as chairperson of the college debating society. A curriculum vitae drawn up with care and attention can dramatically improve your chances of getting a job; one drawn up without any thought isn't worth the paper it's written on. The conventional way to draw up a c.v. is to list details such as education, qualifications, previous employment and so on (*see below* **Table: Information to include on your c.v.**).

By all means be creative with the facts (if it means that you think about your accomplishments in greater detail) and include information which you think will impress, but don't list anything which you won't be able to substantiate at an interview. If it's obvious that you've said something on your c.v. that can't be true, a potential employer will have second thoughts about everything else you have said.

Alternatively, you could opt for a list of 'personal qualities' – administrative skills (such

Information to include on your c.v.

Name, address (both home and at college), **telephone number**(s), **date of birth, marital status and nationality**.

Secondary education, giving the names and addresses of your school and/or college and the dates you attended them.

GCSE, CSE, O, A level, Scottish CSYS, O grades and Higherspasses with dates, grades and examination board.

Higher education, even if not completed.

Other qualifications, such as RSA typing exams.

Work experience, giving the dates of your employment andincluding relevant part-time and holiday work.

Other work-related information, such as positions of

responsibility held at school, voluntary work and certificates in anything, from ballet to the Duke of Edinburgh Award.

Your current hobbies and interests. These tell an employer more about you than your education, qualifications and previous employment ever can, as well as giving a good impression of what sort of person you are. Don't list too many. Single out the most important ones.

The names and addresses of two referees, whom you have checked with first. Ideally, one should be a past employer and one a character witness — your tutor, head teacher or a friend of the family. But read the small print carefully as some organizations specify two character references.

as typing), organizational skills (such as having been on the union ents committee) and so on. This has the advantage of telling a prospective employer more about you and your talents, and can be a good way of selling yourself to someone who may not have a vacancy advertised, but might be persuaded into offering you a job. For formal applications, such information is less useful.

A c.v. should be typed and the information should be clearly presented with no spelling mistakes or typing errors. If you send off a speculative job application with a c.v., you should include a covering letter. You should include in the letter any personal details which you have not mentioned on your c.v. which are relevant to the company or organzation you are writing to.

Interviews

Interviews give your prospective employer a chance to see what you look like and how you conduct yourself. An interview for any kind of job can be a nerve-wracking experience, so it helps to practise first. Think of intelligent questions to ask about the company and the job, as well as the questions you're likely to be asked (and how to respond). You should be sent some background information about the job and the company or organization. However, it's worth undertaking a little research to acquire some additional information as this will impress your interviewers and show that you are serious about getting the job.

First impressions last. You need to appear smart and clean. Never be late for an interview; give yourself plenty of time to find the place. But avoid arriving too early; you end up hanging around in reception, which aggravates the butterflies already looping and diving in your stomach. If you get there early, it's better to find a nearby café to lurk in for half an hour.

Be prepared to tell the interviewer exactly why you want the job; employers almost always ask that question. If you're asked something that stumps you, take a few moments to collect your thoughts before answering. A few seconds of silence is better than saying something you might regret later.

Other Options
Postgraduate courses and further study

After a three year degree and at least sixteen years in the education system, you may think that the last thing you want to do is stay on. Most people assume that postgraduate study consists of courses and qualifications either directly or closely related to your degree subject. However, staying on at college (or, indeed, moving to a different college) doesn't necessarily mean carrying on where your degree left off (although if that's what you want, there's nothing to stop you doing this). Many courses are vocational in nature and, in most cases, dramatically improve your chances of employment – journalism and personnel management are just two examples.

If you decide to carry on with academic study after your degree, you have to start considering it at least a year before you graduate. It's no good deciding after you have graduated that a postgraduate course is what you want to do. If you're planning to specialize in your degree subject, you'll probably need a first or a good upper second, as well as a strong commitment to your chosen subject. For more vocational study, you must show a genuine, practical interest in the course. Work experience or holiday employment at companies operating in your chosen field are good ways of demonstrating your enthusiasm.

Competition for funding for postgraduate study is intense, and there's never enough to go round. The more time you allow yourself for applications (and rejections), the better. The organizations and publications listed at the end of the chapter should be able to help, as should your tutor and careers advisory service.

Enterprise Allowance Scheme

The Enterprise Allowance Scheme pays a weekly amount (about £40 per week, slightly more than the dole) for one year to people starting their own business, and allows them to keep all the profits from the business. It's open to anyone who has been registered unemployed for more than eight weeks, but you have to put up £1,000 of your own money, to show that you're confident that the proposal is financially viable (the high street banks have special loan schemes; alternatively, you can borrow from a friend or member of your family, and return the money when you have been registered onto the scheme). You must also provide a detailed business plan.

The scheme supports everyone from budding Richard Bransons to struggling actors, artists, musicians and anyone else who can't, or doesn't want to, get a job through the 'traditional' channels. If you're waiting for the big break, and need the time, space and opportunity to keep yourself creative, the scheme is worth considering. However, if you plan on becoming a self-made millionaire by the time you're 30, remember that more than half of small businesses go under in their first year. So you need to be very certain that you're doing the right thing before you take the plunge. The local Job Centre will be able to provide you with the relevant information about the scheme.

Taking a year out

All too often, taking a year out between leaving college and joining the rat race is the easy option. It's the excuse you need for not getting a job just yet. You benefit from it only if you know exactly what you want to do and if you plan everything in advance. It's not very constructive to leave college, take a few weeks to have a rest, and then to decide that you might, possibly, try to get a cash-in-hand job to earn a little bit of money to finance a great journey of discovery around the globe. But, of course, you don't want to work too hard – you've just finished your finals and you deserve a rest. So you end up drifting from day to day, with no real chance of saving up the money for the trip. A weekend in Whitley Bay might be on the cards, but a month in Marrakesh, or even a week in Warsaw, is strictly out of bounds.

If you want to take a year out to travel, you must work out how much you need for your trip, and then set yourself a target for earning the money. Be prepared to make sacrifices – if you keep re-adjusting your targets, you may find your holiday of a lifetime remains a lifetime away. But if it's what you want to do, you will find it relatively easy to make sacrifices without too much suffering. For information on travel, *see page 278* **Travel**.

Teaching English as a foreign language (TEFL)

Teaching abroad is a great way to travel the world and earn money (albeit a limited amount) into the bargain. However, it's worth noting at the outset that you must have an approved TEFL qualification. A year off as an English tutor has become an increasingly popular option for graduates in recent years and, as a result, it's now more difficult for unqualified applicants to find teaching posts.

Employment

The main way to obtain a TEFL qualification is through a short course at a private language school. These courses can last for anything from a few days to a month. Different language schools offer different qualifications and some, such as Berlitz, prefer you to teach only at one of their schools abroad, so the qualification may not be valid elsewhere. Jobs are advertised in the *Guardian* on Tuesdays and *The Times* on Fridays. You could also try writing to the British Council (*see below* **Useful Addresses**), although they only take experienced teachers for work abroad. If you're already abroad, call in at the British Consulate to see if the staff know of any vacancies for English teachers. English-language schools in the UK, particularly the less reputable ones, are always looking for teachers for the summer period, and not necessarily just those with formal qualifications. Children's adventure holidays (*see above* **Working Holidays**) often require teachers for their summer camps.

English-language teachers are particularly needed in Brazil, Egypt, Hong Kong, Italy, Japan, Mexico, Peru, Singapore, Spain, Thailand and Turkey. Check with the relevant embassies regarding visa and work permit requirements.

The most widely recognized qualification is the Royal Society of Arts (RSA)/Cambridge Certificate in Teaching English as a Foreign Language to Adults (TEFLA). For a course resulting in this qualification, expect to pay around £600. Alternatively, with a Postgraduate Certificate of Education (PGCE) and TEFL as a subsidiary subject (or even just a PGCE on its own), it's possible to get TEFL work. The Association of Graduate Careers Advisory Services publishes a useful booklet, *Teaching English as a foreign language and teaching abroad* through the Central Services Unit (*see below* **Useful Addresses**).

French-language students and graduates can find work in French schools as an 'Assistant' helping out the teachers with general duties. This work normally lasts for at least a year and you need to apply well in advance. The Central Bureau for Educational Visits and Exchanges (*see below* **Useful Addresses**) can tell you more about it. The Bureau, a Government-funded body, publishes *Working Holidays*, an annual guide which gives information on nearly 100,000 working holidays in 90 different countries.

Further Reading

An A-Z of Careers and Jobs (Kogan Page, £6.95). A mine of information for school-leavers, outlining the qualities and training required for every kind of career, as well as the career prospects of many lines of work.
AGCAS (Association of Graduate Careers Advisory Services) Careers Information Booklets (CSU, all £1.50). AGCAS produces 70 booklets on specific careers for undergraduates, each with details about exams, recruitment, skills required, training and prospects.
Current Vacancies (CSU). A subscription-based fortnightly publication with listings of current jobs for graduate students (£5 for three months). Available in college careers offices.
Equal Opportunities: A Careers Guide (Penguin, £7.95). The essential and best guide to careers, with unbiased and accurate information on entry requirements, prospects, training and the personal attributes required.
Graduate Employment and Training *(GET)* (CRAC/Hobsons). A 1,200 page directory listing 65,000 graduate jobs. It includes the companies around Britain that take on graduates, giving basic factual information

and a short profile of what a graduate or school-leaver has achieved in each company since the time of joining. The same organization produces several handbooks covering specific areas of employment, such as the *Construction Industry Handbook of Professional and Management Careers* and the *Handbook of Tourism and Leisure*. These recruitment directories, the *Student Sponsorship Directory* and other CRAC/Hobsons publications can be consulted in college careers offices.

Great Answers to Tough Interview Questions (Kogan Paul, £4.99).

Hobsons Casebooks (CRAC/Hobsons). A series of nine publications in which graduates give accounts of their experiences. They provide an insiders' view of the technical and personal demands of different jobs. Titles range from *Working Women* to *Biological and Chemical Sciences*.

How to get a Highly-Paid Job in the City (Kogan Paul, £4.95).

Roget Register of Graduate Employment & Training (CSU, £6.25). This is the official compendium of the Association of Graduate Careers Advisory Services, which gives the recruitment and training policies of industries, government bodies and trade and charity organizations. It's published yearly and is available free to all students from college careers offices, or it can be bought from the publishers and large book shops. CSU also publishes the *Roget Register of Legal Employment Training* and *Roget Scot Employment*, both priced £4.25.

Summer Jobs in Britain (Vacation Work, £5.95). An annual directory with information on working holidays in the UK.

Working Holidays (Central Bureau, £6.95). An annual guide which has information on nearly 100,000 holiday jobs at home and abroad.

Useful Addresses

Association of Graduate Careers Advisory Services Crawford House, Precinct Centre, Manchester M13 9EP (061 273 4233).

British Council 65 Davies Street, London W1Y 2AA (071 930 8466).**British Trust for Conservation Volunteers** 36 St Mary's Street, Wallingford, Oxfordshire, OX10 0EU (0491 39766).

BUNAC 16 Bowling Green Lane, London EC1R 0BD (071 251 3472).

Camp America 37 Queen's Gate, London SW7 5HR (071 589 3223).

Central Bureau for Educational Visits & Exchanges Seymour Mews House, Seymour Mews, London W1H 9PE (071 486 5101).

Central Services Unit (CSU) Crawford House, Precinct Centre, Manchester M13 9EP (061 273 4233).

Centre de Documentation et D'Information Royale 92 rue de Dessous des Berges, 75013 Paris (010 331 45 83 04 92).

Federation of Recruitment and Employment Services 10 Belgrave Square, London SW1X 8PH (071 323 4300).

Friends House Euston Road, London NW1 2BJ (071 387 3601).

International Farm Experience Programme National Agricultural Centre, Kenilworth, Warwickshire CV8 2LG (0203 696584).

International Voluntary Service 162 Upper Walk, Leicester LE1 7QA (0533 541 862).

Jobs in the Alps Agency PO Box 388, London SW1X 8LX.

Kibbutz Representatives 1A Accommodation Road, London NW11 8ED (081 458 9235); 11

Employment

Upper Park Road, Salford, Manchester M7 0HY (061 740 1981).
National Youth Bureau 17-23 Albion Street, Leicester, LE1 6GD (0533 471200).
NUS Services Bleaklow House, Howard Town Mills, Glossop, Derbyshire SK13 8PT (0457 868003).
PGL Youth Adventure 974 Station Street, Ross-on-Wye, Herefordshire HR9 7AH (0989 764211).
Project 67 10 Hatton Garden, London EC1N 8OH (071 831 7626).
RADAR 25 Mortimer Street, London W1N 8AB (071 637 5400).
Vacation Work 9 Park End Street, Oxford OX1 1HJ (0865 241978).
Voluntary Service Overseas 371 Putney Bridge Road, London SW15 2PN (081 780 2266).

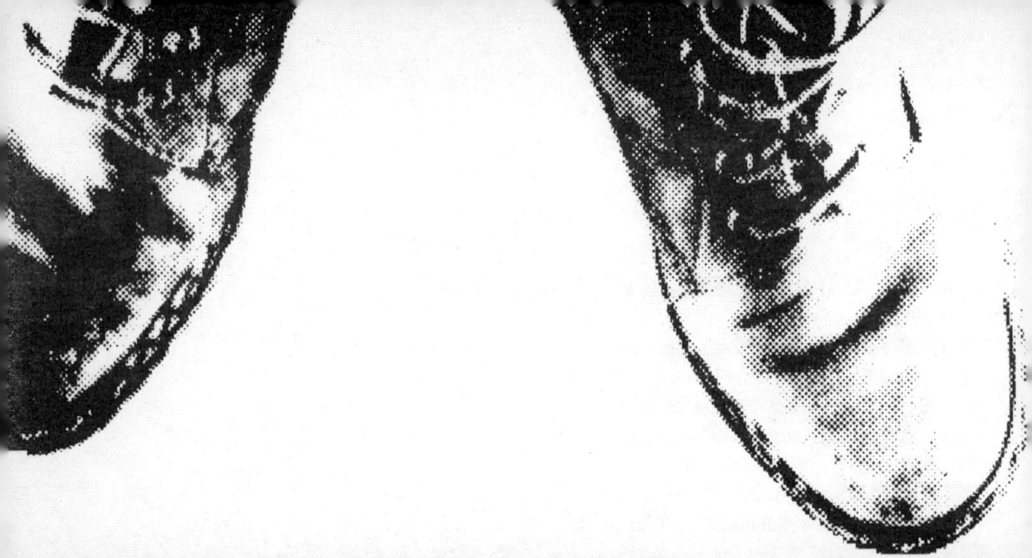
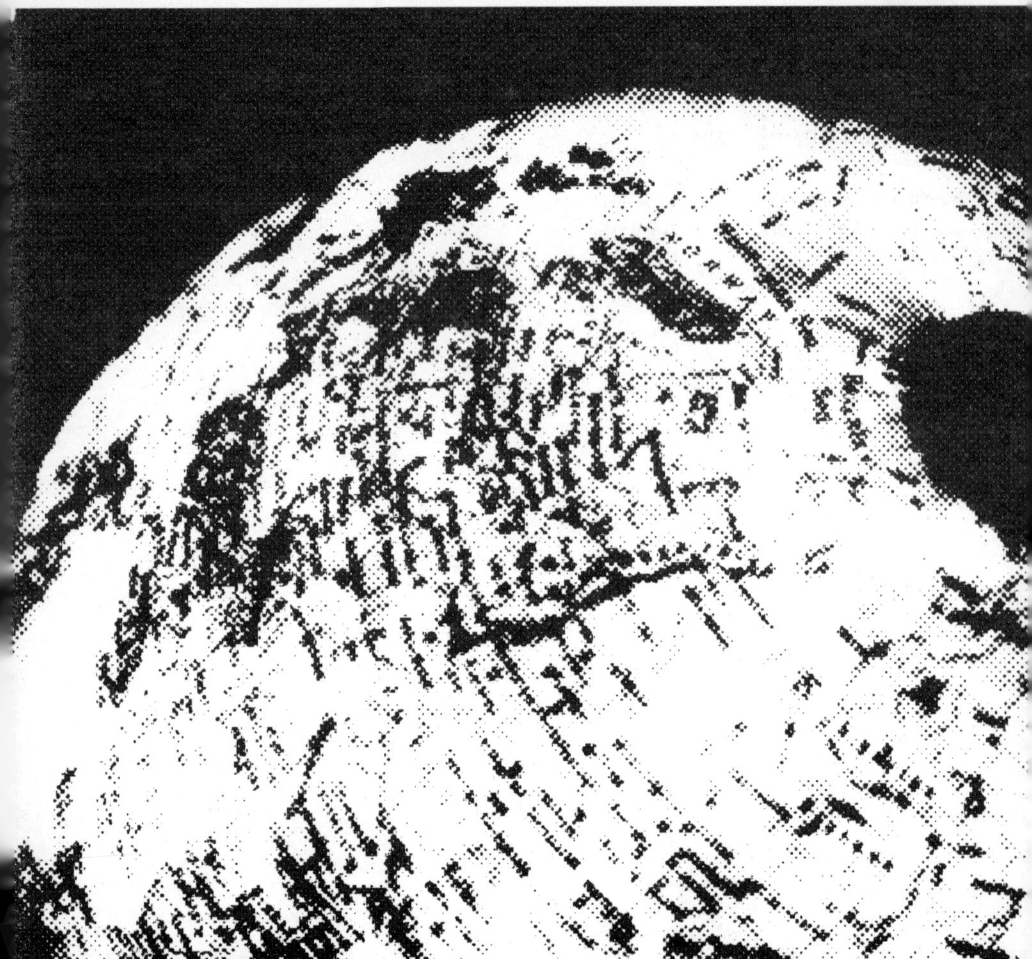

travel

From living it up in Leningrad to basking on a beach in Benidorm, the opportunities for travel as a student are endless. **Gavin Hamilton** explores countries and continents, concentrating on the essential, practical information you will need to ensure that your dream holiday doesn't turn into a nightmare vacation.

The Basics **280**

Europe, North Africa and the Mediterranean **287**

Travel Jargon **288**

Eastern Europe and the Soviet Union **297**

The Long Haul **297**

Useful Addresses **303**

The competition between travel operators for the privilege of sending students to far-off lands is intense – witness the vast sums of money spent on advertising, the discounts offered to students and the lengths to which companies are prepared to go to undercut each other. It's a cut-throat business in which only the fittest survive and many companies, having failed to keep up with the competition, have gone under.

So why the competition? It's true that travel operators have been quick to exploit students' long vacations. It's also true, though, that students are lucky enough to have the time and the freedom to explore foreign lands, but don't have the funds to travel extravagantly. Operators therefore have to make the effort to persuade students that they can afford to travel and must offer packages which are real value for money. It's a cliché, but at no other time will you have the opportunity to see parts of the world that other people only dream about. You could go when you retire, but waiting until then will leave you less likely to have the energy that you now take for granted.

The Basics

First of all, you will need to consider which travel operator you are going to travel with and how, and what you need to do before you leave: all the organizations we mention are listed at the end of this chapter under **Useful Addresses**.

Travel operators

If there's a student travel office in your college or student union, you're only minutes away from the expert knowledge you'll need to find the shortest and cheapest routes. There are numerous travel operators knocking about, but if you don't have a student travel office on campus,

it's best to go to one of the high street offices of the big two student travel companies, Campus Travel and STA Travel. Although they are not strictly student travel operators (they prefer to talk about young, independent travellers), students make up the largest section of their market. They both publish annual, free student travel handbooks, *The Campus Traveller* (Campus Travel) and *The Student Travel Handbook* (STA Travel). Both companies also have subsidiary travel companies: Campus Travel operates Eurotrain, specializing in cheap rail travel to Europe; STA Travel runs WST Charters, offering cut-price holidays in Israel, Egypt and Turkey.

The advantage of booking through STA Travel is that you get access to its 120 travel offices around the world, so if you come a cropper in Kuala Lumpur, you can call in and they will try to sort you out. Also, the knowledgeable staff will not try to foist an unsuitable deal upon you. Sister offices in Europe and cheap train fares offered through Eurotrain make Campus Travel a good bet for travelling on the continent. Both STA and Campus Travel have offices around the UK.

However, should you choose to book your holiday through a different travel company, make sure that they are members of the Association of British Travel Agents (ABTA). ABTA membership is a guarantee that, in cases where the company fails to deliver and/or goes bust, your expenses will be refunded in full.

Transport and tickets

Flights: There's an obvious temptation to go for the cheapest possible flight. In some cases this is sound thinking, in others, less so. Long flights (*see below* **The Long Haul**) are worth discussing with a reliable operator: you might be able to

Travel

make the most of stopovers en route at little extra cost. European flights should be more straightforward, but always ask: whether you can change the return date (often the answer is no); what time the flight arrives (a £10 taxi ride can knock off your savings if the buses aren't running); and whether you are liable to pay any extras, such as airport tax.

Trains: Discounted youth tickets, issued by Eurotrain, are available to anyone under 26. They are valid for two months' travel along a pre-specified route – you can stop off anywhere along it. For the trail around Europe, Morocco and Turkey, the InterRail Card is better value. This is a youth ticket for UK citizens (or residents of six months' standing) aged under 26. It entitles holders to one month's unlimited second-class travel on European (East and West), Scandinavian, Turkish and Moroccan railways. At time of writing, the card costs £175; it is available from all major British Rail stations, from the International Rail Centre at London's Victoria Station, or any student/youth operator.

Coaches: Coach travel is economical if you are going to Paris or Amsterdam, or as far as Denmark, Germany and Switzerland; further afield and a journey can take days rather than hours. Add the cost of the food you'd have to buy and it's often cheaper to fly. The coach company Eurolines is reliable and licensed. Tickets can be bought from any National Express agent around the country and coaches leave from Victoria Coach Station in London, with connections from all major towns and cities in the UK. Many of the other coach companies operating are unlicensed, and although they can be cheaper, you travel at your own risk: an unlicensed company might not observe the rules about changing drivers every so many hours, and a tired driver is a dangerous driver.

Ferries and hovercraft: If you're leaving the country by train or bus, a cross-Channel ferry or hovercraft trip will almost certainly be included in your ticket. If you're driving or hitching, the complexities of routes and costs need thinking about – it's not always cheapest to cross Dover-Calais. Study the brochures, available from just about any travel agent, check what the guide books suggest and be aware of the various discounts on offer: off-peak (day/night) travel; five-day returns; 27 people in one car; and so on. If you're taking your car, you should book in advance (travel agents charge no commission).

Driving: Travelling by car increases your freedom but can isolate you from the locals and be pricier than public transport. However, you can cover long distances quickly via Western Europe's excellent network of motorways, which radiates from the ferry ports. Only Austria, Spain and Greece insist on an International Driving Licence (available from the RAC or AA) although wherever you drive, you'll need insurance and usually a Green Card (issued by your insurers) as proof of having it. Each country has its own rules of the road, given in the guide books we list and in the AA's useful *Traveller's Guide to Europe* (£6.95).

Hitching: Anyone intending to hitch long distances in Europe should get hold of a copy of *Europe: A Manual for Hitch-hikers* by Simon Calder (Vacation Work, £3.95). Obviously, women should take every precaution: never hitch alone.

Cycling: If you're planning on travelling by bike join the Cyclists Touring Club, part of the Alliance Internationale de Tourisme (AIT). Membership of the CTC (£10 per year for students, at time of writing) entitles you to information and advice on cycling in virtually every country in the world, as well as free third-party insurance and legal aid. Essential reading if you're going to Europe is Nicholas Crane's

WHEREVER YOU'RE BOUND, WE'RE BOUND TO HAVE BEEN.

Low cost flights on quality airlines.

Special fares for students and young people.

Well travelled consultants to guide you.

Over 120 offices worldwide.

STA Travel
117 Euston Road, NW1
74 & 86 Old Brompton Rd, SW7.

ULU Travel
University of London Union
Imperial College, LSE, QMWC,
Kings College

North America 071-937 9971. Europe 071-937 9921.
Rest of the World 071-937 9962.

Manchester, Oxford, Cambridge, Bristol, Birmingham.

STA TRAVEL

ABTA
99209
IATA

Travel

Cycling in Europe (Pan, £6.99, currently out of print, but try your local library).

Overland expeditions: Prices may seem astronomical – they're often over £1,000 – but these really are expeditions to parts of the world where ordinary tourists can't or won't go. Organized expeditions include transport in specially equipped buses or jeeps, accommodation and food, so they might be the solution if you're nervous about lone exploration of such out-of-the-way places. Dragoman, Encounter Overland, Guerba Expeditions, Hann Overland and Transglobal are the most established and reliable operators. You can book directly through them or through a student travel office.

ISIC and YHA cards

Your International Student Identity Card (ISIC) will entitle you to discounts on student charter flights, accommodation and admission to art galleries, museums, cinemas and other places of cultural interest. Even if a discount is not advertised, you might be allowed one if you show your card. You are eligible for an ISIC card if you are a full-time student (studying for more than 15 hours a week). The ISIC is valid to the end of the year for which it is stamped. It costs £5 and is available from your student union, from a student travel operator, or by post from ISIC Mail Order.

A Youth Hostels Association (YHA) card is also a wise investment. Membership of the international YHA entitles you to stay in youth hostels across 56 nations. They're not always fun places but they're safe and, in most countries, very cheap. At time of writing, the card costs £8.30, or £4.40 if you're under 21. Non-UK residents can apply for the International Youth Hostel Federation (IYHF) card which costs £9 and gives the same entitlements as the YHA card. The cards are available from YHA's head office and

adventure shops and from youth hostels (if staying overnight). Most hostels will require you to have a sheet sleeping bag (around £10 from YHA adventure shops, or stitch together a couple of old sheets and take a pillow case).

The YMCA is another useful organization, as it operates a series of very cheap InterRail Points across Europe. These are hostels for both sexes, with kitchens, laundries and recreation facilities. Membership to the scheme costs £2: for more information send a stamped addressed envelope to the YMCA InterRail Programme.

Passports and visas

Entry requirements and regulations vary and are complicated, so always ask whether you need a visa. You can't get one at the airport departure desk, or in most towns with a ferry terminal. Always check with embassies if you're unsure, and leave yourself enough time to get a new passport if necessary. If your travel plans are complex – such as for extended African travel – start getting visas well in advance. *See* **Table: Countries for which British Nationals Need an Entry Visa**.

Full British passport holders don't need a visa to visit the USA on holiday, but do need to fill out a visa waiver form, given by the travel agent or on the plane. The lack of support for this scheme, however, means there may soon be a return to the compulsory US tourist visa – check with travel operators for the latest news. Note, too, that the Visitor's Passport (the cheap one, available over the counter at all main post offices for £7.50), although valid for a year, can only be used for trips of up to three months and is not valid outside Europe. Applications for a full British passport (£15 for ten years' validity) take seven to eight weeks by post or two to three weeks if you go to the Passport Office in London. Application forms are available from all post offices.

Countries for which British Nationals Need an Entry Visa

Afghanistan, Argentina, Australia;
Bangladesh, Bulgaria, Burma;
China, Cuba, Czechoslovakia;
Egypt, Ethiopia;
Ghana;
Hungary;
India, Iraq;
Jordan;
Kuwait;
Lebanon, Liberia;
Nigeria;
Pakistan, Philippines, Poland;
Romania;
Saudi Arabia, Senegal, Sierra Leone, Sri Lanka, Sudan, Syria;
Taiwan, Thailand*;
USSR;
Venezuela, Vietnam;
Yemen;
Zaire.

* (for visits of more than 15 days).

Money and insurance

The best ways of carrying money vary greatly from country to country. In the USA you need plastic; in South America, dollars and a money-belt. Travellers' cheques are reliable standbys everywhere: they're available from any high street bank, some building societies, American Express, or Thomas Cook. With a current account and a Eurocheque Card (for which you pay a small annual fee) you can get cash from many European banks, but note that many non-European currencies can only be bought after arrival, most conveniently at the airport.

Insure yourself. For between £4 and £10 a week you can cover your luggage, your tickets and your health – a week in an American hospital could well cost an arm and a leg. Even in Europe, things don't come cheap. Most of the student/youth companies market ISIS Insurance, a thorough, international policy that protects half a million travellers each year. Take it out when you buy a ticket. Once there, be sure to get a certificate of any medical expenses, or a police report if you have anything stolen. You won't be able to claim without them.

Guidebooks

A good guide can pay back its cost in hours, so we've recommended relevant guides under the country/area details that follow. In general, the most consistent, reliable and interesting series are the *Rough Guides* (£5.99 to £10.99) which cover most of Europe, Africa, North and Latin America and parts of Asia too. *Lonely Planet* do similar, if slightly hippyish, guides to most of Asia and Australasia (£4.95 to £10.95) which are good if you are venturing further afield. The *Time Out* Guides to London, Paris, New York and Amsterdam cost £7.99 and are available from all good bookshops.

Travel

Baggage

Try to travel light – it's easier and cheaper. For European flights, you will be allowed 15kg-20kg/33lb-44lb of baggage. If you exceed the allowance, you could be charged extra. You can take 20kg/44lb on long haul flights and no more than two pieces of luggage on transatlantic flights. Carry valuables such as cameras and jewellery in your hand luggage because airlines will not normally compensate you for the full value of anything that goes missing. You won't be allowed to take camping gas cylinders on board a plane and if you take a bicycle up in the air, make sure that you let the tyres down beforehand. You can take as much as you can carry on trains but always ensure that your luggage is properly labelled.

Vaccinations

If you plan to journey to Asia, Africa or South America, you should find out as soon as possible what jabs you will need: they might be a condition of entry to certain countries and are likely to include cholera, typhoid, polio, tetanus, hepatitis, yellow fever and possibly rabies. It's best to have the injections over a number of weeks rather than all in one go, and aim to have them completed at least two weeks before you leave. You have to pay for inoculations; prices range from £5-£6 (typhoid, cholera, polio) to £15-£20 (hepatitis, yellow fever, rabies). Prophylactic (preventive) immunization is free only if, for example, there's a typhoid scare on your street. British Airways runs travel clinics around the UK.

Inoculations must be recorded on an official International Certificate of Vaccination. Your GP can give most vaccinations, but yellow fever jabs must be administered at an approved centre. The doctor's signature must be rubber-stamped by the local area health authority if you have a cholera shot, but if you go to an immunization centre, your ICV booklet can be authorized on the spot. Cholera protection lasts only six months and overlanders might have to be re-vaccinated en route. At best it offers only partial protection, so take no chances even if you've had the jab. The same caution applies to hepatitis.

The Department of Health leaflet T1, *The Traveller's Guide To Health*, contains vital information for people preparing for overseas travel; get it from travel agents, DSS offices and main post offices. The *Health Briefs*, issued from their database by the Medical Advisory Service for Travellers Abroad (MASTA) are up to the minute. They cost from £7 to £25 and an application form is available from Boots dispensaries, or ring MASTA. The service also supplies medical kits, including what is being retailed as an 'AIDS First Aid Kit', essentially a box of sterilized needles and syringes. It's perhaps sensible for parts of Africa. The paperback *Travellers' Health* by Richard Dawood (OUP, £6.99) is comprehensive and readable.

Most ailments can be avoided by taking a few simple precautions: don't drink any water which you are at all unsure of; if in doubt, use water purification tablets. Iodine tablets are safer than the chlorine-based ones but taste awful. Eat in places popular with the locals as they are likely to be hygienic. Find out which malaria tablets are recommended for use at your destination; start taking them before you go and continue for two to three weeks after your return. Use insect repellent where necessary. Take a basic first aid kit with aspirins, plasters and antiseptic, and sun- and anti-histamine creams.

TRAVEL

FROM LONDON TO:

	OW from	RTN from
AMSTERDAM	37	72
BOSTON	111	222
FRANKFURT	40	79
HARARE	280	495
LOS ANGELES	156	296
NAIROBI	235	398
NEW YORK	120	239
ROME	69	155
SYDNEY	430	688
TORONTO	184	236
WASHINGTON	138	276

ACCOMMODATION:

	from
AMSTERDAM	£21
FLORENCE	£23
LOS ANGELES	£16
NEW YORK	£22
ROME	£20
WASHINGTON	£18

PLUS

* EUROTRAIN
* STUDENT CARDS
* TRAVEL GUIDE
* LANGUAGES COURSES
* STUDENT'S ACCOMMODATION IN UK
  (Family & University residence)

YOUTH & STUDENT TRAVEL CENTRE

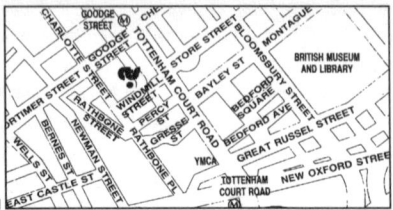

LONDON	W1P1HH - 33, Windmill Street - Metro Goodge Street
	Tel. (071) EUROPE 580 4554 - USA 323 5130 - LONG HAUL 323 5180
PARIS V	20, Rue des Carmes - Tel. (1) 43250076 Metro Maubert Mutualité
ROME	16, Via Genova - Tel. (06):46791
	297, Corso Vittorio Emanuele II - Tel. (06) 6547883/6872560
FLORENCE	11R, Via dei Ginori - Tel. (055) 292150
MILAN	2, Via S. Antonio - Tel. (02) 72001121
NAPLES	25, Via Mezzocannone - Tel. (081) 264800
VENICE	3252, Dorso Duro Cà Foscari - Tel. (041) 5205660

Travel

Europe, North Africa and the Mediterranean

The formation of a single market in 1993 means that trade barriers are about to come crashing down. A single currency might eventually lead to a United States of Europe, but this is still a continent rich in diversity and it remains the most popular holiday destination for students. Whether you make your way around the continent's fashionable cities with the help of an InterRail card, try your luck at island-hopping in Greece, go raving in Ibiza, seek out Scandinavia or soak up the sun on the Costa del Sol, you will find travel operators bending over backwards to pack you off to the Continent. Prices vary considerably, but if you know what you are looking for and are prepared to shop around, you can pick up a real bargain. If in doubt, go to one of the student travel operators (*see above* **Travel Operators**).

The InterRail card (*see above* **Transport and Tickets: Trains**) is the cheapest way to see Europe. It extends as far south as Morocco and as far east as Romania. Much of the Mediterranean coast has now been exploited to saturation point by tourists and developers, but some countries (Portugal and Turkey being the best examples) still have unspoilt beaches where you don't have to endure lager-lout Brits burning and boozing in their Union Jack boxer shorts. Island-hopping in Greece is a cheap and non-touristy way to spend the summer in the sun but if you're after something a bit different, why not try Scandinavia? The landscape is vast, beautiful and just waiting to be discovered. If you're looking for culture, Barcelona and Florence are the cities to head for, while Amsterdam and Paris are unbeatable for a weekend break. Further afield, Israel and Egypt offer more than enough to satisfy most people's appetite for adventure – the Nile, Jerusalem, Galilee, the Dead Sea, the Pyramids.... If you're determined to spend the summer in that part of the world but find that your bank manager doesn't agree, a 'working' holiday on a kibbutz or moshav could be the answer (*see page 254* **Employment**). Main tourist offices are listed below under **Useful Addresses**.

France

Getting there: Most travel operators run regular flights to Paris (from £50 return), Lyon, Marseille (both from £70 return) and Nice (from £75 return). Trains to Paris cost from £60 return, coaches from £50 return. Cross-Channel ferries are the cheapest option if you have your own transport; travel operators will be able to get you the best deal.

Getting around: The *France Vacances* rail pass allows rail travel any four days within a 15-day period, costs from £78 and is available from French Railways. The *Carré Jeune* card costs 147F (about £16) and gives discounts of up to 50 per cent on four single train journeys in one year; the *Carte Jeune* costs 150F and gives a 50 per cent discount on any off-peak rail journey from June to September. The age limit for obtaining both cards is 26. They can be bought at French railway stations. Alternatively, use an InterRail card. Hitching can be difficult if you don't go through an agency such as Allô Stop, *84 passage Brady, Paris 75010 (42.46.00.66)*, which has a list of drivers happy to help impecunious travellers (for a share of the petrol costs).

Accommodation and food: Two associations run student/youth hostels in most major cities, with beds from £5 a night: AJF, *119 rue St Martin, 75004 Paris (43.29.85.00)* and UCRIF, *4 rue Jean-Jacques Rousseau, 75011 Paris (42.60.42.40)*. YHA hostels cost from £2.50 a

apex: An airfare that carries restrictions and 100 per cent cancellation fees.

bucket shops: High street shops (often advertised in magazines and newspaper classifieds) selling cheap and discounted flights, mostly on standby.

charter flights: Flights operated by a tour operator for a specific season and a specific time of the week. They are usually cheaper than scheduled flights but are limited in the frequency of their operation.

long haul: Term used for flights outside of Europe where the journey time and distance covered are considerable.

one way: A straightforward journey from A to B with no return arrangements.

open jaw: An airfare which allows you to travel from A to B and return to A from C. For example: London-Paris, Paris and Amsterdam-London (travel between Amsterdam is not included).

no show: A term used by airlines and operators for passengers who have a confirmed seat but who fail to turn up.

provisional booking/option: A booking held for a certain time limit subject to proper confirmation and payment. If the payment is not made within the time limit, the booking will automatically be released.

standby: A flight obtained at the last minute (if someone cancels for instance). Consequently, they are cheaper than booked flights.

stopover: A point en route to your final destination where you break your journey. For flights, there might be a charge.

RTW: Round The World. RTW tickets are often better value than long haul return tickets.

Via: Not to be confused with stopover. Indicates the flight route, with no guarantee of stopovers being possible.

288

Travel

el jargon

night. Cheap hotels are plentiful, with doubles from £10 a night. It's possible to have a weekend break in Paris (including transport and accommodation) from around £80 for two. As in much of northern Europe, eating out can be pricey, but in cities it's always possible to find restaurants offering set meals of excellent value (*prix fixe*). In the country, small family-run bistros can be remarkably inexpensive. Still, you'll often find the local *boulangerie* (bakery) and deli, or one of the high-quality supermarkets, the best bet. A meal of your own, washed down with cheap, drinkable plonk can be the most economical and delicious of all.

Guidebooks: *The Time Out Paris Guide* (Penguin, £7.99); *Rough Guide to France* (Harrap, £8.99); *Rough Guide to Brittany and Normandy* (Harrap, £5.99); *Rough Guide to Provence and the Côte d'Azur* (Harrap, £6.99).

Germany

Getting there: There are regular flights to Frankfurt (from £70 return) and Berlin (from £100 return). Trains are cheaper: to Hamburg (from £40 single), Berlin (from £55 single) and Munich (from £60 single).

Getting around: Germany is reckoned to be the best place in Europe for hitching. The *German Rail Youth Pass* for people under 25 costs £45 for four days, £70 for nine days and £95 for 16 days (within a 21-day period). The *Tramper Ticket* (for people under 23 and students under 27) gives one month's unlimited travel for £87.20; the *Junior Pass* costs £42 for one year and entitles students under 27 to half price rail travel. All are available from DER Travel Service. Bikes can be rented from most railway stations for DM10 a day.

Accommodation and food: Berlin and the major cities are expensive. Youth hostels are cheap, but generally of poor quality. Try hotels in east Berlin which are still cheap (although they may not be for much longer) or campsites to the west of Berlin. Despite a reputation for stodginess, the quality and variety of German food will surprise you. If you're a carnivore, the sausages, schnitzels and cured meats will keep you more than satisfied; if not, visit the supermarkets, which have some of the freshest and most enticing displays of fruit and veg you'll find anywhere. Prices are among the highest in Europe, though.

Guidebooks: *Rough Guide to West Germany* (Harrap, £8.99); *Rough Guide to Berlin* (Harrap, £5.99).

Greece

Getting there: For an adventure, catch the train to Athens (InterRail or from £180 return). Flights to Athens start from £80 single, £155 return; and there are plenty of charter flights to the islands. The ferry crossing from Brindisi in Italy to Patras is free with the InterRail card. Avoid the ferries to Yugoslavia (they take hours) and coach journeys with unlicensed operators, which are not worth the risk.

Getting around: On the mainland, buses are cheap but the InterRail card won't be much use (except for the long haul to Istanbul); for the islands, ferries are still a relatively cheap option and even some internal flights are affordable, although they fill up very quickly.

Accommodation and food: Rooms offered to you as you leave the ferries are very cheap – around £5 a night per person and often even less if you're prepared to haggle. Meals in island tavernas can be both cheap and filling: *souvlaki* (shish kebabs), salads, chips and vegetables

Travel

cooked in olive oil are standard fare. Be wary of the most touristy areas, especially Athens' port, Piraeus, but do visit the restaurants in Plaka, the city's lively bazaar. A meal with rough local wine should cost you only £2 to £3.

Guidebooks: *Rough Guide to Crete* (Harrap, £5.99); *Rough Guide to Greece* (Harrap, £8.99).

Ireland

Getting there: There are regular flights to Belfast (from £58 return), Dublin (from £70 return) and Cork (from £90 return). The main ferry routes are Holyhead-Dublin/Dun Laoghaire, Pembroke/Fishguard-Rosslare, Liverpool-Belfast and Stranraer-Larne; prices vary according to season and how you travel (car, bicycle or by foot), but are generally a lot cheaper than flights.

Getting around: ISIC holders are entitled to a *CIE Travel Save Stamp*, which gives a 50 per cent reduction on ferries, buses and trains within the Republic, and is well worth the investment. Combined bus and rail passes – *Rambler Tickets* – are available from train stations throughout Ireland and cost IR£75 for eight days, IR£110 for 15 days. Bicycles can be hired from shops throughout Ireland for about IR£6 a day or IR£25 a week. Details are available from the Irish Tourist Board.

Accommodation and food: Information on youth hostels, the best (and cheapest) option, can be obtained from the Irish YHA or the Irish Tourist Board. Restaurants can be very pricey and it's often best to make your own meals, to fill up on fast food, or, especially, to sample some of the excellent pub grub, washed down with a glass of stout. For a splurge, try one of the many wonderful fish restaurants.

Guidebook: *Rough Guide to Ireland* (Harrap, £7.99).

Israel and Egypt

Getting there: Flights to Cairo cost from about £185 return. Ask WST Charters about the onward student flights: London-Tel Aviv and on to Athens (£156), Istanbul (£156) or Cairo (£164). Alternatively, you could fly to Tel Aviv and then catch the bus to Cairo (around £20).

Getting around: In Egypt, opt for the crowded, but cheap and comfortable trains (first class is very cheap). In Israel, the trains are poor – buses and shared taxis are the norm.

Accommodation and food: Rooms in Egypt can cost as little as £5 a night if you can do without air-conditioning. In Israel, youth hostels are your best bet, or you could opt for a kibbutz or moshav (*see page 254* **Employment**). The cooking in Israel and Egypt is healthy, spicy and usually delicious. Both cuisines feature lots of fresh vegetables, beans, chicken and chick-peas. Felafel, fried chick-pea balls served with salad in pitta bread, are an Israeli fast-food favourite. Food is especially cheap in Egypt, a meal typically costing under £2.

Guidebooks: *Rough Guide to Israel and the Occupied Territories* (Harrap, £7.99); *Rough Guide to Egypt* (Harrap, £8.99).

Italy

Getting there: Student flights to Rome, Pisa, Bologna, Genoa, Venice and Verona can cost as little as £50 one way, out of season. The cheapest option is to fly to Milan in the north and then make your way south on the cheap public transport system. Alternatively, a return train ticket to Milan costs from £110. CTS is the specialist student travel operator for all things Italian.

Getting around: Full-time students can get the *Carta Verde* (Green Card) for L8,000 (about £5) which gives up to 30 per cent off rail journeys. People under 26 can purchase reserved *BIJ*

TRAVEL ABROAD

Council Travel

Low-cost student/youth air fares worldwide

On-the-spot ticketing

Airpasses

Eurotrain & InterRail Cards

Adventure Tours

Group Travel Services

International Identity Cards

Youth Hostel Passes

Travel Insurance

Language Programmes

Travel Gear & Guidebooks

Over 40 offices worldwide

A Travel Division of the Council on International Educational Exchange

Council Travel
28A Poland Street
London W1V 3DB
071-437 7767
Hours: Mon-Fri 9:30am-6:00pm
Sat 10:00am-2:00pm (Walk-in only)

STUDY ABROAD

Council on International Educational Exchange

Summer Study in the USA

Wide range of courses available at major American Universities.

Japanese in Japan

Courses from 4 weeks to one semester.

Japan Exchange & Teaching Programme (JET)

Teaching in Japan for graduates.

Internship USA

Course-required work experience in the USA.

Worldwide Study Abroad Opportunities

Academic programmes in Eastern Europe, South America, Asia and Western Europe.

For more information on these and other programmes contact:

Council on International Educational Exchange (CIEE)

33 Seymour Place
London W1H 6AT
071-706 3008

Travel

Tickets, giving between 15 and 40 per cent reductions on second class rail travel. Students under 26 can claim up to 30 per cent off *Voli Notturni* (night flights) and *Voli Nastro Verde* (selected day flights).

Accommodation and food: Youth hostels are cheap and plentiful, particularly in the north. Two or three people together are best off in a shared room in a *locanda*, a fairly basic form of hotel. Both accommodation and food are much better value the further south you go. In the north the food is rich, with the emphasis on breaded meats and heavy sauces, accompanied by pasta or *polenta*, a variety of semolina. In the south you'll find more fish, simply grilled meats and of course, pizza. Everywhere, though, the standard is deliciously high.

Guidebooks: *Rough Guide to Italy* (Harrap, £9.99); *Rough Guide to Sicily* (Harrap, £6.99); *Rough Guide to Tuscany and Umbria* (Harrap, £6.99); *Rough Guide to Venice* (Harrap, £6.99).

The Netherlands

Getting there: London-Amsterdam is a very competitive route, so there are many bargains: flights from £75 return, train from £46 return and coach from £36 return.

Getting around: Bicycles can be hired from railway stations from £2 per day plus around £50 deposit. The *Holland Rail Pass* (£24 for three days' second class rail travel) and the *Rail Rover* (£33.50 for seven days' second class rail travel) are available from Netherlands Railways. Also available is the *Benelux Tourrail Card* (five days' second class rail travel in Belgium, Holland and Luxembourg), which costs £31 for people under 25. Hitching prospects are good.

Accommodation and food: A major expense. Youth hostels and Amsterdam's sleep-ins (£7-£9 per person) are the cheapest options.

For good-value eating, it's best to follow the Dutch and fill up on a café breakfast of bread, cheese and ham. At lunch-time or in the evening, an Indonesian set meal, *rijstafel*, is an exotic but satisfying possibility very popular with the Dutch.

Guidebooks: *The Time Out Amsterdam Guide* (Penguin, £7.99); *Rough Guide to Holland, Belgium and Luxembourg* (£7.99).

Scandinavia

Getting there: The cheapest flights are through Scantours. Scandinavian Seaways runs ferries from Harwich to Gothenburg (Sweden, from £140 return in high season) and Esbjerg (Denmark, from £120 return); student discounts are available. But the cheapest way is by InterRail.

Getting around: InterRail is valid in all four countries; *Nordturist* (around £120 for under-25s but available to anyone) is the Scandinavian equivalent which gives unlimited travel for 21 days and is available from Norwegian State Railways.

Accommodation and food: Cheap accommodation is limited to youth hostels and camping, but Scandinavian youth hostels are the best in Europe; expect to pay £4 to £10 a night. Student cafeterias, youth centre restaurants and self-made meals are the solution to otherwise steep food prices.

Guidebook: *Rough Guide to Scandinavia* (Harrap, £8.99).

Spain and Portugal

Getting there: In the high season, the big charter flight operators virtually give away flights at the last minute to fill their unsold seats, so it's worth leaving it late if you want a bargain. Unless you have an InterRail card, you won't save money travelling there by rail.

TUMI

Latin American Craft Centres

A Taste of Latin America
JEWELLERY, CLOTHING AND CRAFTS FROM THROUGHOUT LATIN AMERICA.

LONDON 23/24 CHALK FARM ROAD
CAMBDEN TOWN NW1 • 071 485 4152

BATH 8/9 NEW BOND STREET PLACE
BA1 1BH • 0225 462367

OXFORD 2 LITTLE CLARENDON STREET
OX1 2HJ • 0865 512307

BRIGHTON TUCAN 29 BOND STREET
BN1 1RD • 0273 26351

WIDEN YOUR CURRICULUM
STUDENT • YOUTH • BUDGET TRAVEL

• COMPETITIVE FARES •

• INTERNATIONAL STUDENT CARD • FLEXIBLE TICKETS •

• RELIABLE CARRIERS • TRAVEL INSURANCE •

LONG HAUL	NORTH AMERICA	EUROPE
071 255 2082	071 637 3161	071 255 1944

TRAVEL CUTS 295a Regent St. London W1R 7YA

Travel

Getting around: The train network in Portugal is reliable and complemented by bus routes; hitching is usually no problem. In Spain, *Tourist Cards* offer unlimited rail travel for eight days (£55), 15 days (£80) or 22 days (£120). On some trains, you have to pay a supplement, normally about 50p.

Accommodation and food: Rooms can be as cheap as £5 per night, though prices have increased since Spain and Portugal joined the EEC. Look in the old quarters of most towns and cities. Campsites are good and camping rough is legal, so long as you don't crash out on tourist beaches or near public water supplies. Away from coastal tourist resorts, food is cheap and authentic. Expect to pay £2 to £3 for a meal in Portugal, where fish dishes are much in evidence, £3 to £4 in Spain. Paella isn't as common as you'd expect, often contains meat instead of shellfish, and tends to be offered as expensive tourist bait. Tapas, snacks taken with a drink or as a meal in themselves, can be very filling and Spanish vegetable markets provide wonderfully fresh produce.

Guidebooks: *Rough Guide to Portugal* (Harrap, £6.99); *Rough Guide to Spain* (Harrap, £8.99).

Turkey

Getting there: Aim to pay between £120 and £150 for a return flight to Istanbul. Turkey is covered by the InterRail card, but it's a long journey by rail. An option is to cross from the Greek Islands.

Getting around: Buses, ferries and shared taxis are very cheap.

Accommodation and food: Rooms are plentiful and inexpensive; outside main resorts, £3 a night should be sufficient. The food is varied, usually excellent, and extremely cheap, if rather meaty. There are many different snacks available from roadside kiosks, but even in Istanbul's restaurants you'll only pay £2 to £3 for a filling meal.

Guidebooks: *Rough Guide to Turkey* (Harrap, £8.99); *Turkey: A Travel Survival Kit* (Lonely Planet, £5.95).

Eastern Europe and the Soviet Union

The collapse of the Berlin Wall, the thawing of the Cold War and the flowering of democracy in the former Stalinist states of the Eastern Bloc have opened up exciting new possibilities for travel. Prague and Budapest are currently topping the travel charts as the most popular destinations for a weekend break. The travel brochures welcome you to their 'free and democratic country', talk of 'killing the past' and apologize for previously misleading people as to the true nature of life under Stalinism. Whether you want to prise away your own piece of the Berlin Wall, take in the architecture of Prague and the delights of the Danube, head for the beaches of Bulgaria, or just drown yourself in Polish vodka, you need to do it soon – in a few years' time, travel and tourism may have gone the same sordid way as in much of the West.

At time of writing, it's still unclear what travel restrictions remain, but currency barriers have been lifted in most countries, visa requirements have been dropped in others and further restrictions are likely to disappear as the old bureaucracies are overhauled. But although the cost of living may be ridiculously low, some countries are more equal than others when it comes to the distribution and availability of goods and services: you'll need to plan your trip well in advance to ensure a happy holiday.

The way some people talk, you might think that the countries of eastern Europe have been under the iron grip of Stalinism for centuries (not

295

"Someone once told me that the difference between tourists and travellers is that travellers go to find out something new, whereas tourists go to see what they know is there already."
John Collee Author of 'A Doctor Writes' in the Observer Magazine (Medicine, Edinburgh Unversity, 1972-79).

just since the Second World War) and that, as a result, they have no history or culture of their own remaining. Nothing could be further from the truth, as anyone who has visited eastern Europe recently will testify. Each country is now rediscovering its rich past and its own distinctive identity. The biggest problem when planning a trip to eastern Europe is deciding where to go. You should make the state travel companies' London offices your first stop – Balkan Holidays (Bulgaria), Cedok Tours (Czechoslovakia), Hungarian Air Tours and Danube Travel (Hungary) and Polorbis Travel (Poland). They can book hotel rooms for you or even set you up with a complete package.

Eastern Europe

Getting there: The InterRail card now covers all countries in what was the Eastern Bloc. Eurotrain's *Eastern Explorer* rail ticket (from £172.50) takes in Berlin, Czechoslovakia and Hungary, as well as parts of western Europe, over a two month period. Expect to pay £150 to £200 for a return flight.

Getting around: The state railway and bus networks are still ridiculously cheap, though this may change if they are privatized. ISIC holders can get student rail discounts.

Accommodation and food: Hotels can be cheap (as little as £5-£10 a night for a double) and rooms in private houses are available in most countries. These can be arranged through the respective State Tourist Office in Britain. Youth and student travel bureaux can give you details of student hostels, and it's best to make advance bookings for hotel rooms in the larger cities. Youth hostels are cheap but you need to book well in advance, as many are reserved for school parties and the like. Food, too, can be good value, but in the USSR, Poland and Romania you're likely to find the choice limited, with restaurants having only one or two dishes on offer, despite a comprehensive menu. Stick to small, family-run restaurants rather than larger tourist-oriented places. Alcohol is cheap, strong and plentiful, good news for you, but a serious social menace.

Guidebooks: *Eastern Europe on a Shoestring* (Lonely Planet, £9.95); *Rough Guide to Berlin* (Harrap, £5.99); *Rough Guide to Czechoslovakia* (Harrap, £7.99); *Rough Guide to Hungary* (Harrap, £6.99); *Rough Guide to Poland* (Harrap, £7.99); *Traveller's Survival Kit Soviet Union and Eastern Europe* (Vacation Work, £8.95).

USSR

Getting there: Intourist Travel, the State Tourist Company, monopolizes travel – even independent travel has to be arranged through it. The packages are expensive, but if you let a small operator like Progressive Tours deal with Intourist, things can be a lot cheaper. A clever alternative is to travel via Scandinavia. From Helsinki in Finland, trains go to Leningrad and Moscow, or you can catch a ferry to the Estonian capital of Tallinin. Most travel operators will book through SSTS and Sputnik, the official student travel agencies of Scandinavia and the Soviet Union.

Getting around: On a package tour, you won't have to worry about getting around. Local transport has a flat fare of 5 kopeck; but it can be a hair-raising experience. In complete contrast, the Trans-Siberian Railway, running from Moscow to the Pacific, a distance of 6,000 miles, is still one of the world's great rail journeys.

Accommodation: Best arranged in advance through Intourist.

Guidebooks: *The Soviet Union: The Independent Traveller's Guide* (Collins, £5.95); *Trans-Siberian Handbook* (Lascelles, £8.95); *Traveller's Survival Kit Soviet Union and Eastern Europe* (Vacation Work, £8.95).

The Long Haul

The key to a successful long haul trip is planning. It's not just a question of getting a cheap flight, hopping on a plane, getting off at the other end and then enjoying your holiday. You'll need to consider visa applications at least three months in advance, the dreaded jabs (*see above* **The Basics**) and, if you plan to cross international borders by land, border restrictions. And that's before you even start to consider what flight to book and where to stay when you get there.

A bewildering array of stopover and RTW fares (*see page 288* **Travel Jargon**) enables you to take in Asia, the USA and the South Pacific for the price of a return fare to Australia. Shop around and don't take the first flight you are offered. Prices of flights may seem astronomical, but will be more than offset by the low cost of living once you are there. If you are at all unsure as to where to go, an overland expedition or organized tour/trek may well be the best bet (*see above* **The Basics**).

As for where to go, pick a destination and someone will be able to get you there. However, there are a number of obvious places to avoid. Since the bloody events of June 1989, China is no longer the desirable destination it was, and seems unlikely to be for some time. Similarly the Middle East (with the possible exception of Israel) is best avoided in the wake of the Gulf War, as are parts of Southern Africa, Peru and Northern India. On the subject of politics, certain stamps in your passport – most notably Israel and South Africa – will deny you access to a host of Middle Eastern and African countries. It's always best to check the latest Foreign Office travel advice if you are at all unsure.

Africa

Getting there: There are plenty of student flights to choose from. Some of the national airlines (such as Sudan Airways) give a notoriously bad service, but are often cheaper. Expect to pay around £400 for a return flight to Nairobi, but closer to £500 if you want to get to Lagos or Harare. North Africa is just a ferry ride from Europe – Marseille to Algiers, Palermo to Tunis, Piraeus to Alexandria.

Getting around: The best way to see Mother Africa is on an overland expedition. These trips are very popular, fairly expensive and need to be booked months in advance. The six-week trip from Nairobi to Harare is a favourite. Local buses and trains vary wildly in price, comfort and efficiency; try flagging down a *matatu*, a shared taxi/minibus. The overnight train ride from Nairobi to Mombasa is a truly memorable experience.

Accommodation and food: Cheap rooms can be found in Nairobi for £3-£5 a night. There are youth hostels in Morocco, Tunisia and Zimbabwe, but generally accommodation in Africa is more expensive than in Asia or South America – camping is the cheapest option. African food is most familiar when from the north, but all the more interesting elsewhere. Grains and meat feature strongly, with wonderfully exotic fish plentiful near the coast.

Guidebooks: *Rough Guide to Kenya* (Harrap, £7.99); *Rough Guide to Morocco* (Harrap, £7.99); *Rough Guide to West Africa* (Harrap, £10.99); *Rough Guide to Zimbabwe and Botswana* (Harrap, £7.95).

Indian subcontinent

Getting there: Expect to pay in the region of £500 for a reliable return flight to Kathmandu and around £400 to get to Delhi and back, although

"Of the two long vacations I had at Oxford, one was spent working for the famous American firm of credit investigators, Dun and Bradstreet, near Cannon Street. I had worked for them in New York the year before, which was an exciting place for a teenager to be: doing translations for them in London in midsummer was dreary work and the only bits of relief I can remember are a) translating a report on a Belgian conman who made a fortune out of selling robes to the clergy but not delivering and b) losing my virginity. It's a strange phrase, losing your virginity, but it happened in such an unexpected way, without my volition, that it seems apt.

Then the summer moved up ten gears, when my brother and I went down south on his scooter to work in the grape-picking season, the *vendage*, at Château Palmer in

Travel

prices can be lower in the bucket shops. Regular flights also go to Bombay, Madras and Karachi. If you want a combined trip to India and Nepal, it's better to fly to Delhi and then take the Delhi-Kathmandu coach (about £20).

Getting around: Travelling around India is very cheap – you can survive on as little as £5 a day – but you need patience. Once you get through the seemingly never-ending queues and hassles at the station, a second class train journey is a great way to see the country. Buses are cheap, but are often unbearably slow and crowded; in Nepal and northern Pakistan, they are the only form of transport. Alternatively, you could book a short tour through a travel operator: 12 days can cost as little as £200.

Accommodation and food: When you get off a train or bus, competing touts are likely to offer you cheap rooms. Ignore them (if you can) and take a look at a number of different places before making a final decision, as prices and quality vary enormously. Alternatively, head for a youth hostel or YMCA. Railway stations have rest rooms for a few rupees and a rooftop bed beneath the stars in a guest house will set you back as little as 10 rupees (about 40p) a night. Recuperate with the occasional blow-out in a good hotel. Indian food is as varied as the subcontinent itself. It is richer, heavier and more meaty in the north, with bread the standard accompaniment; lighter, hotter, and often vegetarian in the south, served with rice or wafer-thin pancakes. A meal will cost no more than £1. Western-style food is widely available, especially in northern cities, but is relatively expensive and of variable quality.

Guidebooks: *Guide to Trekking in Nepal* (Fifth Edition, £8.95); *India – A Travel Survival Kit* (Lonely Planet, £10.95); *Rough Guide to Nepal* (Harrap, £6.99).

Bordeaux. There were six of us English layabouts, and we all slept in one bedroom on iron bedsteads, like in a prep school, and had breakfast in the huge kitchen waited on by an old housekeeper who had no English and little French.

The work was hard, mainly because all the French children who had been doing it every year could pick grapes twice as fast as us hulking grown-ups. I didn't tell my brother I had lost my virginity. He was already under the impression it had happened two years before. Going down south with Stewart on his scooter, as far as Spain, is one of the great memories of my life, even though we skidded on wet sand in Rouen and crashed on the way back."

Miles Kington writes the Moreover.... column in the *Independent* (French and German, Trinity College, Oxford, 1960-63).

CAMPING, WALKING TRAVELLING START WITH US

Tents, rucsacs, sleeping bags, walking boots, outdoor clothing, camping accessories, compasses, OS maps, travel aids.

DISCOUNT WITH STUDENT CARD

WE MAKE THE GOING EASY

camping &outdoor centre

27 Buckingham Palace Road SW1
Tel: (071) 834 6007

22 branches nationwide,
call the above number for your nearest branch

THE OUTDOOR LEISURE SPECIALISTS

• EUROTRAIN • EUROTRAIN • EUROTRAIN •

EUROTRAIN

DISCOUNT RAIL FARES FOR THE UNDER 26'S

	o/w from	rtn from
• Amsterdam	25.30	48.30
• Berlin	61.00	97.90
• Brussels	25.00	43.00
• Paris	31.50	57.80
• Cologne	35.00	62.90
• Rome	84.20	167.00

Eastern Explorer:
London - Amsterdam - Berlin - Prague - Budapest - Vienna - Brussels for £182.50

- Many other destinations
- Tickets Valid at least 2 months
- Stopover anywhere en route
- Ferry Crossing included

NEW! CITY BREAKS FOR GROUPS

Tickets available from:
Your local Student Travel Shop or appointed Eurotrain agent or phone 071 730 3402

* Fares may be subject to change 01 May '91

ROUTE 26 EUROPEAN RAIL FOR UNDER 26's

DISCOVER EUROPE BY TRAIN

TICKET

100's Of Destinations

▶ Great discounts on standard rail fares for those under 26 yrs
▶ Tickets valid for two months
▶ Stop off anywhere along the way
▶ Hundreds of destinations
▶ Offices throughout Europe offering help along the way

▽ WASTEELS

121 WILTON ROAD LONDON SW1V 1JZ Tel: 071-834 7066

START MAKING TRACKS

PARIS	FROM ONLY **£51**	RTN
AMSTERDAM	FROM ONLY **£49**	RTN*
ANTWERP	from only **£46**	RTN*
BRUSSELS	from only **£46**	RTN*
FRANKFURT	from only **£73**	RTN*
BERLIN	from only **£85**	RTN*
NICE	from only **£108**	RTN*
BARCELONA	from only **£115**	RTN

*Youth Fares

Over 200 destinations throughout Europe by coach, with Nationwide connections by **NATIONAL EXPRESS** ▶

Contact your Student Travel Office or local NATIONAL EXPRESS Agent.
Enquiries: London ☎ 071 730 0202, Birmingham ☎ 021 622 4373
Leeds ☎ 0532 460011, Manchester ☎ 061 228 3881
Credit Card Reservations:
London ☎ 071 730 8235, Birmingham ☎ 021 622 4225

eurolines
EUROPEAN EXPRESS COACHES

COACH YOUR WAY ACROSS EUROPE

Travel

South-East Asia

Getting there: The two main gateways to South-East Asia are Bangkok (Thailand) and Singapore, although you could head for Kuala Lumpur (Malaysia) or Jakarta (Indonesia). Flights to Bangkok cost in the region of £400 return; flights to Singapore and Kuala Lumpur start from about £450. Try student travel operators first, and then high street bucket shops. Many people stop over en route to Hong Kong; flights cost from £450 return.

Getting around: Buses are cheap, but if you travel at night it will be uncomfortable, and often downright dangerous. Trains, on the other hand, are warm, cheap and reliable. Flights can be terrific value, often costing little more than trains and buses. Ferries, with the notable exception of those operated to the Philippines, are slow and unreliable. Trekking tours, booked through student travel operators, cost about £250 for 10 days.

Accommodation and food: Shared rooms booked in advance are around £14 in Bangkok, £12 in Kuala Lumpur and £10 in Singapore. Rooms in Bangkok can be found on arrival for as little as £3-£5. A YHA card will prove invaluable in the Philippines. South-East Asian food is now quite familiar to westerners and offers some of the best value and exotic variety in the Orient. Fish dishes and spicy snacks are widely available; a restaurant meal will cost less than £3.

Guidebooks: *Indonesia Handbook* (Moon Publications, £12.95); *Rough Guide to Thailand* (Harrap, £7.99); *Rough Guide to Hong Kong and Macau* (Harrap, £6.99); *South East Asia on a Shoestring* (Lonely Planet, £6.95); *The Tropical Traveller* (Pan, £2.95).

Central and Latin America

Getting there: The indisputable champion of Latin American travel is Journey Latin America, which can arrange flights from around £420 return to Caracas – a relatively gentle introduction. However, prices will be closer to £600 if you want to go to Rio or Lima. If a ticket is all you're after, you might be better off going to a bucket shop or a student travel operator, but don't expect to go anywhere except Mexico for less than £400 return. At the moment Peru is virtually off-limits to all but the bravest of travellers while the present political situation persists – tourists have been killed and parts of the country are very dangerous indeed.

Getting around: It's difficult to generalize about the whole continent, but there are buses everywhere and they are, invariably, excellent value. Trains are cheaper but crowded, unreliable and interminably slow. Internal flights are startlingly cheap – often only twice the bus fare. Flights between countries are more expensive, but are worth considering as part of your flight home.

Accommodation and food: Very, very cheap. In most places, you can survive on as little as £5 a day and live well on £10 a day. Beans and tortillas, minced meat dishes and excellent beer are staples. Eat well for under £2.

Guidebooks: *South America on a Shoestring* (Lonely Planet, £7.95); *Rough Guide to Brazil* (Harrap, £6.99); *Rough Guide to Guatemala and Belize* (Harrap, £7.99); *Rough Guide to Mexico* (Harrap, £7.99); *Rough Guide to Peru* (Harrap, £7.99).

North America

Getting there: There's terrific competition between the transatlantic airlines, so be prepared to shop around. You could try for a courier flight, which will be much cheaper, but hard to get hold of (*see* **Box: Flight Couriers**).

Flight Couriers

For a very cheap flight, you could travel as a courier: you simply deliver a parcel or a sack of documents. You can only take hand baggage with you, but the flights are less than half the standard price. Availability is limited as these flights are very much in demand, but phone one of the major courier firms for the latest deals:

CTS/TNT Skypack Johnson House, Browells Lane, Feltham, Middlesex TW6 2BL (081 844 2626).

Nomad Couriers 224 Great West Road, Heston, Middlesex TW5 9AW (081 570 9277).

Polo Express 208 Epsom Square, Heathrow Airport, Hounslow, Middlesex TW6 2BL (081 759 5383).

Getting around: You can hire a car for about $20 a day, but some states require you to be aged over 25. The best way to see America is on a Greyhound bus. *Ameripass* tickets cost from £85 for seven days to £130 for 30 days, with daily extensions costing £10. They give unlimited bus travel for their duration. The *National Rail Pass* costs about $299 and gives you unlimited travel on the (limited) rail network; it's available from most UK student travel operators. Internal flights are cheaper than you think – the 30-day standby pass from Delta offers unlimited air travel on Delta flights and costs £399.

Accommodation and food: Hotels are pricey in the big cities (upwards of £30 a night and more in New York), but are cheaper in rural areas and motel chains such as Motel 6 and EZ-8, which charge between £15 and £30 for a double room. The few youth hostels there are (from £5 a night) fill very quickly, so it's worth making a reservation. Food can be terribly expensive, although you're always sure of a large helping. Sandwiches are enormous and make good midday fillers. Cooked breakfasts are cheap and reliable, and are usually available all day; coffee is always unlimited. For evening meals, ethnic restaurants are the best value: check out the local Chinatown or Latin Quarter.

Guidebooks: *The Time Out New York Guide* (Penguin, £7.99); *Rough Guide to California and West Coast USA* (Harrap, £8.99); *Rough Guide to San Francisco* (Harrap, £5.99); *Traveller's Survival Kit USA & Canada* (Vacation Work, £6.95).

Australia and New Zealand

Getting there: Many flights include stopovers in Bangkok, Sri Lanka and Hong Kong; others take in Australasia as part of RTW tickets. Aim to pay something in the region of £800 for a return flight.

Getting around: Distances are huge and overland travel can therefore be expensive. Hitching is effective between the cities, but it is worth considering buying a travel pass before you leave. The seven-day Greyhound *Buspass* offers unlimited travel throughout Australia and New Zealand for A$217 (A$536 for 21 days), and the *Capital Connections* ticket gives 30 consecutive days' travel between Brisbane and Melbourne via Canberra and Sydney for A$108; both are available from Deluxe Coachlines. A nine-day Downunder coach pass for both Australia and New Zealand (NZ$269), an eight-

Travel

day coach/rail/ferry New Zealand pass (NZ$120) or a New Zealand air pass valid for four stops (NZ$370) are all available from STA Travel.
Accommodation and food: Backpacker hostels – similar to youth hostels, but with luxury extras such as swimming pools – are everywhere, as are youth hostels. Sydney is a world capital for food, but Melbourne probably offers cheaper eating.
Guidebook: *Traveller's Survival Kit Australia and New Zealand* (Vacation Work, £6.95).

Useful Addresses
Transport and travel
Balkan Holidays Sofia House, 19 Conduit Street, London W1R 9TD (071 491 4499).
British Rail International Rail Centre Victoria British Rail Station, London SW1V 1JV (071 834 2345).
Campus Travel/Eurotrain 52 Grosvenor Gardens, London SW1W 0AG (071 730 3402/8111).
Cedok Tours & Holidays 17-18 Old Bond Street, London W1X 4RB (071 629 6058/071 491 2666).
CTS (Centre Turistico Studentesco) 33 Windmill Street, London W1P 1HH (071 580 4554/071 323 5130/80).
Cyclists Touring Club Cotterell House, 69 Meadrow, Godalming, Surrey GU7 3HS (0483 417217).
Danube Travel 6 Conduit Street, London W1R 9TG (071 493 0263).
Deluxe Coachlines 3 Princetown Street, London WC1R 4AX (071 831 4686).
DER Travel Service 18 Conduit Street, London W1R 9TD (071 408 0111).
Delta Oakfield Court, Consort Way, Horley, Surrey RH6 7AF (0800 414767).
Dragoman Camp Green, Debenham, Suffolk IP14 6LA (0728 861133).
Encounter Overland 267 Old Brompton Road, London SW5 9JA (071 370 6951).
Eurolines 52 Crawley Road, Luton, Bedfordshire LU1 1HX (0582 404511).
French Railways (SNCF) 179 Piccadilly, London W1V 0BA (071 499 2153).
Greyhound Sussex House, London Road, East Grinstead, West Sussex RH19 1LD (0342 317317).
Guerba Expeditions 101 Eden Vale Road, Westbury, Wiltshire BA13 3QX (0373 826689).
Hann Overland 201-203 Vauxhall Bridge Road, London SW1V 1ER (071 834 7337).
Hungarian Air Tours 3 Heddon Street, London W1R 7LE (071 437 1622/9405).
International Rail Centre Victoria Railway Station, London SW1 (071 834 2345).
Intourist Travel Intourist House, 219 Marsh Wall, Meridian Gate, London E14 9FX (071 538 8600).
Irish Rail 185 London Road, Croydon CR0 2RJ (081 686 0994).
Journey Latin America 16 Devonshire Road, London W4 2HD (081 747 3108).
Netherlands Railways 25-28 Buckingham Gate, London SW1E 6LD (071 630 1735).
Norwegian State Railways 21-24 Cockspur Street, London SW1 (071 930 6666).
Polorbis Travel 82 Mortimer Street, London W1N 7DE (071 637 4971).
Progressive Tours 12 Porchester Place, London W2 2BS (071 262 1676).
Scandinavian Seaways I5 Hanover Street, London WIR 9HG (071 491 7256/071 493 6696).
Scantours 8 Spring Gardens, London SW1A 2BG (071 839 2927).

STA Travel/WST Charters Head Office, Priory House, 6 Wrights Lane, London W8 6TA (071 938 4711).
Transglobal 64 Kenway Road, London SW5 0RD (071 244 857l).
Victoria Coach Station Buckingham Palace Road, London SW1 (071 730 0202).
Wasteels 121 Wilton Road, London SW1V 1JZ (sales 071 834 7066/admin 071 834 6744).

Tourist Information
Australian Tourist Commission Gemini House, 10-18 Putney Hill, London SW15 6AA (081 780 2227/1424).
British Airways Travel Clinics (recorded information 071 831 5333).
Danish Tourist Board Sceptre House, 169 Regent Street, London W1 (071 734 2637).
Egyptian State Tourist Office 168 Piccadilly, London W1V (071 493 5282).
Finnish Tourist Board 66-68 Haymarket, London SW1 (071 839 4048).
Foreign and Commonwealth Office King Charles Street, London SW1 (071 270 3000).
French National Tourist Board 178 Piccadilly, London W1 (071 491 7622).
German National Tourist Office Nightingale House, 65 Curzon Street, London W1Y 7PE (071 495 3990).
Greek National Tourist Office 4 Conduit Street, London W1R 0DJ (071 734 5997).
India Government Tourist Office 7 Cork Street, London W1X 1PB (071 437 3677).
Irish Tourist Board 150 New Bond Street, London W1Y 0AQ (071 493 3201).
Irish Youth Hostel Association 14 Upper O'Connell Street, Dublin (0001 747733).

Israel Government Tourist Office 18 Great Marlborough Street, London W1V 1AF (071 434 3651).
Israel Student Travel Office 109 Ben Yehuda Street, Tel Aviv (03 5440111).
ISIC Mail Order NUS Services, Bleaklow House, Howard Town Mill, Mill Street, Glossop SK13 8PT.
Italian Tourist Office 1 Princes Street, London W1R 8AY (071 408 1254).
MASTA (Medical Advisory Service for Travellers Abroad) London School of Hygiene and Tropical Medicine, Keppel Street, London WC1E 7HT (071 631 4408).
Netherlands Board of Tourism 25-28 Buckingham Gate, London SW1E 6LD (071 630 0451).
New Zealand Tourism Office Haymarket, London SW1Y 4TQ (071 973 0360).
Norwegian Tourist Board Charles House, 5-11 Lower Regent Street, London SW1Y 4LR (071 839 6255/2650).
Passport Office Clive House, 70-78 Petty France, London SW1 (071 279 4000/recorded information 071 279 3434).
Portuguese National Tourist Office 1-5 New Bond Street, London W1Y 0NP (071 493 3873).
Romanian National Tourist Office 17 Nottingham Street, London W1M 3RD (071 224 3692).
Spanish National Tourist Office 57 St James's Street London SW1A 1LD (071 499 0901).
Swedish Tourist Board 29-31 Oxford Street, London W1 (071 437 5816).
Turkish Embassy (Consulate Office) 170-173 Piccadilly, London W1C 9DD (071 734 8681).

Travel

US Travel and Tourism Administration 22 Sackville Street, London W1 (071 439 7433).
Youth Hostelling Association (YHA) Trevelyn House, 8 St Stephen's Hill, St Albans, Herts AL1 2DY (0727 55215).
YMCA InterRail Programme Crown House, 550 Mauldeth Road West, Chorlton, Manchester M21 2SJ (061 881 5321).

index

Abortion	pp170-171	
Academic appeals	p208	
Access courses	pp16-17; p16	
Access funds	pp87-89	
students with disabilities	p55	
Accommodation	pp96-115	
for students with disabilities	p53	
AIDS	pp183-186	
HIV antibody tests	pp185-186	
Alcohol	pp188-190; p69	
Alternative prospectuses	p18	
Applying to college	pp4-27	
Mature students	p11; pp47-48	
Students with disabilities	pp52-53	
Arrival at college	pp62-71	
Banks & building societies		
choosing a	pp90-92	
Opening an account	pp63-65	
Bills	pp135-139	
Electricity	p135; pp137-138	
Gas	p138	
Telephone	pp138-139	
Water	p139	
Black students	pp238-243	
Ethnic monitoring	p13	
Budgets	pp132-137	
BUNAC	pp263-264	
Careers	pp267-273	
Milk round	p269	
Careers services	p269	
Interviews	p273	
Childcare & crèches	p231; pp158-159;	
see also **Mature students**		
Changing a course or college	p209	
Choosing a course	pp16-19	
Choosing where to study	pp19-24	
Cleaning & laundry	pp127-129	
Clearing	pp5-7	
College services for students	pp158-159	
Community charge see **Poll tax**		
Complementary therapies	p175	
Consumer rights	pp249-252	
Contraception	pp165-170	
Cooking	pp125-127; p63	
Council housing	pp112-113	
Credit cards	p92	
C.vs	pp271-273	
Debt	p140	
Deferred entry	pp24-25	
Disabled students see **Students with disabilities**		
Dissertations	pp206-207	
Drinking see **Alcohol**		
Drugs	pp186-188	
Overdose	pp187-188	
EC jobs	pp264-265	
Eating disorders	pp193-195	

306

Index

Electoral rights	pp252-253	Benefits	p174		pp246-247
Employment	pp256-277	Dentists	p174	Making a complaint against the	
During a year off	p24	Doctors	p174	police	pp248-249
Overseas students	pp38-39	Opticians	p175	Misleading or offensive	
Voluntary work	p24; p155; p266	Prescriptions	p174	advertising	p250

Electoral rights pp252-253
Employment pp256-277
  During a year off p24
  Overseas students pp38-39
  Voluntary work p24; p155; p266
Enterprise allowance scheme p274
Entrance requirements
  pp16-17; p19
Essays, reports & dissertations pp206-207
Ethnic students see **Black students** and **Overseas students**
Examination & revision
  pp207-209
Executive officers pp156-157

Finance see **Money**
Flatmates p123
Foreign students see **Overseas students**
Freshers' balls p67

Gay students see **Lesbian & gay students**
Grants
  Qualifying & applying for
  pp74-83
  for students with disabilities
  pp53-56
  Rates of pp76-82
  see also **Money**

Halls of residence & college accommodation
  pp100-106
  adapted for students with disabilities p53
Health pp172-199

Benefits p174
Dentists p174
Doctors p174
Opticians p175
Prescriptions p174
Vaccinations for foreign travel
  p285
Help & information see **Useful addresses** and **Useful reading**
HIV see **AIDS**
Home improvement
  pp118-123
  DIY pp118-119
  Draught-proofing p119
  Heating p119; p123
  Painting p119
Hostels p116
Housing associations & co-ops p113

Immigration laws UK pp30-35
Information see **Useful addresses** and **Useful reading**
Insurance p144
  Bike p144
  Life p144
  for foreign travel p217; p284
Interviews
  College pp22-24
  Career p273
ISIC cards p150; p283

Kibbutzim & moshavim p265

Law & Rights pp246-253
  Consumer rights pp249-252
  Electoral rights pp252-253
  Legal rights & Legal Aid

  pp246-247
  Making a complaint against the police pp248-249
  Misleading or offensive advertising p250
  Ombudsmen p253
  Tenancy agreements & tenants' rights pp109-112
Lectures pp204-205
Legal aid p247
Lesbian & gay students
  pp222-227
Libraries & resource centres pp203-204
Lodgings p113

Markets p127
Mature students pp46-49
  Access courses pp16-17; p47
  Entrance requirements p25
  Grants & allowances pp77-79
  Applying to college
  p11; pp47-48
Men's health p179
Money pp74-93
  Access funds see **Access funds**
  Alternative financial assistance
  p89
  for foreign travel p284
  Grants pp74-83
  National Insurance see
  National Insurance
  Student loans see **Student loans**
  for students with disabilities
  pp53-56
  Taxation see **Taxation**
  Transferring money from abroad
  p37
  Welfare benefits, overseas students pp37-38

307

Welfare benefits, student benefits　pp84-87

National Insurance
Overseas students　p41
NHS　pp174-175
NUS　pp148-149
　Campaigns　p154
　Lesbian & Gay Liberation Campaign　pp225-226
　Legal Aid Fund　p247
　Women's Campaign　p234
Nutrition　pp125-127

Ombudsmen　p253
Open days　pp21-22
The Open University　pp20-21; p49
　Applying to　p9
Overseas students　pp30-43
　Ethnic monitoring　p13

Part-time work pp256-260
PCAS　pp5-7
Poll tax
　Discount　p139
　Overseas students　p38
　Registration　p96
Postgraduate study　pp273-274
Prospectuses　p17
Psychological problems　pp193-196
　Depression　p193

Racism & racial harassment　p36; pp239-242
Rag weeks　pp155-156
Registration　pp65-66

Religion in college　p158
Renting a flat　pp107-112
Reports writing a　pp206-207
Resits　p208
Resource centres　pp203-204
Re-taking a year　p209
Revision & examination　pp207-209
Rights　pp246-253
Rotas　pp123-124

Sabbatical officers　p157
Safer sex　p185; see also **Contraception**
Security　pp141-144
　Personal safety　pp142-143
　Home security　pp143-144
　Women　pp231-233
Seminars & lectures　pp204-206
Sex & relationships
　Lesbian & gay students　pp222-227
　Sexuality　p163
　Sexual difficulties　pp164-165
Sexually transmitted diseases　pp179-183; p165
　AIDS see **AIDS**
　STD clinics　p183
Sexism & sexual harassment
　towards lesbians & gays　pp226-227
　see also **Women**
Shopping　pp130-132
　Books　p131
　Clothes　pp130-131
　Household goods　p132
　Stationery　p132
　Toiletries　p132
Skin problems　pp191-193
Smoking　pp190-191

Social security benefits see **Money** and **Welfare benefits**
Sports injuries　p191
Squatting　pp113-114
Student exchanges　p213
Student loans　p74; pp83-83
　students with disabilities　p55
Student media　pp154-155
Student unions & societies　pp277-288
　Alternative prospectuses　p18
　Help and information　p154
　Meetings　p157
　Services　p22; p151
　Campaigns　p154
　Clubs & societies　pp152-153
　Black students　p238-239
　Intro fairs　pp66-67
　Lesbian & gay students　pp224-225
　Mature students　p49
　Overseas students　p36
　Women　p234
　NUS see **NUS**
Student representative councils　p157
Students with disabilities　pp52-59
　Grants & allowances　p77
Studying abroad　pp212-219
Study techniques　pp202-209
　Coursework　pp70-71
Supplementing your income　pp256-280

Taking a year off　pp24-25
Taxation　p92
　Poll tax see **Poll tax**
　Overseas students　p41
TEFL　pp274-275
Temporary work see **Part-**

Index

time work
**Tenancy agreements &
tenants' rights** pp109-112
Transport pp140-141
Travel pp280-305
   Studying abroad pp212-219
Trusts & charities funding
      p89
TV & video hire pp129-130

UCCA pp4-7
Useful addresses
   Accommodation p115
   Applying to college pp26-27
   Basic living p145
   Black students p243
   Employment pp276-277
   Health pp197-199
   Law & rights p253
   Lesbian & gay students p227
   Mature students p49
   Money p93
   Overseas students pp41-43
   Sex and relationships p171
   Students with disabilities
      pp58-59
   Student unions p159
   Studying abroad p219
   Travel pp303-305
   Women p235
Useful reading
   Applying to college p26
   Basic living p145
   Black students p242
   Employment pp275-276
   Health p197
   Law & rights p253
   Lesbian & gay students p227
   Mature students p49
   Money p92
   Sex and relationships p171
   Students with disabilities p58

   Studying abroad pp218-219
   Study techniques p209
   Women p235

Vaccinations for foreign travel
      p285

Welfare benefits
   Overseas students pp37-38
   Student benefits pp84-87
   for students with disabilities
      pp55-56
Women pp230-235
   Safety pp231-233
   Women's officers p230
   Women's press p233
Women's health pp177-179
Work *see* **Employment**
Working abroad p267
Work experience pp269-271
Working holidays pp260-267

Year out p274

Notes on the authors

Paul Allender is the Research Officer (Housing) at NUS. He was previously the Research Officer (Student Financial Support). He has a degree in fine art from Hull College of Higher Education and an MSc in politics and sociology from Birkbeck College, London.

Linet Arthur (34) is the Head of Advice and Training at UKCOSA. Previously the Research Officer (International) at NUS, she studied English literature at Sussex University and has spent time teaching in Zimbabwe.

Tony Balacs (31) has a degree in pharmacology from Sunderland Polytechnic and an MSc in molecular biology from University College London. He has worked as a tutor and is a trained counsellor.

Hazel Bathie (25) studied history of design and the visual arts at North Staffordshire Polytechnic (1987-90), where she was on the union Council for three years and on the union Campaigns Committee for two years. She has recently completed a part-time publishing and editorial skills course at the London College of Printing.

Steve Clamp (23) was elected as a part-time member of the NUS National Executive in 1989, having graduated from Aberystwyth University with a degree in economics. His work on lesbian and gay rights has included: two and a half years running his University Lesbian and Gay Society; two years as UCMC (NUS Wales) Lesbian and Gay Officer; and a year on the NUS Lesbian and Gay Liberation Campaign Committee.

Margaret Davine (52) graduated with an MA in History from Kings College London in 1976 and has been studying for a Phd in medieval history at Westfield College London since 1977. She was Education Officer of the Mature Students Union (MSU) from 1979 to 1982 and from 1986 to 1989; and has been the National Secretary since 1989.

Emma Delap (24) studied combined arts at Leicester University, after which she worked in the information department of a voluntary organization concerned with children with special education needs. She is currently the Information Officer at Skill.

Tim Dawson (27) studied philosophy at the University of East Anglia, after which he edited a magazine for the Student Union Senior Officers Conference (1986-88) and worked as Communications Officer at NUS (1988-90). He currently works at *Marxism Today* and is a contributor to *The Guardian* and *The Times Higher Education Supplement*.

Julie Emery (27) studied French and Spanish at the Polytechnic of Central London and humanities at Thames Polytechnic. She was an executive member of Thames Polytechnic Student Union for three years, including two sabbatical years: one as Entertainments Officer and one as General Secretary. She has worked at *Time Out* for three years; the past two as Editor of the annual *Time Out London Student Guide*.

Dr Anna Graham (28) studied at Kings College London and Westminster & Charing Cross Medical School. She has worked in medicine, surgery and accident and emergency, and is currently a psychiatrist in a London teaching hospital.

Nikki Greenway (22) was elected as a part-time NUS National Executive Member in 1990.

Biographies

While working for NUS she has been studying for her finals in politics and history at Keele University. She ran her University Lesbian and Gay Society for two and a half years, and was a member of the NUS Lesbian and Gay Liberation Campaign Committee before being co-convenor of the Campaign.

Jefferson Hack (20) studied journalism at the London College of Printing (1989-90) and is currently a freelance journalist.

Gavin Hamilton (23) graduated from Bristol University in 1988 with a degree in economics and politics. He then spent a sabbatical year as the NUS Bristol Area Convenor and has been working as a journalist for *Time Out* since February 1990.

Julie Harvey gained a BA in psychology and an MA in women's studies at the University of Warwick. Formerly the Women's Research Officer at Leicester Urban Studies Centre, she is now the Research Officer (Student Awards) at NUS.

Judith Horsfield studied English at Manchester University and worked for eight years in teacher education. She is currently a lecturer in English at Manchester Polytechnic, and is also the Poly's Learning Skills Co-ordinator, and spends much of her time helping students with study problems. She runs seminars and workshops on study techniques.

Hilary Hutcheon (26) studied politics, philosophy and economics at Wadham College, Oxford University. She then studied for diplomas in journalism and production at the London College of Printing where she was president of the student union from 1987 to 1988. She has worked for *Time Out* since July 1990.

Laura Matthews (23) graduated from the London School of Economics in 1988 with a degree in government. She then studied part-time for an MSc in political theory, also at the LSE, and is currently the Press Officer of NUS.

Dr Ann Robinson studied at Middlesex Hospital Medical School and has postgraduate qualifications in obstetrics, paediatrics, family planning and general practice. She works as a GP in Finchley, London.

Maeve Sherlock was president of NUS from 1988 to 1990 and a member of the NUS executive from 1985. Previously she was a student at Liverpool University (1981-84) where she studied sociology and from 1984-85 she was sabbatical treasurer of the student union. She is currently Deputy Director of UKCOSA.

Jane Woolfenden (34) runs the International Student Office at Middlesex Polytechnic. She gained a BA in English and linguistics from Nottingham University and an MA in applied linguistics from Birkbeck College. She has worked for UKCOSA and is the author of *How to Study and Live in Britain* (Northcote House).

Patrick Younge was Vice-President (Education) of NUS from 1987 to 1989 and was the National Organiser for the National Black Students Alliance in 1988. He is currently working as a television journalist in London.

Produced by Time Out Magazine Limited, Fifth Floor, Tower House, Southampton Street, London WC2E 7HD (071 836 4411).

Editorial
Senior Managing Editor Peter Fiennes **Managing Editor** Marion Moisy **Editor** Julie Emery **Assistant Editor** Gavin Hamilton **Copy Editors** Peter Lawson, Ronnie Haydon **Researchers** Tony Balacs, Jefferson Hack, Hilary Hutcheon

Design
Art Director Kirk Teasdale **Design** Iain Murray Warren Beeby

Advertising
Group Advertisement Director Lesley Gill **Sales Director** Mark Phillips **Ad Sales (Time Out)** Andy West, Helen Fireman, Simon Frederick, Karen Poole, Jeremy Saunders. **Advertising Assistant** Ruth Hughes

Administration
Publisher Tony Elliott **Financial Director** Kevin Ellis **Project Co-ordinator** Adele Carmichael

Features in this Guide were written and researched by:
How to Apply Laura Matthews; **Overseas Students** Linet Arthur, Maeve Sherlock; **Mature Students** Margaret Davine; **Students with Disabilities** Emma Delap; **Arrival at College** Gavin Hamilton; **Money** Paul Allender, Julie Harvey, Gavin Hamilton; **Accommodation** Tim Dawson; **Basic Living** Gavin Hamiton, Hilary Hutcheon; **Student Unions** Tim Dawson; **Sex & Relationships** Tony Balacs, Hilary Hutcheon; **Health & Stress** Dr Anna Graham, Dr Ann Robinson; **Study Techniques** Judith Horsfield; **Studying Abroad** Jane Woolfenden; **Lesbian & Gay Students** Steve Clamp, Nikki Greenway; **Women Students** Hazel Bathie, Julie Emery; **Black Students** Patrick Younge; **Employment** Julie Emery, Jefferson Hack, Gavin Hamilton; **Rights** Gavin Hamilton; **Travel** Gavin Hamilton.

The Editors would like to thank the following people and organizations for help and information:
Jules Brown from the Rough Guides; Adam Gaines; Nick Gash; Chris Gottlieb; Ffion Griffith; Michael Herd; Edward King from the Terrence Higgins Trust; Louise Kawakami; Laura Matthews; Mike McCleod; Anne O' Daly; John Offord; the staff and editors of i-D magazine; Doug Taylor; Simon Tuttle; Stephen Twigg; Tim Walker.